W9-BMP-212

OFFICIAL (ISC)²® GUIDE TO THE SSCP® CBK®

SECOND EDITION

OTHER BOOKS IN THE (ISC)2® PRESS SERIES

Official (ISC)2® Guide to the SSCP® CBK®, Second Edition
Harold F. Tipton, Editor
ISBN: 978-1-4398-0483-4

Official (ISC)2® Guide to the ISSAP® CBK®
Harold F. Tipton, Editor
ISBN: 978-1-4398-0093-5

Official (ISC)2® Guide to the ISSMP® CBK®
Harold F. Tipton, Editor
ISBN: 978-1-4200-9443-5

Official (ISC)2® Guide to the CISSP® CBK®, Second Edition
Harold F. Tipton, Editor
ISBN: 978-1-4398-0959-3

CISO Leadership: Essential Principles for Success
Todd Fitzgerald and Micki Krause, Editors
ISBN: 978-0-8493-7943-X

Building and Implementing a Security Certification and Accreditation Program: Official (ISC)2® Guide to the CAP® CBK®
Patrick D. Howard
ISBN: 978-0-8493-2062-3

Official (ISC)2® Guide to the CISSP®-ISSEP® CBK®
Susan Hansche
ISBN: 978-0-8493-2341-X

OFFICIAL (ISC)²®
GUIDE TO THE
SSCP® CBK®
SECOND EDITION

Edited by
Harold F. Tipton, CISSP-ISSAP, ISSMP

(ISC)²®

SECURITY TRANSCENDS TECHNOLOGY®

CRC Press
Taylor & Francis Group
Boca Raton London New York

CRC Press is an imprint of the
Taylor & Francis Group, an **informa** business

AN AUERBACH BOOK

Auerbach Publications
Taylor & Francis Group
6000 Broken Sound Parkway NW, Suite 300
Boca Raton, FL 33487-2742

© 2011 by Taylor and Francis Group, LLC
Auerbach Publications is an imprint of Taylor & Francis Group, an Informa business

No claim to original U.S. Government works

Printed in the United States of America on acid-free paper
10 9 8 7 6 5 4

International Standard Book Number: 978-1-4398-0483-4 (Hardback)

Visit the Taylor & Francis Web site at
http://www.taylorandfrancis.com

and the Auerbach Web site at
http://www.auerbach-publications.com

Contents

Foreword

Information security has become a critical component in the stability and progress of the modern world. With high expectations from the public and stringent regulations from legislative and industry bodies, never have the pressures on corporations, governments and other organizations been so great to protect their own data as well as that of the stakeholders they serve. It is why the information security industry is consistently one of the top performing sectors in the global economy.

Organizations understand that technology alone cannot secure their data. In ever-increasing numbers, they are seeking all levels of information security practitioners throughout the enterprise. The Systems Security Certified Practitioner (SSCP®) certification is the ideal credential for meeting the demand for hands-on practical technicians—the go-to people for information security requirements and policies.

The SSCP provides a solid foundation in the understanding of elementary and advanced security concepts and issues for network security engineers, security systems analysts and security administrators as well as many other IT positions throughout the organization. No matter the position—whether a system or network administrator, information systems auditor, computer programmer or systems analyst, or database administrator—the knowledge that practitioners attain from earning the SSCP will make them an asset to the security posture of an organization.

The road to secure enterprises is often littered with tales of failure and unexpected breaches. All too often, these failures are linked to a lack of understanding of basic tenets of information security. This book is an excellent source of information of best practices, advice and guidance that will prove invaluable in helping your organization prevent errors, avert security breaches, and avoid experiencing a loss of trust by stakeholders and regulators.

As the recognized global leader in the field of information security education and certification, (ISC)²®'s mission is to promote the development of information security professionals throughout the world. With that in mind, we provide you this reference with great pleasure and welcome you to this fast-moving and growing field. We believe you will find the SSCP to be a practical, informative and challenging step in your career development.

As you review the information in this book and study for the SSCP certification exam, remember that earning an (ISC)² credential will also make you a member of an elite network of professionals that will reap benefits throughout your career. You will also be a member of a highly respected organization that is constantly working to raise the profile of the profession through community goodwill programs such as security awareness programs for schoolchildren and an information security career guide for high school and college students.

We wish you success in your journey in becoming a SSCP.

W. Hord Tipton, CISSP-ISSEP, CAP, CISA
Executive Director
(ISC)²

Editor

Harold F. Tipton, currently an independent consultant, was a past president of the International Information System Security Certification Consortium and a director of computer security for Rockwell International Corporation for about 15 years. He initiated the Rockwell computer and data security program in 1977 and then continued to administer, develop, enhance, and expand the program to accommodate the control needs produced by technological advances until his retirement from Rockwell in 1994.

Tipton has been a member of the Information Systems Security Association (ISSA) since 1982. He was the president of the Los Angeles chapter in 1984, and the president of the national organization of ISSA (1987–1989). He was added to the ISSA Hall of Fame and the ISSA Honor Role in 2000.

Tipton was a member of the National Institute for Standards and Technology (NIST), the Computer and Telecommunications Security Council, and the National Research Council Secure Systems Study Committee (for the National Academy of Science). He received his BS in engineering from the U.S. Naval Academy and his MA in personnel administration from George Washington University; he also received his certificate in computer science from the University of California, Irvine. He is a certified information system security professional (CISSP), ISSAP, & ISSMP.

He has published several papers on information security issues for Auerbach (*Handbook of Information Security Management, Data Security Management,* and *Information Security Journal*), National Academy of Sciences (*Computers at Risk*), Data Pro Reports, Elsevier, and ISSA (*Access*).

He has been a speaker at all the major information security conferences including the Computer Security Institute, the ISSA Annual Working Conference, the Computer Security Workshop, MIS Conferences, AIS Security for Space Operations, DOE Computer Security Conference, National Computer Security Conference, IIA Security Conference, EDPAA, UCCEL Security & Audit Users Conference, and Industrial Security Awareness Conference.

He has conducted/participated in information security seminars for (ISC)², Frost & Sullivan, UCI, CSULB, System Exchange Seminars, and the Institute for

International Research. He participated in the Ernst & Young video "Protecting Information Assets." He is currently serving as the editor of the *Handbook of Information Security Management* (Auerbach). He chairs the (ISC)² CBK Committees and the QA Committee. He received the Computer Security Institute's Lifetime Achievement Award in 1994, the (ISC)²'s Hal Tipton Award in 2001 and the (ISC)² Founders Award in 2009.

About the Authors

Samuel Chun, CISSP, is a graduate of Johns Hopkins University in Baltimore, Maryland, where he received his bachelor's and master's degrees in psychology. He is currently the director of the Cyber Security Practice for HP Enterprise U.S., Public Sector. His responsibilities include strategy, portfolio development, and industry messaging of all cyber security solutions. He is also the lead subject matter expert for cyber security policy for the HP Global Government Affairs Division.

Mr. Chun has contributed several chapters in the *Information Security Management Handbook* series, and articles in *Homeland Defense Journal, IT Security Magazine, Roll Call, and Government Security News*. He has also been called on to provide expert testimony at the "State of Federal Information Security" hearing efore the House Subcommittee on Government Management, Organization, and Procurement.

Ken Dunham, CISSP, GCFA (forensics), GCIH Gold (Honors) (incident handling), GSEC (network security), GREM (reverse engineering), is the director of Global Response for iSIGHT Partners. His responsibilities include the oversight of all global cyber-threat response operations. He regularly briefs top-level executives and officials in Fortune 500 companies. Mr. Dunham, who is the author of multiple computer security books, including *Mobile Malware Attacks* and *Defense* and *Bigelow's Virus Troubleshooting*, is a regular columnist for the WildList Organization, and has authored thousands of incident and threat reports over the course his career. He holds a master's degree in teacher education, and is the founder and former president of Idaho InfraGard and Boise ISSA.

Paul Henry, CISSP-ISSAP, has more than 20 years of experience in managing security initiatives for Global 2000 enterprises and government organizations worldwide. He is currently the lead forensic investigator and president of Forensics & Recovery LLC, security and forensics analyst at Lumension Security, chief security consultant at Sipera Systems, and certified trainer for SANS; serves as the board vice president of the Florida Association of Computer Crime Investigators (FACCI) and is the USA board vice president of the International Information Systems Forensics Association (IISFA).

Michael Mackrill, CISSP, has been involved in IT for the past 20 years, and has focused on security for the past 15. At one time or another, he has performed almost every role associated with IT security from IDS monitoring to digital forensics to security management. Throughout his career, Mr. Mackrill has taken every opportunity presented to speak about IT security and has done so at several conferences and special interest groups. He is currently a senior security engineer at Platinum Solutions, an award-winning developer of mission-oriented software systems serving federal customers in law enforcement, health care, and DoD/Intel. In his spare time, Mr. Mackrill enjoys cooking, irritating his children, and online gaming.

Christopher Nowell, CISSP-ISSAP, ISSMP, has more than 16 years of professional information technology and security experience supporting both government and private sector enterprises. Mr. Nowell is currently the chief security officer for Sarum LLC, where he leads the overall corporate Infosec program, and consults with multiple customers on enterprise architecture, security management, and security operations support. Although he has long been an associate editor for the *(ISC)² Journal*, his contribution to this study guide is his first professional publication and reflects his love for all things related to information security.

C. Karen Stopford, CISSP, is an independent security consultant with more than 25 years of experience focusing on information security and IT regulatory compliance. Ms. Stopford has held executive-level positions in both Fortune 500 and public sector organizations with responsibilities of architecting, implementing, and managing day-to-day operations. She is currently concentrating her efforts toward designing and building sustainable security risk assessment and management and metrics programs that are not only aligned, but fully integrated with business process management. She has also designed in-house security specialist and generalist awareness training in the organizations she has served.

Ms. Stopford is an active participant and a speaker at industry conferences in groups that address standards and best practices, and promote awareness of information security efforts. She has been a CISSP in good standing since 1999, has worked as an item writer for the SSCP certification examination, and looks forward to continued efforts to promote education, awareness, and professionalism.

Christopher Trautwein, CISSP, CISM, is currently the information security officer for (ISC)², where he serves as the primary official for protection of all of the organization's privacy data and is responsible for its overarching security policies. With over 14 years of experience in information security, Mr. Trautwein previously served as a director for Sunera LLC in the Information Security and Network Services consulting practice and was a senior security engineer for Check Point Software Technologies and RISCManagement. Mr. Trautwein holds a BA in business administration from Florida Southern College and an MS in management information systems from the University of South Florida.

Introduction

The SSCP credential seems to be the most misunderstood and under appreciated of those certifications offered by (ISC)^2. In actuality, it is one of the most critical and essential in the field. This is because the work of the SSCP is where the effectiveness of information security is implemented. Few CISSPs have the technical skills necessary to perform the hands-on implementation of the information security controls that they determine to be necessary to effectively protect the critical and sensitive resources of the organization.

In a mainframe environment, the SSCP role is usually performed by systems programmers assigned to the security department. Otherwise, it would be the responsibility of a system or network administrator from operations.

The security role of the SSCP is twofold. First, they are responsible for the due care activity of correctly implementing and maintaining designated security mechanisms. Second, they are in the best position to accurately evaluate the effectiveness of the installed controls—the due diligence side of the equation. The following review of the SSCP certification domains identifies of some of the specific SSCP activities.

The SCP certification domains are named after the seven major categories of the SSCP Common Body of Knowledge (CBK). The CBK is a taxonomy of topics and sub-topics that is updated annually by the SSCP CBK Committee composed of international subject matter experts. Currently, the seven categories are:

- Access Control
- Analysis and Monitoring
- Cryptography
- Malicious Code
- Networks and Telecommunications
- Risk, Response, and Recovery
- Security Operations and Administration

Access Control is intended to prevent unauthorized access to system resources and enable security administrators to allow authorized users to access and perform operations on resources according to management approvals. The role of the SSCP is to establish and maintain the confidentiality and integrity of system resources by using access control technology, such as passwords, tokens, biometrics, and certificates, as required by organization policy.

Analysis and Monitoring are the means that are employed by security management to apply due diligence to the security architecture of the organization, that is, how it is determined that appropriate security mechanisms are in place and are performing as expected. The monitoring element provides the ability to observe the results of the mechanisms in operation. Here is where the SSCP, being close to the operation, can be of great help in reviewing and maintaining the records, such as audit trails, created by the system. The analysis element involves the use of the records by security management to evaluate the results of applying the security controls implemented by the SSCP.

Cryptography is one of the most effective mechanisms currently available to protect sensitive data from unauthorized access and detect modification. The role of the SSCP is to implement organization-approved encryption algorithms and maintain the custody and secrecy of keys.

Malicious Code in this context includes viruses, worms, logic bombs, Trojan horses, botnets, spam, phishing and other technical and nontechnical attacks. The incidence of attacks of this nature continues to increase dramatically and presents a serious danger to an organization's data processing activities. It is necessary for the SSCP to thoroughly understand these threats and be prepared to recognize them in time to take effective defensive action. Defensive actions include the implementation and maintenance of antiviral software, for example.

Networks and Telecommunications encompasses the network structure, transmission methods, transport formats, and related security measures. This is the backbone of current-day organizational operations and is the highly technical realm of the SSCP. The SSCP must be alert to both insider and outsider attacks and capable of implementing and monitoring controls, such as DMZs, bastion hosts, and firewalls, as well as intrusion protection and detection mechanisms.

Risk, Response, and Recovery involves identifying risks to data and operations so as to be prepared to respond quickly and correctly to incidents that occur and taking appropriate action to minimize the adverse impact on critical business functions by implementing recovery procedures. The SSCP is a key player in this activity, particularly with respect to business continuity planning and resulting testing and incident response procedures.

Security Operations and Administration is the domain that provides a varied set of responsibilities for the SSCP. These include the monitoring of compliance with legislation requiring information security and the security performance of outsourced contracts; technical input in the development of security policies, procedures, standards and baselines; and security guidance in the development of applications. The SSCP is also expected to assist in change and configuration management. Finally, the SSCP could have an influence upon user security awareness training.

Obviously, the SSCP is a key player on the information security team and responsible for a wide assortment of important security activities. Organization management should ensure that staff members involved in performing the roles described for the SSCP are trained and certified to accept the responsibilities involved.

Chapter 1

Access Controls

Paul Henry

Contents

Access controls permit management to specify what users can do, which resources they can access, and what operations they can perform on a system. Access controls provide system managers with the ability to limit and monitor who has access to a system and to restrain or influence the user's behavior on that system. Access control systems define what level of access that individual has to the information contained within a system based on predefined conditions such as authority level or group membership. Access control systems are based on varying technologies, including passwords, hardware tokens, biometrics, and certificates to name a few. Each access control system offers different levels of confidentiality, integrity, and availability to the user, the system, and stored information.

A Systems Security Certified Practitioner candidate is expected to demonstrate knowledge in how different access control systems operate and are implemented to protect the system and its stored data. In addition, a candidate must demonstrate knowledge in account management, access control concepts, and attack methods that are used to defeat access control systems. Key areas of knowledge include

- Implement logical access controls in terms of subjects
  - Requirements for access controls
  - Account creation and maintenance
- Implement logical access controls in terms of objects
  - Requirements for access controls
  - Object groups
- Implement authentication techniques, for example, single and multifactor authentication, single sign-on, offline authentication
- Apply access control concepts, for example, discretionary access control (DAC), least privilege, and separation of duties
- Manage Internet work trust architectures, for example, extranet, third-party connections.

Access Control Concepts

Access controls are those systems that provide for the ability to control "who" can do specifically "what" with respect to data, applications, systems, networks, and physical spaces. In the simplest of terms (and in a perfect world), an access control system grants system users only those rights necessary for them to perform their respective jobs.

For any access control subject to obtain any access to an access control object, there are three steps that must be accomplished (Figure 1.1).

Figure 1.1 Three steps to access control: identification, authentication, and authorization.

The term "access controls" is very broad in nature and can include everything from a simple password authentication that allows a user to access an e-mail account to a biometric retina scanner that unlocks the door to a critical data center.

What Is a Subject?

An access control subject is an active entity and can be any user, program, or process that requests permission to cause data to flow from an access control object to the access control subject or between access control objects.

Access control subjects include

- Authorized users
- Unauthorized users
- Applications
- Processes
- Systems
- Networks

The authorization provided to the access control subject by an access control system can include but is not limited to the following considerations:

Access Control Subject	Access Control Object
• Temporal—time of day, day of request • Locale from where the access control subject was authenticated • Inside or outside of the network • Password or token utilized • An individual access control subject may have different rights assigned to specific passwords that are used during the authentication process	• Data content of the object • The access control subject may be restricted from accessing all or part of the data within the access control object because of the type of data that may be contained within the object • Transaction restrictions may also apply

The attributes of a subject are referred to as privilege attributes or sensitivities. When these attributes are matched against the control attributes of an object, privilege is either granted or denied.

In a typical access control system, additional subject-specific requirements may include

■ A secure default policy should be applied to any newly created subject.
■ The attributes of the subject should not be expressed in terms that can easily be forged such as an IP address.
■ The system should provide for a default deny on all permissions for the subject, thereby requiring that access to any object be explicitly created by an administrator.
■ In the absence of policy for a given subject, the default policy should be interpreted as default deny.
■ A user ID should remain permanently assigned to a subject.

Subject Group Considerations

The configuration of privileges in access control for an individual subject affords maximum granularity. In systems with perhaps hundreds or thousands of users, this granularity can quickly become a management burden. By incorporating multiple subjects with similar permissions, for example, job titles, within a group, the granularity is thereby coarsened and the administration of the access control system is simplified.

What Is an Object?

An access control object is a passive entity that typically receives or contains some form of data. The data can be in the form of a file, a program, or may be resident within system memory.

Access control objects

- Data
- Applications
- Systems
- Networks
- Physical space, for example, the data center

Typical access control object considerations can include but are not limited to the following:

- Restrict access to operating system configuration files and their respective directories to authorized administrators.
- Disable write/modify permissions for all executable files.
- Ensure that newly created files inherit the permissions of the directory in which they were created.
- Ensure that subdirectories cannot override the permissions of parent directories unless specifically required by policy.
- Log files should be configured to only permit appending data to mitigate the risk of a log file's contents being purposely deleted or overwritten by a malicious user or process.
- Encryption of data at rest can afford additional security and should be a consideration in the determination of the policies for access control objects.

Object Group Considerations

The configuration of privileges to access an individual object affords maximum granularity. It is not uncommon today for the number of objects within an access control system to number in the tens or even hundreds of thousands. While configuring individual objects affords maximum control, this granularity can quickly become an administrative burden. It is a common practice to assign the appropriate permissions to a directory, and each object within the directory inherits the respective parent directory permissions. By incorporating multiple objects with similar permissions or restrictions within a group or directory, the granularity is thereby coarsened and the administration of the access control system is simplified.

Discretionary Access Control

In DAC, the owner of the access control object would determine the privileges (i.e., read, write, execute) of the access control subjects. This methodology relies on the discretion of the owner of the access control object to determine the access control subject's specific rights to afford the security of the access control object. Hence, security of the object is literally up to the discretion of the object owner. DACs are not very scalable; they rely on the decisions made by each individual access control object owner, and it can be difficult to find the source of access control issues when problems occur.

Rule Set–Based Access Controls

Rule Set–Based Access Controls are discretionary controls whereby the owner has the discretion to determine the rules to facilitate access. A Linux-specific open source initiative known as Rule Set–Based Access Control (RSBAC) has been in development since 1996 and in stable production since January 2000. RSBAC is based on the Abrams and LaPadula Generalized Framework for Access Control (GFAC). RSBAC works at the kernel level and affords flexible access control based on several modules:

- Mandatory Access Control module (MAC)
- Privacy module (PM)
- Function Control module (FC)
- File Flag module (FF)
- Malware Scan module (MS)
- Role Compatibility module (RC)
- Function Control module (FC)
- Security Information Modification module (SIM)
- Authentication module (Auth)
- Access Control List module (ACL)

All security relevant system calls in the Linux kernel are extended by RSBAC security enforcement code. The RSBAC security enforcement code calls the central decision component, which then in turn calls all active decision modules (see above listing) and generates a combined decision. This decision is then enforced by the RSBAC system call extensions. One of the original goals of RSBAC was to achieve Orange book B1 certification.

Role-Based Access Controls

Role-based access control (RBAC) is generally considered to be discretionary because the owner determines what roles have access. RBAC is also discretionary because the owner determines the rules. While there are several different implementations of nondiscretionary access controls, most implementations work on the principle of RBAC. RBAC works by assigning roles to access control subjects as well as labels to the access control objects that specify which roles are permitted access to the respective access control objects. Within an RBAC implementation, the ability to permit or deny the inheritance of roles within a given hierarchy is commonly available.

RBAC in many respects is similar to a well-managed work environment. Each employee has an assigned role and job function; they are only permitted access to the information necessary to accomplish their job function. The inheritance aspects of RBAC can be thought of like the organization chart at a well-managed company whereby roles can be inherited across employees at the same organizational level or downward in the organizational chart but perhaps not permitting inheritance of a role moving up the organizational chart to levels above the current assigned role.

Constrained User Interface

Constrained User Interface (CUI) is a methodology that restricts the user's actions to specific functions by not allowing them to request functions that are outside of their respective level of privilege or role. The most common example of CUI can be found in online banking applications and ATMs where the limited menus are readily apparent until after the user has properly authenticated, thereby establishing their respective role/level of privilege.

Another type of CUI is often referred to as View-Based Access Control (VBAC); it is most commonly found in database applications to control access to specific parts of a database. The CUI in VBAC restricts or limits an access control subject's ability to view or perhaps act on "components" of an access control object based on the access control subject's assigned level of authority. Views are dynamically created by the system for each user-authorized access.

Simply put VBAC separates a given access control object into subcomponents and then permits or denies access for the access control subject to view or interact with specific subcomponents of the underlying access control object.

VBAC examples in a medical records database:

- A billing clerk (access control subject) would be able to view the procedures, supplies, and related costs in a database (access control object) to be billed to a patient and would be restricted from seeing the result of any of the underlying tests and perhaps the doctors notes contained within the same database (access control object).
- A nurse (access control subject) would be able to view the results of procedures and tests as well as the doctor's notes but would be restricted from seeing the costs for the procedures and supplies.

VBAC examples in a firewall administrator's management console:

- A firewall user administrator (access control subject) would be able to add new users and reset user passwords in the firewalls database (access control object) but would be restricted from seeing alerts or altering the firewall ACL rules within the same database.

- A firewall monitor (access control subject) would be able to see alerts in the firewall database (access control object) but would not be able to see or alter any information in the database relating to users or ACL rules.
- A firewall virtual private network (VPN) administrator (access control subject) would have the ability to enter VPN-related rules into the firewall database (access control object) to facilitate creating a point-to-point VPN tunnel or perhaps to permit a client to server VPN connection. However, the users would have to already exist in the firewall database (access control object), and the VPN administrator (access control subject) would be restricted from seeing alerts and access control rules that did not specifically relate to the VPN operations within the database.
- A firewall security officer (access control subject) would have full access to all information within the firewall database (access control object). While the view that is given to an access control subject may in fact only be a partial view of the information available from the access control object, it is important in the proper application of VBAC that the views presented to the access control subject appear normal, complete, and in context, without revealing signs of any missing information.

Content-Dependent Access Control

Content-Dependent Access Control (CDAC) is most commonly used to protect databases containing sensitive information; hence, CDAC can be thought of as mechanism for privacy enforcement. CDAC is commonly based on the Abrams and LaPadula GFAC. CDAC works by permitting or perhaps denying the access control subjects access to access control objects based on the explicit content within the access control object. A timely example is that with CDAC in a medical records database application, a health-care worker may have been granted access to blood test records; however, if that record contains information about an HIV test, the health-care worker may be denied access to the existence of the HIV test and the results of the HIV test. Only specific hospital staff would have the necessary CDAC access control rights to view blood test records that contain any information about HIV tests.

While high levels of privacy protection are attainable using CDAC, it comes at the cost of a great deal of labor in defining the respective permissions. It should be further noted that CDAC comes with a great deal of overhead in processing power as it must scan the complete record to determine if access can be granted to a given access control subject. This scan is done by an arbiter program to determine if access will be allowed.

Context-Based Access Control

Context-Based Access Control (CBAC) is primarily used in firewall applications to extend the firewall's decision-making process beyond basic ACL decisions to decisions based on state as well as application-layer protocol session information. A static packet filtering firewall is a good example of a firewall that does not use CBAC. It looks at each and every packet and compares the packet to an ACL rule base to determine if the packet is to be allowed or denied. A stateful inspection firewall is a good example of a firewall that uses CBAC. The firewall also consider the "state of the connection"; i.e., if a packet arrives that is part of a continuing session that had previously been permitted to pass through the firewall then subsequent packets which are part of that session are allowed to pass without the overhead associated with comparing the packet to the ACL rules. CBAC affords a significant performance enhancement to a firewall.

CBAC is often confused with CDAC but they are two completely different methodologies. While CDAC makes decisions based on the content within an access control object, CBAC is not concerned with the content; it is only concerned with the context or the sequence of events leading to the access control object being allowed through the firewall.

In the example of blood test records for CDAC above, the access control subject would be denied access to the access control object because it contained information about an HIV test. CBAC could be used to limit the total number of requests for access to any blood test records over a given period of time. Hence, a health-care worker may be limited to accessing the blood test database more than 100 times in a 24-hour period.

While CBAC does not require that permissions be configured for individual access control objects, it requires that rules be created in relation to the sequence of events that precede an access attempt.

Temporal Isolation (Time-Based) Access Control

Temporal Isolation (Time-Based) Access Control is commonly used to enhance or extend the capabilities of RBAC implementations. This combined methodology is often referred to as Temporal Role-Based Access Control (TRBAC). TRBAC effectively applies a time limitation to "when" a given role can be activated for a given access control subject.

- A high-level "top secret" role would be assigned to a given access control subject during the normal 8:00 A.M. to 5:00 P.M. working hours.
- A lower-level "confidential" role would be assigned to the same access control subject during the 5:00 P.M. to 8:00 A.M. nonworking hours.

To decrease the labor of assigning TRBAC rules to each of many individual access control subjects, most implementations of TRBAC assign the temporal-based classification levels to the perhaps lower number of access control objects rather than to the access control subject. Hence, a given access control object would have a temporal-based classification level that is effective against all access control subjects

Temporal extensions are also used to enhance other access control methodologies. It is common today to find access control devices that support time-based access control rules. The temporal enhancement of the access control rule only allows the rule to be effective during the specified time period.

Nondiscretionary Access Control

The following is a definition of nondiscretionary access control from the National Institute of Standards and Technology (NIST) in May 19, 2006. "Most OS provide what is called discretionary access control. This allows the owner of each file, not the system administrator, to control who can read, write, and execute that particular file. Another access control option is called nondiscretionary access control. Nondiscretionary access control differs from discretionary access control in that the definition of access rules is tightly controlled by a security administrator rather than by ordinary users."

Mandatory Access Control

Mandatory Access Control (MAC) is typically used in environments requiring high levels of security such as government or military systems. In MAC, the inherent problems of trying to rely on each system owner to properly control access to each access control object is eliminated by having the system participate in applying a mandatory access policy; the system owner applies the "need to know" element. This policy affords typically three object classification levels: top-secret, secret, and confidential. Each access control system subject (users and programs) are assigned clearance labels and access control system objects are assigned sensitivity labels. The system then automatically provides the correct access rights based on comparing the object and subject labels. MACs allow multiple security levels of both objects and subjects to be combined in one system securely.

Separation of Duties

This aspect access control establishes guidelines that require that no single person should perform a task from beginning to end, and that the task should be accomplished by two or more people to mitigate the potential for fraud in one person performing the task alone. Separation of duties is a key element in the Clark–Wilson formal model.

Architecture Models

Bell–LaPadula

The Bell–LaPadula confidentiality model provides the "mandatory" component of a MAC system with the following MAC parameters:

Top-Secret-Level Subjects	Secret-Level Subjects	Confidential-Level Subjects
Top-secret-level subject can create as well as write only top-secret-level objects	Secret-level subject can create as well as write secret-level objects and top-secret-level objects	Confidential-level subject can create as well as write confidential-level objects as well as secret- and top-secret-level objects
Can read top-secret-level objects as well as lower-sensitivity level-objects: secret and confidential	Cannot read "up" in top-secret-level objects	Can read only confidential-level objects
Cannot write "down" to lower sensitivity level object: secret and confidential	Can read secret-level objects as well as lower-sensitivity-level objects: confidential	Cannot read "up" in top-secret or secret-level objects
	Cannot write "down" to lower-sensitivity-level object: confidential	

A common theme among applications of MAC is the "no read up–no write down" policy applied to each subject's sensitivity level. This is the "mandatory" part of MAC. It is the implementation of the Bell–LaPadula security model:

- Simple Security Property: The subject cannot read information from an object with a higher sensitivity level than the subjects.
- Star Property: The subject cannot write information to an object with a sensitivity level that is lower than the subjects.

Biba

The Biba formal model was written by K. J. Biba in 1977 and is the basis for the "integrity" aspects of the MAC model. The Biba formal model provides for three primary rules:

- An access control subject cannot access an access control object that has a lower integrity level.
- An access control subject cannot modify an access control object that has a higher integrity level.

■ An access control subject cannot request services from an access control object that has a higher integrity level.

Clark–Wilson

The Clark–Wilson formal model was written by Dr. David D. Clark and David R. Wilson in 1987, and was updated in 1989. Like the Biba formal model, it addresses integrity. However, unlike the Biba formal model, the Clark–Wilson formal model extends beyond limiting access to the access control object by adding integrity considerations to the processes that occur while using the access control object.

The Clark–Wilson formal model effectively provides for the integrity of the access control object by controlling the process that can create or modify the access control object.

Furthermore, the Clark–Wilson formal model also provides for the separation of duties. This aspect of the Clark–Wilson formal model establishes guidelines that require that no single person should perform a task from beginning to end, and that the task should be accomplished by two or more people to mitigate the potential for fraud in one person performing the task alone.

Other Considerations of Clark–Wilson

Well-formed transaction: The well-formed transaction is the basis of the Clark–Wilson model and provides for integrity through the use of rules and certifications applied to data as it is processed through various states. A well-formed transaction also employs the use of separation of duties whereby the implementer of a transaction and the certifier of a transaction must be separate entities.

Access triple. Historically, the Clark–Wilson triple referred to the relationship between an authenticated user, the programs that operate on the data items, and the data themselves. Similarly an access triple refers to an authenticated user having permission to use a given program on a specific set of data.

Brewer–Nash: Chinese Wall

The Chinese Wall adds an additional element: the interrelationships of data to other models. In an example of the addition of a Chinese Wall to the Bell–LaPadula, not only would a given user be restricted to only accessing a specific set of data but also a further consideration of what other data sets the user had previously accessed would be examined before permitting access to the data. In an example of Clark–Wilson augmented with a Chinese Wall, not only is access to data restricted to a given process but also consideration is given to which other data the processes had been used on.

The goal of a Chinese Wall is to mitigate the risk of a conflict of interest. An example of the implementation of a Chinese Wall: access controls within a law office network would allow a consultant to initially have no restriction on which files they were permitted to access. Only after they accessed a given file for a given company would they receive restriction on which other files regarding other companies that they could then have further access to. In the simplest of terms, once you viewed confidential information about one organization, you would not be permitted to have further access to confidential information about any of their competitors.

Identification, Authentication, Authorization, and Accountability

Identity (Who Is the Subject?)

Identification asserts a unique user or process identity and provides for accountability. Identification of an access control subject is typically in the form of an assigned user name. This user name could be public information whether intentional or not. A good example is that in most networks, the user name that identifies the user for network access is also the identification used as the e-mail account identifier. Hence all one would have to do to determine the account holder's user name would be to know the account holder's e-mail address. An access control that relied on the user name alone to provide access would be an ineffective access control. To prove that the individual who presented the user name to the access control is the individual that the user name was assigned to, a secret is shared between the access control system and the respective user. This secret is the user's password and is used to authenticate that the user who is trying to gain access is in fact the user who owns the rights associated with the respective identification.

Methods (User ID, PIN, Account Number)

Unique. Regardless of the method used (userID, PIN, account number), each one must be unique to be valid for any user. Further care must be taken so that users are not readily identifiable from that of another user's userID. An example of this problem would be to simply use the user's first initial and last name as his userID. Anyone knowing the user's first and last name would then easily know the user's userID.

Group. The configuration of privileges in access control for an individual subject affords maximum granularity. In systems with perhaps hundreds or thousands of users, this granularity can quickly become a management burden. By incorporating multiple subjects with similar permissions, such as job titles, within a group, the granularity is thereby coarsened and the administration of the access control system is simplified. However, it is important to note that group IDs are not recommended because individual accountability is lost.

Registration of New Users

Manual user registration provides for the greatest granularity but is also regarded as having too high of an administrative burden to be effective and is today often replaced with an automated provisioning solution. Automated provisioning solutions (identity management) provide a framework for managing access control policies by role, interconnection with IT systems, workflows to guide sign-off, delegated administration, password management, and auditing.

Periodic Review of Access Levels

The periodic review of user access levels is no longer simply a best practice and has been incorporated into current regulations including Sarbanes–Oxley. The mandatory periodic review of user access levels is necessary to ensure that each user's privilege continues to be appropriate and reflects any changes in their access requirements as their role and or responsibilities within the enterprise change.

Clearance

The proper application of clearance is critical in those systems where access controls are based on security labels such as implementations of access control using the Bell–LaPadula model. Access control systems using clearances typically do so using a trusted user directory. Access to the directory is only available after successful authentication, and the directory must be trusted. Clearance levels like other general access levels must routinely be verified against each user's actual requirements, designated access, and status.

Certificates play an important role today in improving trust within a user directory. Instead of simply looking up a user in a directory to determine the level of clearance, a certificate with additional attributes, such as clearance life cycle, can be used to verify by its digital signature that the clearance is valid.

Authentication (Proof of Identity)

Authentication is the process of verification that the identity presented to the access control system belongs to the party that has presented it. The three common factors in authentication are something you know, something you have, and something you are. In network authentication, the identification of the user is authenticated using a secret password that only the user would know. This would be referred to as simple authentication. There are more complex authentication methodologies such as "dual factor authentication" that not only require the secret that the user knows but also requires another layer of authentication in the form of something the user "has" in their possession—such as a security token, or something the user "is"—as in the case of biometric authentication, a fingerprint, or retina scan. We will discuss complex authentication methodologies such as dual factor later in this chapter. Again, the objective of authentication is to prove the identity of the user that is asking for some type of access from the access control system.

Knowledge

Knowledge is something that you know, such as a password.

Static passwords. Static passwords can be a password, a PIN, a passphrase, a graphic, etc. Regardless of length and character construction, static passwords that are not frequently changed are inherently insecure.

Secure storage is a necessity as legacy encryption of passwords in storage is typically easy to crack and makes unauthorized use of accounts a trivial matter for a determined malicious hacker. Tools such as Cain & Able along with Rainbow Tables can defeat the most commonly used password encryption methodologies in seconds.

Password resets when the user forgets his password consume a large volume of time in most IT support departments and also provide an effective entry vector for social engineering attacks. All too often password lockout mechanisms are disabled to reduce the number of required password resets, further increasing the risk of potential compromise. Automated password reset mechanisms range from the user being required to answer a series of personal questions that they previously provided responses for to newer technology-based reset mechanisms that use voice recognition to further automate the process.

Mass lockouts of user accounts are an effective denial of service attack. If a malicious hacker learns that you are using a standard "not unique" user name format making the user names for authentication easy to guess and that your access control system will lock out a user account after a given number of failed login attempts, it is a simple matter to quickly script an attack that walks through a failed login attempt creating a locked-out account for each and every user.

Ownership

Ownership is something the user has in his possession such as a smartcard or a token.

Smartcards. Typically, smartcards are credit card size, contain a tamper-resistant security system, are managed by a central administration system, and require a card reader device, such as the typical card reader on an ATM or fuel pump at a gasoline station. There are contact and contactless smartcards and readers.

A contact card reader requires physical contact with the card reader. There are two primary methodologies for contact card readers. A landing contact requires physical contact with the contacts (landing zone) on the card when it is placed within the reader. Typical standards for landing contact readers include ISO 7816. Landing contact readers are popular in physical access applications. A friction contact requires that the card landing contacts are wiped against the contact reader. Typical friction card readers are those used in credit card transactions at merchants.

Contactless card readers are quickly gaining in popularity and typically rely on radiofrequency identification (RFID) technology to facilitate reading. The additional security mechanisms found in contactless card applications can include challenge/response-based encryption safeguards to reduce the risk of "card skimming" whereby the account information is stolen in an otherwise legitimate transaction. It is believed that users prefer contactless cards because of their inherent ease of use, speed of transaction, and increased security.

Dynamic passwords. Dynamic passwords methodologies, also known as "one-time password," are typically implemented by utilizing hardware or software token technology. Effectively, the password is changed after each authentication session. This effectively mitigates the risk of shoulder surfing or password sniffing as the password is only valid for the one session and cannot be reused.

Tokens. While tokens are available in many different form factors, there are two basic types of tokens in use today: synchronous and asynchronous.

With a synchronous token, time is synchronized between the token device and the authentication server. The current time value is enciphered along with a secret key on the token device and is presented to the access control subject for authentication. A popular synchronous token from RSA called "SecureID" provides for a new six- to eight-digit code every 60 seconds; it can operate for up to 4 years and can be programmed to cease operation on a predetermined date. The synchronous token requires fewer steps by the access control subject to successfully authenticate:

■ The access control subject reads the value from his or her token device.
■ The value from the token device is entered into the login window along with the access control subject's PIN.
■ The authentication server calculates its own comparative value based on the synchronized time value and the respective access control subject's PIN. If the compared values match, access is granted.

An asynchronous token, such as the event-driven, asynchronous token from Secure Computing called SafeWord, provides a new one time password with each use of the token. While it can be configured to expire on a specific date, its lifetime depends on its frequency of use. The token can last from 5 to 10 years and effectively extend the time period typically used in calculating the total cost of ownership in a multifactor authentication deployment. In the use of an asynchronous one-time password token, the access control subject typically executes a five-step process to authenticate identity and have access granted:

1. The authentication server presents a challenge request to the access control subject.
2. The access control subject enters the challenge into his/her token device.

3. The token device mathematically calculates a correct response to the authentication server challenge.
4. The access control subject enters the response to the challenge along with a password or PIN number.
5. The response and password or PIN number is verified by the authentication server and if correct, access is granted.

The use of a PIN together with the value provided from the token helps to mitigate the risk of a stolen or lost token being used by an unauthorized person to gain access through the access control system.

RFID. Early RFID-based products had a reputation for poor security as they were deployed without taking advantage of the integral security mechanisms that are readily available for use with the underlying technology. As RFID technology has evolved, its adoption in access control applications has increased significantly in comparison to traditional friction and contactless card applications. RFID technology effectively provides for a hands-free access control solution. The increased computational capabilities delivered by current-generation RFID technologies allow several security enhancements that are simply not available with the use of legacy technologies.

Characteristic

A characteristic is a physical characteristic of the user, also referred to as "what a person does" or "what a person is," that allows for the confirmation of an individual's identity based on either a physiological condition such as a fingerprint or retina scan or a behavioral characteristic such as keystrokes, speech recognition, or signature dynamics.

Biometrics

Biometrics is classified as behavioral and physiological. Good examples of behavioral biometrics are signature analysis, voice pattern recognition, and keystroke dynamics.

■ *Signature analysis.* The handwritten signature is unique to each individual. Most access control signature analysis access devices use a 3D analysis of the signature, which includes both the pressure and form of the signature. Signature analysis dynamically measures the series of movements, which contain biometric characteristics, such as acceleration, rhythm, pressure, and flow. Signature analysis access control devices have become popular with credit card merchants for authorization of credit card transactions.
■ *Voice pattern recognition.* Voice pattern recognition works by creating a database of unique characteristics of the access control subject's voice. The access

control subject then simply speaks at or near a microphone, and the access control device compares the current voice pattern characteristics to the stored characteristics to determine if access is to be granted. Biology, not technology, is the issue with voice recognition. As the subject ages, the characteristics of the voice naturally change. Voice characteristics can change under stress, and during an emergency situation the access control subject could be denied access simply because of the stress he/she was under at that moment. Further, it is possible to create an error simply by altering the inflection of a given phrase. Voice recognition is an inexpensive methodology to implement, but because of the high probability of error it is best used to compliment another more accurate technology, such as iris scanning, and not to be relied on as a primary access control device.

■ *Keystroke dynamics.* Keystroke dynamics, like the other forms of authentication devices mentioned above, rely on characteristics that are unique to an individual. In the case of keystroke dynamics, it is the characteristics of the access control subject as the user name and password (actually pass phrase) is typed on the keyboard. The normal characteristics of the individual are learned over time and typically can be enrolled with six or eight samples. The individual characteristics used by the typical keystroke analysis device include, but are not limited to:
  – The length of time each key is held down
  – The length of time between keystrokes
  – The typing speed
  – The tendencies to switch between a numeric keypad and keyboard numbers
  – The keystroke tendencies involved in capitalization

■ The accuracy of keystroke dynamics can be easily impacted by hand injuries, fatigue, arthritis, and perhaps temperature. Hence, while keystroke dynamics is regarded as the lowest-cost authentication mechanism, it cannot yet be used reliably in a single-factor or perhaps two-factor (using passphrase) authentication methodology, and is better suited to compliment another technology such as iris scanning in a two-factor authentication scheme. It is important to note however, that, it does provide continuous authentication, if that is desirable.

There are several biometric devices that make use of the user's personal physiological data in access control applications:

■ *Fingerprint verification technology.* Fingerprint verification typically requires seven characteristics or matching points to either enroll a new access control subject or to verify an existing access control subject. The task is not as difficult as it may seem as the human finger contains 30–40 characteristics or matching points. The fingerprint reader does not store an image of the fingerprint. Rather it creates a geometric relationship between the character-istics or matching points and stores and then compares that information.

■ *Hand geometry technology.* Hand geometry verification is typically accom-plished by building a five-element array of finger lengths determined from scanned matching points at the base and end of each finger. The stored five-element array is compared to a new hand scan, and a mathematical calcula-tion is performed to determine the geometric distance between the respective arrays.

■ *Eye features/retina scan.* The retina scan is one of the oldest and most accu-rate biometric authentication methodologies. Dating back to 1930, it was recognized that each human retina had unique characteristics, but it was 1984 before the first commercial retina scanner was released to the public. Traditionally, the retina scan has been reserved only for the most secure appli-cation of physical access control systems. The retina scan simply maps the blood vessels in the back of the eye and only requires 10 or so seconds to complete a scan. There is no known technology that can forge a retina scan signature, and as the blood vessels quickly decay upon death, a retina scan on a dead individual will not create the same signature as that of the live indi-vidual. Hence a retina scan prevents unauthorized access.

■ *Eye features/iris scan.* Iris scanning is based on scanning the granularity of the richly detailed color bands around the pupil. The color bands are well defined at birth and change little over the subject's lifetime. The typical iris scanner maps nearly 247 variables in the iris and can do so at a distance of 19–20 inches. This makes the iris scanner potentially more accurate than a fingerprint, with only 40–80 characteristics, and is less obtrusive then a retina scanner as it does not require the same close proximity to the reading device or a light shining into the eye.

■ *Facial recognition.* Like the fingerprint reader and hand geometry devices, facial recognition uses a mathematical geometric model of certain landmarks of the face such as the cheekbone, tip of the nose, and eye socket orientation, and measures the distance between them. There are approximately 80 sepa-rate measurable characteristics in the human face, but most facial recognition systems only rely on 14–22 characteristics to perform their recognition.

Biometric Implementation Issues

User acceptance is one of the most critical factors in the success of any biometric-based implementation. To minimize the risk of improper use, which can cause failed access, the device should not cause discomfort or concern and must be easy to use.

Biometric accuracy is measured by two distinct rates: the False Rejection Rate (FRR), referred to as type 1 error, and the False Acceptance Rate (FAR), referred to as type 2 error. The actual methodologies of the measurement of accuracy may

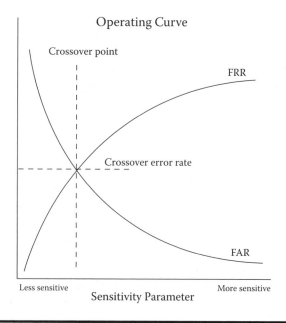

Figure 1.2   The actual methodologies of the measurement of accuracy may differ in each type of biometric device, but simply put, you can obtain a good comparative accuracy factor by looking at the intersection point at which the type 1 error rate (FRR) equals the type 2 error rate (FAR). (From Ruggles, T., A report on the comparison of biometric techniques, http://www.bio-tech-inc.com/bio.htm).

differ in each type of biometric device, but simply put, you can obtain a good comparative accuracy factor by looking at the intersection point at which the type 1 error rate equals the type 2 error rate as shown in Figure 1.2. This value is commonly referred to as the crossover error rate (CER). The biometric device accuracy increases as the crossover value becomes smaller as shown in Table 1.1.

Table 1.1   Biometric Crossover Accuracy

Biometric Crossover Accuracy	
Retinal scan	1:100,00,000
Iris scan	1:131,000
Fingerprint	1:500
Hand geometry	1:500
Signature dynamics	1:50
Voice dynamics	1:50

A further comparison of biometric technologies is provided in Table 1.2.

In reusable password authentication, the access control subject had to remember a perhaps difficult password. In token-based authentication, the access control subject had to retain possession of the token device. In biometric, characteristic-based authentication, the actual access control subject "is" the authentication device.

Physical Use as Identification

Biometrics takes advantage of the unique physical traits of each user and arguably is the most effective methodology of identifying a user. It is important to note that in physical security, biometrics is often used as an identification mechanism, while in logical security biometrics is often used as an authentication mechanism. As biometric technologies evolve, accuracy rates are increasing, error rates are declining, and improved ease-of-use is increasing user acceptance.

The accuracy of biometrics has been found to improve when multiple techniques are combined. The FBI is currently working on a next-generation database that will combine the use of fingerprint, face, iris, and palm matching capabilities to improve overall accuracy.

Multifactor Authentication

For many years knowledge-based authentication in terms of passwords was the most common methodology in use in access control systems. Weakness in the implementation of encryption (hashing) for passwords has effectively rendered these knowledge-based methodologies obsolete.

In October 2005, the Federal Financial Institutions Examination Council provided a recommendation (http://www.ffiec.gov/pdf/authentication_guidance.pdf) to U.S. banks that included, in part, a requirement to replace passwords and single factor authentication with multifactor authentication. The recommendation clearly pointed out that passwords alone were simply no longer a secure methodology for authenticating users in the current Internet environment.

The best practice in access control is to implement at least two of the three common techniques for authentication in your access control system:

- Knowledge based
- Token based
- Characteristic based

Two-Factor vs. Three-Factor Authentication

In two-factor authentication, typically the mechanism used provides for something the user has in the form of a physical token that generates a one-time password and

Table 1.2 Comparison of Biometric Technologies

Comparison of Biometrics

Characteristic	Fingerprints	Hand Geometry	Retina	Iris	Face	Signature	Voice
Ease of use	High	High	Low	Medium	Medium	High	High
Error incidence	Dryness, dirt age	Hand injury age	Glasses	Poor lighting	Lighting, age glasses, hair	Changing signatures	Noise, colds, weather
Accuracy	High	High	Very high	Very high	High	High	High
User acceptance	Medium	Medium	Medium	Medium	Medium	Medium	High
Required security level	High	Medium	High	Very high	Medium	Medium	Medium
Long-term stability	High	Medium	High	High	Medium	Medium	Medium

Source: Liu, S., and Silverman, M., A practical guide to biometric security technology, *IT Professional*, 3, 27–32, 2005. With permission.

something the user knows in the form of a PIN number that is appended to the one-time password that is generated by the token. This methodology is regarded as more secure than historical single-factor methodologies such as traditional passwords; however, it does little to definitively identify the user. This can be significantly improved upon by incorporating a third factor in the form of a biometric that in fact identifies the user. An example of a recent entry in the three-factor authentication market is the RSA AuthenTec Fingerprint device from Privaris. It incorporates a fingerprint reader to identify the user as well as being something the user "has," and also incorporates the traditional one time password and PIN combination found in common two-factor authentication tokens.

Dual Control

Dual control, also referred to as "split-knowledge," is built on the principle that no one person should have access to information that would allow the person to determine the encryption key used to encrypt protected information more quickly than a brute force attack of the entire key-space. Effectively, the determination of any part of the encryption key would require collusion between at least two different trusted individuals. Encryption—splitkeys—is just one example of dual control. It has been said that because of its inherent complexity, dual control is not difficult to accomplish, but is easy to get wrong.

Continuous Authentication

While traditional one-time authentication, otherwise known as transactional authentication, takes place only once before granting access, continuous authentication takes place both before granting access and then continuously through the entire duration of the users connection to maintain the granted access.

Periodic Authentication

The most common use of periodic authentication first provides for traditional challenge/response authentication requiring user interaction and then begins periodically to issue challenge/response authentication queries with the users token to determine if the user has physically left the area where he had authenticated. This methodology aids in reducing the risk that a user would walk away from a device or system he has authenticated access to before properly logging out.

Time Outs

If the user leaves the proximity of the device authenticated after a specific time period, the user is automatically logged off and the authentication process would start over, requiring user intervention to accomplish initial authentication before continuous authentication could again resume. Naturally, the shorter the timeout period, the higher the security that can be provided; however, as always, it comes at the cost of being intrusive to the user.

Reverse Authentication

In the age of the explosive growth in the use of the Internet for financial transactions, we were quickly blindsided by phishing attacks that used social engineering to fool users into authenticating to fake "look-a-like" Web sites, thereby allowing the phisher to steal the user's credentials and then impersonating the user on the actual "real" Web site. With the advent of phishing it is no longer enough to simply authenticate the user in Web-based transactions. Today, it is necessary to also authenticate the Web site/page to the user as part of the authentication process. Bank of America was a pioneer in reverse authentication with their roll-out PassMark, a reverse authentication system that relies on a series of pictures that the user could identify and use to accomplish the authentication of the Bank of America Web site. Some had believed that the picture approach of PassMark was too simplistic and raised doubts about the technology. However, PassMark quickly grew in acceptance and was adopted by more than 50% of the online banking market.

Certificate-Based Authentication

Certificate-based authentication relies on the machine that the user authenticates from having a digital certificate installed that is used in part along with the encrypted user's password to authenticate both the user and the device the user is authenticating from. Effectively, the use of a certificate in the authentication process adds an additional element in security by validating that the user is authorized to authenticate from the device they are using because of the presence of the digital certification within the device. Great care must be taken in the management of the digital certificates by the Certificate Authority to ensure that the use of certificates is properly controlled and certificate renewal and revocations are accomplished in a timely and effective manner.

Authorization

What you can do once you are authenticated is most often controlled by a reference monitor. A reference monitor is typically defined as the service or program where access control information is stored and where access control decisions are made. A reference monitor will typically decide if access is to be granted based on an ACL within the reference monitor. Once access is granted, what the subject can then do is controlled by the authorization matrix or table (see Table 1.3).

Access to Systems vs. Data, Networks

Defining ACLs that only address access to systems can facilitate unintended user access to data that perhaps the user should not have had access to. Including access controls to specific data within a given system increases overall security. Consideration must also be given to a user's access to those networks that are connected to a system that the user is authorized to access to mitigate the risk of the user inadvertently having access to systems and or data accessible through a connected network that they were not necessarily intended to have access to.

Access Control Lists/Matrix

An authorization table is a matrix of access control objects, access control subjects, and their respective rights as shown in Table 1.3. The authorization table is used in some DAC systems to provide for a simple and intuitive user interface for the definition of access control rules. While an authorization table provides for an increase in ease of use, it does not solve the inherent issue of DAC in that you are still relying on the access control object owner to properly define the access control rules. Further, the use of an authorization table does not decrease the instance of errors or violations that may occur when changes are made within the authorization table.

An access control matrix is used in a DAC system to provide for a simple user interface to implement an ACL. The access control matrix determines the access rights for access control objects to access control subjects as shown in Table 1.4. Like the authorization table mentioned above, the access control matrix does not decrease the instance of errors or violations that may occur when changes are made within the access control matrix.

Table 1.3 Authorization Table: Matrix of Access Control Objects, Access Control Subjects, and Their Respective Rights

Access Control Subjects	Access Control Objects					
	Procedure A	Procedure B	File A	File B	File C	File D
Bob	Execute		Read	Read/write		Read
Tom		Execute			Read	
Mary		Execute			Read	
Process A			Read/write			Write
Process B			Write			Read/write

Table 1.4   Access Control Matrix Determines the Access Rights for Access Control Objects to Access Control Subjects

Access Control Subjects	Access Control Objects															
	1	2	3	4	5	6	7	8	9	10	11	12	13	14	15	16
1	X		X	X	X		X						X	X		
2	X		X	X						X	X					
3	X	X				X	X	X						X		X
4			X	X	X											
5		X			X		X	X	X					X	X	
6												X				
7						X	X	X	X	X	X					
8		X	X										X	X		

Directories

Lightweight Directory Access Protocol (LDAP) is an application protocol used for querying and modifying directory services over TCP/IP. An LDAP directory is a logically and hierarchically organized group of objects and their respective attributes using an LDAP Directory Tree. An LDAP directory tree typically starts with domain names at the top of the hierarchy followed by organizational boundaries, then groups followed by users and data, such as groups of documents.

X500 relies also on the use of a single Directory Information Tree (DIT) with a hierarchical organization of entries that are distributed across one or more servers. Every directory entry has what is referred to as a Distinguished Name, which is formed by combining its Relative Distinguished Name (RDN), one or more attributes of the entry itself, and the RDN of the superior entries reaching all the way up to the root of the DIT.

Active Directory (AD, originally called NT Directory Services) stores data and information within a central database, is highly scalable, and provides a wide variety of other network services including LDAP-like directory services, authentication, and Domain Name System–based naming. While AD is primarily used for assignment of policies because of its many attributes, it is commonly used by separate services to facilitate software distribution within a network.

Think of directory structures like LDAP, X500, and AD as a telephone directory where all entries are based on an alphabetical order and have attached addresses and telephone numbers.

Single Sign-On

Single Sign-On (SSO) can best be defined as an authentication mechanism that allows a single identity to be shared across multiple applications. Effectively, it allows the user to authenticate once and gain access to multiple resources.

The primary purpose of SSO is for the convenience of the user. With that in perspective, SSO can also help in mitigating some of the inherent risks of access control subjects using a different password or authentication mechanism for each of the many systems they access in a large network. Simply put, the chances of a security breach naturally increase as the number of passwords and or authentication mechanisms increase. This must, of course, be balanced against the additional risk of using SSO in that once implemented, a malicious hacker now only has to obtain a single set of authentication credentials and then has access to all of the systems that the respective access control subject was permitted to access.

The following advantages as well as disadvantages of SSO must also be considered:

Advantages of SSO	Disadvantages of SSO
More efficient log-on process Easier administration	Difficult to implement across the enterprise
• When a new employee is hired, all of the accounts on all of the systems the new employee needs to access can be quickly added from a single administration point.	• Many systems use proprietary authentication systems that will not work well with standard SSO systems.
• When an existing employee is terminated, all access can be quickly and simultaneously restricted at a single administration point.	Time consuming to implement properly
• If an existing user loses their token or forgets their password, the administrator can quickly update the user's authentication credentials from a single administration point.	• Many underestimate the amount of time necessary to properly implement SSO across all systems in the enterprise.
Can mitigate some security risks	Expensive to implement
• Reduces the inherent risk of a user having to remember passwords for multiple systems, within the enterprise.	• Because of the difficulty and time involved to properly implement SSO, it is expensive. A redundant authentication server is required to avoid a single point of failure.
• Because only a single password is used, the user is more apt to use a much stronger password.	

• Timeout and attempt thresholds are enforced consistently across the entire enterprise. SSO generally offers a good return on investment for the enterprise. The reduced administrative costs can often pay for the cost of implementing SSO in a short period of time. However, it should be noted that if scripting is used to facilitate the implementation of SSO, the typical reduced administration costs associated with SSO could in fact be negated because of the effort required to maintain numerous scripts.	• Proprietary authentication systems may need expensive custom programming to be used in an SSO implementation, and more often than not this cost is not considered in the original estimates and results in SSO implementation cost overruns. Other concerns • In some cases the original authentication system for a difficult to implement system has to be weakened in an effort to get it to work reliably in an SSO system.

Risks

Single point of failure. With all of your users credentials stored on a single authentication server, the failure of that server can prevent access for those users to all applications that it had provided authentication services for.

Single point of access. Because SSO affords a single point of access, it is more prone to mass denial of service attacks where by entire groups of users can be denied access to systems by attacking the single point of access.

Implementation

Kerberos. Kerberos, described in RFC 1510, was originally developed by the Massachusetts Institute of Technology (MIT) and has become a popular network authentication protocol for indirect (third-party) authentication services. It is designed to provide strong authentication using secret-key cryptography. It is an operational implementation of key distribution technology and affords a key distribution center, authentication service, and ticket granting service. Hosts, applications, and servers all have to be "Kerberized" to be able to communicate with the user and the ticket granting service.

Like the previously discussed indirect authentication technologies, Kerberos is based on a centralized architecture, thereby reducing administrative effort in managing all authentications from a single server. Furthermore, the use of Kerberos provides support for:

■ Authentication: You are who you say you are.
■ Authorization: What can you do once you are properly authenticated?
■ Confidentiality: Keep data secret.
■ Integrity: Data received are the same as the data that were sent.
■ Nonrepudiation: Determines exactly who sent or received a message.

The process in the use of Kerberos is substantially different from those indirect authentication technologies we have previously reviewed and is considerably more complex. The following is a simplified explanation of the Kerberos process that was adapted for use here from *Applied Cryptography: Protocols, Algorithms, and Source Code in C* by Bruce Schneier (New York, NY: Wiley, 1993).

1. Before an access control subject can request a service from an access control object, it must first obtain a ticket to the particular target object; hence, the access control subject first must request from the Kerberos Authentication Server (AS) a ticket to the Kerberos Ticket Granting Service (TGS). This request takes the form of a message containing the user's name and the name of the respective TGS.

2. The AS looks up the access control subject in its database and then generates a session key to be used between the access control subject and the TGS. Kerberos encrypts this session key using the access control subject's secret key. Then, it creates a Ticket Granting Ticket (TGT) for the access control subject to present to the TGS and encrypts the TGT using the TGS's secret key. The AS sends both of these encrypted messages back to the access control subject.

3. The access control subject decrypts the first message and recovers the session key. Next, the access control subject creates an authenticator consisting of the access control subject's name, address, and a time stamp, all encrypted with the session key that was generated by the AS.

4. The access control subject then sends a request to the TGS for a ticket to a particular target server. This request contains the name of the server, the TGT received from Kerberos (which is already encrypted with the TGS's secret key), and the encrypted authenticator.

5. The TGS decrypts the TGT with its secret key and then uses the session key included in the TGT to decrypt the authenticator. It compares the information in the authenticator with the information in the ticket, the access control subject's network address with the address the request was sent from, and the time stamp with the current time. If everything matches, it allows the request to proceed.

6. The TGS creates a new session key for the user and target server and incorporates this key into a valid ticket for the access control subject to present to the access control object server. This ticket also contains the access control subject's name, network address, a time stamp, and an expiration time for the

ticket—all encrypted with the target server's secret key—and the name of the server. The TGS also encrypts the new access control subject target session key using the session key shared by the access control subject and the TGS. It sends both messages to the access control subject.

7. The access control subject decrypts the message and extracts the session key for use with the target access control object server. The access control subject is now ready to authenticate himself or herself to the access control object server. He or she creates a new authenticator encrypted with the access control subject target session key that the TGS generated. To request access to the target access control object server, the access control subject sends along the ticket received from Kerberos (which is already encrypted with the target access control object server's secret key) and the encrypted authenticator. Because this authenticator contains plaintext encrypted with the session key, it proves that the sender knows the key. Just as important, encrypting the time of day prevents an eavesdropper who records both the ticket and the authenticator from replaying them later.

8. The target access control object server decrypts and checks the ticket and the authenticator, also confirming the access control subject's address and the time stamp. If everything checks out, the access control object server now knows the access control subject is who he or she claims to be, and the two share an encryption key that they can use for secure communication. (Since only the access control subject and the access control object server share this key, they can assume that a recent message encrypted in that key originated with the other party.)

9. For those applications that require mutual authentication, the server sends the access control subject a message consisting of the time stamp plus 1, encrypted with the session key. This serves as proof to the user that the access control object server actually knew its secret key and was able to decrypt the ticket and the authenticator.

To provide for the successful implementation and operation of Kerberos, the following should be considered:

- Overall security depends on a careful implementation.
- Requires trusted and synchronized clocks across the enterprise network.
- Enforcing limited lifetimes for authentication based on time stamps reduces the threat of a malicious hacker gaining unauthorized access using fraudulent credentials.
- The Key Distribution Server must be physically secured.
- The Key Distribution Server must be isolated on the network and should not participate in any non-Kerberos network activity.
- The AS can be a critical single point of failure.

Kerberos is available in many commercial products, and a free implementation of Kerberos is available from MIT.

Accountability

Accountability is a critical component of any access control system, and the use of unique user and process identities combined with an audit trail is the cornerstone of that accountability.

Standard Format Logs

An *authentication log* contains information about both successful and unsuccessful authentication attempts. An *access control log* contains information about access control requests made on behalf of a client or resource.

ISO 27002 is the replacement for the now obsolete ISO 17799. It is an information security management standard that includes standards for the establishment and maintenance of logs in section 10.10 that includes in part:

■ Recording, when relevant and within the capacity of the logging system, all key events, including the data/time and details of the event, the user ID associated, terminal identity and/or location, network addresses and protocols, records of successful and unsuccessful system accesses or other resource accesses, changes to system configurations, use of privileges, use of system utilities and applications, files accessed and the kinds of access, and alarms raised by the access control or any other protection system, for example, ID/IP.
■ Appropriate privacy protection measures for logged data that is appropriately confidential.
■ Appropriate security protections of a technical, physical, and administrative nature, such as division of responsibilities, to ensure integrity and availability of audit logs.

Security measures are required to protect against the unauthorized changes in access control logs. NIST has published an excellent guide to log management (publication 800-92) that includes a requirement to conduct periodic audits of the security of log management infrastructure that includes the following security objectives:

■ The infrastructure log servers are fully hardened and can perform functions in support of log management only.
■ The systems generating logs are secured appropriately (e.g., fully patched, unneeded services disabled).

- Access to both system-level and infrastructure logs and logging software (both on the hosts and on media) is strictly limited, and the integrity of the logs and software is protected and verified.
- All network communications involving log data are protected appropriately as needed.

The first step after a successful intrusion by a malicious hacker is to clean your access control logs to remove all traces of his actions in the system intrusion.

Remote Access Methods

Centralized Remote Access

With centralized remote access, the access control subject credentials are stored on a central server. This architecture is common in network environments. The centralized server can be positioned within a protected network and therefore offers additional security. Centralized authentication allows both additional access control subjects and access control objects to be added, thereby making this methodology more scalable. Its strength is consistent administration of creating, maintaining, and terminating credentials, but its weaknesses include credentialing delays and single point of failure. Popular centralized implementations are RADIUS, TCACS+, and Diameter.

Remote Authentication Dial-In User Services

Remote Authentication Dial-In User Service (RADIUS) is a popular Internet Engineering Task Force (IETF) implementation of an indirect authentication service. It is similar to Terminal Access Controller Access Control System (TACACS) in that it uses a remote access server to forward the access control subject's information to an authentication server, and then the authentication server either returns the user's associated rights or denies access. Another common feature is that RADIUS centralizes and reduces administrative workload. However, unlike TACACS and Extended TACACS (XTACACS), the RADIUS implementation of indirect authentication utilized encryption by design not as an afterthought.

RADIUS in an IETF configuration offers a set of 255 standard attributes that are used to communicate AAA information between a client and a server. RADIUS in a Vendor-Specific Attribute (VSA) implementation can extend the standard IETF attributes to an additional 255 VSA. RADIUS is used by a number of network product vendors and is regarded as a de facto industry standard for indirect authentication.

Terminal Access Controller Access Control System

TACACS is an older and once popular remote access authentication system and protocol that allows one or more remote access servers to send identification information to a TACACS authentication server for authentication and authorization. The implementation of TACACS provides indirect authentication technology that can be divided into three functional areas known as "AAA" (triple A):

- Authentication
- Authorization
- Accounting

Simplicity was one of the reasons TACACS was once so popular:

- The user attempts to log-in on the remote access server.
- The remote access server forwards the user's identification information to the TACACS authentication server.
- After receiving the identification information from the remote access server, the authentication server either returns authorization information or it denies any access for the user.

Simplicity was perhaps involved in a serious security issue that was built in to TACACS by design. The communications between the remote access server and the authentication server is performed unencrypted (i.e., in clear text). Hence, it is a simple matter for a malicious hacker to see the user's identification information as well as the returned authorization information, thereby dramatically simplifying the potential compromise of the user's account.

Because of its centralized access control architecture, it offers a single point of administration, thereby reducing the effort and associated costs when compared to administering multiple separate authentication systems in decentralized architecture.

Extended Terminal Access Controller Access Control System

A second version of TACACS, called XTACACS, provided extensions to the original TACACS protocol for the support of both SLIP/PPP and CHAP/ARAP authentication.

Terminal Access Controller Access Control System Plus

TACACS+ is a later version of TACACS that among other enhancements is best noted for having solved the original TACACS communications security issues by encrypting the communications between the remote access server and the authentication server.

Diameter

Diameter is defined in RFC3588 and was derived from the RADIUS protocol and is generally believed to be the next-generation AAA protocol. Diameter is a peer-to-peer architecture and every host can act as a client or a server. The primary differences between Diameter and RADIUS are shown in Table 1.5.

Decentralized Remote Access

With decentralized remote access, the access control subject credentials are stored on the local device. This architecture is common on stand-alone devices such as a home PC or some physical access control devices. While local authentication offers easy system maintenance in comparison to a centralized authentication methodology, it can be difficult to add additional access control objects; therefore, it is most often regarded as not scalable.

Table 1.5   Primary Differences between Diameter and RADIUS

	Diameter	*RADIUS*
Transportation protocol	Connection-oriented protocols (TCP and SCTP)	Connectionless protocol (UDP)
Security	Hop-to-hop, end-to-end	Hop-to-hop
Agent support	Relay, proxy, redirect, translation	Implicit support, which means the agent behaviors might be implemented in a RADIUS server
Capabilities negotiation	Negotiate supported applications and security level	Do not support
Peer discovery	Static configuration and dynamic lookup	Static configuration
Server initiated message	Supported, for example, reauthentication message, session termination	Do not support
Maximum attribute data size	16,777,215 octets	255 octets
Vendor-specific support	Support both vendor-specific messages and attributes	Support vendor-specific attributes only

Password Authentication Protocol/Challenge Handshake Authentication Protocol

Both Password Authentication Protocol (PAP) and Challenge Handshake Authentication Protocol (CHAP) are Point-to-Point (PPP) authentication protocols defined in RFC1334. It provides for a method of encapsulating datagrams over serial links. It includes the Link Control Protocol (LCP) to establish, configure, and test the data link connection. It also includes a family of Network Control Protocols (NCPs) for establishing and configuring different network-layer protocols. The primary differences are

PAP	CHAP
• Password required	• Challenge handshake
• Unencrypted password sent via the link	• No password sent via the link
• Allows storage of encrypted passwords	• Need for storing unencrypted secrets

Other Access Control Areas

Physical Security

Physical security plays a significant role in preventing unauthorized access to networks, systems, and data. There are four layers of physical security:

- Environmental design: fences, metal barriers, building and office layout, warning signs, and trenches
- Mechanical and electronic access control: doors, locks, and the keys that control the locks
- Intrusion detection: alarms
- Video monitoring

Portable Device Security

Mobile Phones

Current-generation mobile phones have the processing power of desktop PCs of just a few short years ago. Further, their proliferation and the access that has been granted to network resources to mobile phones are growing at an alarming rate. Of greatest concern is the lack of ability to secure the data stored on the mobile phone as well as to provide for proper access control when permitting access to network resources by mobile phones. Access control policies need to be updated to address the use of current-generation mobile phones to protected network resources.

Previous-generation mobile phones did not have the ability to store large amounts of data and had little capability to access network assets. However, they still required consideration in access control:

- Malicious person can use mobile phones in social engineering attacks to circumvent access controls.
- Eavesdropping on an analog phone is trivial and can require little more than a radio receiver tuned to the correct frequency.
- Eavesdropping on a digital phone is more difficult but is not outside of the realm of possibilities with the right equipment.
- Care needs to be taken in passing credentials using mobile phone conversations.

USB, CD, and DVD Drives

USB drives have been found to be involved in numerous high-profile data breaches. It has been noted that in the TJX breach involving the theft of 45,000,000 customer records had allegedly begun when malicious hackers used USB drives to install malware on employment kiosks in a store's public area in their efforts to gain access into the corporate network.

Current popular operating system software simply provides little, if any, security mechanisms to prevent an unauthorized person from inserting a USB drive into an unattended computer and either install or run programs at the same level of authority as the user or to copy any data accessible from the PC to the USB drive.

USB drive sizes are increasing at the same time their prices are coming down, which will only make their popularity continue to grow.

USB drive risks are not limited to commercial organizations. Recently, a report from the *Mainichi Daily News* noted that Japan's military has confessed to losing a USB device that contained troop deployment maps for a joint Japan–U.S. military exercise. Table 1.6 shows how much data can be potentially removed from your network with an unauthorized USB drive.

Solutions are evolving to provide both control over which approved USB devices can be used on enterprise PCs and what data is permitted to be copied to/from them (data in transit), as well as the enforcement of the use of encryption to safeguard data (at rest) that is permitted by policy to be written to a USB drive.

CD drives have been another vehicle used for both the unauthorized installation of unapproved and potentially malicious software and the theft of both Personally Identifiable Information (PII) and intellectual property (IP). Further, writable CD drives are quickly being replaced by manufacturers of PCs with writable DVD drives. Capacity has quickly gone from 640 MB (CD) to 4.7 GB (DVD). New-technology BlueRay DVD is quickly becoming an affordable commodity and will push the capacity to 50 GB of data that can potentially be written to a single disk.

TABLE 1.6   Amount of Data That Can Be Potentially Removed from Your Network with an Unauthorized USB Drive

Document Type	Average Pages per Document	Average Pages in a 512-MB USB Drive	Average Pages in a 2-GB USB Drive	Average Pages in a 32-GB USB Drive
Microsoft Word	8	32	126	2016
E-mail	1.5	49	194	3104
Microsoft Excel	55	81	322	5152
Microsoft PowerPoint	14	9	34	544

Table 1.7 shows how much data can potentially be removed from your network with a writable CD/DVD/Blue Ray drive.

Bypass of Logical Security

Access to Computers and Equipment

A malicious person that was able to bypass logical security on a user's PC within your enterprise network would obtain all rights and privileges of that user within the network that he compromised. Typically, once gaining a user's level of access,

TABLE 1.7   Amount of Data That Can Potentially Be Removed from Your Network with a Writable CD/DVD/Blue Ray Drive

Document Type	Average Pages Per Doc	Average Pages in CD	Average Pages in DVD	Average Pages in Blue Ray
Microsoft Word	8	40,320	296,100	3,150,000
E-mail	1.5	62,080	455,900	4,850,000
Microsoft Excel	55	103,040	756,700	8,050,000
Microsoft PowerPoint	14	10,880	79,900	850,000

the malicious hacker quickly utilizes escalation of privilege attacks to elevate his level of privilege to that of system administrator. Effectively, what started out as a simple breach of an otherwise low-level user's PC can quickly escalate into a breach where the malicious hacker has administrative privilege of your entire network.

Clear Desk/Clean Screen

The continued growth of the losses associated with insider threats within the enterprise network have shifted a Clear Desk/Clean Screen policy from that of a best practice to that which is now a part of Industry Standards such as BS17799 and others. The elements of a Clean Desk/Clean Screen policy can include, but not be limited to:

- At the end of each day, or when desks and offices are unoccupied, any "confidential" information must be locked away in pedestals, filing cabinets, or offices, as appropriate.
- All wastepaper, which contains any personal or confidential information or data, must be placed in the confidential waste sacks located in each service station. Under no circumstances should this type of wastepaper be thrown away with normal rubbish in the wastepaper bins.
- Whenever you leave your desk and your PC is switched on, it is essential that you ALWAYS "lock" your screen by pressing "Ctrl, Alt, Delete" and then enter, to confirm that you wish to lock your workstation.
- Locking your screen not only prevents someone else from using your PC, which is logged on in your name, but it also prevents someone from reading confidential information left open on your screen.
- If working on sensitive information, and you have a visitor to your desk, lock your screen to prevent the contents from being read.

Sample Questions

1. Which is of the following is not one of the three principle components of access control systems?
   a. Access control objects
   b. Biometrics
   c. Access control subjects
   d. Access control systems
2. Which of the following are behavioral traits in a biometric device?
   a. Voice Pattern
   b. Signature Dynamics

    c. Keystroke Dynamics

    d. All of the above

3. In the measurement of biometric accuracy, which of the following is commonly referred to as a "type 2 error"?

    a. Rate of false acceptance—False Acceptance Rate (FAR)

    b. Rate of false rejection—False Rejection Rate (FRR)

    c. Crossover error rate (CER)

    d. All of the above

4. Which is of the following is not one of the three functional areas of TACACS known as AAA (triple A)?

    a. Authentication

    b. Authorization

    c. Availability

    d. Accounting

5. Which of the following is an International Telecommunications Union—Telecommunications Standardization Sector (ITU-T) recommendation originally issued in 1998 for indirect authentication services using public keys?

    a. Radius

    b. X.509

    c. Kerberos

    d. SESAME

6. Which of the following is NOT one of the three primary rules in a Biba formal model?

    a. An access control subject cannot access an access control object that has a higher integrity level.

    b. An access control subject cannot access an access control object that has a lower integrity level.

    c. An access control subject cannot modify an access control object that has a higher integrity level.

    d. An access control subject cannot request services from an access control object that has a higher integrity level.

7. Which of the following is an example of a firewall that does not use Context Based Access Control?

    a. Application proxy

    b. Static packet filter

    c. Stateful inspection

    d. Circuit gateway

8. In consideration of the three basic types of authentication, which of the following is incorrect?

    a. Knowledge based = password

    b. Token based = smartcard

    c. Characteristic based = biometric

    d. None of the above

9. In the authorization provided to the access control subject by an access control system, which of the following is not a consideration for an Access Control Subject?
   a. Temporal—time of day, day of request
   b. Password or token utilized
   c. False Rejection Rate
   d. Locale from where the access control subject authenticated

10. Password selection is typically based on which of the following criteria?
   a. Minimum password length
   b. Authorizations, rights, and permissions
   c. Required usage of letters, case, numbers, and symbols in the makeup of the password
   d. All of the above

11. Which of the following should be considered in the routine monitoring of an access control system?
   a. The regular monitoring of changes to accounts can help to mitigate the risk of misuse or unauthorized access.
   b. All changes to accounts within the access control system should be logged and reviewed on a regular basis.
   c. Particular attention should focus on any newly created accounts as well as any escalation of the privileges for an existing account to make certain that the new account or the increased privileges are authorized.
   d. All of the above

12. Which of the following is not true in the consideration of Object Groups?
   a. It is a common practice to assign the appropriate permissions to a directory, and each object within the directory inherits the respective parent directory permissions.
   b. Although configuring individual objects affords maximum control, this granularity can quickly become an administration burden.
   c. By incorporating multiple objects with similar permissions or restrictions within a group or directory, the granularity is thereby coarsened and the administration of the access control system is simplified.
   d. Configuring individual objects affords maximum control; this granularity can reduce administration burden.

13. In the three basic types of authentication, which of the following are related to "something you have"?
   a. Synchronous or asynchronous token
   b. Biometric
   c. Smartcard
   d. All of the above

14. Which of the following is an asynchronous device?
   a. Time-based token
   b. Event-based token
   c. All of the above

15. Which of the following are characteristics in biometric behavioral–keystroke dynamics?
    a. The length of time each key is held down
    b. Tendencies to switch between a numeric keypad and keyboard numbers
    c. Acceleration, rhythm, pressure, and flow
    d. All of the above

Chapter 2

Cryptography

Christopher M. Nowell

Contents

Cryptography is often considered the most challenging, foreign, and thus memorable portion of the candidate's certification process. Shrouded in mystery and associated with such concepts as "evil" and "fear," cryptography is the friend of few Systems Security Certified Practitioner (SSCP) candidates. Such drama is far from warranted. To combat these misconceptions, this chapter explains the key foundation concepts you will need to successfully master the cryptography portion of the exam in plain and simple English. Key areas include:

- Understand application of cryptography (e.g., hashing, encryption mechanisms, performance)
- Understand requirements for cryptography (e.g., data sensitivity, regulatory requirements, end-user training)
- Understand concepts of certificates and key management
  - Administration and validation
  - Standards
- Understand secure protocols [e.g., IP Security (IPSec), Secure Socket Layer (SSL)/Transport Layer Security (TLS), Secure/Multipurpose Internet Mail Extensions (S/MIME)]

In reality, cryptography is most often the computerized application of all that high school math you swore you would never use after graduation. This differs slightly from the dictionary definition of, "The enciphering and deciphering of messages in secret code or cipher." To fully understand the concepts associated with this wordy definition, the SSCP candidate must first have a grasp of the basics key to an implementer and operator of cryptographic solutions.

The Basics

The whole of the cryptographic universe revolves around a few key concepts and definitions. Mastering these is fundamental to gaining the understanding necessary to obtain SSCP certification. A successful candidate must understand how cryptography plugs into the overall framework of confidentiality, integrity, and availability. Confidentiality is the most obvious use for cryptography. A message or data stream that is encrypted with even the most basic of techniques is certainly more confidential than one left alone in plaintext. Integrity is the next great area of contribution for cryptography. Hashes and cryptographic hashes are often used to verify the integrity of message as we will learn shortly.

However, if cryptography provides so many benefits, why is it that everything is not encrypted at all times? The answer is unfortunately, availability. Availability is adversely impacted by cryptography by the introduction of extra risk from the loss, distribution, or mismanagement of cryptographic keys. Data that are encrypted must at some point be unencrypted, so losing a decryption key becomes a real problem with the passage of time. In addition, key distribution (the method of getting a key from where it was generated to where it needs to be used) adds another layer of risk and complexity should a key not be transported in time for its use. On top of all of this, cryptography can add a measure of processing overhead and lag time to a data stream or message decryption that may make the data obsolete or unusable. A successful implementer and operator of cryptographic solutions must keep the balance of these three critical aspects in mind at all times to effectively exercise the strengths and minimize the weaknesses involved with this domain.

The following paragraph is full of extremely important definitions. Now would be an excellent opportunity to take a few notes. All too often, cryptographic buzz words are tossed around incorrectly, leading to rampant confusion, mistakes, and the furthering of the unwarranted mythos mentioned earlier. The first of these concepts is the meaning and differences between plaintext and ciphertext. *Plaintext* is quite simple and generally refers to the message or data in its natural unaltered state. *Ciphertext* is that same message or data after the application of cryptosystem. *Cryptosystem* is just a big fancy word for some sort of methodology to encipher or decipher that message or data. The methodology used typically employs at least one cryptographic cipher, algorithm, and cryptographic hash employed either in combination or in multiples. Although often misused interchangeably to mean the same thing, cryptographic ciphers, algorithms, and cryptographic hashes are different concepts.

A *cipher* is a mathematical application of a cryptographic algorithm used to encrypt plaintext or decrypt ciphertext. A cipher that combines a continuous stream of plaintext with a continuous stream of key material is called a *streaming cipher*, while a cipher that combines chunks of plaintext against a chunk of key material is called *block cipher*. This differs critically from a *cryptographic hash*, whose function is generally to take a message of no particular length or type, process it, and return a value with a fixed length and particular structure.

Cryptographic hashes are most often used to quickly scramble important files such as password files, to verify message integrity such as "digital email signatures," and for the construction of cryptographic ciphers. Alternatively, hashes can be employed in a noncryptographic function. This is done by generating a hash value for a particular file and then using it over time to determine if that file has been modified. If the file has changed, regenerating the hash should create a different hash than the original, although this is not always the case.

Algorithms are the rules that govern the use of a cryptosystem's components so that when you say the name of a particular algorithm, other security professionals know which cipher types, key length options, restrictions, and limitations are involved. A *key*, then, is the value used by the cipher to create unique output from the encryption process. Without a key, the cipher will return the same results every time a given set of information is encrypted. *Key space* refers to the set of all possible keys usable by a particular algorithm. All other aspects being equal, an algorithm with a larger key space is considered to be better than one with a smaller key space as the odds of guessing the key becomes substantially smaller with a large space.

Key space differs importantly from *key size*, also called *key length*. Key length refers to the number of bits that can be used in a particular cryptographic key. The size or sizes that an algorithm can use varies widely. Key size has little to nothing to do with an algorithm being considered a strong algorithm. An algorithm that is considered to be strong can greatly benefit from a longer key length, but a longer key length will do little to prop up a faulty algorithm.

Cryptographic algorithms are generally divided into two groups: *symmetric*, also known as private key or secret key, and *asymmetric* cryptography. With regard to symmetric cryptography, ciphers are traditionally divided up into streaming ciphers and block ciphers. For asymmetric cryptography, also referred to as public key cryptography, things are a bit different. With asymmetric cryptography, a combination of multiple cryptographic algorithms, cryptographic hashes, and communications protocols are used to generate, distribute, and implement a cryptosystem that uses two distinct cryptographic keys to securely encrypt, transport, store, and decrypt a particular set of data. Typically, asymmetric cryptography is considered to be quite a bit more challenging to implement and operate. As such, we will focus on this topic in greater detail later in this chapter after we have covered a few more critical concepts.

There are two more concepts critical to understanding the role and value of cryptography. These concepts are *nonrepudiation* and *authentication.* Nonrepudiation is the idea that any action or statement can be tied to a particular individual often at a particular time. Nonrepudiation is not possible to accomplish with symmetric key cryptography on its own as all parties involved in a cryptographic transaction use the same secret key. It is therefore impossible to tie a specific person to a particular cryptographic action using symmetric key cryptography. As we will discuss further in later sections, nonrepudiation is achieved largely through the use or asymmetric or public key cryptography.

With public key cryptography, a person involved in a cryptographic transaction uses his own personal private key along with the shared public key to create a message, thus providing the required nonrepudiation in the form of a digital signature. Effective nonrepudiation can only be achieved through the selection and implementation of a comprehensive public key solution featuring strong algorithms; hashes; protocols; timekeeping; and processes, procedures, and channels for key distribution and management.

Authentication verifies the claimed identity of an individual or process against one or more factors known or processed by the thing being authenticated, hopefully to the exclusion of all other parties. The old-fashioned, traditional method of authentication is the user ID and password. In the cryptographic world, traditional authentication measures such as this are often augmented or replaced by digital certificates: hardware tokens or personal identification numbers.

Block Ciphers

Block ciphers encrypt plaintext in chunks or of a particular size where the block size is the size of the message chunk and the secret key used can vary in length dramatically, with longer keys typically being considered stronger. The key to understanding how a specific block cipher works in a specific implementation revolves around mastering the concept of mode of operation. Mode of operation is a block cipher concept that allows an implementer greater flexibility in selecting a cryptographic solution best suited for the problem at hand. Although there are numerous vendor-specific, nonstandard implementations available, there are generally considered to be five classic modes of operation for block ciphers:

1. Electronic Codebook (ECB)
2. Cipher Block Chaining (CBC)
3. Cipher Feedback (CFB)
4. Output Feedback (OFB)
5. Counter (CTR)

In addition, at the time of this writing, there are three newer standardized modes:

1. Cipher-Based Method Authentication Code Algorithm (CMAC)
2. Counter with Cipher Block Chaining-Message Authentication Code (CCM)
3. Galois/Counter Mode or GCM with its associated specialization

Electronic Codebook

Electronic Codebook (ECB) is by far the simplest of the modes of operation and is often considered to be the least protecting of a message's confidentiality. In ECB, a message is simply divided into blocks and encrypted using the same cipher for the entire message. With ECB, a given block of plaintext encrypted with the same cipher always yields the same results if encrypted multiple times. While this is often a fast method of encrypting and decrypting a message, it makes the message susceptible to something called a replay attack. We will detail attack types later in this chapter, but for now it is important to realize that ECB has serious shortcomings for confidentiality and should only be considered in noncritical situations.

Cipher Block Chaining

Cipher Block Chaining (CBC) is an older but still widely used mode of operation where each block of plaintext is encrypted using a key that is derived from the previous block of ciphertext that had been scrambled using a process called exclusive-OR (Xor) and padded with filler bits where necessary to make blocks of the required size (see Figure 2.1).

Xor is a Boolean logic operation where a condition is true if one of two conditions is true and false if both conditions are either true or false. In this key construction scenario, this means that if the first bit of the plaintext block being used is 1 and the first bit of the ciphertext block being used is 0 then the first bit of the key being built is 1. Likewise if the second bit of the same plaintext block is 1 and second bit of the same ciphertext block is 1, the second bit of the key being created is 0. This process continues until the key is built and ready to go.

The very first block to be encrypted employs a cryptographic device called an initialization vector (IV). An IV is a pseudorandom value of a specific size that is used as starter material in constructing the first key used in encrypting a message. It is also intended to prevent the situation found in ECB where the same data, repeated in a particular message, ends up as identical blocks of ciphertext.

From the perspective of the mode of operation, the IV never needs to be secret but must always be unpredictable for CBC. The problem with a CBC solution occurs when you get an error in one of your blocks. Since each block of plaintext is encrypted with the previous block of ciphertext, an error at any point in the process will create a recursive fault throughout the remainder of the encrypted message.

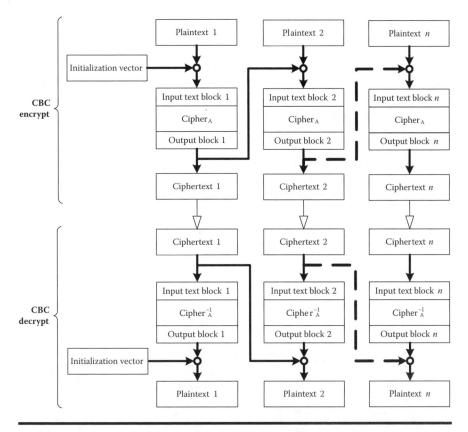

Figure 2.1   CBC is a mode of operation where each block of plaintext is encrypted using a key that is derived from the previous block of ciphertext that been scrambled using a process called exclusive-OR (Xor) and padded with filler bits where necessary to make blocks of the required size.

This error stands a serious chance of rendering the message unrecoverable as there is no ready way to tell where the error occurred and repair the damaged ciphertext.

This is an excellent opportunity to discuss a method that is often employed to combat the problem with errors. Hashed Message Authentication Code, sometimes referred to as Keyed Message Authentication Code, combines a cryptographic hash with a secret key. The goal is to simultaneously validate both the message's integrity along with its authenticity as only the sender and receiver know the secret key. This is most often used to protect the integrity of data transmitted with network security protocols. Occasionally, in secure online commerce, a retailer may require a customer to store a secret key with them in the form of a secret question or a specific file. In these situations, the question or file is the key or key material used along with the hash function to protect and verify the integrity of the data being transmitted.

Cipher Feedback

Cipher Feedback (CFB) is very similar to CBC but the major difference between the two allows for radically different implementations. As with CBC, CFB needs to start with an unpredictable but not necessarily secret IV; padding must be added to the plaintext when it is not long enough for the block size in use and the encryption key for each block is derived from the previous block of ciphertext Xor'd with the chosen cipher for the entire message. Unlike with CBC, CFB decryption forms a steady data stream that allows a block cipher to behave more like a stream cipher, thus making it more flexible than CBC and appropriate for implementation such as encrypted media streams. In addition, CFB suffers from less serious recursive error problems than CBC since an error in the stream will only corrupt that one block and its immediate follow on block. The impact of this error depends entirely on the implementation and so should not be discounted out of hand (Figure 2.2).

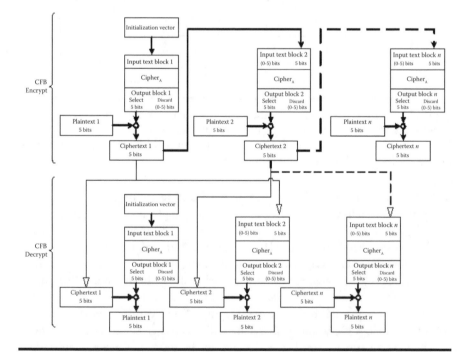

Figure 2.2 CFB is very similar to CBC but their major difference between the two allows for radically different implementations.

Output Feedback

Output Feedback (OFB) differs substantially from CFB and CBC. In OFB, the IV need not be secret nor need it be unpredictable for a given key. Rather, it only needs to be a unique integer for each message encrypted using that particular key. If it is possible for a particular OFB implementation to safely and securely make the IV known to both parties, OFB allows for the key to be precomputed. This allows for a substantial increase in performance as compared with modes of operation that do not support precomputing. In contrast to CBC and CFB, the cipher used to encrypt the blocks is not a modified copy of the previous block of cyphertext. Instead, it is a Xor-modified version of the previous cipher. As a result, OFB Mode block ciphers function as a stream and are thus appropriate for a wide range of implementations where data must be encrypted, transmitted, and decrypted in a rapid, near-real-time fashion (Figure 2.3).

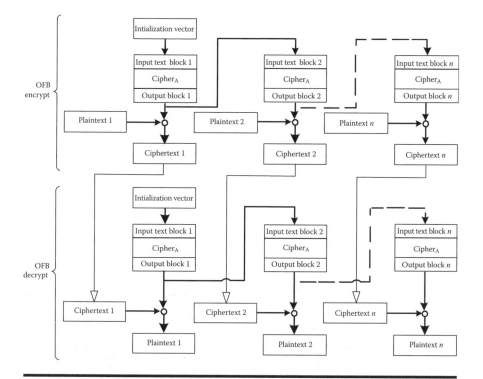

Figure 2.3   OFB differs substantially from CFB and CBC. In OFB, the IV need not be secret nor need it be unpredictable for a given key. Rather, it only needs to be a unique integer for each message encrypted using that particular key.

In addition, because any given block of cyphertext is largely independent from the block before and after it, OFB supports numerous error-correcting protocols to successfully operate. This does not mean that OFB is immune to errors as no mode of operation will fully compensate for a poor-quality data connection. One major problem with OFB implementations can come from the reuse of an IV to initiate the encryption of two or more messages using the same key. When reusing keys, it is imperative that an OFB implementation use a unique IV; otherwise, the confidentiality of the data stream can be easily compromised.

Counter

The final classic mode of operation is Counter (CTR), and it is substantially different from the previously mentioned modes. Although CTR also allows for a block cipher to act as a stream, it does so without the use of an IV or by modifying a previous block of cyphertext for use as the encryption or decryption key. Rather, as the name implies, CTR uses a "counter" function in place of an IV (Figure 2.4).

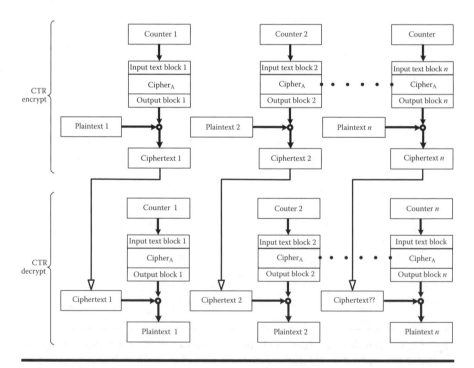

Figure 2.4   The final classic mode of operation is CTR, and it is substantially different from the previously mentioned modes.

Unlike an IV, the counter function must be completely unique and distinct across all messages and keys. In addition, the counter is modified with the encryption of each block in a message and must maintain that unique quality at the same time. The counter can be modified in any number of ways with the most popular method being a simple old-fashioned incremental increase. It is important to note, however, that the cipher must be rekeyed before the counter space is exhausted. If this does not occur, the counter in use will not be unique and a replay attack could result.

Encryption is achieved by combining the counter-modified cipher being used for the message with the block of plaintext once again using Xor. This facilitates the rapid and block-order-independent decryption of a CTR mode data stream. To further enhance usability, CTR mode supports the precomputing of keys in addition to the parallel processing of ciphertext and plaintext blocks in both encryption and decryption functions. This robust flexibility makes CTR mode the most resilient and error resistant of the five classic modes.

Recently, several newer standardized modes have been added to the previously discussed list of classic modes of operation for Block Mode ciphers. The first of these is called CMAC. CMAC is designed to assure the authenticity and integrity of variable length messages encrypted with an underlying block cipher such as Advanced Encryption Standard (AES). CMAC has three key process steps: subkey generation, MAC generation and MAC verification. In CMAC, the primary key generated by the selected cipher function is used to generate two subkeys. These subkeys are secret values and are generated by the Subkey Generation Algorithm using the primary key as source material (Figure 2.5).

While both subkeys are used in MAC generation and MAC verification, they have a third very important role. The first subkey, referred to as K1, is used when the message length is a positive multiple of the block length. The second subkey, referred to as K2, is used when the message length is not a positive multiple of the block length. The illustration included in this paragraph displays the need to make the message a positive multiple of the block length. It is important to note that the implementer potentially has a choice whether to choose storage and precomputation of subkeys to improve performance or to recompute new subkeys with each invocation using a new primary key for increased resistance to cryptanalysis.

The next process step is the MAC generation algorithm. The MAC generation algorithm takes three inputs: a secret key, the message itself, and the length of the message expressed in octets. The message itself is processed with one of the two previously generated subkeys. Which one of the two subkeys is used depends on the previously discussed conditions. The three inputs and the processed messages are combined to form an identically sized MAC to the secret key employed by the selected cipher. The final process step is the MAC verification algorithm. This is the simplest part of the process as it merely recomputes the MAC based on the received message and compares the recomputed MAC to the received MAC. The MAC verification algorithm output is either a response of VALID or INVALID, which either confirms or refutes, respectively, the message's authenticity.

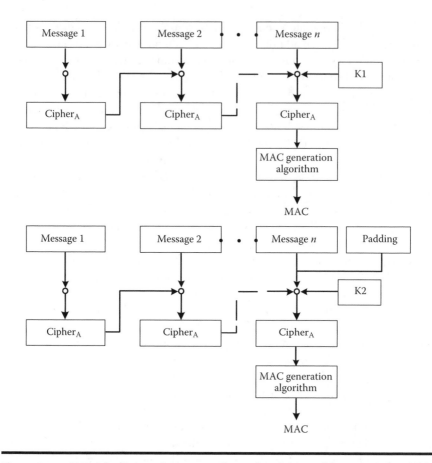

Figure 2.5 CMAC is designed to assure the authenticity and integrity of variable length messages encrypted with an underlying block cipher such as AES.

The next of the newer standardized nodes of operation is Counter with Cipher Block Chaining Message Authentication Code (CBC-MAC) better known as CCM. This mode combines CBC-MAC for authentication with CTR mode for encryption. While CTR and CBC modes have been explained, CBC-MAC provides authentication for messages of a known fixed length by arranging the block segments of a particular message in such a way that modifying one block would cause the following blocks to become obviously altered and the message's integrity destroyed.

With CCM, there are two main variable choices an implementer should understand. The first choice is the size of the authentication field as measured in octets. The choice and implementer makes for this variable result in a trade-off between message expansion and the probability that an attacker can undetectably modify a message with a large number expanding the message more but providing a large degree of protection. The other variable is the size of the Nonce. This value requires a tradeoff between the maximum message size and the size of the number used once, also known as a *nonce*. The nonce is a unique number used to ensure that each message encrypted with a particular key is well protected in terms of privacy. Similar to CCM, the integrity of a message is validated during decryption by recomputing the CBC-MAC value and comparing the value in the received recomputed MAC with the expected result.

Galois Counter Mode (GCM) and its related MAC implementation GMAC is currently the final of the newer standardized modes of operation at the time of this writing. Defined under a single standard due to their close relation and shared founder, GCM provides authentication to an underlying 128-bit block cipher such as AES while GMAC provides the same authentication services but only to unencrypted data. GCM has several unique and advantageous features. The first of these is that the message length need not be fixed nor known in advance. The next feature of note is that the authenticity verification can be performed independently of the decryption process. In addition, if the unique IV is predictable and the length of the encrypted data is known, the block cipher invocations can be precomputed. On top of that, if some or all of the nonencrypted data is fixed, the authentication component can also be precomputed.

GCM is broken down into two main fairly efficient functions, authenticated encryption and authenticated decryption. Both functions can be executed in parallel, and as a result, GCM is capable of high performance operation if the implementer so chooses. All is not perfect with GCM and the implementer must exercise caution, especially when it comes to the IV and the key. For an implementation of GCM to be considered safely resistant to cryptanalysis, the chances that the same IV and the same key being used on two or more sets of input data cannot exceed 2–32. In reality, the IV is a nonce and if even one IV is ever repeated, then the implementation may be vulnerable to the forgery attacks making the uniqueness of the IV almost as important as the secrecy of the key.

Symmetric Cryptography

Stream Ciphers

Stream ciphers operate quite differently than block ciphers. Where block ciphers, even ones capable of performing as stream ciphers, encrypt chunks of plaintext data, turning them into cyphertext before transmitting, stream ciphers encrypt data on the fly usually on a bit-by-bit basis. In stream ciphers, keys are traditionally called *keystreams* and can be either dependent on the plaintext or ciphertext called a *self-synchronizing keystream* or completely independent of both and called a *synchronous streaming cipher*.

Stream ciphers are typically employed for their speed and flexibility benefits more than for their strength of encryption. The first concern with stream ciphers is often their short repeat period. This means that there is a small and definite limit to how much data can be encrypted and transmitted before the keystream is repeated. The comparison of two streams of data where the keystream has repeated can provide a cryptanalyst with the ability to deduce both data streams. To be secure, the amount of data encrypted and transmitted before a keystream repeats must be sufficiently large to make the interception and comparison of encrypted data impractical. With modern computing power being cheap and plentiful, the volume of encrypted and transmitted data that constitutes "impractical" can be extremely large.

Another critical shortcoming of stream ciphers is lack of sufficient bit- or byte-level transposition permutations. What that means is that there is an extremely finite limit to the variety bit or byte positions possible in a stream ciphers. A third material weakness to stream ciphers is their susceptibility to integrity attacks. An example of this can be found in the often used Wired Equivalent Privacy (WEP) security standard. WEP includes an integrity check that uses a 32-bit Cyclic Redundancy Check (CRC) derived from a corresponding RC4 encrypted WEP message. The check compares the message to the CRC value to confirm that the message's integrity has not been compromised during transmission.

The problem originates from the fact that CRCs are well-known nonsecure linear hash functions where the relationship between the RC4 encrypted message and the CRC can be easily determined. This allows an attacker to compromise a message's integrity by altering both the bits in the RC4 encrypted WEP message while altering the corresponding bits in the CRC to make it pass the check. The final flaw in stream ciphers comes from the fact that they are dangerously easy to implement and operate in an incorrect and insecure fashion.

With these limitations in mind, it is understandable why many popular implementations of streaming ciphers are actually block ciphers in a mode of operation that allows for streaming behavior. This is not to say that streaming ciphers are never used. Quite to the contrary, streaming ciphers are often and best employed in situations where the duration requirement for confidentiality is small or the performance considerations are critical. Multimedia transmissions, closed circuit TV, and desktop sharing programs all use streaming ciphers for their encryption needs.

One-Time Pads

One-time pads are more conceptual than practical in the modern business world. That being said, the concept is important to understand as one-time pads have been used in several notable situations. With a one-time pad, a string of bits are generated completely at random at equal length to the message being encrypted. This keystream is then combined with the message using Xor and the result is the encrypted message. The message can be decrypted in the same fashion by somebody who has a copy of the keystream or the ability to recreate it.

In theory, it is near impossible to decrypt such a message without the original random keystream. The problem is, any keystream that can be recreated in little to no time is inherently not random, and any keystream where two or more copies exist lends itself to a number of problems including reuse attacks and old-fashioned thievery. Governments have often used one-time pads in support of intelligence gathering activities, especially before the advent of easily portable electronic encryption/decryption devices.

Introduction to Public Key

Public key cryptography is quite different from symmetric key cryptography in both concept and structure. The intent of public key cryptography is to allow two or more parties to communicate openly across a public infrastructure using publicly available technology through the creation of a secure encrypted channel. The first difficult concept to understand with public key cryptography is that the key used to encrypt a message is different than the key used to decrypt a message. At first examination, this sounds ridiculous and impossible but could not be farther from the truth.

In public key cryptography, every participating party has at least one private key and a public key. The reason for multiple keys is that some keys are used for certain specific functions and not for others. We will go into the details of those functions shortly. As with symmetric key cryptography, the private key is kept secret and hopefully safe from those who wish to break into your cryptosystem. The difference is that the public key is published to a central, sometimes public repository where those who need to send you an encrypted message can get to it. A message's author encrypts his message with the public key of the party who is receiving the message. The recipient then uses her own private key to decrypt the message and read it in plaintext. If the message is intercepted, even by somebody with complete access to all published public keys, the person who intercepted it will not be able to read the plaintext message.

For an extra level of security, it is also possible for the message author to digitally sign a message by creating a hash of the message with his personal private key and attaching it to the message before encrypting it with the recipient's public key. Sounds simple, right? Well, there are a few very important and tricky components to implement that make the incredible benefits of public key cryptography more than a bit challenging to implement effectively.

The next concept sounds like common sense; namely, that the algorithms and hash functions used to create the public and private keys must be easy for a system to computationally generate and use while still being effective and strong. While it would take a normal human an eternity to generate and use the public and private keys in encrypting and decrypting correspondence, a computer should be able to handle the calculations rather quickly. Normally, this is the case; however, when the calculations are scaled up to a large environment with hundreds or thousands of users, speed can become a problem. In addition to the issues associated with complaining users who are never satisfied with the speed of a system, timing issues can be critical in certain implementations as some keys are only good for a short period.

The third concept is a bit more complex than the last. This concept states that if a person or computer knows or has the public key, it should take an impractically large amount of time for a computer to figure out the corresponding private key. This should remain true even when the algorithms used to create the public key are publicly known. This allows for a user to publicly post their public key with a great deal of certainty that their private key will remain safe and known only to them. The final concept is that a unique input, used as a randomly generated key, can be used to generate both the public and private key. This will make the two keys mathematically related to each other yet distinct from all the other public–private key pairs generated by the system.

Hashes and Digital Signatures

We talked briefly about hashes earlier in this chapter but further explanation in the framework of public key cryptography is required. As mentioned before, hashes take a message of variable length and use that data to construct a fixed-length binary output. That output should always be the same every time it is computed against a particular message if that message has not changed. This quality makes hashes excellent for verifying message integrity. It is this integrity-check quality that makes hashes critical in the construction of public key cryptography solutions, especially digital signatures.

Digital signatures can be done with either symmetric or asymmetric cryptography. The problem with using symmetric cryptography is that the digital signature can be easily duplicated by anybody who has the key. With asymmetric cryptography, this is prevented through assurances that a private key is not being shared among multiple persons. The first step in constructing a digital signature is to take the original message and process it with a cryptographic hash function. This will generate something called a message digest that is then encrypted using the sender's private key. This encrypted message digest is referred to as a digital signature, and this signature is appended to the message when transmitted.

When the message is received, the recipient can verify the signature and the message's integrity if they have access to the sender's public key. This is accomplished by running the received message through the same cryptographic hash as the sender used to generate a message digest. The affixed digital signature is then decrypted with the sender's public key, generating another message digest. If these two message digests are compared and found to be identical, then the message integrity has been verified and there is reasonable certainty that the message is from the person it appears to be from. If the message digests do not match up, then it is reasonably certain that either the message has been modified from its original state or the signature is not valid for that sender. This aspect of digital signatures is what allows them to facilitate nonrepudiation as mentioned earlier in this chapter.

It is important to note that a typical implementation will involve the creation and use of signing keys and encryption keys for a particular user. This is to facilitate nonrepudiation as the encryption keys are typically backed up and easily recoverable while signing keys are not. We will further discuss why this is in later sections. Armed with this understanding, we are ready for an in-depth exploration of the next aspect of public key cryptography—digital certificates.

Public Key Infrastructure

Public Key Infrastructure (PKI) is not the same as public key cryptography. While they are indeed related to each other, PKI is an organized coherent collection of policies, processes, hardware, and software used for the purpose of governing certificates and public–private key pairs, including the ability to issue, maintain, and revoke public key certificates. It is imperative to understand for instance that the public key concept of digital signatures, asymmetric algorithms, and certificates are not PKI but rather can be components of a PKI implementation.

As the name implies, PKI is an infrastructure and represents a significant investment of time, money, and materials when implementing it in your environment. For PKI to work, each of the following components must be effectively deployed and managed along with the ability for them to securely interact and share the information necessary to operate the infrastructure. When it does work, a PKI-enabled environment can leverage the high degree of identity assurance, confidentiality, and systems integration to allow for multifactor user and device authentication, physical, logical, and data access control along with the ability to access multiple system components with a single set of credentials. In essence, PKI is the ultimate integration of all the asymmetric cryptography concepts contained in this chapter.

PKI is also all about trusting specific people and organizations with specific trust criteria and for specific lengths of time. In PKI, trust is organized into hierarchical chains that run from a top-level trust authority called a Root down to your organization and then to your devices in that organization. At each link in the chain, each side vouches for the credibility and identity of the other.

PKI trusts are never transitive, meaning that if you trust somebody else and that person trusts a third random person, you do not have any trust obligations to that third random person. Trusts are also not necessarily maintained when a device or the people managing that device relocate to another organization. Who you and your organization decide to trust and why are some of the most important decisions that can be made in a PKI environment. Creating a trust with the wrong party not only can impair the functionality of your PKI environment but also can cause a loss of reputation to you and your organization.

Certificates

Digital certificates, their issuers, and their verifiers are the combination of key several concepts in public key cryptography. Digital certificates employ a digital signature to bind together a public key with an identity. These three elements are required to ensure that the identity associated with the public key is not being impersonated by another. A digital certificate will traditionally include a person or computer's public key, digital signature, and the digital signature of the Certification Authority (CA) that issued the certificate.

Inclusion of the CA's digital signature allows for the authenticity of the certificate to be verified by forming a chain of trust. This chain leads from the recipient, up to the sender's certificate, then up to the issuing CA's certificate, and finally (if applicable) to a trusted third-party root CA that issued the original digital certificate for the CA that issued the sender's certificate containing the public key and signature in use by the recipient. This trusted third-party root CA serves as a verification agent that confirms the identity of the local CA that in turn confirms the identity of the sender through the issuance of their certificate.

The certificate also serves as an excellent encapsulation for distribution as all the information contained within can be contained in a single file for easy circulation. In addition, a typical digital certificate will include other information such as the identity of the person or computer holding the private key, the expiration date of the certificate, and details about the recommended use of the embedded public key.

The CA that issues certificates is often more than just an application running on a computer. The worldwide chain of CAs is a complex collection of systems, software, and people whose sole purpose is to create and issue certificates, maintain status information for existing certificates by building a Certificate Revocation List (CRL), publish that CRL along with active certificates, and finally to maintain an archive of previously issued certificates both expired and active. The CA must also verify the identity of the person or the device for which they are issuing a certificate. When a CA issues a certificate, they are attesting that a person or device is exactly who or what they say they are. This goes double for when a CA issues a certificate to another CA as the issuing CA is vouching for the trustworthy state of the receiving CA.

To ensure that identities are rigorously verified, the CAs will delegate the rolls of identification and authentication of certificate holders by creating an entity called a Registration Authority (RA). The RA is trusted by the CA and registers certificates in the appropriate Certificate Repository while confirming then vouching for the identity of the certificate holder.

Multiple-level identity verification is one of the cornerstone principles behind digital certificates. The idea is that with each level of trust comes a corresponding level of verification. This methodology of continuous "trust but verify" is the cornerstone of public key cryptography. Just as with the CA, the RA's operation is often conducted with a complex set of equipment and software. One of the differences, however, is that there are far fewer people involved in the roll of RA, often just a single person per RA instance. It is important to note that an RA cannot and will not issue or sign certificates. Rather, its role is typically limited to the identification, verification, and authentication of CA-issued certificates.

The next certificate concept to understand was touched on earlier, revocation. Although there are several ways to accomplish this, the two methods most often implemented in a certificate-heavy environment are the previously mentioned CRL or through the inclusion of a secure protocol such as Online Certificate Status Protocol (OCSP) in your certificate implementation. While CRLs are the original traditional method for publishing a comprehensive list of expired certificates, their large size and need to be parsed into usable data from their natural raw text state makes them slow and computationally intensive to use.

OCSP, on the other hand, is a network protocol that handles status check requests from certificate-aware environments while not allowing the pending process to proceed until a response is received affirming the certificates validity. Although multiple repeaters and responders may be required for a large environment, they represent a substantial technological leap over the older CRL-based solution and are often considered key components of a modern PKI environment. Some of the causes of certificate revocation are loss or compromise of the associated private key, the departure of an associated individual from their respective organization or if it is discovered that the issuing CA issued the certificate improperly.

The final certificate concept to understand is that of expiration. Each certificate comes with an expiration date. On that date, the certificate and its associate public key become invalid and depending on the implementation, will cease to function. Issuing new certificates in a manner that minimizes downtime is crucial. While some certificates expire after years of use, there are many short-term certificates and keys that expire after a few minutes or sometimes less. In either case, the certificate-using community affected by the expiration needs to be informed of this. That is why it is so important to have an accurate, synchronized time source across the entirety of your environment.

Key Distribution

The challenges faced with PKI are not only those brought by the components that make up the infrastructure but also those brought by new problems introduced with the integration of those components. In PKI, the single greatest challenge introduced by the integration of digital signature, certificates, algorithms, legacy authentication mechanisms, and human beings is key distribution. The timely, accurate, and authenticated distribution of both private and public key materials is always a great challenge. Often, implementers rely on out-of-band solutions to the distribution problems. This is to say that they rely on some sort of trusted distribution system, outside the PKI environment, to transport their key material to where it needs to go. In PKI, there are three main methods of distributing key material: paper, electronic, and hardware. All three of these concepts are specific methods of establishing a *key exchange.*

Key exchange in PKI is the process of exchanging public keys to facilitate the establishment of secure communication. Paper distribution is almost never used as the alphanumeric representation of a key is too difficult to reliably enter by hand. Also, there is the problem that arises from what happens to the paper after it has been used. Left sitting around, this material can fall into the hands of those who might use it against the key owner. This would force the frequent revocation of certificates, thus defeating the point of automating the process.

Electronic distribution has the challenge of protecting the key material while it is in transit and either ensuring its safe storage or destruction once it has arrived and been used. This can also prove more difficult than it's worth as it suffers many of the same problems that paper does while adding the extra challenge of transmission.

The solution chosen for protection of the key in transit is often itself an encryption-based solution and often using the key material being replaced by a protected key. This workaround involves breaking the key into multiple irregular-length sections and transmitting the sections separately. The idea here is to limit the chances of the entire key being compromised at the expense that part of it might become so. To compensate for this problem, some implementations will create a cryptographic nightmare by encrypting each key segment with a second separate key. If your problem is the expiration, management, and distribution of key material, the solution is never to create even more keys that require management and distribution. Although it is an important concept for a candidate to know as many an implementation of this type exists in the real world, they tend to generate more trouble than solutions.

The third and currently final option for key distribution is a hardware-based solution that passes the key material directly from where it is generated to where it is going to be used. This solution includes smartcards, Trusted Platform Modules, USB drives, or any device of this nature. As with electronic distribution, there is typically a security barrier in place to prevent easy access to the key material on the device. A simple alphanumeric password or personal identification number (PIN) are the two most common barriers, although some of the more elaborate implementations can use biometrics. Hardware-based solutions are gaining popularity as they provide the best balance of safety and ease of management for the currently available solution types.

Key Recovery

We touched on the concept of revocation when we discussed certificates earlier in this chapter. Revocation of keys used to create digital signatures is traditionally considered to be unrecoverable as doing so could introduce sizable doubt as to the nonrepudiation of a signed message. This is not the case for keys used to encrypt messages and files. Revocation of the public encryption key should not mean that any of that information gets deleted or becomes permanently inaccessible. Rather, the encryption key needs to be recoverable should any of the information encrypted with it need to be accessed. The reason for recovering the key could include the termination of an employee who had encrypted messages and files, who has lost their hardware token, or who has forgotten their PIN/password.

The specifics of key recovery are constrained by the type of long-term storage solution chosen with the two most often implemented solutions, simple offline storage or a *key escrow service*. Offline storage is just what it sounds like: private keys are backed up to something like a CD, DVD, tape, or external hard drive, and stored for future use. It is typically an internally run process and comes with the serious risk of an in-house security breach. The individual charged with the backup and storage of the environment's private keys must be somebody who justly garners a great deal of trust.

The other often implemented solution for key recovery is a key escrow service. A key escrow service is often a trusted third-party service provider that is contracted to store your active and legacy private key information. This trusted third party can still be an entity internal to your organization but is typically not one associated with the implementation and operation of your PKI. When your organization requires the use of key that is no longer available through normal channels, the key escrow service is engaged to provide your organization with key or keys they require. In addition, a key escrow service can typically retain information related to the original use of the key, who used the key, and their contact information.

The specific requirements for producing a key that has been escrowed are governed by the service agreement setup between the two groups. The advantage of a key escrow service is that you either eliminate or greatly reduce the insider threat problem while formalizing the key recovery process. The key escrow service is also extremely useful in the settling of legal disputes that involve the recovering of encrypted data by inactive keys as they help to show the concepts of due diligence; that you are properly maintaining and operating your PKI environment and due care; and that you are performing all actions considered to be reasonably responsible in the recovery of your organization's data.

If an organization prefers to keep the key recovery process in-house, an implementer should investigate the use of an "M-of-N" recovery control process. Essentially, this process states that for "N" number of possible people, "M" must be present and consent to the recovery of the private key. In other words, six system administrators (M) of a team of 10 system administrators (N) must be present and consent. The role or group selected to function as the key recovery control group need not be just made up of system administrators but should have sufficient senior-level representation to support whatever decision is made in the key recovery control process.

Key Repository

The concept of a key repository is not exclusive to asymmetric cryptography but is a critical component of PKI. In symmetric key cryptography, the key repository holds all of the private keys used to sign and encrypt information. Typically, each person maintains and updates a personal key repository. In PKI, the key repository is a centralized database of active current certificates and their associated public keys designed to be accessible by all users and devices in PKI environments. This repository, sometimes referred to as a key directory or just directory, contains only active public keys and their associated certificates. The location of the private key depends on the implementation selected but can take the form of key repository local to the machine of a particular user, a hardware token such as a smart card, or other similar device.

The key repository must be implemented in such a fashion that the users and devices in the environment can readily access the keys but only those tasked with managing the repository can add or remove keys and digital certificates. When a key and certificate combo expires or is expired, the key should be removed from the active repository, especially if it is being replaced by a new set. This prevents a message from being sent out with the expired key and potentially being rejected by the recipient upon receipt. If the system has not been set up properly, it is possible for a revoked key and certificate to be accepted and used so proper management of your repository is critical to the safe and effective operation of your PKI environment.

General Cryptography

Problems, Weaknesses, and Concerns

We have already covered a number of problems, weaknesses, and concerns associated with cryptography but there are a few more that need to be addressed. The first issue is called *hash collision* and occurs when two different inputs are processed with the same hash function and end up producing the same hash value. While this will happen from time to time with any hash function, one that has been well designed will not have it happen often. Similarly, *key clustering* is what occurs when two or more keys generate identical ciphertext from identical plaintext using the identical algorithm. As discussed earlier, the function of a key is to introduce a random event into an otherwise predictable equation. Regularly occurring key clustering is the utter failure of the key to provide that functionality and is a sign of a faulty algorithm that should not be used for or as part of protecting anything important. Key clustering makes the cryptanalyst's job easier by dramatically reducing the number of attempts an attacker must go through to determine the correct key to decrypt a message.

The next issue with cryptography is that of algorithm aging. While a particularly well-designed algorithm can last for decades, it is inevitable that the armies of evil doers out there will find a way to either break it completely or to reduce its level of provided protection substantially. In addition, older algorithms often use less sophisticated math, smaller key spaces, and shorter key lengths. This makes them susceptible to the next two issues, cryptanalysis and attack.

Cryptanalysis refers to the study of ways and means to either bypass or break a cryptographic algorithm, hash, protocol, or function. Methods for accomplishing this are referred to as cryptographic attacks. These attacks usually revolve around extremely complex mathematics and ciphertext comparisons where the attacker attempts to reveal some form of predictability in the random number generation, hash function, or flaw in the construction of the algorithm. Unwanted predictability is the death of any cryptographic function and is an inevitable result of large amounts of time, often years, spent doing cryptanalysis.

Another method of cryptographic attack is good old-fashioned brute force where an attacker tries random combination after random combination of bits in an attempt to decrypt or un-hash a particular chunk of plaintext. Given the complexity, options, and layers involved in modern cryptography, brute force attacks can take tremendous amounts of time to execute and yield very little information about the cryptographic functions used. As a result, brute force is most often used to reveal the contents of a specific message.

A second type of attack is called a "man-in-the-middle" attack. This attack requires an attacker to impersonate one of the members of a conversation to the satisfaction of the other members. The attacker then intercepts the message traffic and interjects new traffic where appropriate. The end goal is to compromise the confidentiality of the encrypted channel, collect any relevant information, and if need be, spread disinformation to the parties on the trusted encrypted channel. This is often thwarted by requiring each party on an encrypted channel to authenticate themselves before communicating on that channel.

If the public key used to create an encrypted message is unsigned, it is possible for an attacker to modify the public key in such a way as to change the destination address while still displaying the correct name. It is important for the implementer to sign public keys when confidentiality and availability are critical because if this modified unsigned public key is widely disseminated, the owner of the certificate will not receive messages encrypted with it. Instead, the address inputted by the attacker will receive the supposedly confidential messages. We will discuss some examples of this authentication in the following section.

A *related key attack* is where an analyst observes the operation of a cipher in an effort to understand the mathematic relationships between the encrypted messages. The best known instance of this attack was the highly successful effort to break the WEP. A *side channel attack* is study of a cryptographic function based on the details of its implementation; how much power or cooling does the system require, how many people are needed to operate it, what information is being leaked electromagnetically into the surrounding environment, and vectors of that nature. These types of attack typically require an extreme level of technical skill and are less likely to yield a direct compromise of the cryptographic function but rather will provide an attacker with clues to use along with other forms of attack.

A *chosen plaintext attack* is an attack where the analyst generates numerous chunks of chosen plaintext and uses them to create corresponding cyphertext. The idea here is that if the analyst has access to the cryptographic function, they can generate enough chosen plaintext vs. cyphertext comparisons to eventually predict the outcome of future operations.

The final two attacks we will discuss are not really attacks at all, but rather are more academic fields of cryptanalysis. The first called a *Birthday Attack*. This attack is based on the statistical probability that in a group of 23 or more random people, there is a 50% or greater chance that two of them will have been born on the same day. This is why no matter how strong your hash function is, a certain number of hash collisions are going to occur. In a group of a certain size, there is a certain chance that two messages will end up with the same hash. This is not so much an attack as an inevitable concept that keeps digital signatures from being the be-all, end-all of asynchronous cryptography.

The final type of problem with modern cryptography comes from the implementation. This can take the form of either a poor vendor implementation of an otherwise secure standard or a poorly executed installation of an otherwise secure vendor installation. One major industry vendor that implements a remote access solution will probably implement it slightly differently from another major vendor. It is extremely important for the implanting security engineer to keep current on the security flaws of the various vendor providers. The other issue of poorly executed or configured implementation is more difficult to address. It is extremely important that an implementer be extremely familiar with industry best practice for installation and configuration of a particular solution while being equally careful that all the specifics of your environment are attended to. While large-scale, vendor-based product flaws are more likely to make the national news, the flawed particulars of a mistake ridden implementation is far more likely to impact your organization's day-to-day operation.

One last issue to note with cryptography is speed. Even the fastest encryption type is slower than an equivalent message that is unencrypted. As a rule of thumb, streaming ciphers are faster than block ciphers, even those behaving as streaming ciphers. Also, synchronous cryptographic standards are faster than asynchronous cryptographic standards, often by orders of magnitude.

The natural instinct with encryption of any sort is to use the most comprehensive and rigorous settings possible. While the intention is noble, an overzealous implementation may very well deprive you of that much loved functionality you were trying to protect. This is why numerous asynchronous implementations use the initial public key exchange to create an encrypted channel before switching to a synchronous solution for bulk data transfer. This is one of the most powerful and important features of asynchronous cryptography. The ability for two distinct and disparate systems with different owners to first establish and then maintain secure communications over a network that neither group owns either in part or in full is the fundamental success scenario of asynchronous cryptography.

The following sections deal with technical specifics of numerous algorithms, ciphers, hashes, and protocols involved in modern cryptography. Having mastered the foundational concepts discussed above, we should be ready to discuss specific cryptographic functions and implementations. This list is not all-inclusive and is intended as a source of examples standards.

Algorithms, Ciphers, and Types

Data Encryption Standard and Triple Data Encryption Standard

Data Encryption Standard (DES) was first created in the early to mid 1970s, making it quite possibly older than you are. Generally, it is considered a cryptographic antique suitable for only the most modest of security requirements. It is a symmetric block Feistel algorithm that is capable of using multiple modes of operation (ECB, CBC, CFB, and OFB) so as to operate as both a block and a stream style cipher. While it can be made to operate in a streaming mode, it is always a block cipher. In its original form it uses a key size of 56 bits and a block size of 64 bits.

By the late 1970s, a more complicated and stronger version of DES had been developed called Triple DES (3DES). Sometimes referred to as TDES, 3DES is also still in use today with a better reputation than DES has. It is still considered an aged algorithm and should not be used if there are newer more robust algorithms to choose from. 3DES has an actual key length of 168 bits and a block size of 64 bits. The 168-bit key is constructed from three 56-bit DES keys that successively encrypt the message one after another. With 3DES, there is a difference between the total number of bits in a key and the effective number of bits. When all three keys are the same, the effective number of bits is the same as single DES and provides no better protection. With the other two options, either two or three keys out of a total of three are independent. When 3DES's susceptibility to multiple forms of cryptanalytic attack is factored in, the two or three independent key options yield 80 and 112 bits of relative key strength, respectively. The last major advocate of the DES family of standards is the payment card industry where it is often employed to secure credit and debit card operations.

Advanced Encryption Standard

AES was first envisioned by the U.S. government as a competition to replace multiple aging algorithms, including DES. Of the 15 designs submitted to the competition, the design referred to as Rijndael was selected as the winner. Now referred to as AES, this design is a symmetric substitution block algorithm with key length options of 128, 192, or 256 bits, and encrypts/decrypts in 10, 12, and 14 rounds, respectively, to the listed key lengths in standard compliant implementations. AES has a block size of 128 bits and can be used in most modes of operation. This flexibility and robust security has contributed to making AES one of the most popular algorithms currently available. This is not to say AES is perfect, as several academic efforts have revealed potential weaknesses of AES against chosen plaintext and related key attacks.

International Data Encryption Algorithm

International Data Encryption Algorithm (IDEA) was developed in the early 1990s and intended as a replacement for DES. IDEA is a symmetric block substitution algorithm and has a key size of 128 bits and a block size of 64 bits. The core mathematical operations used by IDEA make it a fairly robust cryptographic standard, but the computational complexity makes it somewhat slower than its competition, often achieving speeds similar to DES when implemented using a software-based solution.

Blowfish

Blowfish is a keyed symmetric block Feistel algorithm developed in the early mid 1990s that provides a substantial amount of protection to confidential information. Blowfish provides a wide diversity of key lengths ranging from 32 to 448 bits with a constant block size of 64 bits where the message is encrypted and decrypted over 16 rounds of operation. The speed at which Blowfish operates is generally faster than DES, is considered to be stronger than DES, and is completely unencumbered by patents of any sort. This combination has made Blowfish a popular choice for cryptography solutions in the open source community.

Twofish

One of the final candidates for the AES contest, Twofish is a symmetric block Feistel algorithm that was first published in the late 1990s. Derived from Blowfish, Twofish has a key length of 128, 192, or 256 bits with a block size of 128 bits where the message is encrypted and decrypted over 16 rounds of operation. Depending on the key length selected for a particular implementation, Twofish is either slightly slower than AES for shorter keys or slightly faster for longer length keys. As with Blowfish, Twofish has no patents restricting its use, thus making it a popular choice for open-source cryptography solutions.

RSA

Invented in 1977, RSA, which stands for Rivest, Shamir, and Adleman, its inventors, was the first asymmetric key cryptography solution suitable for both signing and encrypting a message, meaning it can be used to generate both public and private keys. RSA key lengths are 1024 to 3072 bits long, with a size of 2048 to 3072 being recommended by most implementations for rigorous long-term security. Due to its age and substantial key lengths, RSA is tremendously slower than just about any equivalent symmetric solution.

Skipjack

Skipjack was originally invented by the U.S. National Security Agency for use in voice communications equipment. It is a symmetric block Feistel algorithm with an 80-bit key size and a 64-bit block size over 32 rounds of cryptographic operation. Declassified in 1998, it was shortly thereafter partially compromised using an Impossible Differential Cryptanalysis attack. The most important aspect of Skipjack pertains to its mandatory use of a government-run key escrow service that would have maintained a copy of each user's encryption key, ostensibly as a privacy enhancement feature. In reality, this feature would have potentially permitted government circumvention of user attempts to keep their data private. The requirement for a government-run encryption key escrow service received a very poor reception from security industry vendors and professionals when the idea was first proposed by National Institute of Standards and Technology in the mid 1990s. Skipjack is not widely used but serves as a rare example of government-developed cryptography available in the public domain.

Digital Signature Algorithm and Digital Signature Standard

Digital Signature Algorithm (DSA) is one of the many asymmetric standard-based choices available to the Digital Signature Standard (DSS) for the creation of reliable robust digital signatures. The standard for DSA and DSS outline the variables required for inclusion in a digital signature, recommendations for the bit length of certain variables, and recommendations for selecting hash functions. The recommended key length is 1024 to 3072 bits with a hash length of 224 to 256 bits.

Elliptical Curve Cryptography

Elliptical Curve Cryptography (ECC) is a type of asymmetric cryptography that uses high-powered algebra to calculate elliptical curves over a finite field. Typically in asymmetric cryptography, the goal is to create a puzzle where it is close to impossible to solve the puzzle without the secret of how the puzzle was created. In ECC, the larger the finite field is, the harder the puzzle is to solve, and so the implementation is considered harder to break. This mathematical complexity allows for ECC to have shorter key lengths than most asymmetric cryptographic standards typically achieving a safe operating state with about twice the bit length of an equivalent symmetric implementation.

Public Key Cryptography Standards

Public Key Cryptography Standards (PKCS) were created by RSA Security in an attempt to standardize and advance the field of public key cryptography. Those standards that are still in use govern such things as the math behind public and private key construction, public key exchanges, password-based cryptography, digital signatures, certificate requests, cryptographic tokens, and key storage.

Rivest Ciphers 2, 4, and 5

Rivest Cipher 2 (RC2) is a symmetric Feistel block algorithm designed in the mid to late 1980s by RSA Security. RC2 has a variable key length ranging from 8 to 128 bits, with a fixed block length of 64 bits. Due to its age, relatively small key length and widely published source code, RC2 is no longer widely used, especially in new implementations.

Rivest Cipher 4 (RC4) is a widely used symmetric stream algorithm developed in the mid to late 1980s by RSA Security. RC4 is used in numerous implementations including SSL and WEP. Although RC4 is largely considered to be secure, it is critically important to implement it correctly as serious vulnerabilities can ensue from improper implementation. RC4 has a variable key length of 40 to 256 bits, but the specifics of an implementation can constrain that bit length from its maximum.

Rivest Cipher 5 (RC5) is a clever symmetric block Feistel algorithm created in the mid 1990s by RSA Security. RC5 has a variable block length and key length, and performs a variable number of rounds of operation to encrypt and decrypt a message. The block size is 32, 64, or 128 bits, with the key length being anything from 0 bits to 2040 bits and the number of rounds being anything from 0 to 255. RC5 is used as part of the Wireless Transport Layer Security standard, which in turn is part of the first version of the Wireless Application Protocol security standard. In addition, it is used as an encryption option in some remote access solutions such as Citrix.

Feistel Cipher

Named for its creator, IBM cryptographer Horst Feistel, a Feistel cipher is a symmetric structure used to construct numerous different block ciphers. The major advantage to a Feistel-type cipher is that the encryption and decryption operations are very similar and sometimes identical. This allows an encryption and decryption operation to reverse the key schedule, sometimes with a minimum of modification, to perform the desired functions with much simpler hardware components than would otherwise be required.

Specific Hashes

Message Digest 2, 4, and 5

Message Digest (MD) 2, 4, and 5 are hash functions used to create message digests for digital signatures. MD2 was first created in 1989 and forms a 128-bit message digest using a 128-bit block through 18 rounds of operation. Although it is considered to be older than is ideal, MD2 is still used in certain PKI environments where it is used in the generation of digital certificates. MD4 was created in 1990 and also generates a 128-bit message digest using a 512-bit block, but does so through only three rounds of operation. MD4 is a popular choice among file sharing and synchronization applications, although there are several well-published compromises that severely limit the nonrepudiation qualities of an MD4 hash. MD5 uses a 512-bit block and generates a 128-bit message digest as well, but does so over four rounds of operation along with several mathematical tweaks including a unique additive constant that is used during each round to provide an extra level of nonrepudiation assurance. That being said, there are numerous easy and well-published exploits available for creating hash collisions in an MD5-enabled environment.

Secure Hash Algorithm 0, 1, and 2

Secure Hash Algorithm (SHA) is a collection of hash functions created by the U.S. government starting in the early mid 1990s. SHA-0 was the first of these hash standards, but was quickly removed and replaced by SHA-1 in 1995 due to some rather fundamental flaws in the original SHA-0. SHA-1 uses a block size of 512 bits to create a message digest of 160 bits through 80 rounds of operation. SHA-1 does not provide a great deal of protection against attacks such as a birthday attack, and so the SHA-2 family of hash functions was created. With SHA-2, the often employed naming convention is to use the size of the created message digest to describe the particular SHA-2 implementation. In SHA-2, the possible message digests are 224, 256, 384, and 512 bits in length. SHA-224 and SHA-256 use a block length of 512 bits while SHA-384 and SHA-512 use a block length of 1024 bits.

HAVAL

HAVAL was created in the in the mid 1990s as a highly flexible and configurable hash function. With HAVAL, the implementer can create hashes of 128, 160, 192, 224, and 256 bits in length, using a fixed block size of 128 bits and 3, 4, or 5 rounds of operation.

RIPEMD-160

Research and Development in Advanced Communications Technologies in Europe (RACE) Integrity Primitives Evaluation Message Digest (RIPEMD) is a hash function that produces 160-bit message digests using a 512-bit block size. RIPEMD was produced by a collaborative effort of European cryptographers and is not subject to any patent restrictions.

Specific Protocols

Diffie–Hellman Key Exchange

Diffie–Hellman Key Exchange is a cryptographic concept used for two parties to establish a secured communication channel over a public or insecure network connection by exchanging secret keys without knowledge of each other or any previous arrangement. Diffie–Hellman has no authentication mechanism built in by default so it is highly susceptible to a man-in-the-middle attack. In response to this major problem, Station-to-Station (STS) was created by several members of the original team. STS provides both two-way key authentication along with authentication of both parties involved in the cryptographic function.

SSL and TLS

SSL and its successor, TLS, are protocols that provide confidentiality and integrity protection for data being transmitted over a TCP/IP network connection. SSL and TLS operate between layers 3 and 4 of the OSI model. TLS is in the process of superseding SSL with many implementations of TLS being accidentally referred to as SSL out of confusion or bad habit.

There are three general steps in creating a TLS or SSL connection. The first step is for both parties to negotiate a common compatible algorithm version to use. Typically, the server and client will support multiple versions of SSL and TLS; thus, during this process, a common compatible standard will be chosen. The next step involves the exchanging of public keys via digital certificates and the establishment of a secure communications tunnel. The authentication is most often handled by the application being used such as an internet browser after the secure tunnel is created. If the authentication is mutual, both parties must be components of an integrated PKI environment. This is quite common in a TLS VPN implementation. The TLS protocol is secure in that whatever cipher and key length is selected for use with the protocol will bring its strengths and weaknesses along with it.

Secure Shell

Secure Shell (SSH) is a network cryptography protocol used mostly to create connections for remote systems administration and remote application use, and to bypass network security devices. SSH is actually three components in one standard. The first, which is called the Transport Layer Protocol, handles authentication, integrity, and confidentiality of the data stream. The second part, called the User Authentication Protocol, authenticates the client to the server. The third part, called the Connection Protocol, breaks the connection into multiple channels to further scramble and obfuscate the data. SSH can use a wide variety of mechanisms to authenticate a user or device, including password-based, host-based, and asymmetric cryptography–based methods. There are two versions of SSH currently in operation: SSH-1 and SSH-2. SSH-1 has several well-published design flaws that make it quite easy to compromise. Therefore, SSH-1 should be avoided in favor of SSH-2 if at all possible.

IP Security, Internet Key Exchange, and Internet Security Association and Key Management Protocol

IPSec is a framework of protocols for communicating securely with IP, by providing mechanisms for authenticating and encryption. IPSec can be implemented in two modes: transport mode, which is designed for end-to-end protection, and tunnel mode, which protects traffic between networks. The main difference between the two modes is that with transport mode, only the payload of the IP packet is encrypted and/or authenticated. In tunnel mode, the entire original packet is encrypted and wrapped with a new IP packet. The way two parties come to an agreement as to the type of connection, configuration options, algorithms, key sizes, and security measures to be used is called a security association (SA). This gives a great deal of flexibility and customization to an IPSec implementation by allowing the implementer to choose the options right for their scenario.

Within IPSec, the identity of the sender can be ensured through the use of an authentication header (AH). AH accomplishes this by incorporating an unpredictable sequence number and a hash of the packet's payload into itself based on a prenegotiated hashing standard. The option for an implementer to choose is Encapsulating Security Payload (ESP). ESP is one of the mechanisms used by IPSec to protect the integrity or confidentiality of a data packet using many of the same features of AH such as sequence numbering. In ESP, the header contains the information necessary for the selection of an SA while the payload section contains the encrypted data payload and the authentication section contains the information necessary for the recipient to authenticate the packet.

In IPSec, the roll of a negotiator between the two parties attempting to establish an SA is performed by Internet Key Exchange (IKE). IKE is a protocol used by IPSec to set up SAs through a Diffie–Hellman-style exchange to establish a secure session and generate the necessary key material. The first step involves the two parties authenticating each other by exchanging a previously shared secret key, a digital certificate, or a randomly generated unique number called a nonce. After both parties have successfully authenticated themselves to each other over the temporary

IKE connection, the more permanent SA is established. The specifics for the key generation and SA formation are governed by Internet Security Association and Key Management Protocol (ISAKMP). In an effort to limit the types of data that can pass between IPSec connected parties, IP Security Policy is used to restrict a connection to only the data types desired.

X.509

There are numerous types of digital certificates; however, for the world of public key cryptography, the most prolific and important certificate type is the X.509 formatted certificate. X.500 is a widely adopted international set of standardized recommendations and specifications for directory services that are independent of platform, business model, or geographic location. These directory services are in turn responsible for the storage, distribution, and management of digital certificates. X.509 is the resultant standard for certificates in an X.500 compliant environment.

X.509 certificates are not created equal as there are numerous mandatory, optional, and version-related fields to fill out when creating these certificates that require the implementer to understand the restrictions and interoperability issues associated with a particular environment. First, certificates are issued in five different categories called *classes*. Class 1 certificates are issued to individuals and are considered to be appropriate for email signatures. Class 2 certificates are provided to organizations looking to prove their identity online. Class 3 certificates are used for digitally signing software and drivers along with providing an identity to servers that require it. Class 3 certificates are used for software signing, driver signing, and often in support of Digital Rights Management or other rights management schemes. Class 4 certificates are used to secure Internet commerce transactions, while Class 5 certificates are used exclusively by governments and large corporations.

Sample Questions

1. Applied against a given block of data, a hash function creates
    a. A chunk of the original block used to ensure its confidentiality
    b. A chunk of the original block used to ensure its integrity
    c. A block of new data used to ensure the original block's confidentiality
    ▾ d. A block of new data used to ensure the original block's integrity
2. In symmetric key cryptography, each party should use
    a. A previously exchanged secret key
    b. A secret key exchanged with the message
    c. A publicly available key
    d. A randomly generated value unknown to everyone

3. Nonrepudiation of a message ensures that
   a. A message is always sent to the intended recipient
   b. A message is always received by the intended recipient
   c. A message can be attributed to a particular author
   d. A message can be attributed to a particular recipient
4. Digital signatures can afford
   a. Confidentiality
   b. Encryption
   c. Nonrepudiation
   d. Checksums
5. In Electronic Code Book (ECB) mode, data is encrypted using
   a. A different cipher for every block of a message
   b. The same cipher for every block of a message
   c. A user-generated variable length cipher for every block of a message
   d. A cipher-based on the previous block of a message
6. In cipher block chaining (CBC) mode, the key is constructed by
   a. Reusing the previous key in the chain of message blocks
   b. Generating new key material completely at random
   c. Modifying the previous block of ciphertext
   d. Cycling through a list of user defined choices
7. Cipher feedback (CFB) mode allows for data to be
   a. Transmitted and received in a stream
   b. Encrypted in no particular order
   c. Decrypted in no particular order
   d. Authenticated before decryption
8. Stream ciphers are normally selected because of
   a. The high degree of strength behind the encryption algorithms
   b. The high degree of speed behind the encryption algorithms
   c. Their ability to encrypt large chunks of data at a time
   d. Their ability to use large amounts of padding in encryption functions
9. Asymmetric cryptography uses
   a. One of five modes of operation
   b. Keys of a random or unpredictable length
   c. One single key for all cryptographic operations
   d. One or more pairs of public and private keys
10. A key escrow service is intended to allow for the reliable
    a. Recovery of inaccessible private keys
    b. Recovery of compromised public keys
    c. Transfer of inaccessible private keys between users
    d. Transfer of compromised public keys between users
11. Cipher-based method authentication code (CMAC) subkeys 1 or 2 is respectively used when

a. The first subkey is a negative multiple of the block length or the second subkey when the message length is a negative multiple of the block length.

b. The first subkey is a positive multiple of the block length or the second subkey when the message length is not a positive multiple of the block length.

c. The first subkey is not the positive inverse of the block length or the second subkey when the message length is not the negative inverse of the block length.

d. The first subkey is the positive inverse of the block length or the second subkey when the message length is the negative inverse of the block length.

12. In Counter with Cipher Block Chaining Message Authentication Code Mode (CCM), choosing the size of the authentication field is a balance of

a. Message content and availability

b. Message content and confidentiality

c. Message size and integrity

d. Message size and privacy

13. The correct choice for encrypting the entire original data packet in a tunneled mode for an IPSec solution is

a. Authentication Header (AH)

b. Encapsulating Security Payload (ESP)

c. Point-to-Point Tunneling Protocol (PPTP)

d. Generic Routing Encapsulation (GRE)

14. Security concerns with Rivest Cipher 4 (RC4) stem from

a. The commonly known nonce hashed with the key

b. A faulty pseudo random number generator

c. Slow rates of operation in block mode

d. A weak key schedule

15. A significant advantage to selecting a Feistel Cipher for implementation is that

a. All encryption functions rely on a complex random shuffling of the key schedule before attempting operation.

b. All decryption functions rely on a complex random shuffling of the key schedule before attempting operation.

c. The encryption and decryption functions are often the reverse of each other.

d. An implementer can choose from multiple native stream ciphers.

16. The AES standard fixes the size for a block at

a. 96 bits

b. 128 bits

c. 256 bits

d. 512 bits

17. When implementing an MD5 solution, what randomizing cryptographic function should be used to help avoid collisions?
    a. Salt
    b. Message pad
    c. Modular addition
    d. Multistring concatenation
18. Key Clustering represents the significant failure of an algorithm because
    a. A single key should not generate the same ciphertext from the same plaintext, using the same cipher algorithm.
    b. Two different keys should not generate the same ciphertext from the same plaintext, using the same cipher algorithm.
    c. Two different keys should not generate different ciphertext from the same plaintext, using the same cipher algorithm.
    d. A single key should not generate different ciphertext from the same plaintext, using the same cipher algorithm.
19. A related key attack occurs when a cryptanalyst
    a. Exploits impossible differences at some intermediate state of the cipher algorithm
    b. Attempts to use every combination and permutation possible for a given key
    c. Studies a cryptographic function based on the details of its implementation, such as performance, power consumption, and user load
    d. Observes the operation of a working cipher in an effort to understand the mathematical relationships between the encrypted messages
20. Elliptical Curve Cryptography achieves acceptable levels of security with comparably shorter key lengths in asymmetric cryptography through
    a. The algebraic calculation of an elliptical curve over a large but finite field
    b. The algebraic calculation of an elliptical curve over an infinite field
    c. The natural logarithmic calculation of an elliptical curve using noncyclic subgroups
    d. The natural logarithmic calculation of an elliptical curve using cyclic subgroups

Chapter 3

Malicious Code

Ken Dunham

Contents

The number and types of attacks using malicious code are increasing. The requirement for an individual or an organization to protect himself from these attacks is extremely important. The malicious code domain addresses computing code that can be described as being harmful or destructive to the computing environment. This includes viruses, worm, logic bombs, Trojans, and other technical and nontechnical attacks.

While there are a variety of methods available to build a virus, many viruses are still targeted at a specific computing platform. With the availability of platform-independent languages, such as Perl, ActiveX, and Java, it is becoming easier to write malicious codes that can run across different platforms. The Systems Security Certified Practitioner (SSCP) candidate is expected to demonstrate knowledge in the concepts of malicious and mobile codes, types of malicious code threats, how malicious code is introduced into the environment, and various protection and recovery methods. Key areas of knowledge include

- Identify malicious code
  - Viruses
  - Worms
  - Trojan horses
  - Rootkits
  - Malware and spyware
  - Trapdoors and backdoors
  - Botnets
  - Logic bombs
  - Mobile code
- Implement malicious code countermeasures
  - Scanners (e.g., heuristic, integrity checker, signatures)
  - Antimalware
  - Containment and remediation
  - Software security (e.g., code signing, application review)
- Identify malicious activity (e.g., social engineering, insider threat, data theft)
- Implement malicious activity countermeasures (e.g., user awareness, system hardening)

Introduction to Windows Malcode Security Management

Malcode, short for MALicious CODE or software, runs rampant on Windows and other operating systems by the twenty-first century. System administrators are no longer protecting the perimeter of a network but managing an ever-porous network constantly under attack from within and by external actors. My unique role in malicious code and geopolitical intelligence has given me the opportunity to be the first responder for the largest networks in the world during a time when corporate networks and home computers are most under siege from malcode attacks.

In 2008, a network was successfully exploited multiple times using an exploit framework tool created by Russians called Neosploit. Multiple malicious codes continued to hammer away at the network, causing massive headaches for both system administrators and security experts responding to the incidents. An in-depth analysis revealed that a policy change rolled out by administrators left systems vulnerable to known exploits and attacks in the wild. This is a real-world example of how business units must work together in tandem to best manage risk. It is a challenge that exists in every major network requiring excellent communication skills, strong leadership skills, and technical capabilities within business units.

In 2007, a major enterprise environment suffered a large-scale botnet attack with dozens of infected hosts within the network. Multiple acquisitions and merging of networks left the network vulnerable to attack. No clear chain of command and control (C&C) for security measures existed on the global network. The bot attack significantly disrupted the business and was very expensive in view of loss of productivity and mitigation staff expenses. System administrators quickly reimaged the computers and got the computers back online. Unfortunately they did not know how to protect against the original vector of attack and were soon successfully attacked AGAIN. This is a hard lesson in properly understanding how to mitigate a threat.

In 2008, a Trojan was installed on a computer in a major network. It also installed a rootkit that was undetected by updated antivirus software. System administrators updated their antivirus and detected and removed the Trojan from multiple desktops using antivirus software. The rootkit remained undetected in the system. It also remained undetected over the network communicating with a remote C&C server through encrypted TCP port 80 communications. The integrity of the entire network was compromised for several months before the rootkit was discovered and mitigation actions were taken accordingly. This is a hard lesson in properly understanding the impact of an attack to restore integrity to an infected host.

These first real-world examples are what you can expect throughout this book to help apply critical malcode knowledge and working concepts for the SSCP candidate. It is designed to empower the SSCP candidate in a job as a systems administrator, security personnel, or manager. We focus on the technical understanding each individual needs to have to properly identify, respond to, analyze, and mitigate malicious code within a network environment. This covers infection vectors like exploit frameworks such as Neosploit and how to de-obfuscate JavaScript exploits and payloads to analyzing samples within a test environment to identify the payloads and impact of malcode.

Related areas, such as monitoring and managing network traffic, are touched on but not fully developed due to the specific emphasis of this chapter on malcode. Additionally, proprietary solutions and multiple architectures exist for lowering and managing risk related to malcode, which vary widely, and are not appropriate for this context. Additionally, little to no information exists for non-Windows environments in which malcode also exists, such as Macintosh and Linux, since the concepts and principles in general apply other than obvious changes required for behavioral analysis of binaries for non-Windows operating systems.

Perhaps of greatest relevance are the first-hand examples of how to under-stand and work with malcode in an enterprise environment. This chapter provides authoritative and updated emergent malcode risks that are impacting top networks in 2008. Each sample used in examples and case studies has been carefully selected to best prepare you for the real world rather than a theoretical study of malcode. SSCP candidates that successfully employ concepts and working knowledge from this chapter can be counted on for managing malcode risks facing any Windows network.

CIA Triangle: Applicability to Malcode

The CIA triangle shown in Figure 3.1 is the central component of all 10 domains of computer security and especially pertinent to malcode risk. Table 3.1 gives exam-ples of how all elements of the triangle are applicable to malcode.

Malcode Naming Conventions and Types

There is no international standard for malcode naming conventions. Some names, like the infamous Storm worm from 2007 and later, get traction in public media reports and become popularized over time. Others, such as Code Red, are assigned as a family name by individuals analyzing a new worm while staying up late at night drinking Code Red soda. In general, the antivirus industry follows CARO-like naming standards.

CARO-Like Naming Standards

CARO is short for the Computer AntiVirus Research Organization and was estab-lished in the early 1990s to research malcode. In 1991 a committee was formed

Figure 3.1   The CIA triangle is the central component of all 10 domains of com-puter security and especially pertinent to malcode risk.

Table 3.1 CIA Elements as They Apply to Malcode

Confidentiality	A Trojan infects a host and provides a remote attacker with access to sensitive documents, breaching confidentiality.
Integrity	A bot is installed in the computer and immediately installs several other files from private locations that are not detected by antivirus. While the known file is later removed by updated antivirus, the additional payloads remain on the system.
Availability	A computer that is infected with malicious code is instructed by a remote actor to perform a distributed denial of service (DDoS) attack against a remote Web server. The Web server becomes unavailable due to network congestion or overloading the server with the DDoS attack. The infected host also suffers degraded performance due to large volumes of egress traffic.

to develop a naming convention to help organize the technical classifications of malicious code. What they came up with was a way to classify codes based on the following general structure:

Platform.Type.Family _Name.Variant[:Modifier]@Suffix

We have to note that the above syntax has been modified slightly to best reflect the combined usage and terms related to the original CARO naming standard proposed years ago. This can be debated, but the above syntax is how malcode is generally named today based on CARO discussions in the early 1990s and later.

PLATFORM commonly denotes the operating system, such as W32 for a Windows 32-bit platform malicious code. It can also be an application specific to that threat, such as PPT for PowerPoint-based malicious code. Proposed prefixes from 1999 are below, taken from http://members.chello.at/erikajo/vnc99b2.txt:

BOOT—MBR, DOS-BR, Floppy-BR
DOS—DOS file
BAT—DOS Batches
OS2—IBM's OS/2 viruses
MAC—Macintosh viruses
W3X—Windows 3.x files
W95—Windows 95 files
WNT—Windows NT files
W2K—Windows 2000 files
W32—Windows 95/98/NT/2K files
WM—MS Winword Macro viruses

XM—MS Excel Macro viruses
W97M—MS Word97 viruses
X97M—MS Excel97 viruses
PPT—MS PowerPoint
WORK—MS Works
AM—MS Access
A97M—MS Access97
O97M—MS Office97
HLP—MS Helpfile viruses
VBS—MS Visual Basic
JS—Java Script
JAVA—Java viruses
COR—Corel Draw viruses
AMI—AmiPro viruses
ELF86—ELF x86 binary viruses
BASH—Bash viruses
PERL—Perl viruses

Obviously technology has changed since this original "suggestion" was made by CARO in the early 1990s. These platform rules are roughly followed by antivirus companies helping computer professionals to extract some meaning from the CARO-like name of a sample. Applying what you have learned, what does the example name below mean?

W32.Rispif.A

W32 indicates that it is malcode that spreads on Windows 32-bit operating systems (Windows 95 and later). Rispif is the family name. ".A" indicates that this is the first variant in this family to be reported.

Details on this code can be found at http://www.symantec.com/business/ security_response/writeup.jsp?docid=2008-081915-2311-99&tabid=2.

TYPE is the next major category that sometimes appears first in a malcode name, such as Trojan.FamilyName.Variant. Types correlate to the types seen in this chapter, such as Trojan, Worm, Virus, Joke, Dropper, etc. Each antivirus company uses its own naming schemes or abbreviations that roughly follow this model.

FAMILY NAME is the name given to the family. There is a "group name" that can also be assigned according to older proposed standards, but this is not used today. The family name is the area where antivirus companies have had great variance in the past. Family names vary based on how each company or reporter references a malcode. In the early part of this century there was a rush to get our signatures and information on codes, which led to great diversity in names given to codes. When things are slower, coordination could take place first and names were selected to be consistent. Family names are selected for a variety of reasons, such as a string seen in egress packets to a remote C&C, strings within the binary, text related to the author or target of attack, etc. In general, professionals try not to honor bad actor names for code or promote virus authoring group names to avoid any gratification for bad actors. To look at how family names can vary greatly, take a look at Backdoor.Win32.Breplibot.b (Kaspersky):

CA: Win32.OutsBot.U
F-Secure: Breplibot.b
Kaspersky: Backdoor.Win32.Breplibot.b
McAfee: W32/Brepibot!CME-589
Microsoft: Backdoor:Win32/Ryknos.A!CME-589
Norman: W32/Ryknos.A
Panda: Bck/Ryknos.A
Sophos: Troj/Stinx-E
Symantec: Backdoor.Ryknos
Trend Micro: BKDR_BREPLIBOT.C
Source: http://cme.mitre.org/data/list.html

Notice in the preceding example CARO-like naming standards. Unfortunately, naming conventions and family names vary greatly among antivirus companies. Some start with the operating system, such as W32, and others with the type, such as Backdoor or Troj (short for Trojan). Some spell out W32 to Win32, etc. Also notice that some use slashes instead of dots (or underscores and hashes), and some an exclamation point to then include the common malware enumeration (CME) value assigned to the code, 589 (see Common Malware Enumeration for more information on this program). Family names are even worse for this sample with names such as OutsBot, Breplibot, Brepibot (no L), Ryknos, and Stinx. This makes correlation of samples very difficult, if not impossible, with binaries in hand for proper comparisons.

VARIANTS, also referred to as identifiers and with major and minor classification possibilities, identify each unique member of a family. In some cases antivirus companies use a .GEN signature for code to generically handle a certain code family. In other cases, especially with companies like Kaspersky, unique individual variant names are assigned to each variant of code within a family. Variants may be minor, like a small repacking of a Trojan, or major, like an upgrade from AgoBot to PhatBot code justifying an entire new family name. However, antivirus companies all handle such situations differently, resulting in some using one family name forever if the code is based on the same source code, such as AgoBot, while others differentiate based on major changes in functionality or similar malcode characteristics.

Variants are typically done with A–Z assignments, using the structure ".AAA..." as needed for variants of a family. For example, the first new variant of a family is

".A." The next variant is ".B." When the ".Z" variant is used, the next variant is ".AA," then ".AB," and so on. Numbers and symbols can also be used for naming of malcode but were not the norm in 2008.

@SUFFIX may be attached to some CARO-like naming conventions to identify how a malcode spreads. Common suffixes include @M for mailing virus or worm code by Symantec, and @MM for a mass mailing virus or worm. Symantec defines a mailing malcode as one that only sends out malicious e-mails as the user sends out e-mails, appending or hijacking the mail code. A mass-mailing malcode is one that sends messages to every e-mail found within the address book of the infected computer or addresses harvested from multiple other locations on the computer.

Cross-Referencing Malcode Names

A lot of manual work is the best effort to fully qualify and identify documentation related to a specific malcode binary of interest. This generally involves looking at multiscanner results, looking up available documentation on specific antivirus vendor sites, open source intelligence (OSINT) queries for incidents and data related to the threat and more. To get started, a few cross-referencing and documentation tools exist on the Internet, which every professional should properly understand: CME, multiscanners, and VGrep.

Common Malware Enumeration

CME is yet one of many such failed efforts to coordinate naming conventions to date. A public site for the initiative first appeared in late 2005. The goal of the group is to reduce public confusion in referencing malcode threats, enhance communications between antivirus vendors, and improve communication and information sharing for the information security community at large. In short, many names and a lack of sharing lead to confusion during a malcode outbreak.

CME included a group of experts who submitted, analyzed, and shared threats to evaluate them for CME inclusion. If accepted, a CME number or identifier is assigned in a semirandom order (not 1, 2, 3, but 711, 416, etc.). Each participating vendor then assigns their unique name to that same sample shared within CME to help produce an authoritative laboratory-qualified correlation of names to a specific binary. A list of all the samples managed by the CME effort while still funded is available online at http://cme.mitre.org/data/list.html.

Unfortunately, the group lost funding and momentum by 2007. Today, CME is nonfunctional other than a historical reference on their public Web site. This is sadly the reality when it comes to information sharing and especially code sharing within the antivirus industry to date. Competitive interests and costs associated with having to rename samples for standardization greatly hinder global coordination. For this reason it is important to learn how to cross-correlate names for malcode to properly analyze code.

Public Multiscanners

Public multiscanners (multiple antivirus engines scan the code) exist today that make it trivial for any user to upload and quickly identify names assigned to a specific binary. Analysts can then look up specific malcode names on each vendor site to identify any documentation related to the sample in question. If no specific information is available on a specific variant of a family, sometimes a family report may exist or a similar variant within the family (if you cannot find FamilyName.C, FamilyName.A may be documented).

VGrep

VGrep is another tool that has been used by antivirus professionals for many years that helps to correlate codes by name. Once registered on the site, users may freely use VGrep to correlate samples of interest. Figure 3.2 is a screenshot of what it looks like when one searches for a common family name like "MyDoom," one of the most prolific mass mailing worm families in the history of computing.

Today VGrep also includes hyperlinks to vendor reports rendered in VGrep results. This makes it easy to quickly correlate codes and look up information on multiple vendor sites related to a variant or family of code. Unfortunately it is a database and may not include emergent threats of interest to a SysAdmin. In short, it is a fantastic tool for looking at historical codes, but may not help with the latest variants to be spread in the wild.

Malcode Types

Classification of malcode into types forces a hierarchy of definitions that are somewhat forced in a very fast changing and fluid world of technology. Some prefer to classify codes based on how they spread, such as "File Infector" for malcode that infects existing files to spread. Others classify malcode based on their payload or impact, such as a Nuker (Trojan) that overwrites or corrupts data on a hard disk.

Classification schemes were heavily debated in the 1990s as the malcode scene significantly changed and matured. Shortly after the turn of the century, the term "blended threats" became popularized through white papers and media. A blended threat is one that combines multiple characteristics of malcode (viruses, worms, Trojan, etc.) to initiate, transmit, and spread an attack. In short, lots of codes with varied functionality are used in an attack.

The days of a single backdoor Trojan attack on a computer quickly faded into the sunset as criminals sought financial gain. Within a few years attacks became increasingly large scale, automated by bad actors, including multiple minor variants and multiple codes in an incident. In some cases hundreds of files are installed on a computer for maximum financial gain and abuse. The advent of such attacks has quickly dissolved traditional classification schemes, largely rendering them useless.

Home > Resources > VGrep > Search Results

Summary

Over 100 results found.
Showing results 1 to 5.
PLEASE NOTE: We're currently trying to integrate vendors' virus encyclopedias into VGrep. You'll notice that some vendors' results are clickable. Clicking on the links will take you to the search results on that vendor's website - whether anything useful is found there is largely dependent on the vendor - if you have any feedback, please email webmaster@virusbtn.com.

Search Again

Terms: MyDoom   Match **Whole String**: ☐

Search by **Vendor**: Any ▾   Search

Results

Results: 1-5, 6-10, 11-15, 16-20, 21-25, 26-30, 31-35, 36-40, 41-45, 46-50, 51-55, 56-60, 61-65, 66-70, 71-75, 76-80, 81-85, 86-90, 91-95, 96-100

Alwil	[undetected]	Avira	[undetected]
AVG (Grisoft)	[undetected]	Kaspersky Lab	[undetected]
SOFTWIN	[undetected]	Frisk Software	[undetected]
McAfee	Generic.dx	IKARUS	Email-Worm.Win32.**Mydoom**.AI
Microsoft	Worm:Win32/**Mydoom**.BI@mm	Symantec	W32.**Mydoom**.BI@mm
Norman	W32/**MyDoom**.AX@mm	Trend Micro	PE_Generic
Rising RavScan	[undetected]	Sophos	W32/**MyDoom**-BS
CA VET	Win32/**Mydoom**.BM	VirusBuster	[undetected]

Alwil	[undetected]	Avira	[undetected]
AVG (Grisoft)	[undetected]	Kaspersky Lab	[undetected]
SOFTWIN	[undetected]	Frisk Software	[undetected]
McAfee	W32/**Mydoom**.dam	IKARUS	[undetected]
Microsoft	[undetected]	Symantec	[undetected]
Norman	[undetected]	Trend Micro	[undetected]
Rising RavScan	[undetected]	Sophos	[undetected]
CA VET	[undetected]	VirusBuster	[undetected]

Alwil	[undetected]	Avira	[undetected]
AVG (Grisoft)	[undetected]	Kaspersky Lab	[undetected]
SOFTWIN	[undetected]	Frisk Software	[undetected]

Figure 3.2   VGrep reveals more than 100 results for MyDoom, a popular worm family to date.

For example, what do you call a threat that includes a downloader Trojan horse, a mass mailing worm, a rootkit to conceal files and activity on a computer, ad/spyware illegally installed on the computer but has a legal end user license agreement included, and a backdoor Trojan that steals sensitive information? Most companies have since moved to an itemized approach, naming and handling each threat individually. Unfortunately this greatly hinders the SysAdmin, who needs to know the entire scope of the attack to prevent, identify, and mitigate all the codes and vectors of vulnerability used in such an attack.

It is also noteworthy to identify common misuse of the term virus. The term virus is popularized and is frequently used to describe anything malicious. It is a technical term within the antivirus community describing malcode that infects an existing host file. Even this definition, within the technical community, is debated and varies among professionals and organizations. In short, professionals should be specific and technical in how they name malcode instead of using generic terms like virus, which are not specific or necessarily accurate.

Also, slang terms used by some, such as Brazilian bad actors like Virii, are not generally recognized or used. Terms and types in this document do not specify such slang.

An excellent professional source for technical terms of malcode exists on the Virus Bulletin site (http://www.virusbtn.com/resources/glossary/index). It includes many names not included in this overview, such as Data Diddler and Zip Bomb, and is an excellent source for reference. Virus Bulletin is also a leading professional malcode research organization of high interest to any professional who specializes in malcode-related work.

Vector

The vector of attack is how transmission of malcode takes place, such as e-mail, a link sent to an instant messenger user, or a hostile Web site attempting to exploit vulnerable software on a remote host. This is one of the most important components of a malcode incident for a SysAdmin to understand to properly protect against reinfection or additional attacks on infrastructure of a corporate network.

Payload

A payload is the primary action of a malicious code attack. This generally refers to the end point or primary impact rather than smaller components of an attack. For example, a downloader Trojan may be used to install and run a Nuker Trojan horse that attempts to overwrite or corrupt files on the local disk. In such an incident both payloads could be itemized out, downloader and Nuker components. However, in most cases, incident managers refer to the primary payload, the Nuker component of the attack.

Virus

A virus is a malicious software that infects a host file to spread. It is commonly used in a general sense to refer to all sorts of malcode, but this is not technically accurate. Fred Cohen is credited with first using this term officially in 1983.

Logic Bomb

A logic bomb is a type of Trojan that typically executes a destructive routine when certain conditions are met, such as date and time. A logic bomb can be planted by a disgruntled employee within a network to then launch a destructive routine, such as overwriting or corrupting data, several weeks after the employee leaves the company.

Worm

A worm is malicious software that creates a copy of itself (or clones itself) to spread. For example, a mass-mailing worm sends out copies of itself via e-mail. Some individuals prefer to call worms any code that traverses across a network through various means.

Trojan

A Trojan is a malicious software that masquerades as something it is not. It does not replicate. One of the most common Trojans in the wild in 2008 is downloader Trojans from generic family names like Agent, Small, and Delf.

Dropper

A dropper is a malicious file used to install malicious code on a computer. Downloader Trojans are sometimes also called droppers.

Keylogger

Keylogger is a type of Trojan used to capture data keylogged on a system. It may also include sophisticated Trojans that can capture all keystrokes and take pictures of the screen at specific points in time to steal online credentials and other sensitive information. It may also refer to physical keylogger devices that can be placed in line between keyboards and a computer to steal sensitive information. An example of a physical keylogger device is KeyGhost, available at http://www.keyghost.com/keylogger/.

Bot

A bot is malicious code that acts like a remotely controlled "robot" for an attacker, with other Trojan and Worm capabilities. This term may refer to the code itself or an infected computer, also known as drone or zombie. Other related terms are botherder or botmaster, for the bad actor that manages the botherd or botnet (typically thousands of infected zombies). Some also refer to automation as a key component differentiating bots from other types of code. However, that definition then can be confused with worms that can be fully automated rather than carefully controlled like a bot.

File Infector

File infector, mostly a historical term, generally refers to viruses that infect files. Perhaps the most well known historical file-infecting virus is Jerusalem, which infects all executable files run except for command.com in DOS. Figure 3.3 shows how a file can be modified by a file-infecting virus:

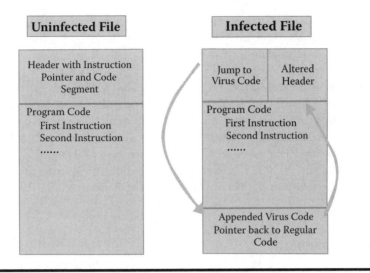

Figure 3.3   A file-infecting virus may append virus code.

File-infecting viruses may prepend code to the front of the file, append code to the end of the file as shown in Figure 3.3, or creatively inject into various locations of the file. File-infecting viruses that inject into various locations of the body are also known as "Cavity Viruses," such as the infamous Elkern. Removal of such code can be quite difficult, and multiple file infections often corrupt files beyond repair.

Modern-day file-infecting viruses are rare but are sometimes included with blended threats that install Trojans, spreading as worms across the network, and infecting specific files types of interest on the host, such as EXE or even Web content such as HTML pages (with script injects).

Macro Viruses

Macro viruses first emerged with Concept in 1995, spreading within Microsoft Office software. They are created within Visual Basic for Applications or WordBasic, and spread through Office documents such as DOC files. Macro viruses spread like wildfire for several years until changes in technology and security responses to the threat, in addition to a competitive criminal marketplace with Trojans and bots, essentially removed them from the wild as a prevalent threat shortly after the turn of the century.

Boot Sector Virus

A boot sector virus is malcode that spreads in the wild by copying itself to the Master Boot Record (MBR) of a hard disk and boot sectors of floppy disks. Brain, the first PC virus, is a boot sector virus. Other notable examples include Form, Joshi, and AntiCMOS. Figure 3.4 shows how a clean disk is modified to become infected by a traditional boot sector virus.

In 2007, a new threat emerged against the MBR, where Mebroot modifies the MBR of hard disks and installs into the slack space (unused space at the end of a drive) to load a kernel level rootkit before the operating system even boots up! It is possible that such stealthy code is installed in available memory on hardware, pushing the boundaries of software-based threats on hardware loading before the operating system. Removal of such threats is extremely challenging within a network environment in 2008 not used to such new threats, requiring that the MBR be overwritten with new data in addition to reimaging or reinstalling the operating system.

Windows Rootkit

There are many definitions for a Windows rootkit that are still debated today. The historical definition of a rootkit comes from Linux computers that had been hacked, where the attacker wanted to maintain "root" or administrator privileges on a computer after a compromise. To accomplish this feat, the attacker installed a variety of modified Linux tools to function as normal but not show the compromise, such as an open port to the attacker or malicious files installed on the computer. As a result the name "rootkit" makes sense, where a "kit" or suite of tools was used to maintain root.

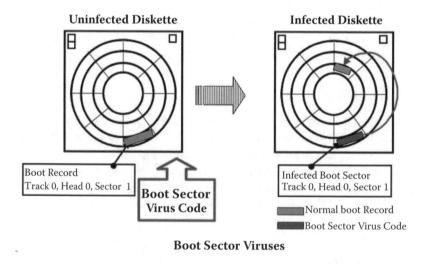

Boot Sector Viruses

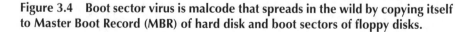

Figure 3.4   Boot sector virus is malcode that spreads in the wild by copying itself to Master Boot Record (MBR) of hard disk and boot sectors of floppy disks.

Some have defined Windows rootkits as codes that mask intrusion as well as being used in the compromise of a system. Strictly speaking, rootkits are used to maintain elevated privileges on a system by being stealthy. In Windows the term rootkit is more generalized to identify malcode that attempts to conceal the presence of code (stealth techniques) on a system by injecting processes, concealing files on the system, hiding registry keys from users attempting to analyze keys on the system, and more. Windows rootkits are not necessarily a suite of tools but are often one or two files. There are two types of Windows rootkits, userland and kernel, as shown in Figure 3.5.

- *Userland*: These rootkits only have user access rights to the outer ring of permissions known as userland. Userland rootkits typically have a DLL extension name and are stored in the Windows System32 directory. Bad actors typically attempt to install a hostile DLL as a legitimate file and then use it to control various function calls made by Windows or other programs to maintain stealth on an infected computer.
- *Kernel*: Kernel level rootkits are the more powerful of the two rootkit types because they have the same level of power as an administrator (root on Windows). Software attempting to identify and remove rootkits on a system is in a race condition to not be manipulated or controlled by hostile code operating on the same layer of access control and permissions. Kernel level rootkits are typically installed as a SYS or VXD file type in the Windows or Windows System32 directories.

Adware, Spyware, and Potentially Unwanted Programs

Adware, spyware, and potentially unwanted programs are technically legal software, but frequently illegally installed without user consent, to display advertisements or monitor behavior or sensitive data. To avoid litigation, several antivirus companies started calling these Potentially Unwanted Programs (PUPs) and do not scan for these by default within antivirus programs.

These programs are technically legal, including an End User License Agreement (EULA). However, affiliate abuse frequently involves such software being illegally installed by bad actors who seek financial rewards per install. As a result, the legal software is illegally installed on computers. In the beginning of this new type of threat, end users simply ignored the EULA to view an online greeting card and found out later that their computer mass mailed all their contacts to visit the same site.

Adware is software funded for advertising, such as pop-up advertisement for porn sites.

Spyware is legal software that is used to report user information to a remote party. For example, the code used tracks user habits online such as search terms and then reports it to a remote agency. This is different from malicious Trojans, which keylog or steal sensitive information, because spyware includes a valid EULA agreement.

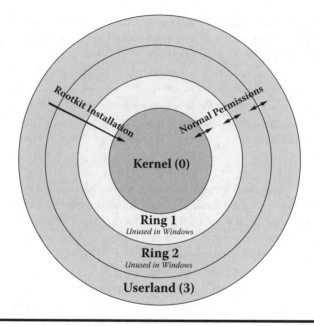

Figure 3.5 Rootkits either infect userland or kernel layers on Windows. (Image ©2007–2010 Ken Dunham.)

Rogue software, also known as goadware, is a new subset of this type of malcode in the wild in 2008 that may or may not include a EULA. They are illegal due to their deceptive business practices and court cases to date. They first emerged in the wild in 2002 and are now major criminal enterprises used to goad users into purchasing software that is nonfunctional or crippled. Rogue software is commonly installed illegally through exploitation or through deceitful user interaction procedures. Once installed, they goad the user in an aggressive fashion, such as changing the desktop image, displaying frequent pop-ups, and windows with no easy close options. They frequently masquerade as antivirus, ad/spyware software, and performance-improving software programs, making it difficult for consumers to identify what is legitimate and what may be rogue software.

Polymorphic

Polymorphic viruses assume many (poly) shapes and forms (morphic) by encrypting code differently with each infection. This term caught on in the mid 1990s with tools emerged to generate thousands of new minor variants of code based on mutation routines to subvert signature technology used by antivirus software at the time.

Proof of Concept

Proof of concept (POC) is a functional code used to prove exploitation or function-ality. POCs are sometimes created by authors of exploits to prove that exploitation of a vulnerability is possible. POC malcode are also created to show that malcode can spread in new environments.

Brief History of Malcode

Historical facts around malcode vary and can be highly debated at times. Fred Cohen is frequently credited with first coining the term virus with his work in the early 1980s. Brain marks the first PC virus in 1986. When Robert Morris spread the "Internet Worm" on November 2, 1988, the "anti" virus industry got a lot of media attention and a new industry was well underway to what we see in the twenty-first century today.

The Internet Worm

The story behind Robert Morris is an interesting one, especially in light of contin-ued issues of debate and ethics that we see still today in computing. Robert "Bob" Morris is his father who is an American cryptographer who was involved in the cre-ation of the Rainbow Series of computer security standards. Morris had warned of security issues in government servers but was brushed off by experts of the day. His son, Robert Morris, created a POC code to vindicate his father, with no inherent malicious payloads. When he tested it on the MIT network, it got out of hand and began to spread quickly. Take note that other less plausible statements exist regard-ing his motive, such as Morris attempting to "measure the size of the Internet."

It was not long before an approximately 6000 UNIX computers became infected with his worm creation, indirectly resulting in disruption of service to infected servers and networks. The U.S. General Accounting Office put the cost of the dam-age at about $10–100 million, which obviously includes downtime, repair costs, and multiple other soft costs related to the incident. Robert Morris was the first individual tried and convicted of violating the 1986 Computer Fraud and Abuse Act. He eventually served 3 years probation, 400 hours of community service, and paid a fine of $10,000.

At about this same time, viruses ran rampant on the Macintosh platform and began to take off on the PC platform. Viruses such as WDEF, a boot sector–infecting virus on Macintosh, quickly spread as people copied files to and from disks and on computers with hard disks (hard disks were a big deal in the late 1980s for personal computers!). Professionals began to create antivirus software solutions, with Norton (now Symantec) emerging as one of the leaders with a clean boot disk option and antivirus scanner option with great effectiveness for PC viruses of the day.

Notable Firsts

Several notable "firsts" for virus history for this early period are in the list below:

- The first file-infecting virus to target executables is the Lehigh virus discovered at Lehigh University in 1987.
- Jerusalem, one of the most prevalent families in the wild for several years, emerged in 1987, infecting both COM and EXE files. It included a destructive payload to activate on Friday the 13th.
- Cascade is the first encrypted virus, discovered in 1988. It greatly hindered mitigation.

Polymorphism and Virus Creation Kits

Polymorphic viruses, also known as self-mutating viruses, became the next focus of concern for the antivirus industry. Dark Avenger's Mutating Engine and Mutating Engine (MtE) appeared in the wild in 1991. Antivirus efforts quickly countered by using emulators to essentially sandbox code in memory to look at the decrypted virus.

Virus creation kits also emerged in the early 1990s. These tools made it easier for bad actors to create variants of code. Perhaps one of the most infamous, shown in Figure 3.6, is "Virus Creation Lab," also known as VCL, published by "Nowhere Man," a member of a group called NuKE, in 1992.

In its day VCL was impressive, featuring a full-color graphical interface with mouse control and drop-down menus (Figure 3.7).

VCL includes extensive documentation and examples of various types of viruses that it can create. For the expert it includes Assembly language source code for viruses created by the tool to enable editing by the bad actor before deploying the virus in the wild. While these tools promoted the concept of virus writing, organized criminal efforts were far off in the horizon. At this point in time, virus writing was mostly interesting and POC-type creations. Some were destructive, but the dawn of financially motivated malicious code attacks as the norm did not come along for several more years.

Another famous creation kit at the time, dueling for pride points with VCL, is the Phalcon-Skism Mass-Produced Code Generator. While not as developed on the GUI front, it was considerably more functional than the virus creations made with VCL. It is capable of creating memory-resident viruses that infect both COM and EXE files with support for encryption.

Michelangelo

In 1992, Michelangelo, one of the most infamous early viruses of its day, emerged in the wild. This virus carried a destructive payload that executes on March 6 of any

Figure 3.6   VCL was published by Nowhere Man in 1992.

year, the birthday of the famous painter. It caught the attention of the media and helped to fan the flames of virus writing in the 1990s.

Mac Viruses

Macintosh viruses also continued to grow strong into the early 1990s. A new strain of application-specific HyperText viruses began to spread within the HyperCard freeware application bundled with each Mac, discovered by the author of this chapter. Merryxmas and Merryxmas2 viruses worked to infect the Home "stack" (or file) of HyperCard, a central file used within HyperCard. Each stack or HyperCard file

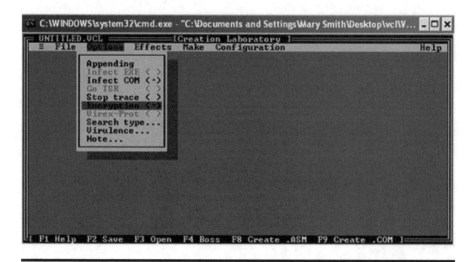

Figure 3.7 VCL features full-colored menus and many powerful options in its day.

opened after infection was then infected from the code stored in the Home stack. If a user removed the virus code from the Home stack, infected stacks quickly reinfected the Home stack. As long as the Home stack stayed infected, every stack opened was quickly reinfected. This type of virus was very prevalent within the Macintosh world for several years, a predecessor in principle functionality and operation to the world of Macro viruses that later followed on the PC in 2005.

In May of 1991, Mac viruses suffered a major blow with the advent of a major operating system upgrade to Mac OS 7. Most Mac viruses only worked properly in Mac OS 6 and earlier. As a result the upgrade to the 32-bit Mac OS 7 removed many of the traditional threats. However, application-specific threats like HyperText viruses continued to thrive until programs like MerryxmasWatcher 2.0 appeared on the freeware market to help identify, remove, or inoculate against traditional strains of the virus (programmed by Ken Dunham). Few threats emerged against Macs for the rest of the decade that had any major significance in the wild (Autostart being one of those).

Hacktivism Moving toward Cyberwar and Cyberterrorism?

Yaha worms emerged as a top threat in 2003. These worms were unique, authored by Indian Snakes out of India as part of the India–Pakistan Kashmir border conflict in the region. The group created a special patch utility to modify Yaha worm binaries (Figure 3.8). Their code proved to be highly effective, spreading as a worm in the wild and then performing DDoS attacks against Pakistan Web servers. The tool could also be used to overwrite hard drives based on a logic bomb component

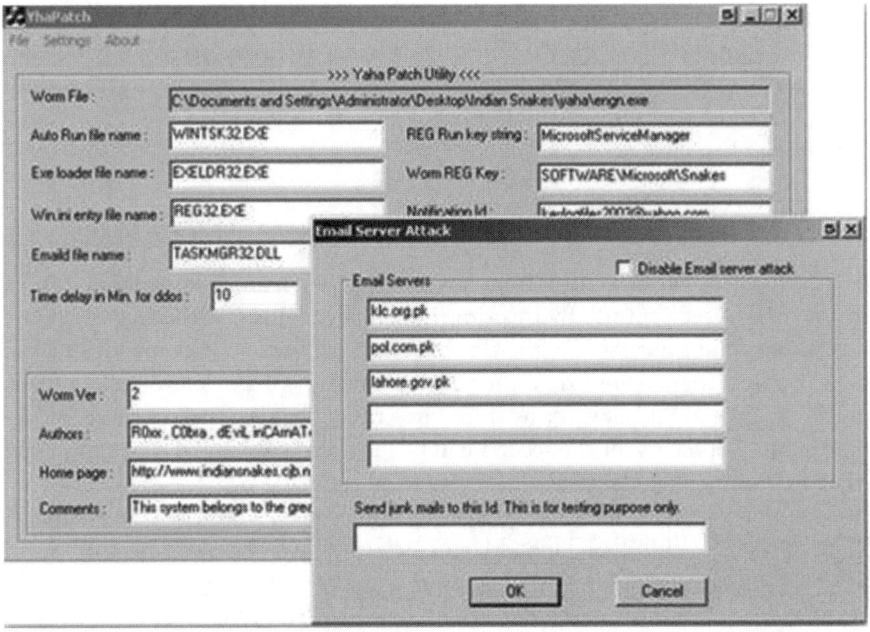

Figure 3.8   Indian Snakes patch utility targeted Pakistan resources by default.

that targeted computers using a Pakistan time zone configuration. It also included an exploit to locate and crash computers in the Pakistan IP space, steal sensitive information, and much more. The Indian Snakes successfully weaponized malcode to target a specific country moving up from traditional hacktivism, which is hacking for a religious or political ideology, toward cyberwarfare-type tactics.

The concept of cyberterrorism also took the stage of many discussions following the attacks on the United States on 9-11. No true acts of cyberterrorism took place for the next few years even though many claimed some actions to be terrorist related. In 2007, major attacks on Estonia, from within their own country and by Russians, were caused through a political issue related to the moving of a statue. Some called this cyberterrorism, but again, this was heavily debated by many. In 2008, a Georgia–Russia conflict and DDoS attacks on Georgian resources raised questions over possible cyberwarfare tactics utilized by the Russians against Georgia. One thing is clear by 2008; cyberwarfare is considered a very real threat by major powers globally.

1994: Virus Hoaxes

By 1994 Internet access became a reality for many U.S. citizens. Along with it came virus hoaxes spreading through e-mail. Infamous hoaxes include "Good Times," spreading fear, uncertainty, and doubt to many. It is known by many names, including Join the Crew, PenPal Greetings, Deeyenda, Irina, and Win a Holiday, based on the variants that emerged over the years. Others also emerged, like "It Takes Guts to Say Jesus," warning users of an e-mail that erases everything on a hard drive when opened.

1995: Turning of the Tide and a New Threat, Macro Viruses

By 1995 the tide began to turn, from fame to disruption, and eventually to fortune by the turn of the century. By this time in computing history, the Internet boom was taking off in a huge way in the United States and viruses were growing quickly. New opportunities abounded on the new Windows 95 platform, which bad actors quickly sought to take advantage of for virus opportunities. One of the most significant developments for the second half of the decade was the release of the first Macro virus in 1995, Concept.

Concept was a new sort of virus that was authored in Word Basic for Microsoft Word to spread within DOC files. Macros are powerful features of Microsoft Word that enable users to create scripts (macros) to automate tasks, such as pressing a hotkey to quickly turn a selection into a color, font, size, and style of interest. Because it spread within DOC files, it was able to be spread in files that existed on both Macintosh and PC operating systems. Macro viruses quickly became the most prevalent type of threat in the wild for several years until major updates to Microsoft Office, including significant security updates, essentially removed Macro viruses from the wild shortly after the turn of the century.

Anti-Trojan Utilities

The late 1990s also experienced a boom in Trojans and the development of specific anti-Trojan software programs. Antivirus software was not keeping up with Trojan threats as closely as other types of threats, like Macro viruses and traditional viruses. As a result several Trojan-specific utilities emerged and became popularized until antivirus companies later gained ground on the emergent Trojan threat in the wild. This same type of niche utility development also took place with the advent of ad/spyware and Windows rootkits in the first part of the twenty-first century.

Worm Wars

Near the turn of the century major changes took place in the computing industry related to Y2K fears, online commerce threats, and increased reliance on e-mail by millions globally. In 1999, David Smith (30 years old at the time) released the Melissa worm into the wild, spreading as both a Macro virus and e-mail worm to hundreds of thousands of computers in a very short period of time. A rash of worms followed, including ILoveYou (VBS.LoveLetter) in 2000, Nimda in 2001 (Admin backwards), and Code Red in 2001. The "Year of the Worm" was 2003, with more major worm outbreaks in this year than any other in the history of computing to date. It included major threats: Slammer, BugBear, Blaster, Welchia, SoBig.F, Dumaru, and Swen, to name a few. Microsoft Corp. also created a bounty program, and law enforcement agencies like the FBI were now handling these major threats. Over the next few months several major arrests took place, including Blaster.B author Jeffrey Lee Parsons; Sven Jaschan, author of NetSky and Sasser worms in 2004; and Ago, a German male father of bots and author of Agobot and Phatbot codes. As a side note, 2004 was called the "Year of the Worm War" where Bagle worm authors battled out Netsky (Jaschan) for who could create the most prevalent and sophisticated worm code. Jaschan won the war with his creation of Sasser, but got arrested shortly thereafter. These events significantly changed the malcode scene forever, whittling away those that feared enforcement and hardening those that were financially motivated to launch such attacks.

DDoS Attacks on Major Web Properties

At the turn of the century, MafiaBoy (Mike Calce), a high school student from Montreal, Canada, successfully took major Web sites offline, including Yahoo, Amazon, Dell, E*Trade, eBay, and CNN. By this time in Internet history, these sites were all considered a core part of the infrastructure of online services and Internet usage. MafiaBoy successfully launched his attacks using a tool called Tribe Flood Network (TFN). Several other similar tools emerged during this period, such as Trinoo and Stacheldraht. These tools were later superseded by bots, proving to be much more effective, flexible, and desired by the maturing criminal market in the twenty-first century.

2004 is known as the "Year of the Bot" by some because the source code for PhatBot (and other top malcode) was spread in the underground in the spring. This was followed with an explosion of bot variants and attacks in the wild in 2004 and later. DDoS extortion cases against small online gambling sites became a major issue, especially in the United Kingdom.

Legal and Law Enforcement Challenges

In 2000, an interesting legal issue began to emerge with ILoveYou, CIH, and VBSWG. Onel de Guzman was one of the authors of the ILoveYou worm in the Philippines. No law existed to hold him accountable for his crimes and global damage caused by his malicious creation. As a result, no justice could be executed against Guzman for his crimes, but was later outlawed partly due to global pressure on lawmakers to change laws in the country. Other countries also began to implement such laws, slowly but surely.

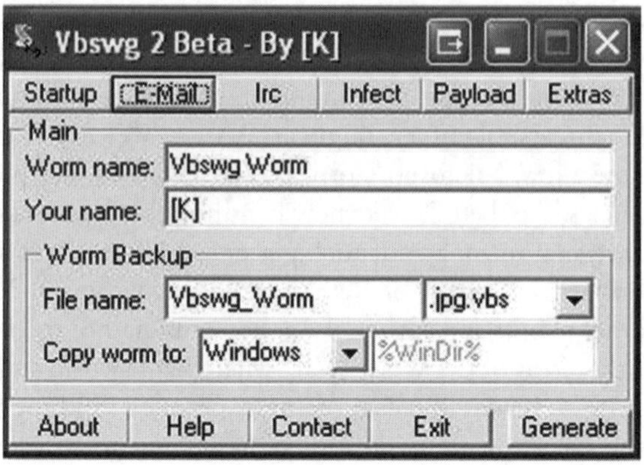

Figure 3.9   VBSWG 2 Beta is easy to use with many features.

CIH was a very destructive file-infecting virus that attempted to overwrite data on hard drives and corrupt the system BIOS on vulnerable devices on specific dates. Chernobyl was the most destructive variant easily impacting at least 500,000 or more computers on a single day in 1999. Chen Ing-Hau, author of the virus, admitted to creating the virus and got a job with a company called Wahoo. No charges were ever pressed against him within his country in 1999, so he could not be prosecuted. In 2000 the virus struck again, on April 26, and he was charged and arrested.

VBSWG was created by [K]Alamar, an Argentinean male, boldly posted on a public Internet home page in 2000 (Figure 3.9). He aggressively updated his code with many features.

Later, Jan de Wit, also known as OnTheFly, used his toolkit to create the Anna Kournikova worm. He was quickly arrested and ended up serving 150 hours of community service. Many thought he deserved greater consequences and that [K] Alamar also should be held accountable for his malicious toolkit. Such events continued to exert pressure on the international community to develop the law authorities required to coordinate global investigations to hold such actors accountable.

Mobile Malcode

Scares of mobile malcode, on PDA and smartphone devices, started in 2000 with Timfonica. It spread on PCs and then spammed phones. It was not until 4 years later that this new medium started to experience significant malcode growth in the wild with the advent of the Cabir worm source code spread by a group called 29A and others. CommWarrior followed, spreading through both Bluetooth and MMS vectors, able to spread globally instead of just locally. Some mobile malcode are destructive and most inadvertently drain the battery on the device as it attempts to spread to other devices. There are now mobile malcode impacting multiple operating systems and some that perform financial fraud by dialing outbound to premium line numbers.

Maturation of an Internet Criminal Marketplace

After the turn of the century, the criminal marketplace began to mature and drive malcode threats seen by 2005 and later. Malcode threats now turned from fame to fortune, and legal consequences existed for anyone diddling in the field. Adware and spyware emerged to legalistically abuse End User License Agreements (EULA) that click-happy Internet users ignore. Then affiliate abuse followed, where illegal installations without any EULA displayed took place, rewarding fraudsters with payment for each installation illegally performed on computers. Both authors, who were always more sophisticated, calculated, and controlled than Trojan actors, quickly automated attacks for financial gain. DDoS attacks, extortion, industrial espionage, spam, pharmaceutical fraud, 419 scams, phishing, and many other types of attacks now run rampant in an information age.

Trojans and bots served as the primary genesis of malcode identity theft. In the beginning, Trojan attacks were kids trying to compromise a system and grab an image of a girl on a webcam. Then they got credit card numbers and registration keys. This led to Warez (illegal software), credit card fraud, and related identity theft. Over time the market matured to where fraudsters pay for "full details" to get social security numbers, addresses, medical history, and anything else they can find on a victim to best perform various identity theft collection, monetization, laundering, and marketplace actions.

Concurrent with these marketplace developments is the advent of exploit kits for sale on the underground. These include but are not limited to MPack, Neosploit, Firepack, Icepack, Fiesta, and others. These kits typically include a C&C to enable easy management of the exploit kit and payloads.

By 2008 the malcode arena is largely dominated by leaders of the criminal marketplace. Top threats include the infamous rogue host provider "Russian Business Network," Wicked Rose, and the NCPH Hacking Crew launching targeted attacks out of China, Step57.Info Russian malcode team, rogue security products like "Antivirus XP 2008/9," Prg for state-of-the-art man-in-the-middle financial fraud, extortion-ware that encrypts files on a system and only decrypts for a fee, Torpig and Mebroot for advanced stealth and financial fraud, and many more.

Vectors of Infection

As aforementioned, the vector is where the malcode comes from, which can be a form of media transfer such as e-mail or P2P networks, or exploitation combined with Web browsing. Various techniques exist to trick users into executing code or revealing sensitive information, covered in this section. For example, default view settings of Windows do not show the true extension of a file. "report.doc" may only appear as "report" to the end user. Various methods exist to then trick users into thinking malicious files are safe, exploiting this default behavior of Windows, when it is actually malicious.

An interesting new vector emerged around Christmas of 2007, where digital frames were infected with malcode. These new gifts enabled users to transfer malcode through a USB-based thumb drive.

Social Engineering or Exploitation

Social engineering is a big term for discussing how bad actors trick users or "con" them. For opportunistic attacks, angles of promising something sexual is a popular theme to get someone to click on a link, open a file, or perform some other sort of desired action. After all, most pornography is accessed during the business week during business hours (epidemic). Other angles may be fear, like claiming that your services are terminated or that there is a problem of some sort, attempting to trick the user into revealing sensitive information (phishing-type scams) or perform actions to install malcode.

Training can be highly effective in helping those who are naive to not be taken advantage of easily. Simply training people to never trust unsolicited e-mails, instant messages, or other communications is essential. Up-training is also effective for any higher-risk issues that emerge that are specific to a date and time, such as a new e-mail-borne threat with various subjects and body characteristics easily identified by individuals within an organization. However, an acceptable use policy and support from management must be in place to give any such training teeth and follow up. With such a combination, the "user-to-keyboard" error (human issues) risk can be lowered. This is important since many high-profile successful threats to date still rely on social engineering to spread in the wild, such as the recent Storm worm of 2007/2008.

Long File Extensions

Long file extensions have been around for many years. On Windows NTFS-based operating systems, the filename can be up to 255 characters long (http://en.wikipedia.org/wiki/Filename). Filenames that are very long are abbreviated with three dots "...," concealing the true extension of the file as shown in Figure 3.10.

Double File Extensions

Another easy trick on the filename is to add two extensions to it. This is often combined with long filenames to show only the first extension, such as "Madonna.

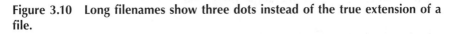

Figure 3.10   Long filenames show three dots instead of the true extension of a file.

jpg" followed by many spaces and then the real extension, such as .exe: "Madonna. jpg.exe."

Fake Related Extension

Sometimes a fake related extension is what works best for an attack vector. In December of 2005 a new major threat emerged related to Windows MetaFile (WMF). Bad actors quickly deployed exploits with WMF files. Security experts and SysAdmins countered by blocking WMF files until a patch could be deployed. Bad actors then started sending out hostile WMF files but used the JPG extension. The JPG extension worked to launch a vulnerable program that would then properly interpret the header of the hostile WMF file (ignoring the filename extension), and exploitation took place. This is a prime example of how knowing the minute details of exploitation makes a huge difference in understanding and protecting against possible threat vectors.

Fake Icon

Fake icons are often given to files to make them appear as something safe or trusted. Some actors will give filenames that appear to be something like a PDF or similar file, and then an icon for PDF files, but configure the file so that it runs as an executable. Figure 3.11 shows an example of how a notepad icon is given to an executable, making it appear as safe. Fortunately, this computer was configured to show the real extension of a file so as to avoid being easily fooled by computers that, by default, do not show the extension.

Password-Protected ZIP Files/RAR

Some malcode attacks send compressed or encrypted files to potential victims. This helps to bypass some gateway filters that exist to block EXE, COM, SCR, and

engn.EXE

Figure 3.11 Engn is all that appears on default configured Windows XP computer and notepad Icon.

similar file types known to be of high risk. Such attacks will normally include text or an image to provide the password to a possible victim, instructing them to open the file. Figure 3.12 shows an example from 2008.

Hostile Codecs (Zlob)

Zlob is one of the most infamous families of code to date in 2008. This family of code spreads through multiple vectors, but always ends up with a user installing a hostile

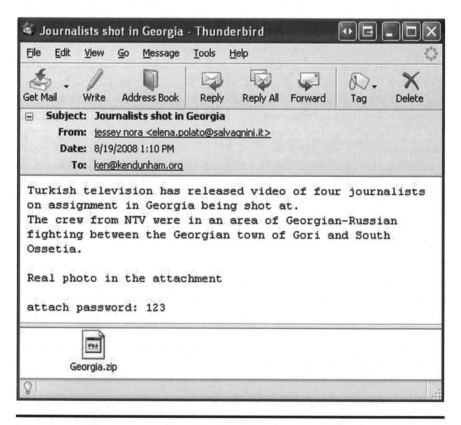

Figure 3.12 Recipient of e-mail is given a password and prompted to open a hostile attachment.

codec. Various posts are made to forums or users may be directed via e-mail or some other vector to visit a pornography site. Upon visiting the pornography site, or similar such content, they are told they cannot view the video without installing a codec first. Installation of the codec gives permission to install Zlob or similar malicious code.

E-Mail

E-mail is one of the most well-known vectors for spreading malcode. It is heavily used and depended upon by millions daily. It is also the written word and is highly trusted by many. Sometimes e-mail threats can involve a vulnerability related to e-mail clients or even Web browsers, such as Internet Explorer, that are used to view HTML-based content. Some have argued that the e-mail vector will die away, but the reality is malcode still successfully spreads in 2008 through social engineering e-mail-borne threats. It is here to stay but will highly likely be increasingly less of an impact in the future as it is replaced with mobile solutions that have high asset values to fraudsters targeting new mediums.

Web-Based Attacks

Web-based attacks are one of the most popular in 2008 to spread malcode in the wild. Internet browsing is one of the most popular uses of the Internet. Social network sites can have vulnerabilities exploited to spread code through profiles. Web-based vectors commonly spread through social engineering and through exploitation of Internet Explorer and now Firefox and other browsers. Web vectors have a multitude of possibilities. For example, a Web site can have a Zlob code prompting the user to download code to view a movie. A hostile Web site can include an exploit to automatically install code on vulnerable computers.

Brute Force Attacks

Bots are infamous for attempting to spread through a network via brute force attacks. By attempting to log in to remote computers as "Admin" or "Admin123," etc., thousands of passwords can be checked quickly for authentication. Since passwords are typically weak they are easily guessed on many systems, leading to a compromise. Targeted malcode attacks involve an attacker creating a customer library of possible credential values related to the target or compromised data to further compromise a computer or network.

Instant Messaging

Instant messaging (IM) threats may involve exploitation of software to spread code but more frequently rely on social engineering. Kelvir is one such bot, infamous for spreading as a bot through traditional means and also through IM. Historically,

IM threats are less likely to be trusted and followed compared to e-mail threats. Most involve a user receiving a message with a link, required to click on the link to visit the hostile site. The remote hostile site may involve social engineering or include an exploit to attack the computer.

Peer-to-Peer Networks

Peer-to-peer (P2P) networks involve hosts sharing files with one another, either directly or through a centralized P2P server. A wide variety of files are shared on P2P networks, including those that are unintentionally shared and pirated, illegal, and warez-type media. Most P2P downloads are not malicious. However, risk escalates to more than 75% on average once a user starts to search for terms like famous women used in social engineering, like "Paris," or pornography related terms and illegal terms like "warez" and "crack." Most organizations block the use of P2P software for security and liability concerns. SysAdmins need to be diligent to monitor network traffic for possible rogue P2P installations, famous for unintentional sharing and abuse historically.

Internet Relay Chat

Internet Relay Chat (IRC) was a big part of how people "chatted" or communicated near the turn of the century. Today, social networking sites and forums are dominating the scene as IRC falls into the background. IRC is still used by thousands daily and has similar threats to several years ago. It is common to receive spammed messages within IRC chat rooms, private messages from bots by bad actors, and more. Sometimes bad actors attempt to exploit vulnerable software (chat clients) or may send malcode through IRC to the user via links or files directly through a DCC connection.

Rogue WAP

WAPs are allowed in some organizations and can be a vector for malcode to travel through into an enterprise network. For such organizations they typically invest in solutions to manage their WAPs and employee use thereof. However, some organizations do not allow wireless solutions and fail to monitor for rogue WAPs. It is not uncommon for mobile devices in 2008 to include a wireless option or for employees to own their own inexpensive WAP. It is important that SysAdmins be looking for WAPs on a regular basis to audit their own airspace. It is trivial with freeware tools on both Windows and Linux.

Contractors over Virtual Private Network

Contractors typically do not have the same level of rigor applied to their computers as that of an enterprise. It is all too common for contractors to connect into a network over a Virtual Private Network (VPN) to only infect the network. For example, in 2004, the Sasser worm infected a contractor computer. The contractor later established a VPN connection with a network that allows no Internet access. Sasser spread to the closed network and immediately imploded when it found no Internet connection, taking the entire network offline.

Rogue Products and Search Engines

There are literally hundreds of rogue security products, such as Antivirus XP 2008/9, Antivirus Pro, and many others. They have legitimate sounding names and GUIs but are not legitimate programs. They have even successfully hosted advertisements for short periods of time on major Web sites. Parked domains and manipulated search engine results and abuse can also be used to help spread malcode to computers via social engineering and exploitation. One tip is to scan files before installation with a free multiscanner like VirusTotal (http://www.virustotal .com) to see if it is detected as malicious.

Infected Factory Builds and CDs

Should you scan your plastic-wrapped CDs for malcode? While it is fairly rare, major cases of brand new media gets reported to be infected every year. Infected CDs and computers are a possibility, especially as major changes take place in highly competitive industries with outsources or overseas operations. Sometimes core builds of various downloads on the Internet are also hacked or compromised by bad actors leading to malicious installations of software. Again, these cases are rarer than other vectors but do happen and are normally communicated clearly and globally when such incidents take place.

Insider Hardware Threats

Insider hardware threats are a huge problem in a world where mobile solutions with powerful and affordable hardware are available to the consumer. For example, Knoppix can be loaded on to a thumb drive and then used to boot up a computer and possibly gain unauthorized access to files on the drive or make changes in Linux mode. One of the most common police issues related to keyloggers is not the software malcode variety but that of the hardware variety put between the keyboard and the computer to steal information. Insiders can also use a thumb drive to steal information, load hostile code onto computers, and perform various nefarious activities within the workplace.

Web Exploitation Frameworks

Web exploitation frameworks are tools that include many exploits and a user interface to launch attacks against computers visiting a Web site. They are frequently developed and sold as a kit on the Russian underground for hundreds or thousands of U.S. dollars. They can be quite sophisticated, including encryption and a C&C center for the bad actor using the tool. In 2008 one of the leading frameworks is Neosploit. However, more inexpensive and good performing frameworks competing with Neosploit are applying pressure in the Russian underground marketplace for Neosploit authors. Competing products are many but also include IcePack and FirePack as examples.

Payloads

There is a wide range of payloads with malcode. In the early days, payloads were more related to fame, such as promoting an alias of a virus writing author. Early codes often asked for permission to spread or simply spread and notified the user. Then destructive payloads followed, resulting in a loss of data. Common payloads are overviewed in this section.

Backdoor Trojans

Backdoor Trojans provide an attacker with full remote access to a computer. This is a full breach of integrity. It is common for more than one code to be installed, to increase survivability on an infected computer. If one code is detected a new private undetected code may have been installed on the computer to maintain access and control. Backdoor Trojans first had "fun stuff" options to open the CD tray, flash the lights on the keyboard, and mess with the mind of a victim. Today they may include a remote C&C server that tracks how many infections per country and log files by IP address. Trojans are sometimes specialized, only grabbing online gaming credentials or software license keys. Others grab everything they can capture. Payloads from a backdoor Trojan are as creative as malcode authors can be with their attacks since they have full remote control over the computer.

DDoS Types

There are several tactics used to disrupt or deny service to a computer, such as congesting netflow traffic to a computer or attempting to overwhelm a server on the application level. Common methods of DDoS attacks are shown in the table that follows.

Man-in-the-Middle Malcode

Man-in-the-Middle (MITM) refers generically to any agent that is in between communications or processing and is able to influence it in some

Type of DDoS	Annotation
TCP SYN	This is one of the most common types of attacks performed today because of how successful it is in taking down Web sites of interest. Filtering out hostile from legitimate traffic for a Web server can be a very difficult process, hindering anti-DDoS attack efforts significantly. In this attack sequence, multiple TCP SYN packets are sent to the target from many computers simultaneously to overload it. A TCP handshake takes place for each attack sequence generated in the attack, involving a SYN (synchronization) packet, an ACK (acknowledgement) packet, and a final SYN-ACK packet.
Push-Ack	This attack is similar to a TCP SYN attack but sends out TCP packets with PUSH and ACK bit values set to one. This forces the target to load all data into a TCP buffer and then send an ACK when it is finished processing packets. Sending multiple packets of this nature may overload the buffer of the target computer causing it to crash.
Teardrop (Teardrop2, Targa, SYNdrop, Boink, Nestea Bonk, NewTear)	This classic and much older style of DDoS attack attempts to overlap IP fragments between packets to cause a vulnerable host to crash. Many minor variations of this attack exist today, and they are closely related. Updated firewalls and systems easily mitigate this type of attack today.
Land	An attacker modifies an IP packet to have the same source and destination address and port, causing vulnerable computers to crash.
Naptha	An attacker creates a large number of TCP connections to a target, leaving them in various states to overwhelm the target. This type of attack does not keep a record of the connection state and responds only to packets based on the flags in the packet received from the target.
UDP	UDP is a send-and-forget protocol that does not use a TCP handshake like that of TCP. This type of attack frees up the zombie computer to simply send out large volumes of UDP packets, never having to manage the standard TCP handshake that is required with the TCP protocol.

(continued)

Type of DDoS	Annotation
ICMP Flood	A large number of ICMP packets are sent to the target to overload it, causing it to crash or become inaccessible during the attack.
Ping of Death	A single ICMP ECHO request packet is sent to the target exceeding 65,535 bytes. This is an older attack that has been largely abandoned, given the more successful modern attacks now being used, such as TCP flood attacks.
ICMP Nuke	Especially crafted packets are sent to vulnerable operating systems in an attempt to crash the computer. This attack is similar to the ping of death (ICMP attacks) but attempts exploitation of the target operating system instead of attempting to overload the target with many ICMP packets.
Echo (Chargen)	An attacker creates packets spoofed with the target address, appearing to come from the local system's ECHO service, forcing the chargen service on the computer into a loop. If successful, the chargen service, responsible for character generation, becomes overloaded, causing the system to crash.
Smurf and Fraggle	Smurf and Fraggle attacks are dirty cousins that use a similar technique to overload a target with many packets over a short period of time. To orchestrate a Smurf attack, many ICMP packets are sent to multiple computers using a spoofed IP source address. These computers respond to the ICMP packets, quickly overloading the target (the spoofed IP used in the original packets). Fraggle attacks work in a manner similar to Smurf attacks but utilize UDP ECHO packets.

Recursive HTTP (Spidering)	Using scripts or utilities, attackers are able to perform recursive HTTP requests of a Web site, depleting resources on a targeted Web server. Spidering is sometimes performed against dynamic sites to identify the slowest loading page. Attackers then use this information to perform a DDoS against the exact resource that will likely result in DDoS success, for both the front-end of a Web site and the backend.
DNS Recursion (Amplification Attacks)	A DNS query spoofed with a victim source address is sent to a DNS server.[a] This results in the DNS server sending back a reply to the spoofed address. When large domains are queried, amplification can be significant. For example, a 30-byte query can receive up to 512 bytes of DNS response before the server truncates the response. Attackers can use the EDNS DNS protocol extension and submit multiple DNS queries to hundreds of thousands of recursive DNS servers to quickly generate massive DDoS attacks.

Source: Ken Dunham and Jim Melnick, *Malicious Bots: An Inside Look into the Cyber-Criminal Underground on the Internet*, Auerbach Publications, New York, NY, 2008. With permission.

[a] U.S. CERT. March 2006. The continuing denial of service threat posed by DNS recursion. http://www.us-cert.gov/reading_room/DNS-recursion033006.pdf.

regard. It is traditionally used to describe communication flows across the Internet. With regard to malcode, it is more commonly used to describe malcode that infects a host and then plays MITM locally to manipulate traffic and events.

MetaFisher is a famous code for playing MITM on a computer following an infection. It installs as a Browser Help Object (BHO) for Internet Explorer. The following infection can perform the following MITM actions:

■ Display a local phishing page related to a URL entered or clicked on by a user. For example, the user tries to go to bank.com and a local phishing page designed to look like bank.com is displayed instead, unbeknownst to the user.
■ Inject HTML to add extra fields or manipulate existing data. For example, when a Spanish user attempts to log onto a bank, only one password is required to view account data, but a second password to perform account transactions. MetaFisher is able to generate an extra field for the second password upon the user attempting to view account data. This is not that questionable to an end user and providers the fraudster with all the necessary data required to steal funds from the account.
■ Subvert true two factor authentication for Transaction Authorization Number (TAN) systems utilized by German banks. The malcode simply displays an error message that the TAN number is not valid, prompting the user to enter a new TAN number along with their logon and password. Meanwhile the malcode has captured a valid TAN number, logon, and password.

There are now phishing attacks that are controlled by malcode that are very sophisticated. In one instance the malcode monitors URLs. If it sees a URL that it targets for phishing, it sends encrypted data over TCP port 80 to a remote C&C. The remote C&C returns customized phishing data to the code in real time to display in the browser instead of the URL accessed by the end user. Endpoint attacks are the future of malcode attacks in many respects and pose significant challenges to overcome compared to traditional attacks to date.

Domain Name Servers

Domain Name Servers (DNS) are critical to how users typically browse the Internet, typing in a domain name that is then translated into an IP number. Unfortunately, DNS servers have various features and protocols that are vulnerable to attack. DNS servers can be hacked, poisoned, or compromised in a multitude of ways. In 2006 an estimated 400,000 or more such servers were considered misconfigured and vulnerable to abuse in large-scale DDoS attacks. In 2003 a massive ad/spyware campaign took place on thousands of DNS servers redirecting users to hostile sites that installed close to 50 malicious files on each "drive-by installation." In 2008, major issues emerged related to DNS poisoning, and even the servers for H.D.

Moore, author of MetaSploit, found his server compromised. One of the main ongoing issues with DNS is that everyone must depend on all DNS servers globally. While we can all do a good job of maintaining our own DNS server, what do you do about the one overseas that is poisoned and directing your consumers to hostile sites instead of your trusted site?

Identifying Infections

Identification of infections often takes place through scant network alerts or antivirus results. Unfortunately these alerts all too often do not include enough details to enable a thorough response by a SysAdmin. For example a network tool may identify a hostile IP address and sample traffic but may not include the domain or original Universal Resource Identifier (URI). As a result the SysAdmin may need to perform open source intelligence queries against the IP alone in hopes of identifying possible related malicious activity to know how to follow up on the malcode threat.

In addition, an investigation of cache data and logs from the local host may also be required to investigate a possible infection. SysAdmins need to review policies to ensure that logs are detailed enough and not deleted too quickly to empower malcode mitigation and investigations. For example a decision to delete detected malicious code removes any samples that could have been quarantined instead and then captured for laboratory analysis.

If antivirus software on a host identifies malcode, it may only be detecting part of the incident. New private code may have been installed following the infection, a common practice by 2008. A second antivirus program and specialty programs like anti-rootkit software may be required to quickly identify other binaries on the system of question. In addition, manual inspection of drive contents or mounting the drive and identifying changes to the system may be required.

Security Solutions

A wide variety of security solutions exist to help fight malcode on multiple layers. A brief annotation of common areas of concern is outlined in this section. Configuration options of solutions like antivirus software are not covered here since that is specific to each application and policies implemented by individual organizations.

Network Layer

A large number of solutions and managed services exist for working with the network layer of an enterprise. It is very important to be able to monitor and manage all network traffic across an enterprise. Best practices lock down ports that are not used, encourage the use of nonstandard ports to avoid brute force attacks against

FTP and SSH and similar services, and more. Administrators also need network monitoring in place to identify questionable egress traffic made by hosts, such as excessive DNS requests, port scanning activities, worm behavior related to the network, and IRC traffic over TCP port 6667. For example, if a backdoor Trojan is discovered on a computer, monitoring for egress traffic can help to identify the C&C server and activity of the code. Monitoring can take place with tools like FPort (FoundStone) for mapping processes to ports on the host as well as network solutions like Snort.

TCP port 80 is the most difficult to manage in terms of malcode in 2008. Unlike IRC, which is often not used in an enterprise environment and can be easily identified on a network, TCP port 80 is the default port used to browse the Internet. Malcode now makes regular use of TCP port 80 to perform malicious C&C and related malcode actions. If deep filtering is applied over TCP port 80 it will not likely catch encrypted communications with more sophisticated malcode. Unfortunately this is a trend that is growing due to mature criminal organizations driving such attacks in 2008 and beyond.

Deep-analysis capabilities are also required to help identify and mitigate code. For example, if an incident takes place, the SysAdmin benefits greatly from having a PCAP file of how the malcode functions within a laboratory environment. That information can then be used to develop customer Snort signatures or similar solutions across the network. SysAdmins can work with intelligence agencies like iSIGHT Partners to acquire support for malcode incidents of interest and deep data required to develop Snort signatures or coordinate MSS providers.

Application Layer

Antivirus software is the top solution employed on the application layer of hosts within a network. Some question in 2008 if the death of antivirus is upon us. The reality is that antivirus software successfully detects and removes hundreds of thousands of known malicious files. While antivirus is not very effective in 2008 in detecting new samples, it does have value in protecting against historical threats. Heuristics, if properly employed, can improve detection by 7–10%. Still, the reality is that malicious code attacks are successful daily because antivirus software did not detect the threat and this trend will continue. Host-based Intrusion Detection Systems (HIDS) are what some believe to be the next big application to play a role in the war against malcode on the endpoint.

Any solid antivirus solution involves a multilayered approach that is part of a greater enterprise security plan. For example, use one antivirus engine on the gateway and another on the host. This greatly improves the chances of detecting the malcode since one single antivirus solution is limited to its unique detection capabilities. Two or more layers of antivirus protection helps to improve overall detection and mitigation rates.

When selecting antivirus, a host of needs must be identified and evaluated, specific to an organization. From a corporate strategy there are several solid and proven antivirus solutions available, but contracts may vary greatly on customer support, costs, and other important contract items. These business decisions often drive decisions between two or more solid antivirus solutions.

Third-Party Certifications

To identify what is a solid antivirus solution, research is required. First, identify those solutions that provide the type of centralized management and options required to fulfill your enterprise needs. It is then appropriate to consider demonstrations of products as well as reviewing third-party certifications of antivirus software. Several reliable third-party certification sources exist online:

- AV-Test.org: http://www.av-test.org/
- Virus Bulletin VB100 Awards: http://www.virusbtn.com/vb100/index
- Virus Research Unit: http://www.uta.fi/laitokset/virus/
- West Coast Labs: http://www.westcoastlabs.org/

Look for consistency in certifications. Those that regularly obtain certification are generally considered more robust for functionality than those that do not. One of the challenges is how samples are acquired and then used in tests performed by such agencies. One of the key components of this historically is what is known as the Wildlist.

The Wildlist

Malcode that actually infects a computer is considered "in the wild" in loose terms. This is different from POC code that may only exist within a laboratory environment, or some new code created by an author but not launched against a victim. The technical definition for malcode in the wild is derived from an age-old group known as the Wildlist. The Wildlist maintains a Web site at http://www.wildlist.org/. When two or more Wildlist reporters, experts in the industry, submit the same code it is considered "in the Wild." A monthly Wild list is published, and samples are shared among WildCore participants of which this author is a member.

The Wildlist has been plagued with significant challenges by 2008, with many complicated attacks that operate under the radar with high degrees of randomness or polymorphism-like characteristics. As a result some submitted codes may be part of the same family but not the same variant, and, therefore, may not make the Wildlist as a result even if they were part of the same wave of attack. Experts are now working on ways to improve the Wildlist or create new programs to help authenticate real-world threats that can then be used in qualifying antivirus software effectiveness and what codes are actually in the wild.

Questionable Behavior on the Computer

Questionable behavior may indicate many things, including possible malicious behavior. In the early days one could look for excessive drive activity, but that is difficult to notice on modern-day computers that are so fast. The same is true for a slower Internet connection, with users rarely noticing any extra activity over a broadband connection. Still, questionable activity can lead to some research on the Internet to help a SysAdmin identify possible malicious code. The SysAdmin can then go back to a computer in question and attempt to identify and capture malicious code, analyzing it to then qualify the nature and impact of the code.

Pop-Ups

Pop-ups are one of the most common issues that users will report to a Help Desk. Take for example ad/spyware warnings like the one in Figure 3.13.

The pop-up shown in Figure 3.13 may just be another goading message to get a user to install Antivirus 2009. If it appears while Web surfing but no obvious changes take place on the computer, and does not later reappear, there may be no infection. This is where research is required to follow up on such threat reports by end users. In this instance, this is what takes place before a user may download and install the rogue security product known as Antivirus 2009.

Degraded Performance

Degraded performance is rarely seen in 2008 with host computers compared to the 1990s. The change in technology has resulted in very fast machines with a large number of memory resident programs, making it difficult to identify what is legitimate and what is malicious. Degraded performance could be due to memory-handling issues that frequently occur with Microsoft Products. It could be due to working with large files, like an unmanaged Microsoft Outlook PST file/inbox or graphics heavy Microsoft Word document. Naturally, performance is never as good as one would want when it comes to high-demand environments such as

Figure 3.13 Popup for Antivirus 2009 that may indicate possible malicious activity.

AutoCAD or high-end gaming needs. Still, if a *noticeable* change in performance takes place it may be worthwhile to investigate egress traffic on a computer as well as look at performance and process information on the host. This may lead to an investigation to discover an injected rootkit and malicious process or perhaps optimization of a computer.

Modified HOSTS File and DNS Changes

Malicious codes may modify the HOSTS file to block or redirect traffic on the host. The HOSTS file is located in the Windows\System32\Drivers\ETC directory. It normally has just a few entries, like the sample below showing a printer, Exchange, and a Shared drive for VPN access:

```
127.0.0.1                localhost
HP001635578986           HP001635578986
10.1.100.5               exchange.local
192.168.155.5            SharedDrive
```

However, if it has additional entries that point to questionable content or loopback it may indicate a malicious code infection. Data below are from an actual HOSTS-related file from a malcode in 2008:

```
0.0.0.0      avp.ch
0.0.0.0      avp.com
0.0.0.0      avp.ru
0.0.0.0      avast.com
```

The above changes block access to known antivirus domains such as AVP.ch and others. They are redirected to 0.0.0.0, which goes nowhere.

Also be on guard for changes to the DNS server used by the client. Some malicious codes now change the DNS server to point to a remote rogue server that then plays MITM to monitor or manipulate traffic from the infected host.

Inspection of Processes

Inspection of processes on a computer can be very time consuming and difficult. First, a SysAdmin needs to have a baseline of what should be expected on the computer per the enterprise build for that type of host. Then, the SysAdmin can look for nonexistent processes such as Explorer.exe in the Windows Task Manager. If such a program (Windows itself) is not visible, it is being hidden by a Windows rootkit (should always be visible).

The more traditional approach to looking for malcode in processes is to look for new processes taking up lots of memory or finding a new or unexpected process in the list. Programs like ProcessExplorer help the analyst to dive deep into the code, terminate it, and perform actions not possible within Windows Task Manager.

Other programs such as EnCase Enterprise include a response component that enables a SysAdmin to log in remotely to any host within the network. EnCase then includes MD5 solutions to quickly identify known good (whitelisted) processes, known malicious processes, and those that are in question (unknown). EnCase also includes its own anti-rootkit process that helps subvert such threats. This provides a SysAdmin an excellent remote view into what needs to be looked at on a system, possibly captured, and then analyzed for malicious behavior.

Inspection of the Windows Registry

SysAdmins can create Perl scripts to audit a network for possible malicious changes to the Windows registry on hosts of a network. This is a very efficient way for a SysAdmin to quickly identify any questionable or known malicious entries that may exist in the traditional AutoRun areas of the Windows registry such as HKLM\ SOFTWARE\Microsoft\Windows\CurrentVersion\Run and RunServices.

When dealing with known questionable or malicious executables, a manual search of the Windows registry can be very useful. Simply type "regedit" into the Start\Run location on a Windows computer to pull up the Windows registry editor program. Then use the Edit menu to perform a Find for the executable name of interest. Press F3 to move to the next instance, quickly searching the entire Windows registry.

Tools such as Autoruns (Figure 3.14), cports, and "HiJack This!" are excellent freeware programs that may also be useful in quickly identify autostart entries.

Since the functionality of Windows registry keys are often not known or well documented, one must perform queries on the Internet or within various Windows registry guides to identify what the role of a specific entry may be. For example, if one enters a suspect key into an Internet search engine and gets back many replies related to malicious code, a quick review may highly suggest a malicious entry for the host computer being investigated. Once this can be correlated back to a specific code, the SysAdmin can then look for files of interest, capture, and qualify the threat in a laboratory environment.

Inspection of Common File Locations

A manual inspection of files is also helpful, but can be subverted by Windows rootkits that may conceal files. Malicious code changes are typically performed in the Windows and Windows System32 directories. Files are also frequently stored in temporary Internet locations, the user directory, and the root directory of the drive (C:\). It is also common to find files stored within a Windows\System32 subdirectory, such as drivers or a custom directory created by the malcode.

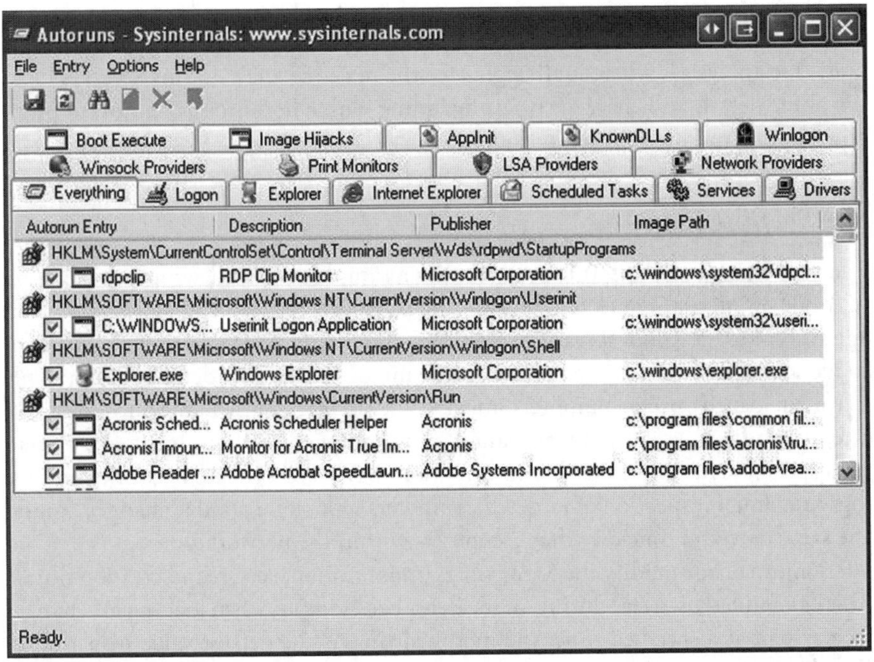

Figure 3.14 Autoruns is a freeware program that helps a SysAdmin to quickly audit autostart entries.

When a Windows rootkit is present on the system, it has the ability to conceal files from the end user. IceSword, a free anti-rootkit program authored by a Chinese programmer, is the best freeware program currently available to inspect a system and locate hostile rootkit files on the system. It also includes an analytical interface with color coding and "creation time" lists that are essential for the first responder.

Behavioral Analysis of Malcode

A test system must be in place to properly analyze malcode behaviorally. This system should contain a known set of applications, processes, and tools that establish a behavioral baseline. Changes to the system can then be identified manually as well as through various tools useful in behavioral analysis of malcode. It is important to remind SysAdmins that they must perform their work carefully so as to not bridge networking and spread a threat in the wild. In addition, any laboratory computer should be separated from the normal network to avoid any possible contamination or unwanted impact, such as a network worm attempting to exploit or spread to other computers on the network.

Static File Analysis

Static file analysis is where it all begins for the malcode analyst. This involves looking at file details and characteristics, including with a hexadecimal editor, to properly identify and investigate the code.

File Properties

File properties can be useful in correlating a sample to related samples or data on malcode of interest. For example, a specific threat may have a static file size or average size related to codes spread by the threat. The analyst can correlate the file sizes to identify if it may be related or not. More importantly, exact details about the file may help identify other computers infected with a different filename but similar file size, or modified or created time values. For example, if a worm infected a system on a specific date and time, that information may help correlate network and host logs or manual inspection of targeted computers to look for similar changes around the same date and time on other computers within the network.

Some malcode modify the MAC times (modification, access, and creation times). This can hinder discovery during an incident. For example, when looking for changes to a system at a specified time, the modified time is the default value displayed in Windows. If the modified time is modified by the malcode to be something fairly old, it will not show up at the top of the modified time listing when sorted. This is an easy and highly effective way for malcode to subvert code identification by time stamps alone. For this reason, all MAC times should be looked at carefully when attempting to find code that may have infected a system at a specific point in time.

Behavioral tests can also be performed on code, and then a directory dump and difference analysis can be performed to identify what is different pre and post installation of the code, to identify what is new on the system. Realize, though, that if a Windows rootkit is involved, the postinfection directory dump must be done from a disk mount or boot disk rather than from within the infected operating system itself.

Hash

Hash values, such as MD5 and SHA1, are a cryptographic hash function used to calculate a unique value of a file. Even a minor change in 1 byte of a file results in a new hash value. MD5 is one of the most popular hashes to use in 2008. Many freeware tools are available to calculate the hash value, such as HashCalc for Windows. In addition, malcode experts are moving toward naming binaries by MD5 values for large malcode archives. If two binaries have the same hash value, they are exactly the same! There are ways to subvert hash systems, but this is not common nor should it be considered a major problem for a malcode analyst attempting to identify and correlate malcode binaries of interest.

Portable Executables Header

Portable Executables (PE files) for Windows 32-bit systems have a header that tells the analyst much about the file. Tools such as LordPE and PEiD (Figure 3.15) help the analyst to identify what type of file and packer is being analyzed. Such tools may also include the EntryPoint, File Offset, EP Section, TimeDateStamp data, and other information useful in initiating reverse engineering of a binary.

String Analysis

A string analysis can be performed on both packed and unpacked files. Strings provide clues to the functionality and various system calls made by code. Comments within the original source code may also be visible in part helping to explain actor attribution or other functionality. Performing a string analysis on packed and unpacked, including memory captures, may provide many clues as shown in Figure 3.16.

In this figure, notice the first line talking about a program and DOS mode. This helps to further validate that the binary is indeed an executable. Then, notice a reference to a DLL, mscoree.dll, and other strings of interest. This string dump does not reveal much because the binary is still packed with UPX. However, if it is unpacked, notice how the strings change (Figure 3.17).

Strings are very useful to the reverse engineer who understands how to correlate seemingly cryptic data to what one sees while disassembling malcode. The average analyst and SysAdmin can look for common signs of infection, common system calls of interest, URLs, and other data used for initial triage. If detailed string files are captured by the SysAdmin, they can then be later shared with a reverse engineer to facilitate a deep analysis of the malcode.

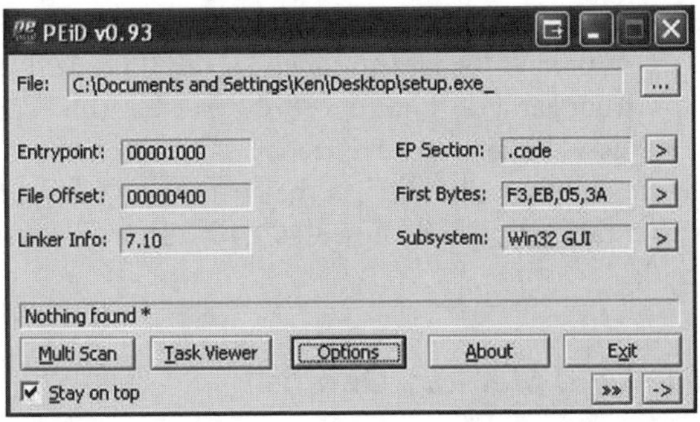

Figure 3.15   PEiD identifies data related to an Antivirus XP 2008 rogue security application.

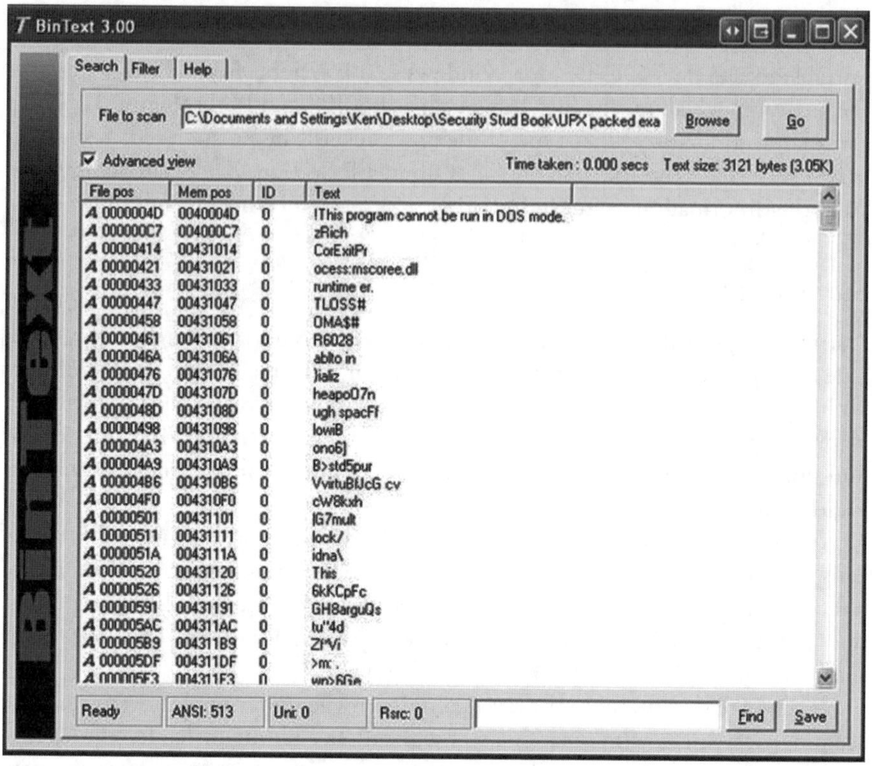

Figure 3.16   BinText reveals strings of a packed binary.

Hex Editors

There are both freeware and commercial hex editors available to look at the binary contents of a file. This may look confusing at first glance until you know what to look for. The first few characters identify the true file type, irrespective of the extension assigned to the Windows filename (remember the JPG file that was actually a WMF file example from earlier?). Figure 3.18 shows what you expect to see when working with a Windows binary: an MZ header.

Notice in Figure 3.18 that the file has the string "UPX," indicating that it is likely packed with a famous packer known as UPX. This is useful in identifying how to unpack a file.

Unpacking Files and Memory Dumps

Unpacking files can be a difficult process involving some patching of files captured. It may also result in the accidental execution of a binary, so it should always be done within a safe test environment to avoid accidental execution of code. Unpacking

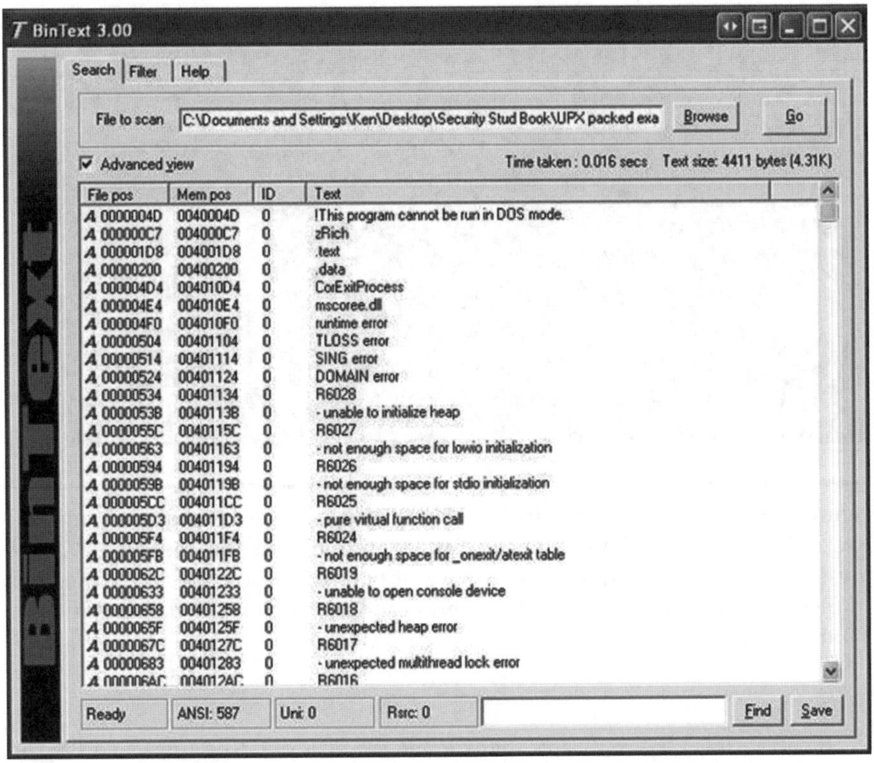

Figure 3.17 BinText reveals many more strings of interest in unpacked binary.

files first involves trying to identify what the code was packed with, such as UPX
with our former example. In the case of UPX, one must simply locate an updated
version of it online and run the command "upx -d filename," where "-d" is for
decompress and filename is the name of the file, 1D.tmp in Figure 3.19.

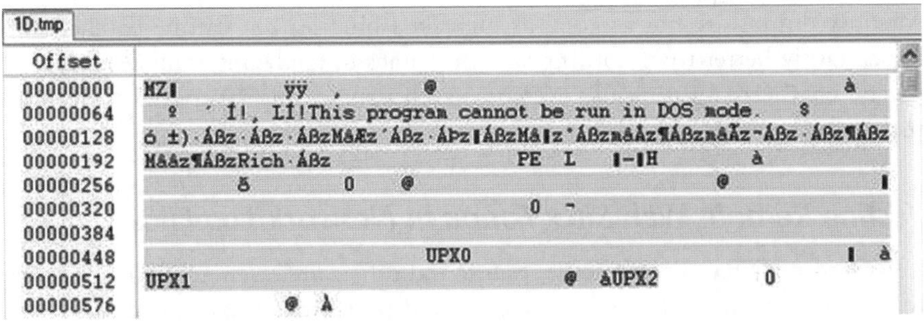

**Figure 3.18 MZ header reveals this is an executable, not a TMP file. We also see
it is packed with UPX.**

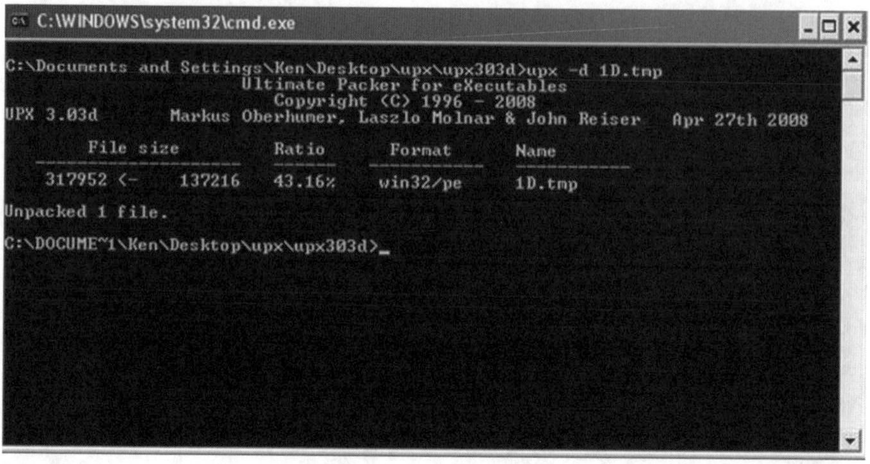

Figure 3.19 Unpacking files first involves trying to identify what the code was packed with, such as UPX with our former example. In the case of UPX, one must simply locate an updated version of it online and run the command "upx -d filename," where "-d" is for decompress and filename is the name of the file, 1D.tmp.

If successful, UPX indicates that the file is unpacked. The unpacked file can then be used for additional string analysis and disassembly.

Warning: Locating a packer and unpacker online may result in an analyst traveling to high-risk areas of the Internet, such as crack sites and hacker zines. It is important to always run such tools in a test environment, since they may harbor malcode themselves and cannot be trusted. Some packers are very difficult to work with, requiring more creative efforts in unpacking or capturing code from memory.

Memory dumps can be performed with tools like LordPE and OllyDbg. Memory dumps are not as good as unpacked binaries but can be patched and are certainly better than nothing when it comes to analyzing samples. A strong reverse engineer can typically overcome such issues using a variety of advanced techniques.

Testing Remote Web Sites Found in Network Log Files

Log files from firewalls, IDS, IPS, Snort, and others are often configured to only report the basic facts, like the IP address and packet details. Unfortunately, this often leaves out important information like the exact path or domain visited by a victim during an attack. Performing an open source intelligence query is helpful in identifying possible malicious behavior related to the address. Behavioral analysis of the sample may also reveal domains or IPs and related data of interest to a malcode attack. Extensive time-consuming research may be required to best understand an attack and related attack data.

When looking at remote hostile servers, always check into each public directory. For example, http://badsite.com/images/badfile.exe may allow a directory list of the image's subdirectory. It is not uncommon in such situations to then locate additional binaries or log files or scripts of interest in an investigation.

Passive DNS Queries

Passive DNS queries exist within private and public databases. The best open source passive DNS replication database available at the time of this writing is http://www.bfk.de/bfk_dnslogger.html. This Web site makes it easy for a query to be entered and to then see what information has passively been stored related to that IP or domain. This information must be interpreted carefully.

Passive DNS records are similar to who has rented an apartment previously. If it is a drug house, then the tenants may be related. However, they may not be related even if both have had issues related to drugs (do not draw conclusions easily!). The same is true for passive DNS servers, where former domains and IP addresses associated with a domain may provide clues and connections to further substantiate an investigation, but with great discretion and a robust investigation.

WHOIS, Reverse IP, Name Servers

There is a wealth of information available on domains, their IPs, reverse IPs, name servers, historical IP addresses, WHOIS registrant name or company affiliations, open source correlation, and more. This can be one of the most time-consuming and difficult components of an investigation to properly understand and follow. This is especially true when working large-scale criminal operations where thousands of domain and fake aliases may exist. Several sites of interest are helpful in collecting such data:

■ Robtex: Large volumes of information and also what servers are shared with other domains or IPs. Great for looking up related data within various IP ranges or shared resources.
■ DomainCrawler: Lots of interesting information on domains unique to this server.
■ SpamHaus: Excellent for identifying if a server is related to known abuse in the past.
■ DNSstuff: A suite of tools with powerful research options.
■ DomainTools: A commercial site that offers excellent data including name server spy reports, domain history, domain monitoring, historical IP information, and more. Essential for the intelligence analyst.

Warning: Abuse notifications should also be done through an alias instead of from a SysAdmin directly because some abuse notifications are sent directly to the offender.

Scans of a server in question, such as with nMap, can be debated as legal or ethical. Scans are generally considered legitimate within the international security community and may be useful in identifying a remote server or the ports it has open related to potential malicious behavior. Accessing various services, such as opening an FTP connection, may also help to capture banner data of interest in an investigation.

Deobfuscation of Scripts

Obfuscated JavaScript and similar content may prove to be difficult to decipher. Fortunately, a few tools exist to help make this easier. Simply running VMware and then a sniffer on the host machine helps to identify all important network communications performed during an attack against a site or when code is run. Irrespective of any obfuscation that takes place, the links to executables and communications with remote C&Cs cannot be hidden from the sniffer on the host.

Using FireFox "Live HTTP Headers" add-on (an extension) is also helpful in sniffing and sorting through traffic related to specific sessions of interest. It is a free and powerful tool that allows the analyst to save HTTP headers from a session, replay, and quickly triage data from a session (see Figure 3.20).

Manual deobfuscation of JavaScript can be time consuming, but fast with a few simple templates and tricks. Use the example below, in a safe test environment, to copy and paste obfuscated strings from escape strings into the template (using Notepad), then open it up within Internet Explorer and see what the text area script reveals.

```
<html>
<script language=javascript>
document.write("<textarea rows=100 cols=100>");
//paste document.write or unescape string below:

document.write("</textarea>");
</script>
</html>
```

Realize that it is now common for *multiple* layers of obfuscation to exist possibly requiring a repeat of such operations or converting from various data representations several times to get to the real script. Additionally, more advanced scripts with internal self-checks now exist to hinder such efforts, forcing true debugging techniques to be utilized instead of the text area trick and similar techniques illustrated briefly above. There are several such methods and advanced tools

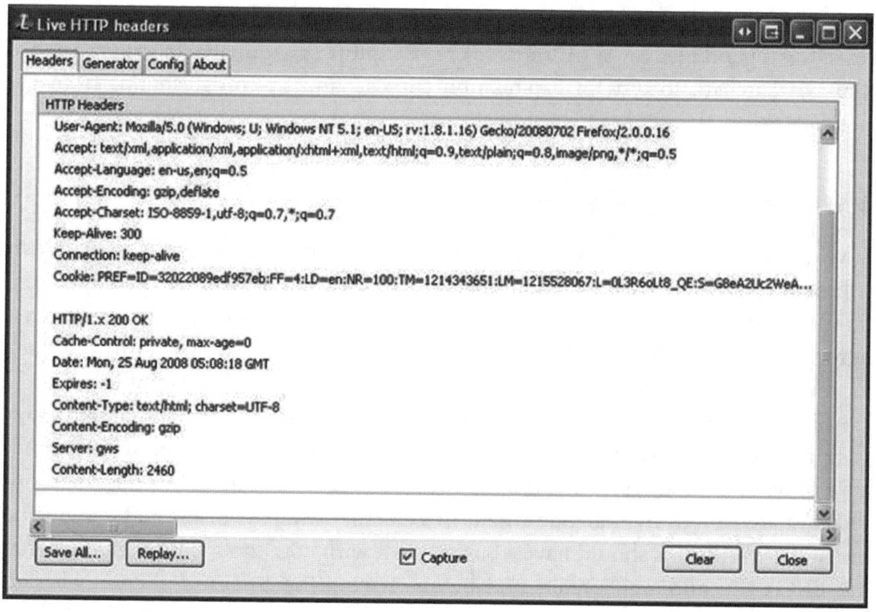

Figure 3.20 Live HTTP Headers is a free tool for analyzing traffic within FireFox.

for working with such scripts, available on sites like the SANS Internet Storm Center.

Interpreting Data

When working with a remote hostile site, do not make assumptions about the behavior or capabilities. Many malcode and exploit sites now check for the IP and render different behaviors if the IP visits a site a second time. Even 404 errors are sometimes bogus as a way to drive security experts away, while C&C activities take place for communications from a bot with a special HTTP header used to identify bot traffic. It is increasingly common for internal self-checks, browser IDs, IP checking, and other antisecurity expert scripts to be running on remote hostile servers.

Anti-VMware is another example of being on guard for interpretation of data. If code is anti-VMware, it may detect the virtual environment and then exit. Thus, if nothing happens or unexpected behavior takes place within a virtual environment, the test may need to be performed again on a native "goat" computer used to test out malcode on a real computer.

Native goat machines must be able to be restored quickly through imaging solutions like Acronis software or Ghost. They ideally mirror the images used in the corporate environment and are put on a separate network for SysAdmin laboratory tests. It is a good idea for SysAdmins to create multiple goat images based on patched and not patched, to test for exploitation success, and up-to-date builds from the network.

VMware Testing of Samples

VMware is one of the most popular tools used to analyze code in a virtual environment today. Other solutions also exist, like Qemu and Truman for Linux and Parallels for Macintosh. These tools typically require that you own our own license agreements for operating systems installed within a virtual environment. Each essentially uses a special drive to write data to a software file instead of to a disk.

Simple behavioral analysis, where one runs the code in a virtual environment, is fairly straightforward but does involve measured and experienced interpretation of data. For example, it is easy to misinterpret data and believe that snapshot changes are caused by malcode when, in fact, they are part of normal computing changes. SysAdmins should have a base system with core tools and techniques that are PROVEN and well understood before attempting to run any code with an unknown behavior.

A good way to get started is to simply run various tools on a clean VMware system and interpret the changes when Internet Explorer is opened, or files are opened or deleted, etc. Follow this up with testing of malcode captured in quarantine from antivirus that is from a well-documented family that is easy to understand. Run the code and look for documented features to help learn tools and techniques for analyzing malcode. When an unknown sample comes across your desktop, follow the same procedures and also use a third-party sandbox solution to compare results against.

Warning: Always be very careful in the network setting of a virtual environment to avoid accidental worm spreading through shares or a bridged network connection.

Core tools vary greatly within the industry, but should include basic snapshot and real-time monitoring tools for processes, files, and network activity. This also includes anti-rootkit programs. A list of helpful tools is given below to help get your core laboratory of tools established:

- InstallWatchPro and InCTRL for snapshot views of a system that can survive a restart
- Autoruns, HiJack This!, and cports for quick views of open ports and auto-run entries
- Anti-rootkit programs—as many as possible since no single scanner can detect all rootkits; IceSword and GMER are two essentials
- File analysis tools like HashCalc, PEiD, LordPE, a WinHex, and others

- Monitoring tools from Microsoft (formerly SysInternals): Filemon, Regmon, TdiMon, Tcpview, and ProcessExplorer
- Wireshark, Fport, nMap, NetCat for working with networking and remote servers
- Proxy tools or services so that a behavioral machine can have different IP for multiple tests against a site that checks for the IP. Freecap is a great tool to help make some programs proxy aware if they are not. Tor is also a good freeware solution to meet some needs.
- Firefox, Adobe Reader, and similar programs that may be useful in tests or exploit research
- OllyDbg or other debugger or disassembly type for reverse engineering.

It is also advisable to create a test image that has certain configurations useful for malcode research, such as changing view settings to show the full extension, show system files, and do not hide known file types or system files. It is also helpful to create shortcut links to common malcode locations such as C:\, Windows, Windows System32, Drivers, Drivers\ETC, and similar directories.

Advanced File Capture Techniques

Sometimes files are difficult to identify or capture from a computer. For example, some files may not allow copying or moving from a virtual machine or may not be visible. Advanced techniques are then required to capture such files.

DiskMount. DiskMount is a free utility provided by VMware that enables a SysAdmin to mount a virtual machine that is not currently loaded within VMware. Simply infect a virtual machine and then shut it off (no shut down required). Then use DiskMount to mount the drive on the HOST machine. It can then be accessed with the full control of the HOST machine.

Warning: Once a drive is mounted on the HOST, malicious files on the infected guest could be accidentally executed! Handle with extreme caution. Defang any captured files by renaming their extension to something like badfile.exe_.

A quick way to find files that have been changed on a drive is to use the Windows search function. After mounting the drive, right click on the mounted drive and Search... Look for files via a modified date, or created date, for the current day. All the files are loaded and easily captured. However, MAC times can be modified and, therefore, such files potentially missed requiring a manual inspection for any lingering files not yet identified through such methods.

Suspend Memory Captures. VMware supports what is known as a suspense mode. When VMware is put into suspense mode, all data from what is running in memory are then stored in a special temporary file created within the directory of the virtual machine on the HOST computer. SysAdmins can locate the special VMEM file type and then analyze it within a hex editor or similar tool to locate files within memory of interest. This is a time-consuming and complicated process that can yield excellent rootkit analysis when necessary.

Linux DD Captures. Linux builds like Knoppix easily boot from a CD or thumb drive. Booting up a system from Linux enables a user to use a tool called "DD" to capture the MBR or other data from a drive. This can be useful if a machine is suspected of being under the control of a Windows rootkit.

Anti-VMware Code Techniques. Anti-VMware code exists to detect the presence of a virtual machine. In most cases such code simply exists and does nothing to hinder the analysis of the code. A native goat machine can be used to analyze such code. SysAdmins may also modify default VMware settings to remove common detection vectors used by malcode in the wild. By disabling hardware acceleration and similar components on a virtual machine, and then testing code a second time, many malcode fail to detect the virtual environment and then run as expected.

Free Online Sandbox Solutions

There are several free online sandbox solutions available to the public today. When using these scanners, realize that they capture and share or sell the code submitted. Do not use such solutions for sensitive codes. Current online reputable sandbox solutions include the following:

- Norman: http://www.norman.com/microsites/nsic/
- Sunbelt Malware Research Labs: http://research.sunbelt-software.com/Submit.aspx
- ThreatExpert: http://www.threatexpert.com/submit.aspx
- Anubis: http://anubis.iseclab.org/

Reports from such sandboxes are invaluable in comparing against laboratory results to confirm or help explain malicious behavior related to a specific binary.

Interactive Behavioral Testing

Interactive behavioral testing is a very time-consuming process and is part of a more advanced reverse engineering process in most cases. Take for example a malcode that attempts to connect to a remote IRC server. A SysAdmin can create a Linux virtual environment with Snort and an IRC server on the box. The SysAdmin can then modify the HOSTS file of the Windows virtual machine to point to the IRC server for the domain requested by the malcode. When the malcode is run, it will be redirected to the internal Linux server and will attempt to log into the IRC server. If properly configured the SysAdmin can then interact with the malcode in the IRC server, trying out different commands and watching what it does when various conditions or commands change. The possibilities are almost endless on various virtual networks and solutions that can be implemented to test specific components of code within a laboratory environment.

Malcode Mitigation

Malcode mitigation can be a daunting topic of great scope. This overview provides both strategic and tactical direction.

Strategic

A defense-in-depth architecture (Figure 3.21) and CEO down support for security is essential for every enterprise. Individuals in charge of security need to identify ways to best communicate regularly the value of security decisions made by and supported by executive staff. It can be difficult to translate the world of geek to the world of business, but it is critical to successfully communicate and position security decisions into the infrastructure of any company.

Best-practice guidelines exist for policies on various platforms. These guides are becoming increasingly authoritative and helpful in securing enterprise networks against common malcode attacks. Work toward prevention and lowering

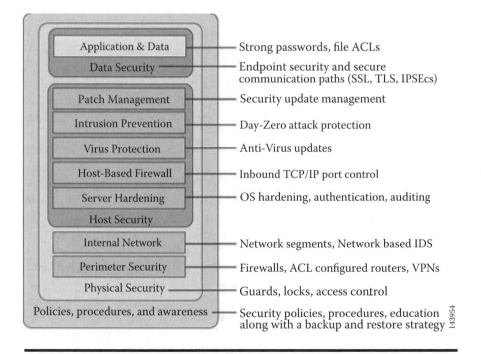

Figure 3.21 Defense-in-depth architecture involves many layers of protection.

risk (not completely removing it) is a process that should be highly valued in the work place.

An emergency response team and procedures, with the necessary power to act, should be in place before an incident takes place. Ideally an internal CERT should exist as part of a greater disaster recovery plan.

Again, these general guidelines are very brief and should only be considered a few highlights of essential components for successful strategic management in fighting malcode.

Tactical

Obviously, hardening systems against attack, including operating system, application, and antivirus updates, and properly backing up and protecting data is core to the tactical front against malcode. The rest of this section will focus on common mistakes made by SysAdmins in the field. Never remotely log in to a possibly infected computer with admin rights. If you are dealing with a worm, it will likely spread through your admin account into the rest of the network.

If a malcode incident is discussed in the media, you will need to know about it. Executives want to get the scoop and make sure that they are covered. Be proactive in how you monitor and report such issues to your management. Do all that you can to help executives know that they will not be the next name in the press due to your security management and their wise business decisions to support security.

Never make the mistake of simply reimaging a box and moving one from a malcode incident to never understand the original vector of attack or payloads related to the attack. This simply removes evidence and data of great value to the individual who seeks to deal with the original source of the problem rather than just the symptom (the payload or malcode attack itself). Take the time to dive deep into the code as appropriate to qualify the threat and properly mitigate risk.

Do not rely on antivirus to solve all your problems. Just because an update signature now detects code that has infected a host on your network does not mean that your problems are over. Do not forget that other codes that remain undetected may exist on the computers. Use anti-rootkit tools, and take nothing for granted when the integrity of a system has been compromised.

After a malcode incident, put special alerts in place to watch for egress traffic related to known attack data points such as remote C&C IPs or domains. Again, take nothing for granted as you seek to fully mitigate malcode from a network.

When working with file-infecting viruses that also have worm components, recognize the great challenge that lies ahead. These types of infections within a network environment can be almost impossible to remove unless the SysAdmin is highly organized and very diligent in looking at the MD5 values of all targeted files on a drive, such as all EXE and SCR file types. Without such diligence, legitimate files that are infected with malcode may go undiscovered, reinfecting cleaned boxes.

Forget about manual disinfection after a malcode break unless it is a short-term fix on a computer that cannot be taken offline for some serious business reason. If you must perform manual disinfection, carefully monitor the computer over the network and consider using extra utilities on the host itself to identify any remnant activity or related payloads.

Realize that safe mode can be undermined by some malcode. If you boot up in safe mode, you may still have a malcode running in memory hindering disinfection efforts! Also realize that some malcode now remove all former restore points on a Windows backup solution and then install a new restore point that includes the malcode! Using a clean image from a protected location is important in maintaining the integrity of a system. This works best when user files are not stored on hosts but on a network server, making machine wipes much easier. Additionally, realize that MBR kernel level threats exist (Mebroot with Torpig) and may require that the MBR of a disk be cleaned before attempting to install a clean image on a computer.

Just because you do not allow WAPs within the enterprise does not mean they do not exist on the network. Audit everything to know what is going on inside and in and out of a network!

Design networks to maximize intelligence load balancing, bandwidth, and upstream host provider anti-DDoS capabilities or throttling and tarpitting techniques to help manage DDoS attacks against one or more network resources.

Configure routers within internal networks to explicitly limit ingress traffic to allow IP addresses. Also configure filtering to take place between Network Address Translation devices and the ISP to explicitly allow only authorized sources. Deny private, server, and unroutable traffic and direct broadcast packets as appropriate within the network topology.

Configure routers to block spoofed traffic from within a network.

Consider using a Honeypot to trap bot traffic, analyze it, and ensure countermeasures and auditing is in place over the network to prevent similar attacks on legitimate network resources.

Finally, a complete package of training and technology is required to best mitigate malware. Humans are often the last link and the weakest link, but they can help significantly in mitigating malcode. Technology also has much to offer but is not a silver bullet. By working both angles together, risk is significantly lowered.

There are a wide variety of products available to help detect and manage add-on devices, such as thumb drives and similar USB devices. To manage USB storage devices with policy, follow the instructions offered by Microsoft Corp. at http://support.microsoft.com/default.aspx?scid=kb;en-us;823732. Other policy solutions also exist, such as disabling autoplay for all devices to avoid INF spreading malcode via USB-infected devices.

To find various software solutions, look for products related to Data Loss Protection or endpoint security. Cisco Security Agent and Preventia Desktop Endpoint Security both attempt to prevent the loss of sensitive data through various endpoint solutions that include intrusion detection, firewall, and application management. Products like Safend Protector and Reflex Disknet Pro are global solutions that offer robust management of removable I/O devices, such as USB, printers, and PDAs.

Both solutions are also able to force encryption of data of removal devices when such devices are allowed to be used, further enhancing security measures for increasingly mobile solutions. Many other products also exist in this space, including solutions by Lumension Sanctuary Device Control, Utimaco Safeguard Enterprise, and Symantec Endpoint Protection.

When looking at various software solutions, be sure to look for price, support, functionality, and flexibility. This is a fairly new space with some products providing more functionality than others. Some products are reported as having poor installation features and bugs in their software. Others offer granular control over policies, while others only allow for global policies with little fine tuning possible. Performing due diligence when considering such a solution greatly helps in qualifying the best solution at the time of purchase.

Of course, software solutions mentioned above can be subverted with the right tools and techniques. As a result, some have turned toward hardware solutions. For example, some security professionals have use epoxy or soldering kits to permanently block access to USB drives on devices.

Sample Questions

Select the best answer for each question below. Some questions may include possible answers that are correct but not the "best."

1. A blended threat infects legitimate documents within the My Documents directory and sends them to users in the address book of the victim to spread in the wild. This is primarily an example of a security breach of which CIA element?
   a. Confidentiality
   b. Integrity
   c. Availability
   d. None of the above
2. What is the name of the international malcode naming standard used by all antivirus vendors today?
   a. Common Malware Enumeration (CME)
   b. Computer AntiVirus Research Organization (CARO)
   c. VGrep
   d. None of the above

3. "VBS" is used in the beginning of most antivirus vendors to represent what component of the CARO general structure?
   a. Modifier
   b. Suffix
   c. Platform
   d. Family
4. W32.Rispif.AB is what variant of this malcode?
   a. Rispif
   b. A
   c. B
   d. AB
5. W32.Sober.O@mm spreads through what primary vector, according to Symantec naming conventions?
   a. Mass Mailer
   b. Windows 3.X
   c. Windows 95/98/ME
   d. Windows 32-bit
6. A SysAdmin discovers an antivirus message indicating detection and removal of Backdoor.win32.Agent.ich. What should the SysAdmin do to monitor to the threat?
   a. Use Rootkit detection software on the host
   b. Update antivirus signature files
   c. Run a full host scan
   d. Monitor egress traffic from the computer
7. Antivirus software detects malcode on a computer. Why would a SysAdmin want to perform additional antivirus scans on the infected host using different antivirus software?
   a. To locate additional threats that may exist, not detected by the host antivirus
   b. To identify a second antivirus vendor name for the code
   c. To identify and remove any threats found on the system
   d. None of the above
8. Which of the following assists an analyst in cross-correlating malcode samples by name?
   a. VGrep
   b. Public Multiscanners
   c. CME
   d. All of the above
9. Malcode that infects existing files on a computer to spread are called what?
   a. Trojans
   b. Viruses
   c. Worms
   d. Rootkit

10. A Trojan that executes a destructive payload when certain conditions are met is called what?
    a. Keylogger
    b. Data Diddler
    c. Logic Bomb
    d. None of the above

11. Where does a cavity virus infect a file with malcode?
    a. Prepends Code
    b. Appends Code
    c. Injects Code
    d. None of the above

12. What is the family name of the first Macro virus discovered in the wild in 1995?
    a. Concept
    b. AntiCMOS
    c. Melissa
    d. Bablas

13. Mebroot is unique because it modifies what component of a computer to load upon system startup?
    a. Windows registry keys
    b. Startup folder
    c. MBR
    d. Kernel

14. SYS and VXD hostile codes are commonly associated with what type of threat?
    a. Trojans
    b. Worms
    c. Userland Rootkits
    d. Kernel Rootkits

15. A PUP refers to software that may include what?
    a. EULA
    b. Monitoring
    c. Capture Sensitive Data
    d. All of the above

16. What is the name of the first highly destructive malcode designed to activate a payload on Friday the 13th?
    a. Jerusalem
    b. Lehigh
    c. Internet Worm
    d. Cascade

17. Onel de Guzman is known to be one of the authors for ILoveYou who could not be prosecuted for his crimes because he lived in a country without laws prohibiting his behavior. What is the name of his country of residency?
    a. Indonesia
    b. Philippines

    c. United Kingdom

    d. Germany

18. Social engineering refers to what?

    a. Social networking sites like MySpace and Facebook

    b. Individuals who study the behavior and actions of specific people groups

    c. Training techniques useful in a corporate environment

    d. Techniques and communication strategies for deceiving people

19. What is an example of rogue security software?

    a. Antivirus Pro

    b. AntiVir

    c. VirusTotal

    d. GREM

20. What is one of the most common types of DDoS attacks to take place on the Internet today?

    a. Teardrop

    b. Naptha

    c. TCP SYN

    d. Smurf

21. To evade detection by SysAdmins, malcode typically uses what TCP port in 2008 for remote C&C communications?

    a. 80

    b. 443

    c. 6667

    d. 65000

22. "0.0.0.0 avp.ch" is a string found within a Trojan binary indicating that it likely performs what changes to a system upon infection?

    a. Communicates with a remote C&C at avp.ch

    b. Contains a logic bomb that activates immediately

    c. Modifies the HOSTS file to prevent access to avp.ch

    d. Downloads code from avp.ch

23. Which of the following programs is useful in identifying common modifications made to the Windows registry by malcode?

    a. Autoruns

    b. FPort

    c. Filemon

    d. PeID

24. What does it mean when a SysAdmin does not see explorer.exe in the Windows Task Manager on a host machine?

    a. It is normal for explorer.exe to not appear in Windows Task Manager

    b. Explorer.exe is likely injected and hidden by a Windows rootkit

    c. Explorer.exe does not need to be visible if svchost.exe is visible

    d. Internet Explorer is open and running in memory

25. If a SysAdmin attempts to analyze code within VMware and nothing executes, what might be the next steps to further analyze the code?
    a. Modify advanced settings of VMware to disable hardware acceleration and similar components and execute the code again
    b. Run the malcode in a native test environment to see if it is anti-VMware
    c. Submit the code to an online sandbox scanner to compare behavioral results
    d. All of the above

Chapter 4

Monitoring and Analysis

Mike Mackrill

Contents

Monitoring and analysis play key roles in the security life cycle. Monitoring is an activity that collects information and provides a method of indentifying security events, taking the appropriate action to maintain the security of the system, and report the pertinent information to the appropriate individual, group, or process. The analysis function provides a security manager with the ability to determine if the system is being operated in accordance with accepted industry practices and with any specific organizational policies and procedures.

Understanding the audit components prepares the candidate to work with either internal or external auditors during a formal audit review. The Systems Security Certified Practitioner (SSCP) candidate is expected to demonstrate knowledge in the various methods of data collection, including data logging, sampling, and reporting in addition to analysis and audit review and compliance check techniques. It is also essential to understand the legal requirements for monitoring and audit activity. Key areas of knowledge include:

- Understand principles, practices, and mechanisms
- Perform audits
- Maintain effective monitoring systems
- Conduct analysis of exploits

Policy, Controls, and Enforcement

Security Framework

Where do you start? To properly ensure that your network and infrastructure are secure, you need to have a plan. There are certain things that you know you will need to do, such as enforce user passwords, detect intrusion, or set up firewalls on critical segments, but how can you be sure that you have not overlooked anything? Once you have everything in place, how can you communicate your security plan to your end users, upper management, and auditors? The security framework is the answer.

A security framework is composed of the following:

Organizational policies. These policies are a formal statement by upper management that describes the company's dedication to security, the reporting structure of the security organization, how the security framework will work within the organization, how the policies will be enforced, how they will be checked for compliance, and the ramifications for noncompliance.

Functional policies. These policies describe how organizational assets are to be used and protected. Functional policies can be issue-centric, focusing on such items as acceptable use, remote access, e-mail usage, etc. Functional policies can also be system-centric focusing on such items as operating system, antivirus, IDS deployment, firewall rules, etc.

Standards. Standards define compulsory requirements for the organization. They can include specifics on hardware, specific vendors for software, and operating system versions among others. For example, a standard might require that all workstations to run a vendor-supported version of the Microsoft desktop operating system.

Baselines. Baselines define the minimum requirements to achieve a desired security level for a system or business practice. Baselines are critical in an environment where different groups may place hosts onto the network. When a baseline is developed and followed, the risk to the company will be kept at a minimum. A baseline could be as simple as requiring the latest version of a server operating system with all security patches applied and the latest antivirus software installed. It could also go into great detail outlining which services will be on/off and defining access control lists for critical directories.

Procedures. Procedures are the step-by-step instructions on how to implement a policy, standard, or baseline. Procedures are the details to support a policy, standard, or baseline. With properly developed procedures, any IT staff familiar with your systems should be able to implement the policy, standard, or procedure with little or no outside assistance. Procedures also tie nicely into disaster recovery documentation.

Guidelines. Guidelines are recommendations made to improve security but are not a requirement to be in compliance with the security framework. In many instances, a guideline is used in lieu of a policy to gain acceptance throughout the user community. For example, a company can have a guideline that suggests using a mixture of alpha characters, numeric characters, and symbols in a password, yet does not require them.

A security framework needs to be reviewed periodically to ensure that it is up to date with current business practices, new technology, and new threats. Thus, what does a security framework do? A security framework allows security professionals to see the big picture of the security environment and identify potential areas that might have been missed. It gives evidence that the company is exercising "due care" in its day-to-day operating environment. It also gives auditors a reference for conducting audits.

What is a control and how does it tie into the security framework? A control is a specific activity, process, or technology that is implemented to reduce the risk of a security event from adversely affecting an organization. Administrative controls make up the steps that define a policy, procedure, or guideline. For example, a company has a policy that states "All workstations will be secured from unauthorized access at all times." The controls that would help enforce that policy could include account password complexity, inactivity logout timers, access control lists for the workstation, time/day login restrictions, mandatory security event logging, and physical security. Controls fall into seven categories.

Control Categories

Preventive controls. Preventive controls do just what the name suggests: prevent something from happening. The main issue with preventive controls is user acceptance. Because these controls can be seen as bothersome to the end user, you must ensure that the community understands the function of such a control and its rationale, and accepts its use. For example, if you set a preventive control that locks user workstations after 5 minutes of inactivity to prevent unauthorized access and your user community does not see the value in such a short lock out, they will find a way around the control such as putting a stapler on the space bar to keep the lockout from ever taking place.

Detective controls. Detective controls are used to identify unwanted activity after the fact. Log files are a good example of a detective control. They allow you to track down the details of an event (like a user account lockout) after it has happened.

Corrective controls. Corrective controls either fix an issue or return a system back to its original state before an event occurred. System restore points are an example of a corrective control.

Directive controls. A directive control is a control that is mandated by a higher authority. These usually occur through corporate directives, industry regulation, or laws. Document retention rules are often dictated by industry regulations and the controls (e.g., Records Management and Retention Policy) that dictate proper document retention would be a directive control.

Deterrent controls. Deterrent controls are any control that makes it difficult or undesirable for a user to perform an activity. Several companies publish proxy logs to an internal Web site. This allows other users to see where someone has been surfing on the Web. It can be considered a deterrent control because it would certainly make a user think twice before going to a site that was prohibited by company policy.

Recovery controls. Recovery controls are all about getting back to normal after an event. These events do not necessarily have to be security related; for example, a power failure. Backups and system restore points are two examples of recovery controls.

Compensating controls. Compensating controls reinforce or replace normal controls that are unavailable for any reason. For example: Your company requires smart cards for login; however, you have a procedure in place for using passwords in case the smart cards are unavailable. The password procedure would be a compensating control.

Summary

Policies applied together form the security framework for the company. While it is possible to create your own security framework in-house, it is advisable to use one of the nationally or internationally known standards and guidelines to form your security framework to ensure that your framework covers the most scenarios possible. Standards and guidelines for good security practice come from several organizations and are often adapted by other organizations to form their own security frameworks. They include the following:

International Organization for Standardization

- ISO 17799 (now 27001)—A high-level security guideline (often referred to as a standard) not meant for the certification of systems but for high-level security framework assistance. It was passed as a standard late in 2000 (based on British Standard 7799-1). It is a management standard that deals with an examination of the nontechnical issues relating to installed security systems within organizations.
- ISO GMITS (Guidelines for the Management of Information Technology Security)—A five-part technical report guideline currently in revision that discusses many facets of security frameworks.

Governmental Bodies

- British Standards Institute
  BS 7799 Part 1—A high-level checklist oriented security guideline
  BS 7799 Part 2:2002—A standard against which a system may be certified because it uses a lot of "the organization shall do . . . ," words. It has fewer implementation suggestions than Part 1. An organization may be accredited as complying with the BS7799-2.
- U.S. National Institute for Standards and Technology (NIST)
  NIST Special Publications 800-12, 800-14, 800-26, 800-30, 800-37, and others provide a wealth of strategic and tactical information for developing, running, and certifying security frameworks.

Audit Organizations

- Information Systems Audit and Control Association (ISACA)™
- Developers of Control Objectives for Information and Related Technology (COBIT)™—Generally applicable and accepted standards for good IT

security and control practices. Their goal is to provide a reference framework for management, users, IT auditors, and IT security practitioners.

Professional Organizations

- American National Standards Institute (ANSI)—U.S. liaison committees to ISO committees. Technical Committee T4 participates in the standardization of generic methods for information technology security.
- Information Systems Security Association (ISSA)—An international organization of information security professionals and practitioners whose purpose is education, peer interaction, and professional growth.
- Computer Emergency Response Team (CERT)—A variety of advice on secure computing practices and incident response techniques is offered.

Compliance Techniques

So, you now have the security framework and all of its controls, policies, procedures, and guidelines in place, but how do you know that your company is following the framework and implementing it correctly? What good does it do to have a security framework that nobody follows? What can you use to ensure compliance with your security framework? The following methods can be used to ensure compliance with your framework. It should be noted that there are other ways of ensuring compliance other than those listed and that you may not employ all of these methods depending on your security framework and the emphasis placed on security by upper management.

Observations

Observations are not necessarily used to confirm that the company is following the security framework as much as it is used to confirm that what is being done is consistent with the security framework. Conflicts between the written procedure and what is actually being done can be seen as a benefit as well as a security violation.

Security is an exercise in risk management and security decisions need to be based on the business needs. For example, if your security framework is based on a sensitive environment such as banking, it would probably have procedures and standards dealing with the mandated use of digital signatures. If your company's stance on security is more lax, the business may not feel that digital signatures are worth the time, training, and management overhead. By observing that digital signatures are not being used in regular transactions by the business, you are given the evidence you need to either take your case to the business and explain why you feel it is needed, or (and sometimes this is harder) you have the evidence before you to re-evaluate your decision to require digital signatures in the security framework.

Testing

There are two separate types of testing that can be used to ensure compliance. The first not only confirms compliance with your security framework but should also be in your security framework as a policy. Let us call it methodical testing.

Methodical testing are tests that are done on a scheduled or triggered event, for example, vulnerability assessment scanning. Hosts (servers) change over time, either from changes pushed to the system through patches or through configuration changes made to the host. A policy that requires vulnerability assessment scans on a regular basis will cause quick identification of hosts that have vulnerabilities that create exposure for the company. Vulnerability testing could also be triggered as part of a policy for new hosts coming onto the network.

The second type of testing is periodic testing. Periodic testing is random testing of policies and procedures to ensure that they are operating correctly and as anticipated. Want to confirm that your new user account procedure is operating correctly? Put in a request for a fake user and watch it go through the system. Not sure if your Web content filters are working correctly? Try getting to a Web location that would normally be blocked. There are a few important things to remember before doing any periodic testing. The first is to ensure that you have written permission from management to conduct periodic testing. By testing some of your policies (especially the "Thou shall not" policies), you are likely to occasionally violate your company policies. The second (and this should be done for any testing) is to document the test and the results of the test. Evidence of passing a test is just as important as evidence of failing one. The third is to remember to spread your tests out. Do not focus your testing on any particular host, group, or service.

Penetration Testing

Penetration testing, which will be discussed more in depth later in the chapter, can be considered the bullying big brother of vulnerability testing. While vulnerability scanning points out flaws, missing patches, and configuration errors on a device, penetration testing takes those vulnerabilities and exploits them to demonstrate the ability to gain access into the system. Although penetration testing can be harshly realistic, it is a necessary part of an all encompassing security programs.

Social Engineering

Social engineering can be a difficult issue for security practitioners to work with. What is social engineering? Unlike most things in the digital security realm, social engineering has very little to do with computers and networks. Social engineering is all about people. Namely, getting people to give you confidential information, or perform actions on a system that they normally would not do, or is against policy. Social engineering is not as much a test against your security framework as it is an attack against your user's awareness of, acceptance of, and compliance with the framework.

For example, your company has a policy about not sharing passwords. You pose as a help desk technician and call the end user making up some story about how you need to log in as the user to test a program remotely and then ask for their password. If your users KNOW your policy, and UNDERSTAND the importance of it, they will not give you their password. However, if it is common practice for IT to ask for a user password when performing maintenance, the user is unfamiliar with the policy, or does not think that it is important not to share their password, you will get their password.

Another example of social engineering that has been on the rise the past few years is phishing. Phishing involves sending the user an official looking e-mail, typically from an institution that would be important to the user such as a bank. This e-mail is written so that it has a sense of urgency. It is also written in such a way as to make the user think that they will lose something if they do not perform the task. The task in the e-mail is usually something like "log in and change your password now" or "verify your account information now" complete with a handy Internet link to where the user can make those changes. So the user merrily clicks on the link thinking they are going to their bank Web site to make their account safe, when what they are really doing is going to a hacker Web site and entering their bank account information for the hackers to use.

Logging

Logging, which is covered in depth later in this chapter, is a primary tool for monitoring the security state of your network. Of course, logging only works if you have it turned on for the right events, and you can manage the size of the logs reviewed to a reasonable size.

Audit

Security Auditing Overview

You have been told that your organization is going to have a security audit. Panic sets in, or does it not? Just what is a security audit and what does it mean to you? A security audit is nothing more than an evaluation of how well the objectives of your security framework are being met and a review to make sure that your security framework is not missing anything. Nothing that comes out of an audit should surprise security practitioners if they have been doing their routine monitoring. Think of it this way. Monitoring is an ongoing evaluation of your security framework done by the folks who manage the security day-to-day while an audit is an evaluation of the security framework performed by someone outside of the day-to-day security operations. Security audits serve two purposes for the security practitioner. First, they point out areas where security controls are lacking, policy is not being enforced, or ambiguity exists in the security framework. The second benefit of security audits is that they emphasize security things that are being done right. Auditors, in general, should not be perceived as the bad guys that are out to prove what a bad job you are doing. On the contrary, auditors should be viewed as professionals who are there to assist you in driving your security program forward and to assist you in making management aware of what security steps are being correctly taken and what more needs to be done.

So, who audits and why? There are two categories of auditors who perform a security audit. The first are internal auditors. These people work for the company and these audits can be perceived as an internal checkup. The other type of auditor is an external auditor. These folks are either under contract with your company to perform objective audits or are brought in by other external parties. Audits can be performed for several reasons. This list is by no means inclusive of all the reasons that an audit may be performed, but covers most of them.

- Annual audit—Most businesses perform a security audit on an annual basis as dictated by policy.
- Event triggered audit—These audits are often conducted after a particular event occurs, such as an intrusion incident. They are used to both analyze what went wrong and, as with all audits, to confirm due diligence if needed.
- Merger/acquisition audit—These audits are performed before a merger/acquisition to give the purchasing company an idea of where the company they are trying to acquire stands on security in relation to its own security framework.
- Regulation compliance audit—These audits are used to confirm compliance with the IT–security-related portions of legislated regulations such as Sarbanes–Oxley and HIPAA.
- Ordered audit—Although rare, there are times when a company is ordered by the courts to have a security audit performed.

What are the auditors going to use as a benchmark to test against? Auditors should use your security framework as a basis for them to audit against; however, to ensure that everything is covered, they will first compare your framework against a well-known and accepted standard (see Policy, Controls, and Enforcement for a partial list of standards organizations).

What methodology will the auditors use for the audit? There are many different methodologies out that are used by auditors worldwide. Here are a few of them:

- ISO/IEC 27001:2005 (formerly BS 7799-2:2002), Specification for Information Security Management

- ISO/IEC 27002:2005 (previously named ISO/IEC 17799:2005), Code of Practice for Information Security Management
- NIST SP 800-37, "Guidelines for the Security Certification and Accreditation of Federal Information Technology Systems," which can be retrofitted for private industry
- CObIT (Control Objectives for Information and related Technology) from the Information Systems Audit and Control Association (ISACA)

Auditors may also use a methodology of their own design, or one that has been adapted from several guidelines. What difference does it make to you as a security practitioner which methodology they use? From a technical standpoint, it does not matter; however, it is a good idea to be familiar with the methodology they are going to use so that you can understand how management will be receiving the audit results.

So what does an auditor do? Auditors collect information about your security processes. Auditors are responsible for:

- Providing independent assurance to management that security systems are effective
- Analyzing the appropriateness of organizational security objectives
- Analyzing the appropriateness of policies, standards, baselines, procedures, and guidelines that support security objectives
- Analyzing the effectiveness of the controls that support security policies
- Stating and explaining the scope of the systems to be audited

What is the audit going to cover? Before auditors begin an audit, they define the audit scope that outlines what they are going to be looking at. One way to define the scope of an audit is to break it down into seven domains of security responsibility; that is, to break up the IT systems into manageable areas upon which audits may be based.

These seven domains are:

- User domain—the users themselves and their authentication methods
- Workstation domain—often considered the end-user systems
- System/application domain—applications that you run on your network, such as e-mail, database, and Web applications
- LAN domain—equipment required to create the internal LAN
- LAN-to-WAN domain—The transition area between your firewall and the WAN, often where your DMZ resides
- WAN domain—Usually defined as things outside of your firewall
- Remote Access Domain—How remote or traveling users access your network

Auditors may also limit the scope by physical location, or just choose to review a subset of your security framework.

So what is your job during an audit? As an IT security practitioner you will probably be asked to participate in the audit by helping the auditors collect information and interpret the findings for the auditors. Having said that, there may be times when IT will not be asked to participate. They might be the reason for the audit and the auditors need to get an unbiased interpretation of the data. When you are asked to participate in an audit, there are several areas that you will probably be asked to participate in. Before participating in an audit, you need to ensure that you have the controls, policies, and standards in place to support these areas and that you are sure they are working up to the level prescribed. An audit is not the place to realize that your logging or some other function is not working like you thought it would be. In truth, these items should be an ongoing activity, not just to prepare for an audit.

Documentation

As part of an audit, the auditors will want to review system documentation. This can include:

- Disaster/business recovery documentation—While some IT practitioners and auditors do not see this as part of a security audit, others feel that because the recovery process involves data recovery and system configuration, it is an important and often overlooked piece of information security.
- Host configuration documentation—Auditors are going to want to see the documentation on how hosts are configured on your network both to see that everything is covered and to verify that the configuration documentation actually reflects what is being done.
- Baseline security configuration documentation for each type of host—As with the host configuration, this documentation does not just reflect the standard configuration data, but specifically what steps are being done related to security.
- Acceptable use documentation for the host if applicable. Some companies spell out acceptable use policy under the user responsibilities policy and the administrator use policy. Some also include it for particular hosts. For example, a company may say that there is to be no transfer of business confidential information over the FTP (file transfer protocol) server within the user policies and reiterate that policy both in an acceptable use policy for the FTP server, as well as use it as a login banner for FTP services. As long as the message is the same, there is no harm in repeating it in several places.
- Change management documentation—There are two different types of change management documentation that you may need to produce for auditors. The first one would be the policy outlining the change management process. The other would be documentation reflecting changes made to a host.

- Data classification—How are your data classified? Are there some data that you should spend more effort on securing than others? Having data classification documentation comes in handy for justifying why some hosts have more security restrictions than others.
- Business flow documentation—Although not exactly related to IT security, documentation that shows how business data flow through the network can be a great aid to auditors trying to understand how everything works. For example, how does your order entry data flow through the system from when the order is taken until it is shipped out to the customer? What systems do data reside on and how do data move around your network?

Log Files

Log files can be cumbersome and unwieldy. They can also contain critical information within them that can document compliance with your security framework. Your security framework should have the policies and procedures to cover log files, namely, they need to spell out:

- What devices and hosts might contain critical log data.
- What information gets logged.
- Where and how the log files are going to be stored.
- Retention schedule for log files.
- What security measures are going to be employed to ensure the integrity of the log files in storage and in transit.
- Who has access to modify or delete log files.

Detailed resources for building logging infrastructure include:

- http://www.loganalysis.org/
- http://csrc.nist.gov/publications/nistpubs/800-92/SP800-92.pdf
- http://www.serverwatch.com/tutorials/article.php/3366531.

Links to tools that allow for periodic and real-time analysis can be found at the following Web sites:

- http://www.securityfocus.com/infocus/1613
- http://www.dmoz.org/Computers/Software/Internet/Site_Management/Log_Analysis.

Reviewing of Host Logs

Auditors are going to want to review host logs as part of the audit process. As a security professional, you are going to want to regularly review host log files as part of your security program. Remember that an audit is a snapshot in time, so you will not want to use live log files for an audit review. It is best to save the log file off to a separate file and present that to the auditors for them to review. Likewise, if they want historical data, you can give them a copy of a log file that has been rotated out of production. As part of your log processes, you should establish guidelines for log retention and follow them to the letter. If your policy states that you retain standard log files for only 6 months, that is all you should have. During normal log reviews, it is acceptable to use live log files as long as your review does not disrupt the normal logging process.

Review Incident Logs

Any time that you have an incident (see Section 4.3 for definition), you should save the log files of all devices that have been affected, or are along the network path the intruder took. These files need to be saved differently than your standard log retention policy. Since it is possible that these log files might be used in a court case against the intruder, there are several guidelines that should be followed:

- Create a hash value for the log files. This hash value can be used to show that the files have not been altered.
- Copy the log files to a read-only type of media such as CD or DVD.
- Maintain chain of custody on the log files. Document who saved the files and where they were saved and who has access to them.
- The data retention rules might change for potential legal evidence, so ensure that you check with your legal department for guidance on how long to retain incident logs.

During an audit, auditors might want to review these files both to check on your incident response policy and to identify any trends in the intrusions.

Log Anomalies

So you have these log files that you are either reviewing yourself, or helping review them as part of an audit process. What is it you are looking for? Identifying log anomalies is often the first step in identifying security-related issues both during an audit and during routine monitoring. What constitutes an anomaly? A log anomaly is basically anything out of the ordinary. Some will be glaringly obvious. For example: gaps in date/time stamps, or account lockouts. Others will be harder to detect, such as someone trying to write data to a protected directory. While it would seem that you would want to log everything so that you would not miss any important data, you would soon drown under the amount of data that you collected.

Log Management

Log files can grow beyond your means to gather meaningful data from them if they are not managed properly. How can you ensure that you are getting the data you need without overburdening your resources with excessive log events? The first thing to remember is that you need to start with your most critical resources. Then you need to be selective in the amount of data that you receive from each host. Finally, you need to get the data somewhere that you can easily access them for analysis.

Clipping Levels

Clipping levels are a predefined criteria or threshold that sets off an event entry. For example, you do not want to be notified on every failed login attempt, because everyone mistypes their password occasionally. Thus, you set the clipping level to only create a log entry after two failed password attempts. Clipping levels usually have a time property associated with them. For the logging process to not have to keep track of every single failed password attempt in the off chance that the next time that account is logged in the password is mistyped, you can set the time limit to a reasonable amount of time; for example, 30 minutes. Now the system only has to keep track of an invalid login attempt on a particular account for 30 minutes. If another invalid attempt does not come in on that account, the system can disregard the first one. Clipping levels are great for reducing the amount of data that you accumulate in your log files. Care must be taken to ensure that you are not skipping important data, and like everything else, your clipping levels need to be documented.

Filtering

Log filtering usually takes place after the log files have been written. Clipping reduces the amount of data in the log; filtering reduces the amount of data viewed. Filters come in extremely handy when trying to isolate a particular host, user account, or event type. For example, you could filter a log file to only look at invalid login attempts, or for all entries within a certain time window. Care must be taken when filtering that you do not filter out too much information and miss what you are looking for.

Log Consolidation

Log consolidation gives you one-stop shopping for log file analysis. Log file consolidation is usually done on a separate server from the one that actually generates the log files. Most logging systems have the ability to forward log messages to another server. Thus, the entry not only appears in the log file of the server but it also appears in the consolidated log on the "consolidation server." Log consolidation is extremely useful when you are trying to track a user or event that reaches across multiple servers or devices. Log consolidation is discussed further below in the centralized versus distributed log management section.

Log Retention

Now that you have all your systems logging, and you are reviewing those logs for anomalies, how long are you required to keep the logs? How are you going to store the logs?

Automated log tools. Automation is one of the keys to successful log file management. There are many different tools both commercial and open source that can automate different phases of log file retention. Scripts are available on the Internet, or can be written in-house, which can automate some of the processes needed in log management. Some key areas that you might want to research for log file automation tools:

- Log consolidation tools—tools that automatically copy log entries to a central server.
- Log retention tools—tools that will move old log files to separate folders for backup and purge old data from log files.

Business and legal requirements. Business and legal requirements for log retention will vary from business to business. Some businesses will have no requirements for data retention. Others are mandated by the nature of their business, or by business partners to comply with certain retention data. For example, the Payment Card Industry (PCI) Data Security Standard requires that businesses retain 1 year of log data in support of PCI with a minimum of 3 months worth of data available online. Some federal regulations have requirements for data retention as well. If you are unsure if your business has any requirements for log file retention, check with your auditors and legal team. They should know for sure. So, if your business has no business or legal requirements to retain log data, how long should you keep it? The first people you should ask would be your legal department. Most legal departments have very specific guidelines for data retention, and those guidelines may drive your log retention policy. If you still do not have any guidance on how long to keep logs, try this technique.

Maintain 3 months' worth of logs online. Once the 3-month threshold has passed, move the log files off to tape or other backup media. Keep offline backup files for a year, keeping track of how far back you are ever asked to look into the log files. At the end of the year, see how far back was the longest that you had to look for data, add 3 months to that time, and utilize that for the maximum length of time to retain offline log files.

Centralized versus distributed log management. Centralized log management is where you copy the log files onto a central server that is then used for all log analysis. There are several advantages to utilizing a central server for log management:

- Provides one place to access all pertinent log files
- Allows creation of a timeline of events that cross multiple devices
- Enables simplification of moving log files offline
- Helps prevent tampering of log files

There are also several issues that arise when using a centralized log management server:

- Results in a single point of failure for log file retention if not appropriately backed up
- Increases bandwidth requirements between servers
- Raises the need for encrypted and/or secure transfer of log files

Storage. Now that you have determined where you are going to keep your log files, and for how long you are going to keep them, the question arises: where you are going to store all this data? Log files can become quite large, very fast. Several gigabytes of log data per day is not uncommon for log files on a busy network. Be prepared to add more disc space to your log repository if needed. You are also going to need some backup methodology and media to move log files offline for retention.

Response to Audit

Once the security practitioner has finished helping the auditors gather the required data and finished assisting them with interpreting the information, their work is not over. There are still a few more steps that need to be accomplished to complete the audit process.

Exit interview. After an audit is performed, an exit interview will alert personnel to glaring issues they need to be concerned about immediately. Besides these preliminary alerts, an auditor should avoid giving detailed verbal assessments, which may falsely set the expectation level of the organization with regard to security preparedness in the audited scope.

Presentation of audit findings. After the auditors have finished tabulating their results, they will present the findings to management. These findings will contain a comparison of the audit findings versus the company's security framework and/or industry standards or "best practices." These findings will also contain recommendations for mitigation or correction of documented risks or instances of noncompliance.

Management response. Management will have the opportunity to review the audit findings and respond to the auditors. This is a written response that becomes part of the audit documentation. It outlines plans to remedy findings that are out of compliance, or explain why management disagrees with the audit findings.

As a security practitioner you should be involved in the presentation of the audit findings and assist with the management response. Even if your input is not sought for the management response, you need to be aware of what issues were presented and what the management's responses to those issues were.

Once all these steps are completed, the security cycle starts over again. The findings of the audit need to be fixed, mitigated, or introduced into your security framework.

Monitoring

Security Monitoring Concepts

Few professionals would believe that any system is completely safe, no matter how extreme the measures that are employed to ensure protection of its confidentiality, integrity, and availability. You should assume that all systems are susceptible to attack, and at some point will be attacked. This mindset helps an IT security practitioner prepare for inevitable system compromises. Comprehensive policies and procedures and their effective use are excellent mitigation techniques for stemming the effectiveness of attacks. Security monitoring is a mitigation activity used to protect systems, identify network patterns, and identify potential attacks.

Terminology

Monitoring terminology can seem arcane and confusing. The purpose of this list is to define by example and reinforce terminology commonly used when discussing monitoring technology.

- Safeguard—a built-in proactive security control implemented to provide protection against threats.
- Countermeasure—an added-on reactive security control.
- Vulnerability—a system weakness.
- Exploit—a particular attack. It is named this way because these attacks exploit system vulnerabilities.
- Signature—a string of characters or activities found within processes or data communications that describes a known system attack. Some monitoring systems identify attacks by means of a signature.
- False positive—monitoring triggered an event but nothing was actually wrong, and in doing so the monitoring has incorrectly identified benign communications as a danger.

- False negative—the monitoring system missed reporting an exploit event by not firing an alarm. This is bad.
- True positive—the monitoring system recognized an exploit event correctly.
- True negative—the monitoring system has not recognized benign traffic as cause for concern. In other words, it does nothing when nothing needs to be done. This is good.
- Tuning—customizing a monitoring system to your environment.
- Promiscuous interface—a network interface that collects and processes all of the packets sent to it regardless of the destination MAC address.

Implementation Issues for Monitoring

You should remember the security tenets *confidentiality*, *integrity*, and *availability*. IDS can alert to these conditions by matching known conditions (signatures) with unknown but suspect conditions (anomalies).

- Confidentiality—unauthorized access may breach confidentiality
- Integrity—corruption due to an attack destabilizes integrity
- Availability—denial of service keeps data from being available

The security organization must make decisions concerning the deployment of monitoring systems. What types to deploy and where to deploy are functions of budget and system criticality. Implementation of monitoring should be supported by policy and justified by the risk assessment. The actual deployment of the sensors will depend on the value of the assets.

Monitoring control deployment considerations include:

- System criticality drives deployment.
- Choose one or more monitoring technique types—HIDS/NIDS/logging.
- Choose an analysis paradigm—statistical anomaly/signature.
- Choose a system that meets timeliness objectives—real-time/scheduled (non-real-time).
- Choose a reporting mechanism for incident response—push or pull; that is, does a management system query the monitoring devices for data or does the device push the data to a repository where it is stored or analyzed?
- Make the update mechanisms part of policy with well-defined procedures, especially for signature-based devices.
- Tune monitoring systems to reflect the environment they support.
- Choose automatic response mechanisms wisely.
- Maintenance and Tuning—for the long-term use and effectiveness of the monitoring controls, systems should be cared for like any other mission critical component.

Keep IDS signatures (if applicable) current—Signature-based IDS must be kept up to date as previously unknown vulnerabilities are revealed. Take, for example, the ineffectiveness of a host antivirus system with virus signatures that are a year old. Since several new viruses emerge each week, a system with old signatures may be effective for the old exploits but the system is defenseless for new viruses. IDS systems operate on the same principle. IDS vendors often have notification systems to alert you about new signature definitions or the capability for automatic update.

Keep IDS subsystems current—As new generations of IDS subsystems (the operating systems and software engines that drive the system) become available, consider testing, then deploying, these to know if they add to your capability to detect exploits but do not introduce instability.

Tune IDS—NIDS systems have limitations on how much processing they can handle; therefore, limit what the NIDS must monitor based on your environment. For example, if you do not have any Windows-based hosts, consider disabling monitoring for Windows-based exploits. Conversely, if you have a UNIX environment and UNIX-based signatures are not enabled, you will likely miss these events.

As system changes are made, the security systems that protect them should be considered. During the change control process, new changes should factor in how the security systems will handle them. Some sample questions are as follows:

- Will the host configuration change require a reconfiguration of the HIDS component?
- Will the addition of a database application of a host require the HIDS agent to be configured to screen database transactions for validity?
- Will the network change require alterations to the way the NIDS collects data?
- Will the new services offered on a host require the NIDS to be tuned to have the appropriate active or passive responses to exploits that target those new services?
- Will the DMZ to management network firewall rules need to be changed to accommodate the logging stream from the new Web server placed on the DMZ?

Collecting Data for Incident Response. Organizations must have a policy and plan for dealing with events as they occur and the corresponding forensics of incidents. Ask yourself the following:

- How do I plan to collect event and forensic information from the IDS/IPS?—Organizations cannot expect IDS/IPS to be a "set it and forget it" technology. Human interaction is required to interpret events and high-level responses. IDS can organize events by priority and can even be set to react in a certain way to an observed event, but humans will periodically need to decide if the IDS is doing its job properly.

■ How will I have the IDS/IPS respond to events?—Depending on your IDS/IPS capabilities, you will need to decide how you want it to react to an observed event. The next section discusses active versus passive IDS response.

■ How will I respond to incidents?—What investigative actions will the security staff take based on singular or repeated incidents involving one or more observed events? This is a function of your security policy.

When organizations suffer attacks, logging information, whether generated by a host, network device, IDS/IPS, or other device, may be at some point considered evidence by law enforcement personnel. Preserving a chain of custody for law enforcement is important so as not to taint the evidence for use in criminal proceedings. See the SSCP Risk, Response, and Recovery section for a discussion of these rules in detail.

Monitoring Response Techniques. If unauthorized activity is detected, IDS/IPS systems can take one or both of the following actions:

■ Passive response—notes the event at various levels but does not take any type of evasive action. The response is by definition passive because the event is merely noted.

■ Active response—notes the event and performs a reaction so as to protect systems from further exploitation.

The following are examples of passive IDS/IPS response:

■ Logging the event to a log file
■ Displaying an alert on the console of an event viewer or security information management system
■ Logging the details of a packet flow that was identified to be associated with an unauthorized event for a specified period of time, for the purpose of subsequent forensic analysis
■ Sending an alert page, text message, or e-mail to an administrator.

The following are examples of active IDS/IPS response:

■ In the case of an unauthorized TCP data flow on a network, initiate a NIDS reset the connection (with a TCP reset) between an attacker and the host being attacked. This only works with TCP-based attacks because they are connection oriented.
■ In the case of any IP data flow (TCP, UDP, ICMP), initiate a NIDS, instruct a filtering device like a firewall or router to dynamically alter its access control

list to preclude further communications with the attacker, either indefinitely or for a specified period.

■ In the case of a disallowed system call or application-specific behavior, initiate the HIDS agent to block the transaction.

With TCP resets, often the IDS will send a TCP packet with the FIN flag set in the TCP header to both the attacker and the attacked host to gracefully reset the connection from both host's perspective. By resetting the attacker, this discourages future attacks (if they keep getting resets). By resetting the attacked host, this frees up system resources that may have been allocated as a result of the attack.

With system calls, if a process that does not normally need to access the Web server's data tries to access the data, the HIDS agent can disallow this access.

Response Pitfalls. Active IDS response pitfalls include:

■ Cutting off legitimate traffic due to false positives
■ Self-induced denial of service.

Many monitoring systems provide the means to specify some sort of response if a particular signature fires, although doing so may have unintended consequences.

Entertain the notion that a signature has been written that is too generic in nature. This means that it sometimes fires as a result of exploit traffic and is a true positive but sometimes fires as a result of innocent traffic and is a false positive. If the signature is configured to send TCP resets to an offending address and does so in a false-positive situation, the IDS may be cutting off legitimate traffic.

Self-induced denial of service can also be a problem with active response systems. If an attacker decided to spoof the IP address of your business partner and sends attacks with the partner's IP address and your IDS reacted by dynamically modifying the edge router configuration, you would cut off communications with the business partner.

Take note that active response mechanisms should be used carefully and be limited to the types of actions listed above. Some organizations take it upon themselves to implement systems that actively counter attack systems they believe have attacked them as a response. This is highly discouraged and may result in legal issues for the organization. It is irresponsible to counter attack any system for any reason.

Who Are These People Attacking Us?

Attackers are generally thought of as persons who perform overt and covert intrusions or attacks on systems, who are often motivated by one of the following:

■ Notoriety, ego, or sport—exemplifies the attacker's "power" to his or her audience, whether to just a few people or to the world. To the attacker, the inherent challenge is "I want to see if I can do it and I want everyone to know about it."

■ Greed and profit—the attacker is attempting personal financial gain or financial gain of a client; that is, an attacker might have been hired by a business to furtively damage a competitor's system or gain unauthorized access to the competitor's data. An attacker may use or resell information found on systems, such as credit card numbers.

■ Political agenda—attacking a political nemesis physically or electronically is seen as a way to further one's own agenda or ideals or call attention to a cause.

■ Revenge—the overriding motivation behind revenge in the attacker's eyes is, "I've been wronged and I am going to get you back." Revenge is often exacted by former employees or those who were at one point in time trusted by the organization that is now being attacked.

■ Curiosity—They do not really want to do any damage. They just want to see how it works.

There is one category of "attacker" that is often overlooked by security professionals, and while it may seem unfair to some to lump them in with attackers, it seems to fit. These are the individuals within your company either through ignorance, ego, or stress cause unintended intrusions to occur. They could be the IT system administrator that finds it easier to grant everyone administrative rights to a server rather than take the time to define access controls correctly, or the administrative assistant who uses someone else's login into the HR system just because it was already logged in. These individuals can cause as much damage to your company as someone who is trying to attack you and the incidents they create need to be addressed like any other intrusion incident.

What Is an Intrusion?

Intrusions are acts by persons, organizations, or systems that violate the security framework of the recipient. In some instances, it is easier to identify an "intrusion" as a "violation." For example, you have a policy that prohibits users from using computing resources while logged in as someone else. While in the true sense of the definition, the event is an intrusion, it is more acceptable to refer to the event as a violation. Intrusions are considered attacks but are not just limited to computing systems. If something is classified as an intrusion, it will fall into one of following two categories:

Intrusions can be overt and are generally noticeable immediately. Examples of overt intrusion include the following:

■ Someone breaking into your building and stealing computing hardware
■ Two people robbing a bank

- Someone stealing copper wiring out of the electrical closet
- Flooding an E-commerce site with too much data from too many sources, thereby rendering the site useless for legitimate customers
- Attackers defacing a Web site

Intrusions can be covert and not always noticeable right away, if at all. These, by their nature, are the most difficult to identify. Examples of covert intrusions include the following:

- A waiter stealing your credit card number after you have paid your bill and using it on the Web that evening
- An accounting department employee manipulating financial accounts for illegal and unauthorized personal financial gain
- An authorized user that improperly obtains system administrator login credentials to access private company records to which he is not authorized
- An attacker who poses as an authorized computer support representative to gain the trust of an unknowing user, to obtain information for use in a computer attack
- A hacker that gets hired as IT staff so he can gain access to your systems

So, What Is an Event?

An event is a single occurrence that may or may not indicate an intrusion. All intrusions contain events, but not all events are intrusions. For example, a user account is locked for bad password attempts. That is a security event. If it was just the user forgetting what she changed her password to last Friday, it is not an intrusion; however, if the user claims that they did not try to login before their account was locked, it might be an intrusion.

What Kinds of Monitoring Are There?

There are two basic classes of monitoring devices: real-time and non-real time.

Real-time monitoring provides a means for immediately identifying and sometimes stopping (depending on the type of system used) overt and covert events. They include some types of network and host intrusion detection systems. These systems keep watch on systems and (can) alert administrators as unauthorized activity is happening. They can also log events for subsequent analysis if needed. A real-time monitor for computers is like the burglar alarm for your home. When someone breaks in, it sounds the alarm.

Non-real-time monitoring provides a means for saving important information about system events and possibly monitoring the integrity of system configurations after the fact. These technologies include application logging, system logging, and integrity monitoring. Logging and integrity systems might tell you that a burglar was at your home, but he is likely gone by the time you find out. This does not mean that non-real-time systems are not as good as real-time systems. Each fulfills a different niche in monitoring. These system logs would be more like the footprints or fingerprints a burglar would leave behind.

Monitoring should be designed to positively identify actual attacks (true positive) but not identify regular communications as a threat (false positive), or do everything possible to increase the identification of actual attacks and decrease the false-positive notifications.

Monitoring event information can provide considerable insight about possible attacks perpetrated within your network. This information can help organizations make necessary modifications to security policies and the supporting safeguards and countermeasures for improved protection.

Monitoring technology needs to be "tuned," which is the process of customizing the default configuration to the unique needs of your systems. To tune out alarms that are harmless (false positives), you must know what types of data traffic are considered acceptable. If you still have your security framework, data classification documentation, and business flow documentation, you should have a good idea of what information should be on your network, and how it should be moving between devices.

Deploying monitoring systems is one part of a multilayer security strategy comprised of several types of security controls. By itself, it will not prevent intrusions or give you all the information you need to analyze an intrusion.

IDS/IDP

What is an IDS and an IDP and how do they differ? IDS stands for Intrusion Detection System. It is a passive system that detects security events but has limited ability to intervene on the event. An IDP is an Intrusion Detection and Prevention system. It is capable of both detecting a security event and stopping the event from continuing on to the targeted host.

There are two types of IDS/IDP devices. Network-based IDS or NIDS generally connect to one or more network segments. It monitors and interprets traffic and identifies security events either by anomaly detection or based on the signature of the event. Host-based IDS, or HIDS, usually reside as a software agent on the host. Most of the newer NIDS are IDP devices and not IDS. Active HIDS can do a variety of activities to protect the host from intercepting system calls and examining them for validity to stopping application access to key system files or parameters. Active HIDS would be considered an IDP. Passive HIDS (IDS) take a snapshot of the file system in a known clean state and then compare that against the current file system on a regular basis. They can then flag alerts based on file changes.

Where should you deploy HIDS and NIDS? Still got your business data flow diagrams and data classification policy? Those are good starting points. HIDS and NIDS need to be deployed where they can best protect your critical business assets. Of course, in a perfect world with unlimited budget, all your devices would be protected by HIDS and NIDS, but most IT security staff have to deal with limited personnel and limited budget. Protect your critical assets first and protect the most you can with the fewest devices. A good starting point would be to place HIDS on all systems that contain financial data, HR data, and any other data for which protection is mandated. NIDS should be placed on all ingress points into your network and on segments separating critical servers from the rest of the network. There used to be some debate among security practitioners as to whether your NIDS should be placed outside your firewall to identify all attacks against your network, or inside your firewall to only identify those that made it past your firewall rules. The general practice now appears to be to not worry if it is raining outside; only worry about what is dripping in your living room. In other words, keep the NIDS inside the firewall.

Both HIDS and NIDS are notoriously noisy out of the box and should be tuned for your environment. They also need to be configured to notify the responsible people via the approved method if they identify a potential incident. These, like the alerts themselves, must be configured properly to ensure that when something really does happen, the designated people know to take action. For the most part, low-priority events can send alerts via e-mail, while high-priority events should page, or call, the security personnel on call.

Vulnerability Assessment

Vulnerability assessment is simply the process of checking a system for weaknesses. These vulnerabilities can take the form of applications or operating systems that are missing patches, misconfiguration of systems, unnecessary applications, or open ports. While these tests can be conducted from outside the network, like an attacker would, it is advisable to do a vulnerability assessment from a network segment that has unrestricted access to the host you are conducting the assessment against. Why is this? If you just test a system from the outside world, you will identify any vulnerability that can be exploited from the outside; but what happens if an attacker gains access inside your network? Now there are vulnerabilities exposed to the attacker that could have easily been avoided. Unlike a penetration test, which is discussed later in this chapter, a vulnerability tester has access to network diagrams, configurations, login credentials, and other information needed to make a complete evaluation of the system. The goal of a vulnerability assessment is to study the security level of the systems, identify problems, offer mitigation techniques, and assist in prioritizing improvements.

The benefits of vulnerability testing include the following:

- It identifies system vulnerabilities.
- It allows for the prioritization of mitigation tasks based on system criticality and risk.
- It is considered a useful tool for comparing security posture over time especially when done consistently each period.

The disadvantages of vulnerability testing include:

- It may not effectively focus efforts if the test is not designed appropriately. Sometimes testers "bite off more than they can chew."
- It has the potential to crash the network or host being tested if dangerous tests are chosen. (Innocent and noninvasive tests have also been known to cause system crashes.)

Note that vulnerability testing software is often placed into two broad categories:

- General vulnerability
- Application-specific vulnerability

General vulnerability software probes hosts and operating systems for known flaws. It also probes common applications for flaws. Application-specific vulnerability tools are designed specifically to analyze certain types of application software. For example, database scanners optimized to understand the deep issues/weaknesses of Oracle databases, Microsoft SQL Server, etc., and can uncover implementation problems therein. Scanners optimized for Web servers look deeply into issues surrounding those systems.

Vulnerability testing software, in general, is often referred to as V/A (vulnerability assessment) software, and sometimes combines a port mapping function to identify which hosts are where and the applications they offer with further analysis that pegs vulnerabilities to those applications. Good vulnerability software will offer mitigation techniques or links to manufacturer Web sites for further research. This stage of security testing is often an automated software process. It is also beneficial to use multiple tools and cross-reference the results of those tools for a more accurate picture. As with any automated process, you need to examine the results closely to ensure that they are accurate for your environment.

Vulnerability testing usually employs software specific to the activity and tends to have the following qualities:

OS fingerprinting—This technique is used to identify the operating system in use on a target. OS fingerprinting is the process where a scanner can determine the operating system of the host by analyzing the TCP/IP stack flag settings.

These settings vary on each operating system from vendor to vendor or by TCP/IP stack analysis and banner grabbing. Banner grabbing is reading the response banner presented for several ports such as FTP, HTTP, and Telnet. This function is sometimes built into mapping software and sometimes into vulnerability software.

Stimulus and response algorithms—These are techniques to identify application software versions, then referencing these versions with known vulnerabilities. Stimulus involves sending one or more packets at the target. Depending on the response, the tester can infer information about the target's applications. For example, to determine the version of the HTTP server, the vulnerability testing software might send an HTTP GET request to a Web server, just like a browser would (the stimulus), and read the reply information it receives back (the response) for information that details the fact that it is Apache version X, IIS version Y, etc.

Privileged logon ability—The ability to automatically log onto a host or group of hosts with user credentials (administrator-level or other level) for a deeper "authorized" look at systems is desirable.

Cross-referencing—OS and applications/services (discovered during the port mapping phase) should be cross-referenced to more succinctly identify possible vulnerabilities. For example, if OS fingerprinting reveals that the host runs Red Hat Linux 8.0 and that portmapper is one of the listening programs, any pre-8.0 portmapper vulnerabilities can likely be ruled out. Keep in mind that old vulnerabilities have resurfaced in later versions of code even though they were patched at one time. While these instances may occur, the filtering based on OS and application fingerprinting will help you better target systems and use your time more effectively.

Update capability—Scanners must be kept up-to-date with the latest vulnerability signatures; otherwise, they will not be able to detect newer problems and vulnerabilities. Commercial tools that do not have quality personnel dedicated to updating the product are of reduced effectiveness. Likewise, open-source scanners should have a qualified following to keep them up-to-date.

Reporting capability—Without the ability to report, a scanner does not serve much purpose. Good scanners provide the ability to export scan data in a variety of formats, including viewing in HTML or PDF format or to third-party reporting software, and are configurable enough to give the ability to filter reports into high-, mid-, and low-level detail depending on the intended audience for the report. Reports are used as basis for determining mitigation activities at a later time.

Problems that may arise when using vulnerability analysis tools include:

False positives—When scanners use generalized tests or if the scanner does not have the ability to somehow look deeply at the application, it might not be able to determine whether the application *actually* has vulnerability. It might result in information that says the application *might* have vulnerability. If it sees that the server is running a remote control application, the test software may indicate that you have a "High" vulnerability. But if you have taken care to implement the remote control application to a high standard, your vulnerability is not as high.

Crash exposure—V/A software has some inherent dangers because much of the vulnerability testing software includes denial of service test scripts (as well as other scripts) which, if used carelessly, can crash hosts. Ensure that hosts being tested have proper backups and that you test during times that will have the lowest impact on business operations.

Temporal information—Scans are temporal in nature, which means that the scan results you have today become stale as time moves on and new vulnerabilities are discovered. Therefore, scans must be performed periodically with scanners that are up-to-date with the latest vulnerability signatures.

Scanner tools

- Nessus open source scanner—http://www.nessus.org
- Internet Security Systems' (ISS) Enterprise Scanner—http://www.iss.net
- eEye Digital Security's Retina—http://www.eeye.com
- SAINT—http://www.wwdsi.com
- For a more in-depth list, see http://sectools.org/web-scanners.html

Weeding out false positives. Even if a scanner reports a service as vulnerable, or missing a patch that leads to vulnerability, the system is not necessarily vulnerable. Accuracy is a function of the scanner's quality; that is, how complete and concise the testing mechanisms are built (better tests equal better results), how up-to-date the testing scripts are (fresher scripts are more likely to spot a fuller range of known problems), and how well it performs OS fingerprinting (knowing which OS the host runs helps the scanner pinpoint issues for applications that run on that OS). Double check the scanner's work. Verify that a claimed vulnerability is an actual vulnerability. Good scanners will reference documents to help you learn more about the issue.

The following scenario illustrates verification of vulnerability results: A host running Red Hat Linux 7.0 is scanned over a network connection with an open-source vulnerability scanner. Port enumeration techniques show that the host is listening on TCP port 123 (NTP—network time protocol). A vulnerability scanner may reference an NTP daemon (service) vulnerability that exists in *some* NTP implementations. Keep in mind that scanners should know about this common NTP issue, although not all scanners know about this vulnerability (note comments about scanner quality mentioned earlier).

The point here is to verify whether the tool correctly pinpointed this potential problem as a true problem. In other words, is this a true positive or a false positive?

Issues that affect the scanner's accuracy include:

Is the detected listening port, in this case TCP port 123, really running the service commonly seen on that port? Or was some other service redefined to run on port 123? Scanners often use test techniques like banner grabbing to ensure that the service that generally is listening on a particular port is indeed that service. Was the scanner able to correctly fingerprint the OS? If no NTP vulnerability exists in Red Hat Linux 9, for example, then there should be nothing to report. Making this claim depends heavily on the scanner's confidence that Red Hat 9 is in use.

Was the scanner able to ascertain through some test whether the NTP service has been upgraded to a fixed version? Scanners can derive more information from a system if it has logon credentials to that system. If it has no algorithm to determine whether the NTP service is the default (vulnerable) one or an upgraded one, the reports may show that the NTP service *may* be vulnerable, not that it *is* vulnerable.

Common Vulnerabilities and Exposures (CVE) references are definitions of vulnerabilities that try to note which vendor products and application versions are potentially vulnerable. Note that the CVE references Red Hat Linux advisory RHSA-2001.045-05 for more vendor-specific information. Many other vendors had the same problems and their sites are referenced as well.

Red Hat Linux advisory RHSA-2001.045-05 notes that two of its software distributions, versions 6.2 and 7.0, contained NTP services vulnerable to exploitation and that patched versions exist for download and subsequent upgrade. The tool correctly identified the OS and the problem with the NTP service. Mitigation measures were linked in the reporting output.

You should come away from this with the idea that all scanner reports should be treated with skepticism until the results are verified.

Other examples include:

■ "Patch 008-132 is missing." Verify that this is actually the case using the operating system's patch management systems or some other third-party tool engineered specifically for patch management.
■ "Sendmail may be vulnerable." Reference the vendor's Web site to see if there are known issues with your OS and sendmail versions.
■ "Windows remote registry connection is possible." Look at the host's appropriate registry key to see if this is true.

Host scanning—Organizations serious about security create hardened host configuration procedures and use policy to mandate host deployment and change. There are many ingredients to creating a secure host but you should always remember that what is secure today may not be secure tomorrow, as conditions are ever-changing. There are several areas to consider when securing a host or when evaluating its security:

Disable unneeded services—Services that are not critical to the role the host serves should be disabled or removed as appropriate for that platform. For the services the host does offer, make sure it is using server programs considered secure, make sure you fully understand them, and tighten the configuration files to the highest degree possible. Unneeded services are often installed and left at their defaults but since they are not needed, administrators ignore or forget about them. This may draw unwanted data traffic to the host from other hosts attempting connections, and it will leave the host vulnerable to weaknesses in the services. If a host does not need a particular host process for its operation, do not install it. If software is installed but not used or intended for use on the machine, it may not be remembered or documented that software is on the machine and therefore will likely not get patched. Port mapping programs use many techniques to discover services available on a host. These results should be compared with the policy that defines this host and its role. One must continually ask the critical questions, for the less a host offers as a service to the world while still maintaining its job, the better for its security (because there is less chance of subverting extraneous applications).

Disable insecure services—Certain programs used on systems are known to be insecure, cannot be made secure, and are easily exploitable; therefore, only use secure alternatives. These applications were developed for private, secure LAN environments, but as connectivity proliferated worldwide, their use has been taken to insecure communication channels. Their weakness falls into three categories:

– They usually send authentication information unencrypted. For example, FTP and Telnet send username and passwords in the clear.
– They usually send data unencrypted. For example, HTTP sends data from client to server and back again entirely in the clear. For many applications, this is acceptable; however, for some it is not. SMTP also sends mail data in the clear unless it is secured by the application (e.g., the use of Pretty Good Privacy [PGP] within Outlook).
– Common services are studied carefully for weaknesses by people motivated to attack your systems.

Therefore, to protect hosts, one must understand the implications of using these and other services that are commonly "hacked." Eliminate them when necessary or substitute them for more secure versions. For example:

■ To ensure privacy of login information as well as the contents of client to server transactions, use SSH (secure shell) to login to hosts remotely instead of Telnet.

- Use SSH as a secure way to send insecure data communications between hosts by redirecting the insecure data into an SSH wrapper. The details for doing this are different from system to system.
- Use SCP (Secure Copy) instead of FTP (file transfer protocol).
- Ensure least privilege file system permissions—Least privilege is the concept that describes the minimum number of permissions required to perform a particular task. This applies to services/daemon processes as well as user permissions. Often systems installed out of the box are at minimum security levels. Make an effort to understand how secure newly installed configurations are, and take steps to lock down settings using vendor recommendations.
- Make sure file system permissions are as tight as possible.
- For UNIX-based systems, remove all unnecessary SUID (set used ID) and SGID (set group ID) programs that embed the ability for a program running in one user context to access another program. This ability becomes even more dangerous in the context of a program running with root user permissions as a part of its normal operation.
- For NT-based systems, use the Microsoft Management Center (MMC) "security configuration and analysis" and "security templates" snap-ins to analyze and secure multiple features of the operation system, including audit and policy settings and the registry.
- Establish and enforce a patching policy. Patches are pieces of software code meant to fix a vulnerability or problem that has been identified in a portion of an operating system or in an application that runs on a host. Keep the following in mind regarding patching:
  - Patches should be tested for functionality, stability, and security. You should also ensure that the patch does not change the security configuration of your host. Some patches might reinstall a default account, or change configuration settings back to a default mode. You need a way to test whether new patches will break a system or an application running on a system. When patching highly critical systems, it is advised to deploy the patch in a test environment that mimics the real environment. If you do not have this luxury, only deploy patches at noncritical times, have a back-out plan, and apply patches in steps (meaning one-by-one) to ensure that each one was successful and the system is still operating.
  - Use patch reporting systems that evaluate whether systems have patches installed completely and correctly and which patches are missing. Many vulnerability analysis tools have this function built into them, but be sure to understand how often your V/A tool vendor updates this list versus another vendor who specializes in patch analysis systems. You will probably find that some vendors have better updating systems than others.
  - Optimally, tools should test to see if once a patch has been applied to remove a vulnerability, the vulnerability does not still exist. Patch application sometimes includes a manual remediation component like a registry

change or removing a user and if the IT person applied the patch, but did not perform the manual remediation component, the vulnerability may still exist.

■ Examine applications for weakness—In a perfect world, applications are built from the ground up with security in mind. Applications should prevent privilege escalation and buffer overflows and myriad other threatening problems. However, this is not always the case, and applications need to be evaluated for their ability not to compromise a host. Insecure services and daemons that run on hardened hosts may by nature weaken the host. Applications should come from trusted sources. Similarly, it is inadvisable to download executables from Web sites you know nothing about. Some programs can help evaluate a host's applications for problems. In particular, these focus on Web-based systems and database systems:

- Nikto from http://www.cirt.net evaluates Web CGI systems for common and uncommon vulnerabilities in implementation.
- Web Inspect from http://www.purehacking.com.au is an automated Web server scanning tool.
- AppDetective from http://www.appsecinc.com evaluates applications, especially various types of databases, from vulnerability.
- ISS Database Scanner from http://www.iss.net evaluates databases for security.

■ Ensure that antivirus is installed and is up-to-date with the latest scan engine and pattern file offered by the vendor.

■ Use products that encourage easy management and updates of signatures; otherwise, the systems may fail to be updated, rendering them ineffective to new exploits.

■ Use products that centralize reporting of problems to spot problem areas and trends.

■ Use system logging. Logging methods are advisable to ensure that system events are noted and securely stored, in the event they are needed at a later time.

■ Subscribe to vendor information. Vendors often publish information regularly, not only to keep their name in front of you but also to inform you of security updates and best practices for configuring their systems. Other organizations such as http://www.securityfocus.com and http://www.cert.org publish news of vulnerabilities.

Firewall and Router Testing—Firewalls are designed to be points of data restriction (choke points) between security domains. They operate on a set of rules driven by a security policy to determine what types of data are allowed from one side to the other (point A to point B) and back again (point B to point A). Similarly, routers can also serve some of these functions when configured with access control lists (ACLs). Organizations deploy these devices to not only connect network segments together, but also to restrict access to only those data flows that are required. This can help protect organizational data assets. Routers with ACLs, if used, are usually placed in front of the firewalls to reduce the noise and volume of traffic hitting the firewall. This allows the firewall to be more thorough in its analysis and handling of traffic. This strategy is also known as layering or defense in depth.

Changes to devices should be governed by change control processes that specify what types of changes can occur and when they can occur. This prevents haphazard and dangerous changes to devices that are designed to protect internal systems from other potentially hostile networks, such as the Internet or an extranet to which your internal network connects. Change control processes should include security testing to ensure the changes were implemented correctly and as expected.

Configuration of these devices should be reflected in security procedures and the rules of the access control lists should be engendered by organizational policy. The point of testing is to ensure that what exists matches approved policy.

Sample baseline for the Internet perimeter systems is given below.

Edge routers will have the following qualities:

- For management—Telnet disabled; SSH enabled.
- An authentication system that verifies that the person logging onto the router (for managing it) is who they say they are; accomplished with one-time password system.
- An authorization system that verifies that the logged on administrator has the privileges to perform the management routines they are attempting to invoke.
- An accounting system that tracks the commands that were invoked; this forms the audit trail.
- Basic intrusion detection signature recognition functionality.
- Syslog event reporting to an internal host.
- Blocking of RFC1918 (nonroutable addresses) and packets sourced from 0.0.0.0 inbound and outbound.
- Blocking of inbound MS networking, MS SQL communication, TFTP, Oracle SQL*Net, DHCP, all types of ICMP packets except for path MTU and echo replies. It should be noted that some of these ports may be necessary for business operations and they must be examined on a case by case basis before blocking.

Firewalls will have the following qualities:

- For management—Telnet disabled; SSH or SSL enabled.
- An authentication system that verifies that the person logging onto the firewall (for managing it) is who they say they are; accomplished with one time password system.

- An authorization system that verifies that the logged on administrator has the privileges to perform the management routines they are attempting to invoke.
- An accounting system that tracks the commands that were invoked (this forms the audit trail).
- Event report logging to an internal host.
- Network address translation functionality, if required, is working properly.
- Enabling inbound transmissions from anywhere to the organizational Web server, FTP server, SMTP mail server, and e-commerce server (for example).
- Enabling inbound transmissions back to internal users that originally established the connections.
- Enabling outbound HTTP, HTTPS, FTP, DNS from anyone on the inside (if approved in the policy).
- Enabling outbound SMTP from the mail server to any other mail server.
- Blocking all other outbound access.

With this *sample* baseline in mind, port scanners and vulnerability scanners can be leveraged to test the choke point's ability to filter as specified. If internal (trusted) systems are reachable from the external (untrusted) side in ways not specified by policy, a mismatch has occurred and should be investigated. Likewise, internal to external testing should conclude that only the allowed outbound traffic can occur. The test should compare devices logs with the tests dispatched from the test host.

Advanced firewall testing will test a device's ability to perform the following (this is a partial list and is a function of your firewall's capabilities):

- Limit TCP port scanning reconnaissance techniques (explained earlier in this chapter) including SYN, FIN, XMAS, NULL via the firewall.
- Limit ICMP and UDP port scanning reconnaissance techniques.
- Limit overlapping packet fragments.
- Limit half-open connections to trusted side devices. Attacks like these are called SYN attacks, when the attacker begins the process of opening many connections but never completes any of them, eventually exhausting the target host's memory resources.

Advanced firewall testing can leverage a vulnerability or port scanner's ability to dispatch denial of service and reconnaissance tests. A scanner can be configured to direct, for example, massive amounts of SYN packets at an internal host. If the firewall is operating properly and effectively, it will limit the number of these half-open attempts by intercepting them so that the internal host is not adversely affected. These tests must be used with care, since there is always a chance that the firewall will not do what is expected and the internal hosts might be affected.

Security Monitoring Testing—IDS systems are technical security controls designed to monitor for and alert on the presence of suspicious or disallowed system activity within host processes and across networks. Device logging is used for recording many types of events that occur within hosts and network devices. Logs, whether generated by IDS or hosts, are used as audit trails and permanent records of what happened and when. Organizations have a responsibility to ensure that their monitoring systems are functioning correctly and alerting on the broad range of communications commonly in use. Documenting this testing can also be used to show due diligence. Likewise, you can use testing to confirm that IDS detects traffic patterns as claimed by the vendor.

With regard to IDS testing, methods should include the ability to provide a stimulus (i.e., send data that simulate an exploitation of a particular vulnerability) and observe the appropriate response by the IDS. Testing can also uncover an IDS's inability to detect purposeful evasion techniques that might be used by attackers. Under controlled conditions, stimulus can be crafted and sent from vulnerability scanners. Response can be observed in log files generated by the IDS or any other monitoring system used in conjunction with the IDS. If the appropriate response is not generated, investigation of the causes can be undertaken.

With regard to host logging tests, methods should also include the ability to provide a stimulus (i.e., send data that simulates a "log-able" event) and observe the appropriate response by the monitoring system. Under controlled conditions, stimulus can be crafted in many ways depending on your test. For example, if a host is configured to log an alert every time an administrator or equivalent logs on, you can simply log on as the "root" user to your UNIX system. In this example, response can be observed in the system's log files. If the appropriate log entry is not generated, investigation of the causes can be undertaken.

The overall goal is to make sure the monitoring is configured to your organization's specifications and that it has all of the features needed.

The following traffic types and conditions are those you should consider testing for in an IDS environment, as vulnerability exploits can be contained within any of them. If the monitoring systems you use do not cover all of them, your systems are open to exploitation:

■ Data patterns that are contained within single packets—this is considered a minimum functionality since the IDS need only search through a single packet for an exploit.

■ Data patterns contained within multiple packets—this is considered a desirable function since there is often more than one packet in a data stream between two hosts. This function, stateful pattern matching, requires the IDS to "remember" packets it saw in the past to reassemble them, as well as perform analysis to determine if exploits are contained within the aggregate payload.

■ Obfuscated data—this refers to data that is converted from ASCII to Hexadecimal or Unicode characters and then sent in one or more packets. The IDS must be able to convert the code among all of these formats. If a signature that describes an exploit is written in ASCII but the exploit arrives at your system in Unicode, the IDS must convert it back to ASCII to recognize it as an exploit.

- Fragmented data—IP data can be fragmented across many small packets, which are then reassembled by the receiving host. Fragmentation occasionally happens in normal communications. In contrast, overlapping fragments is a situation where portions of IP datagrams overwrite and supersede one another as they are reassembled on the receiving system (a teardrop attack). This can wreak havoc on a computer, which can become confused and overloaded during the reassembly process. IDS must understand how to reassemble fragmented data and overlapping fragmented data so it can analyze the resulting data. These techniques are employed by attackers to subvert systems and to evade detection.
- Protocol embedded attacks—IDS should be able to decode (i.e., break apart, understand, and process) commonly used applications (DNS, HTTP, FTP, SQL, etc.) just like a host would, to determine whether an attacker has manipulated code that might crash the application or host on which it runs. Therefore, testing should employ exploits embedded within application data.
- Flooding detection—an IDS should be able to detect conditions indicative of a denial of service flood, when too many packets originate from one or more sources to one or more destinations. Thresholds are determined within the configuration. For example, an IDS should be able to detect if more than 10 half-open (embryonic) connections are opened within 2 seconds to any one host on your network.

Intrusion Prevention Systems Security Monitoring (IPS). IPSs are technical security controls designed to monitor and alert for the presence of suspicious or disallowed system activity within host processes and across networks, and then take action on suspicious activities. Likewise, you can use testing to confirm that IPS detects traffic patterns and reacts as claimed by the vendor. When auditing an IPS, its position in the architecture is slightly different than that of an IDS; an IPS needs to be positioned inline of the traffic flow so the appropriate action can be taken. Some of the other key differences are: the IPS acts on issues and handles the problems, while an IDS only reports on the traffic and requires some other party to react to the situation. The negative consequence of the IPS is that it is possible to reject good traffic and there will only be the logs of the IPS to show why the good traffic is getting rejected. Many times the networking staff may not have access to those logs and may find network troubleshooting more difficult.

Security Gateway Testing. Some organizations use security gateways to intercept certain communications and examine them for validity. Gateways perform their analysis on these communications based on a set of rules supplied by the organization—rules driven by policy—and pass them along if they are deemed appropriate and exploitation-free, or block them if they are not. Security gateway types include the following:

Antivirus gateways—These systems monitor for viruses contained within communications of major application types like Web traffic, e-mail, and FTP.
Java/ActiveX filters—These systems screen communications for these components and block or limit their transmission.
Web traffic screening—These systems block Web traffic to and from specific sites or sites of a specific type (gambling, pornography, games, travel and leisure, etc.).

Security testing should encompass these gateway devices to ensure their proper operation. Depending on the device, the easiest way to test to ensure that it is working is try to perform the behavior that it is supposed to block. There are "standard" AV test files available on the Internet that do not contain a virus but have a signature that will be discovered by all major AV vendors. While this file will not ensure that your AV will catch everything, it will at least confirm that the gateway is looking into the traffic for virus patterns.

Wireless Networking Testing. With the proliferation of wireless access devices comes the common situation where they are not configured for even minimal authentication and encryption because the people deploying them generally have no knowledge of the ramifications. Therefore, periodic wireless testing to spot unofficial access points is needed.

Adding 802.11-based wireless access points (AP) to networks increases overall convenience for users, mostly because of the new mobility that is possible. Whether using handheld wireless PDA devices, laptop computers, or the newly emerging wireless voice over IP telephones, users are now able to flexibly collaborate outside of the office confines—ordinarily within the building and within range of an AP—while still remaining connected to network-based resources. To enable wireless access, an inexpensive wireless access point can be procured and plugged into the network. Communication takes place from the unwired device to the AP. The AP serves (usually) as a bridge to the wired network.

The problem with this from a security perspective is that allowing the addition of one or more AP units onto the network infrastructure will likely open a large security hole. Therefore, no matter how secure your wired network is, when you add even one AP with no configured security, basic security, or even what seems to be high security, this is similar to adding a network connection in your parking lot allowing anyone with the right tools and motivation access to your internal network. The implication here is that most APs as originally implemented in the 802.11b/g standard have security that is easily breakable. Security testers should have methods to detect rogue APs that have been added by employees or unauthorized persons. By doing so, these wireless security holes can be examined. The following wireless networking high points discuss some of the issues surrounding security of these systems:

- Wireless-enabled devices (e.g., laptops) can associate with wireless access points or other wireless devices to form a bridged connection to the wired network.
- Without some form of authentication, rogue devices can attach to the wireless network.
- Without some form of encryption, data transferring between the wired and the wireless network can be captured.

With this information, a security tester can test for the effectiveness of wireless security in the environment using specialized tools and techniques as presented here.

To search for rogue (unauthorized) access points, you can use some of the following techniques:

- Use a network vulnerability scanner with signatures that specifically scan for MAC addresses (of the wired port) of vendors that produce AP units, and then attempt to connect to that interface on an HTTP port. If the unit responds, analyze the Web code to determine if it is a Web page related to the management of the AP device. This requires periodic scanning and will leave you vulnerable until the time you have the opportunity to scan again.
- Use a laptop or handheld unit loaded with software that analyzes 802.11x radio frequency (RF) transmissions for SSIDs and WAP wired side MAC addresses that do not belong to the company or are not authorized. Make sure discovery tools pick up all bands and 802.11x types; that is, if you only test for 802.11b, you may miss rogue 802.11a units. This requires periodic scanning by physically walking through the organization's grounds and will leave you vulnerable until the time you have the opportunity to scan again.
- Up and coming solutions allow for authorized APs and wireless clients to detect unauthorized RF transmissions and "squeal" on the rogue access point. This information can be used to automatically disable an infrastructure switch port to which a rogue has connected.

To lock down the enterprise from the possibility of rogue APs, you can do the following:

- Enable MAC address filtering on your infrastructure switches. This technique matches each port to a known MAC address. If someone plugs in an unapproved MAC to a switch port expecting another MAC address, the AP will never be able to join the network from the wired side.

To gauge security effectiveness of authorized APs:

- Discover authorized APs using the tools described herein and ensure they require encryption.
- Ensure discovered APs meet other policy requirements such as the type of authentication (802.1x or other), SSID naming structure, and MAC address filtering.
- Ensure APs have appropriate layer 2 ethernet type filters, layer 3 protocol filters, and layer 4 port filters (to match your configuration procedures) so that untrusted wireless traffic coming into the AP is limited to only that which is needed and required.

Wireless Tools:

- Netstumbler (http://www.netstumbler.com)—Windows software that detects 802.11b information through RF detection including SSID, whether communication is encrypted, and signal strength.
- Kismet (http://www.kismetwireless.net)—Linux software that detects 802.11b and 802.11a information through RF detection including SSID, whether communication is encrypted, and signal strength. It features the ability to rewrite MAC address on select wireless cards.
- Wellenreiter (http://www.remote-exploit.org)—Linux software that detects wireless networks. It runs on Linux-based handheld PDA computers.
- Nessus (http://www.nessus.org)—Linux software for vulnerability assessment that includes 30 plus signatures to detect WAP units.
- Airsnort (http://airsnort.shmoo.com)—Linux software that passively collects wireless frames and exploiting WEP weakness, derives the WEP.

War Dialing

War dialing attempts to locate unauthorized, also called rogue, modems connected to computers that are connected to networks. Attackers use tools to sequentially and automatically dial large blocks of numbers used by the organization in the hopes that rogue modems will answer and allow them to make a remote asynchronous connection to it. With weak or nonexistent authentication, these rogue modems may serve as a back door into the heart of a network, especially when connected to computers that host remote control applications with lax security. Security testers can use war dialing techniques as a preventative measure and attempt to discover these modems for subsequent elimination. Although modems and war dialing have fallen out of favor in the IT world, a security practitioner still needs to check for the presence of unauthorized modems connected to their network

War Dialing Tools:

Tmap—ftp://ftp.immutec.com/pub/tmap/
THC-Scan—http://freeworld.thc.org/
Phone Sweep—http://www.sandstorm.net/products/phonesweep

War Driving

War driving is the wireless equivalent of war dialing. While war dialing involves checking banks of numbers for a modem, war driving involves traveling around with a wireless scanner looking for wireless access points. Netstumbler was one of the original products that people used for war driving. From the attacker perspective, war driving gives them a laundry list of access points where they can attach to a network and perform attacks. The best ones in a hacker's eye are the unsecured wireless access points that allow unrestricted access to the corporate network. The hacker will not only compromise the corporate network, but will then use the corporate Internet access to launch attacks at other targets which are then untraceable back to the hacker. From a security standpoint, war driving enables you to detect rogue access points in and around your physical locations. Is an unsecured wireless access point that is NOT on your network a security threat to your network? It certainly is. If a user can connect their workstation to an unknown and unsecured network, they introduce a threat to the security of your network.

Penetration Testing

Penetration testing takes vulnerability assessment one step farther. It does not stop at identifying vulnerabilities; it also uses those vulnerabilities to expose other weaknesses in the network. Penetration testing consists of five different phases:

- Phase 1: Preparation
- Phase 2: Information gathering
- Phase 3: Information evaluation and risk analysis
- Phase 4: Active penetration
- Phase 5: Analysis and reporting

Penetration testing also has three different modes. Those modes are:

- White box—tester has complete knowledge of the systems and infrastructure being tested
- Gray box—A hybrid between white and black box. This mode can vary greatly.
- Black box—Assumes no prior knowledge of the systems or infrastructure being tested.

White Box. These testers perform tests with the knowledge of the security and/ or IT staff. They are given physical access to the network and sometimes even a normal username and password. Qualities include:

- Full cooperation of organization
- Planned test times
- Network diagrams and systems configurations are supplied

Pros—You should get good reaction and support from your organization being tested and fixes can occur more rapidly. It is also good to use as a dry run for testing your incident response procedures.

Cons—You may get an inaccurate picture of your network response capabilities because the organization is prepared for the "attack."

Black Box. These testers generally perform unannounced tests that even the security and/or IT staff may not know about. Sometimes these tests are ordered by senior managers to test their staff and the systems for which the staff are responsible. Other times the IT staff will hire covert testers under the agreement that the testers can and will test at any given time, such as four times per year. The object is generally to see what they can see and get into whatever they can get into, without causing harm, of course. Qualities include:

- Play the role of hostile attacker
- Perform testing without warning
- Receive little to no guidance from the organization being tested

Pros—You will get a better overall view of your network without someone "being prepared" for the testing.

Cons—The staff may take the findings personally and show disdain to the testing team and management.

Phase 1: Penetration Testing Goals. Without defined goals, security testing can be a meaningless and costly exercise. The following are examples of some high-level goals for security testing, thereby providing value and meaning for the organization:

- Anyone directly or indirectly sanctioned by the organization's management to perform testing should be doing so for the purpose of identifying vulnerabilities so that they can be quantified and placed in a ranking for subsequent mitigation.
- Since a security test is merely the evaluation of security on a system at a point in time, the results should be documented and compared to the results at other points in time. Analysis that compares results across time periods paints a picture of how well or poorly the systems are being protected across those periods (otherwise known as base lining).
- Security testing can be a form of self audit by the IT staff to prepare them for the "real" audits performed by internal and external auditors.
- In the case of covert testing, testers aim to actually compromise security, penetrate systems, and determine if the IT staff notices the intrusion and an acceptable response has occurred.

It is extremely important as a security practitioner to ensure that you have business support and authorization (in accordance with a penetration testing policy) before conducting a penetration test. It is advisable to get this support and permission in writing before conducting the testing.

Penetration test software tools. Software tools exist to assist in the testing of systems from many angles. Tools help you to interpret how a system functions for the purpose of evaluating its security. This section presents some tools available on the commercial market and in the open source space as a means to the testing end. Do not interpret the listing of a tool as a recommendation for its use. Likewise, just because a tool is not listed does not mean it is not worth considering. Choosing a tool to test a particular aspect is a personal or organizational choice.

Some points to consider regarding the use of software tools in the security testing process:

- Do not let tools drive the security testing. Develop a strategy and pick the right tool mix for discovery and testing based on your overall testing plan.
- Use tools specific to the testing environment. For example, if your aim is to test the application of operating system patches on a particular platform, analyze the available ways you might accomplish this process by seeing what the vendor offers and compare this against third-party tools. Pick tools that offer the best performance tempered with your budget constraints.
- Tool functions often overlap. The features found on one tool may be better than those on another.
- Security testing tools can make mistakes, especially network-based types that rely on circumstantial evidence of vulnerability. Further investigation is often necessary to determine if the tool interpreted an alleged vulnerability correctly.
- Network tools sometimes negatively affect uptime; therefore, these tests should often be scheduled for off-hours execution.
  - By increasing network traffic load
  - By affecting unstable platforms that react poorly to unusual inputs
- Network scanners are affected by network infrastructure.
- Placement of probes is critical.
- When possible, place them on the same segment you are testing so that filtering devices and intrusion detection systems do not alter the results (unless you plan to test how your intrusion detection systems react).
- Be aware that the models for detection of vulnerabilities are inconsistent among different toolsets; therefore, results should be studied and made reasonably consistent among different tools.

Analyzing testing results. It is often easier to understand the testing results by creating a graphical depiction in a simple matrix of vulnerabilities, ratings for each, and an overall vulnerability index derived as the product of vulnerability and system criticality. More complicated matrices may include details describing each vulnerability and sometimes ways to mitigate it or ways to confirm the vulnerability.

Tests should conclude with a report and matrices detailing the following:

- Information derived publicly
- Information derived through social engineering or other covert ways
- Hosts tested and their addresses
- Services found
- Possible vulnerabilities
- Vulnerability ratings for each
- System criticality
- Overall vulnerability rating
- Vulnerabilities confirmation
- Mitigation suggestions

Testers often present findings matrices that list each system and the vulnerabilities found for each with a "high, medium, low" ranking. The intent is to provide the recipient a list of what should be fixed first. The problem with this method is that it does not take into account the criticality of the system in question. You need a way to differentiate among the urgency for fixing "high" vulnerabilities across systems. Therefore, reports should rank true vulnerabilities by seriousness, taking into account how the organization views the asset's value. Systems of high value may have their medium and low vulnerabilities fixed before a system of medium value has any of its vulnerabilities fixed. This criticality is determined by the organization and the reports and matrices should help reflect a suggested path to rectifying the situation. For example, the organization has received a testing report listing the same two high vulnerabilities for a print server and an accounting database server. The database server is certainly more critical to the organization; therefore, its problems should be mitigated before those of the print server.

As another example, assume the organization has assigned a high value to the database server that houses data for the Web server. The Web server itself has no data but is considered medium value. In contrast, the FTP server is merely for convenience and is assigned a low value. A security testing matrix may show several high vulnerabilities for the low-value FTP server. It may also list high vulnerabilities for both the database server and the Web server. The organization will likely be interested in fixing the high vulnerabilities first on the database server, then the Web server, and then the FTP server. This level of triage is further complicated by trust and access between systems. If the Web server gets the new pages and content from the FTP server, this may increase the priority of the FTP server issues over that of the usually low-value FTP server issues.

Phase 2: Reconnaissance and Network Mapping Techniques. Basic security testing activities include reconnaissance and network mapping.

Reconnaissance—collecting information about the organization from publicly available sources, social engineering, and low-tech methods. This information forms the test attack basis by providing useful information to the tester.

Network mapping—collecting information about the organization's Internet connectivity and available hosts by (usually) using automated mapping software tools. In the case of internal studies, the internal network architecture of available systems is mapped. This information further solidifies the test attack basis by providing even more information to the tester about the services running on the network and is often the step before vulnerability testing, which is covered in the next section.

Note: Security testing is an art. This means that different IT security practitioners have different methods for testing. This chapter attempts to note the highlights to help you differentiate among the various types and provides information on tools that assist in the endeavor. Security testing is an ethical responsibility and the techniques should never be used for malice. This information on tools is presented for the purpose of helping you spot weaknesses in your systems or the systems you are authorized to test so that they may be improved.

Reconnaissance. Often reconnaissance is needed by a covert penetration tester who has *not* been granted regular access to perform a cooperative test. These testers are challenged with having little to no knowledge of the system and must collect it from other sources to form the basis of the test attack.

Reconnaissance is necessary for these testers because they likely have no idea what they will be testing at the commencement of the test. Their orders are usually "see what you can find and get into but do not damage anything."

Once you think you know what should be tested based on the information you have collected, always check with the persons who have hired you for the test to ensure that the systems you intend to penetrate are actually owned by the organization. Doing otherwise may put delicate systems in harms way or the tester may test something not owned by the organization ordering the test (leading to possible legal repercussions). These parameters should be defined before the test.

Social Engineering and Low-Tech Reconnaissance. Social engineering is an activity that involves the manipulation of persons or physical reconnaissance to get information for use in exploitation or testing activities. Low-tech reconnaissance uses simple technical means to obtain information.

Before attackers or testers make an attempt on your systems, they can learn about the target using low-technology techniques such as:

■ Directly visit a target's Web server and search through it for information.
■ View a Web page's source for information about what tools might have been used to construct or run it.
■ Employee contact information.
■ Corporate culture information to pick up internally used "lingo" and product names.
■ Business partners.
■ "Googling" a target. "Googling" a target refers to the reconnaissance activity whereby an attacker uses search engines that have previously indexed a target

site. The attacker can search for files of a particular type that may contain information they can use for further attacks. Google and other search engines can be very powerful tools to a cracker because of the volume of data they are able to organize. Example: Search a particular Web site for spreadsheet files containing the word "employee" or "address" or "accounting."

- Make sure that Web servers are configured correctly and require authentication to access private information.
- Dumpster diving—Retrieving improperly discarded computer media and paper records for gleaning private information about an organization.
- Computer hard drives and removable media (floppies, CDs, etc.) thrown away or sold without properly degaussing to remove all private information.
- Equipment (routers, switches, and specialized data processing devices) discarded without configuration data removed without a trace.
- Shoulder surfing—Furtively collecting information (e.g., someone else's password)
- Social engineering using the telephone—Attackers often pose as an official technical support person or fellow employee and attempt to build a rapport with a user through small talk. The attacker may ask for the user's assistance with (false) troubleshooting "tests" aimed at helping the attacker collect information about the system. If the attacker finds a particularly "helpful" user, he might be bold enough to ask for their username and password because "we've been having trouble with the router gateway products interfacing with the LDAP directories where your username and password are stored and we think it is getting corrupted as it passes over the network, so if you could just tell me what it is that would be great," or some such nonsense aimed at gaining the user's confidence. The other possible scenarios that can be used with social engineering to gain information are only limited by your imagination.
- Usenet Searches—Usenet postings can give away information about a company's internal system design and problems that exist within systems. For example: "I need advice on my firewall. It is an XYZ brand system and I have it configured to do this, that, and the other thing. Can anyone help me?— signed joe@big_company_everyone_knows.com"

Mid-Tech Reconnaissance

Whois Information. Mid-tech reconnaissance includes several ways to get information that can be used for testing.

Whois is a system that records Internet registration information, including the company that owns the domain, administrative contacts, technical contacts, when the record of domain ownership expires, and DNS servers authoritative for maintaining host IP addresses and their associated friendly names for the domains you are testing. With this information, you can use other online tools to "dig" for information about the servers visible on the Internet without ever sending a single probing packet at the Internet connection. The contact information provided by Whois can also be used for social engineering and war dialing.

The following are example attacks:

- Using Whois, collect information about DNS servers authoritative for maintaining host IP addresses for a particular domain. Use the tools like those found at http://www.samspade.org to dig for information about hosts and IP addresses associated with the domain.
- Using Whois, identify the administrative contact and his telephone number. Use social engineering on that person or security-unaware staff at the main telephone number to obtain unauthorized information.
- Using Whois, identify the technical contact and her area code and exchange (telephone number). Using *war dialing* software against the block of phone numbers in that exchange, you attempt to make an unauthorized connection with a modem for the purpose of gaining backdoor entry to the system.

There are many sources for Whois information and tools, including:

- http://www.internic.net
- http://www.networksolutions.com
- http://www.samspade.org (includes other tools as well)

DNS Zone Transfers. In an effort to discover the names and types of servers operating inside or outside a network, attackers may attempt zone transfers from DNS servers. A zone transfer is a special type of query directed at a DNS server that asks the server for the entire contents of its zone (the domain which it serves). Information that is derived is only useful if the DNS server is authoritative for that domain. To find a DNS server authoritative for a domain, Whois search results often provide this information. Internet DNS servers will often restrict which servers are allowed to perform transfers but internal DNS servers usually do not have these restrictions.

Secure systems should lock down DNS. Testers should see how the target does this by keeping the following in mind:

- Attackers will attempt zone transfers; therefore, configure DNS's to restrict zone transfers to only approved hosts.
- Attackers will look for host names that may give out additional information—accountingserver.bigfinancialcompany.com.
- Avoid using Host Information Records (HINFO) when possible. HINFO is the Host Information Record of a DNS entry. It is strictly informational in nature and serves no function. It is often used to declare the computer type and operating system of a host.

■ Use a split DNS model with internal DNS and external DNS servers. Combining internal and external functions on one server is potentially dangerous. Internal DNS will serve the internal network and can relay externally bound queries to the external DNS servers that will do the lookup work by proxy. Incoming Internet-based queries will only reveal external hosts because the external hosts only know these addresses.

■ There are a variety of free programs available that will resolve DNS names, attempt zone transfers, and perform a reverse lookup of a specified range of IPs. Major operating systems also include the "nslookup" program, which can also perform these operations.

Network Mapping. Network mapping is a process that "paints the picture" of which hosts are up and running externally or internally and what services are available on the system. Commonly, you may see mapping in the context of external host testing and enumeration in the context of internal host testing, but this is not necessarily ironclad, and mapping and enumeration often seem to be used interchangeably. They essentially accomplish similar goals and the terms can be used in similar ways.

When performing mapping of any kind, the tester should limit the mapping to the scope of the project. Testers may be given a range of IP addresses to map, so the testers should limit the query to that range. Overt and covert testing usually includes network mapping, which is the activity that involves techniques to discover the following:

■ Which hosts are up and running or "alive"?
■ What is the general topology of the network (how are things interconnected)?
■ What ports are open and serviceable on those hosts?
■ What applications are servicing those ports?
■ What operating system is the host running?

Mapping is the precursor to vulnerability testing and usually defines what will be tested more deeply at that next stage. For example, consider a scenario where you discover that a host is listening on TCP port 143. This probably indicates the host is running application services for the IMAP mail service. Many IMAP implementations have vulnerabilities. During the network mapping phase, you learn that host 10.1.2.8 is listening on this port but you tend not to learn which IMAP implementation it is. IMAP vendor X may have an ironclad implementation whereas IMAP vendor Z's system may be full of bugs and vulnerabilities. Network mapping may provide insight about the operating system the host is running which may in turn narrow the possible IMAP applications. For example, it is unlikely that the Microsoft Exchange 2000 IMAP process will be running on a Solaris computer; therefore, if network mapping shows a host with telltale Solaris "fingerprints" as well as indications that the host is listening on TCP port 143, the IMAP server is probably not MS Exchange. As such, when you are later exploring vulnerabilities, you can likely eliminate Exchange IMAP vulnerabilities for this host.

Mapping results can be compared to security policy to discover rogue or unauthorized services that appear to be running. For example, an organization may periodically run mapping routines to match results with what should be expected. If more services are running than one would expect to be running, the systems may have been accidentally misconfigured (therefore opening up a service not approved in the security policy) or the host(s) may have been compromised.

When performing mapping, make sure you are performing the mapping on a host range owned by the organization. For example, suppose an nslookup DNS domain transfer for bobs-italianbookstore.com showed a mail server at 10.2.3.70 and a Web server at 10.19.40.2. Assuming you do not work for bobs-italianbookstore.com and do not have intimate knowledge of their systems, you might assume that they have two Internet connections. In a cooperative test, the best course of action is to check with their administrative staff for clarification. They may tell you that the mail is hosted by another company and that it is outside of the scope of the test. However, the Web server is a host to be tested. You should ask which part of the 10.0.0.0 bobsbookstore.com controls. Let us assume they control the class-C 10.19.40.0. Therefore, network mapping of 10.19.40.1 through 10.19.40.254 is appropriate and will not interfere with anyone else's operations. Even though only one host is listed in the DNS, there may be other hosts up and running.

Depending on the level of stealth required (i.e., to avoid detection by IDS systems or other systems that will "notice" suspected activity if a threshold for certain types of communication is exceeded), network mapping may be performed very slowly over long periods of time. Stealth may be required for covert penetration tests.

Network mapping can involve a variety of techniques for probing hosts and ports. Several common techniques are listed below:

- ICMP echo requests (ping)—If you ping a host and it replies, it is alive (i.e., up and running). This test does not show what individual services are running. Be aware that many networks block incoming echo requests. If the requests are blocked and you ping a host and it does not reply, you have no way of knowing if it is actually running or not because the request is blocked before it gets to the destination.
- TCP Connect scan—A connect scan can be used to discover TCP services running on a host even if ICMP is blocked. This type of scan is considered "noisy" (noticeable to logging and intrusion detection systems) because it goes all the way through the connection process. This basic service discovery scan goes all the way through a TCP session setup by sending a SYN packet to a target, receiving the SYN/ACK from the target when the port is listening, then sending a final ACK back to the target to establish the connection. At this point, the test host is "connected" to the target. Eventually the

connection is torn down because the tester's goal is not to communicate with the port, but only to discover whether it is available.

- TCP SYN scan—SYN scanning can be used to discover TCP services running on a host even if ICMP is blocked. SYN scanning is considered less noisy than connect scans. It is referred to as "half-open" scanning because unlike a connect scan (above), you do not open a full TCP connection. Your test host directs a TCP SYN packet on a particular port as if it were going to open a real TCP connection to the target host. A SYN/ACK from the target indicates the host is listening on that port. An RST from the target indicates that it is not listening on that port. If a SYN/ACK is received, the test host immediately sends an RST to tear down the connection to conserve resources on both the test and target host sides. Firewalls often detect and block these scan attempts.

- TCP FIN scan—FIN scanning can be used to discover TCP services running on a host even if ICMP is blocked. FIN scanning is considered a stealthy way to discover if a service is running. The test host sends a TCP packet with the FIN bit on to a port on the target host. If the target responds with an RST packet, you may assume that the target host is not using the port. If the host does not respond, it may be using the port that was probed. Caveats to this technique are Microsoft, Cisco, BSDI, HP/UX, MVS, and IRIX-based hosts that implement their TCP/IP software stacks in ways not defined by the standard. These hosts may not respond with an RST when probed by a FIN. However, if you follow up a nonreply to one of these systems with, for example, a SYN scan to that port and the host replies, you have determined that the host is listening on the port being tested and a few possible operating systems (see OS fingerprinting).

- TCP XMAS scan—XMAS scans are similar to a FIN scan (and similarly stealthy) but they additionally turn on the URG (urgent) and PSH (push) flags. The goal of this scan is the same as a TCP FIN scan. The additional flags might make a packet be handled differently than a standard packet so you might see different results.

- TCP NULL scan—NULL scans are similar to a FIN scan (also stealthy) but they turn off all flags. The NULL scan is similar to the others noted above; however, by turning off all TCP flags (which should never occur naturally), the packet might be handled differently and you may see a different result.

- UDP scans—A UDP scan determines which UDP service ports are opened on a host. The test machine sends a UDP packet on a port to the target. If the target sends back an ICMP port unreachable message, the target does not use that port. A potential problem with this methodology is the case where a router or firewall at the target network does not allow ICMP port unreachable messages to leave the network, making the target network appear as if all UDP ports are open (because no ICMP messages are getting back to the test host). Another problem is that many systems limit the number of ICMP messages allowed per second, which can make for a very slow scanning rate.

Available mapping tools include:

■ Nmap—http://www.insecure.org
■ Solarwinds—http://www.solarwinds.net
■ Superscan—http://www.foundstone.com
■ Lanspy—http://lantricks.com/lanspy

Another technique for mapping a network is commonly known as "firewalking," which uses traceroute techniques to discover which services a filtering device like a router or firewall will allow through. These tools generally function by transmitting TCP and/or UDP packets on a particular port with a time to live (TTL) equal to at least one greater than the targeted router or firewall. If the target allows the traffic, it will forward the packets to the next hop. At that point, the traffic will expire as it reaches the next hop and an ICMP_TIME_EXCEEDED message will be generated and sent back out of the gateway to the test host. If the target router or firewall does not allow the traffic, it will drop the packets and the test host will not see a response.

Available firewalking tools include:

■ Hping—http://www.hping.org/
■ Firewalk—http://www.packetfactory.net/projects/firewalk/

By all means, do not forget about the use of basic built-in operating system commands for discovering hosts and routes. Basic built-in and other tools include:

■ Traceroute (Windows calls this tracert)—Uses ICMP or TCP depending on the implementation of a path to a host or network.
■ Ping—See if a host is alive using ICMP echo request messages.
■ Telnet—Telnetting to a particular port is a quick way to find out if the host is servicing that port in some way.
■ Whois—Command line Whois can provide similar information to the Web-based Whois methods previously discussed.
■ System Fingerprinting. System fingerprinting refers to testing techniques used by port scanners and vulnerability analysis software that attempt to identify the operating system in use on a network device and the versions of services running on the host. Why is it important to identify a system? By doing so, you know what you are dealing with and later on, what vulnerabilities are likely for that system. As mentioned previously, Microsoft-centric vulnerabilities are (usually) not going to show up on Sun systems and vice versa.

Phase 3: Information Evaluation and Risk Analysis. Before active penetration, you need to evaluate our findings and perform risk analysis on the results to determine which hosts or services you are going to try and actively penetrate. It is not a good use of time to perform an active penetration on every host that you have identified in Phase 2. You must also identify the potential business risks associated with performing a penetration test against particular hosts. You can and probably will interrupt normal business processes if you perform a penetration test on a production system. The business leaders need to be made aware of that fact, and they need to be involved in making the decision on which devices to actively penetrate.

Phase 4: Active Penetration. This bears repeating. Think twice before attempting to exploit a possible vulnerability that may harm the system. For instance, if the system might be susceptible to a buffer overflow attack, it might be enough to identify the vulnerability without actually exploiting it and bringing down the system. Weigh the benefits of succinctly identifying vulnerabilities against potentially crashing the system.

Here are some samples:

- Vulnerability testing shows that a Web server may be vulnerable to crashing if it is issued a very long request with dots (i.e., ../../../../../../../../../ 1000 times). You can either try to actually crash the server using the technique (although this may have productivity loss consequences) or alternatively and perhaps for the better you can note it for further investigation, perhaps on a test server. Make sure you have permission before attempting this type of actual exploitation.
- Vulnerability testing shows that a UNIX host has a root account with the password set to root. You can easily test this find to determine whether this is a false positive.
- Vulnerability testing shows that a router may be susceptible to an SSH attack. You can either try the attack with permission or note it for further investigation.

Penetration Testing High-Level Steps

The following outline provides a high-level view of the steps that could be taken to exploit systems during a penetration test. It is similar in nature to a vulnerability test but goes further to perform an exploit.

1. Obtain a network address (usually center on internal testing when you are physically onsite)—With the advent DHCP on the network, a tester can often plug in and get an IP address right away. DHCP assigned addresses usually come with gateway and name server addresses. If the tester does not get a DHCP address, the system may be setup for static addresses. You can

sniff the network for communications that detail the segment you are on and guess at an unused address.

2. Reconnaissance—Verify target information
   - DNS information obtained via DHCP
   - DNS zone transfer when allowed by the server
   - Whois
   - Browsing an internal domain
   - Using Windows utilities to enumerate servers
   - Pings sweeps
   - Traceroute
   - Port scans (TCP connect, SYN scans, etc.)
   - OS fingerprinting
   - Banner grabbing
   - Unix RPC discovery

3. Target vulnerability analysis and enumeration
   - Using techniques that are less likely to be logged or reported in an IDS system (i.e., less "noisy" techniques) evaluate the vulnerability of ports on a target.
   - For NT systems, gather user, group, and system information with null sessions (NT), "net" commands, nltest utility.
   - For UNIX systems, gather RPC information.

4. Exploitation—Identify and exploit the vulnerabilities
   - Buffer overflows
   - Brute force
   - Password cracking
   - Vulnerability chaining
   - Data access

Phase 5: Analysis and Reporting. As with any security testing, documentation of the test, analysis of the results, and reporting those results to the proper managers are imperative. There are many different methods that can be utilized when reporting the results of a vulnerability scan. A comprehensive report will have separate sections for each management/technical level involved in the test. An overview of the results with a summary of the findings might be ideal for management, while a technical review of specific findings with remediation recommendations would be appropriate for the device administrators. As with any report that outlines issues, it is always best to offer solutions for fixing the issues as well as reporting their existence.

Penetration Testing Example—NT Host Enumeration Example

- Gain access to the network.
- Enumerate NT operating system details.

- Identify domain controllers for the purpose of attempting password file access.
- Attempt NULL connections to servers to enumerate vital information.
- Attempt administrator access based on the user list obtained.
- If administrator access is obtained, use utilities to obtain the password file.
- Crack the password file.
- Explore other trusted domains using password derived from the crack.

This example shows an overview of a Microsoft Windows penetration test. The premise is that security consultants have been hired by the CIO to perform a penetration test to discern whether reasonable security controls are in place. The IT staff is not aware that this covert test is scheduled. Their goal is to attempt access on the NT domain system. They are not supposed to use penetration techniques likely to damage data or systems. The following steps show how the testers might go about their task. Keep in mind that this is an example and that conditions might be different in your situation.

1. The testers arrive at the organization's headquarters and sign in with physical security. They make small talk and claim they are from an office in another city. The testers are granted access and make themselves at home in a conference room.
2. They plug into the LAN ports. One of two ports is live. The PC on the live port receives a DHCP IP address along with domain name information, gateway, WINS, and DNS server addresses.
3. Using built-in Windows commands and NT Resource Kit commands, the tester begins to gather useful network information and identify potential targets. By design, Windows systems offer up rich content about the details of systems on the network. This detail, while used for normal operation, can also be used against the servers. Since many of the net commands found on Windows systems do not require authenticated access, information can be obtained from any NT workstation on the network. The tester identifies NT domains (this also came as part of the DHCP address details but this command shows *all* the domains in the domain browser list) using the built-in net command:

```
C:\sectools>net view /domain
Domain
---------------------------------------------------------
HQ
HQ-ACCOUNTING
WORKGROUP
```

The tester now identifies computers belonging to the HQ domain specifically:

```
C:\sectools>net view /domain:HQ
Server Name                Remark
-------------------------------------------------
\\CAD                      Administrators remarks
\\OFFICESERV               Application server
\\RND                      Research Server
\\IT                       Server
\\IT2                      Server
```

Identify HQ domain controllers with the Windows resource kit "nltest" utility. Note that nltest includes the means to obtain a huge array of domain information:

```
C:\sectools>nltest /dclist:HQ
```

Get list of DCs in domain 'HQ' from '\\OFFICESERV '.

```
officeserv.hq.com [PDC] [DS] Site: Default-First-Site-Name
```

Once the available systems in the domain are identified, the tester will select potential targets usually based on their name and whether they are domain controllers. The tester can generally determine the IP address or name of the target server using the following ping technique if a name server (DNS or WINS) was specified as part of the DHCP address information:

```
C:\sectools>ping officeserv

Pinging officeserv.hq.com [10.90.50.5] with 32 bytes of data:

Reply from 10.90.50.5: bytes=32 time<1ms TTL=128
Reply from 10.90.50.5: bytes=32 time<1ms TTL=128
Reply from 10.90.50.5: bytes=32 time<1ms TTL=128
Reply from 10.90.50.5: bytes=32 time<1ms TTL=128

Ping statistics for 10.90.50.5:
Packets: Sent = 4, Received = 4, Lost = 0 (0% loss),
Approximate round trip times in milliseconds:
Minimum = 0ms, Maximum = 0ms, Average = 0ms
```

The tester can enumerate the role of server in the domain using the "netdom" tool found in the Windows resource kit. In this example, the tester queries for the role of member server RND and its relationship to its domain controller OFFICESERV:

```
C:\sectools>netdom query \\rnd
NetDom 1.8 @1997-98.
Querying domain information on computer \\RND...
```

```
Computer \\RND is a member of HQ.
Searching PDC for domain HQ...
Found PDC \\OFFICESERV
Connecting to \\OFFICESERV...
Verifying secure channel on \\RND...
Secure channel established successfully with \\officeserv.
hq.com for domain HQ.
```

The tester decides to target the domain controller because it maintains the password file (also known as the SAM file) for the entire domain. To get detailed information from the target server, the tester has to, at a minimum, establish a "null session" to the server. A null session is an anonymous, nonauthenticated connection to a Windows host. Once the connection is established, detailed information about the system can be obtained. Note that support for null sessions can be disabled, which makes the job of exploiting the host more difficult.

```
C:\sectools>net use \\officeserv\ipc$"/user:"
The command completed successfully.
```

With an established null session, the tester can use a tool like SomarSoft's DumpSec to derive vital domain controller information, including domain user names, password policy information, permissions, and trusted domains. DumpSec allows for the retrieval of information using an anonymous connection to a computer including the following:

- "Dumping" of user names to identify administrators, accounts used for application services, and other user accounts
- Detailed user information including last logon, password last changed times, account status, RAS permissions, SID, etc.
- Group information including which ones exist and which users are contained within them
- File permissions including user and group permissions and file level auditing
- Registry permissions including user and group permissions and key level auditing
- Share permissions including user and group permissions for existing shares

DumpSec allows for the retrieval of information using an administrator connection to a computer including the following:

- Policies including account policy, trusts, audit policy, replication, and null sessions
- Rights including detailed rights assigned to groups and individuals
- Services including which services are installed and running on the host

Once all user information is enumerated via DumpSec (remember that at this point the tester only has an anonymous connection to the target), the tester terminates the null session.

```
C:\sectools>net use \\officeserv\ipc$ /delete
```

The tester now attempts to logon as administrator (or some other username they learned from DumpSec) and manually guesses passwords for the account on the target domain controller using the "net use" command. If the tester were to target a member server (i.e., a nondomain controller), he would be attempting access on the local user database (SAM) file. Domain-wide SAM files are only resident on domain controllers.

```
C:\sectools>net use \\officeserv\ipc$ * /user:HQ\administrator
Type the password for \\officeserv\ipc$:{password guess 1}
Logon failure: unknown user name or bad password
C:\sectools>net use \\officeserv\ipc$ * /user:HQ\administrator
Type the password for \\officeserv\ipc$:{password guess 2}
Logon failure: unknown user name or bad password

C:\sectools>net use \\officeserv\ipc$ * /user:HQ\administrator
Type the password for \\officeserv\ipc$:{password guess 3}
Logon failure: unknown user name or bad password

C:\sectools>net use \\officeserv\ipc$ * /user:HQ\administrator
Type the password for \\officeserv\ipc$:{password guess 4}
Logon failure: unknown user name or bad password
```

Administrator accounts do not normally have a lockout feature that deactivates the account if too many bad logon attempts are made. However, the "passprop" utility adds this function and forces administrators to go to the host's console to unlock the administrator account. The tester, who does not have physical server access, checks to see if the passprop utility is being used to lock the administrator account remotely if excessive bad logon attempts are made. Using DumpSec via another anonymous IPC$ connection, she determines whether the administrator account has been locked after two to six attempts. If it is not, she again deletes the IPC$ connection to the server and begins using automated password guessing tools.

Using Secure Networks Inc.'s NAT (NetBIOS Auditing Tool—there are others like this including Brutus and SMBGrind), the tester attempts to guess passwords in an automated fashion by specifying one or more administrator accounts learned from DumpSec. Assuming that at least one of those accounts has a weak password, the tester will learn the password and get privileged access. The section in this chapter—Password Testing—explains this activity more fully.

```
C:\sectools>nat -o <output_file> -u <user_list> -p <password_
list> <ip_address>
```

Next the tester uses the "pwdump3" utility to make an administrative-level connection to the host with the administrator credentials learned from cracking activities and extracts the SAM file out of the server's running memory (the SAM file itself is locked during operation because it is always in use). Pwdump3 logs onto the host, installs itself as a service, turns itself on, grabs the information from memory, copies it back to the tester's host, stops itself from running in host memory, and uninstalls itself.

```
C:\sectools\pwdump3v2>pwdump3 officeserv sam-hashes.txt
administrator
pwdump3 (rev 2) by Phil Staubs, e-business technology, 23 Feb
2001 Copyright 2001 e-business technology, Inc.
```

This program is a free software based on pwpump2 by Todd Sabin under the GNU General Public License Version 2 (GNU GPL); you can redistribute it and/or modify it under the terms of the GNU GPL, as published by the Free Software Foundation. NO WARRANTY, EXPRESSED OR IMPLIED, IS GRANTED WITH THIS PROGRAM. Please see the COPYING file included with this program (also available at http://www.ebiz-tech.com/pwdump3) and the GNU GPL for further details.

```
Please enter the password >*********

Completed.
```

Now that the tester has the domain controller's SAM file, he can use a password cracking utility like John the Ripper or L0phtcrack to crack the passwords for many of the users. The following is the contents of the hash file obtained by pwdump3:

```
Administrator:500:CFB4021690DA871A944E2DF489A880E4:179BE7084BB
B5FFA2D96AB59F6AA6D96:::
bill:1002:E52CAC67419A9A22F96F275E1115B16F:E22E04519AA757D12F1
219C4F31252F4:::
Guest:501:NO PASSWORD*********************:NO
PASSWORD*********************:::
IUSR_HQ:1004:E0C510199CC66ABDAAD3B435B51404EE:352DFE551D62459B
20349B78A21A2F37:::
mary:1001:FB169B026D5B9DE72CFBD46F2C07EC6B:6AD16A97C219C6DB8AA
AAC8236F769E0:::
roger:1003:62B4F4E39B2EF8637F8E43D4EB012C81:A4D9F515587778C30F
31ACD76844AE56:::
```

While the password cracker is running, the test team can access this host and other hosts with trust relationships and look around for "interesting" data. Within a few hours, 40–90% of the passwords in the SAM file are likely to be cracked, providing access from host to host in any allowable user context. Perhaps one of the most damaging exploitation activities is accessing an organizational leader's e-mail with their user credentials learned from the SAM file-cracking activity.

Penetration Testing Example: Closing Notes. Penetration testers will often use the information learned to perform further host and domain exploitation. Often when one administrator or equivalent account falls, it is only a matter of time before they all fall. Furthermore, any trusting domain of the compromised domain can in turn be compromised. Access at this level allows a penetration tester access to potentially sensitive system files and data files. It allows for the installation of backdoor programs like NetCat and VNC (among others) for continued easy access into hosts thought to be secure.

Sample Questions

1. A security audit is best defined as:
   a. A covert series of tests designed to test network authentication, hosts, and perimeter security
   b. A technical assessment that measures how well an organization uses strategic security policies and tactical security controls for protecting its information assets
   c. Employing Intrusion Detection Systems to monitor anomalous traffic on a network segment and logging attempted break-ins
   d. Hardening systems before deploying them on the corporate network
2. Why is it important for organizations to have a security framework?
   a. To show that the organization has exercised "due care"
   b. So they can adhere to regulations developed by an institutional or governmental body
   c. To avoid possible legal action or financial penalties
   d. All of the above
3. Creating Incident Response policies for an organization would be an example of an:
   a. Administrative Control
   b. Technical Control
   c. Physical Control
   d. Logical Control
4. Which of the following would be a good example of a host isolation security control?
   a. Encrypting syslog activity on the network
   b. Applying the most recent patches to a system
   c. Installing antivirus on a local machine
   d. Setting up a DMZ between the public and private network

5. What is the most important reason to analyze event logs from multiple sources?
   a. They will help you obtain a more complete picture of what is happening on your network and how you go about addressing the problem.
   b. The log server could have been compromised.
   c. Because you cannot trust automated scripts to capture everything.
   d. To prosecute the attacker once he can be traced.
6. Security testing does not include which of the following activities?
   a. Performing a port scan to check for up and running services
   b. Gathering publicly available information
   c. Counterattacking systems determined to be hostile
   d. Posing as technical support to gain unauthorized information
7. Why is system fingerprinting part of the security testing process?
   a. Because it is one of the easiest things to determine when performing a security test.
   b. It shows what vulnerabilities the system may be subject to.
   c. It shows the auditor whether a system has been hardened.
   d. It tells an attacker than a system is automatically insecure.
8. What is the difference between vulnerability and penetration testing?
   a. Vulnerability testing attempts to exploit a weakness found from penetration testing.
   b. Penetration testing attempts to exploit a weakness found in vulnerability testing.
   c. Vulnerability testing uses scripts to find weaknesses while penetration testing uses a GUI-based program.
   d. Penetration testing is used to uncover vulnerabilities without harming the system
9. The following are benefits to performing vulnerability testing except:
   a. They allow an organization to study the security posture of the organization.
   b. They identify and prioritize mitigation activities.
   c. They can compare security postures over a period of time when done consistently.
   d. It has the potential to crash the network or host.
10. What is the primary purpose of testing an Intrusion Detection System?
    a. To observe that the IDS is observing and logging an appropriate response to a suspicious activity.
    b. To determine if the IDS is capable of discarding suspect packets.
    c. To analyze processor utilization to verify whether hardware upgrades are necessary.
    d. To test whether the IDS can log every possible event on the network.
11. Which of the following is true regarding computer intrusions?
    a. Covert attacks such as a Distributed Denial of Service (DDOS) attack harm public opinion of an organization.

b. Overt attacks are easier to defend against because they can be readily identified.

c. Network Intrusion Detection Systems (NIDS) help mitigate computer intrusions by notifying personnel in real-time.

d. Covert attacks are less effective because they take more time to accomplish.

12. The main difference in real-time versus non-real-time monitoring is:

a. Non-real-time monitoring is not as effective as real-time monitoring.

b. Real-time monitoring provides a way to immediately identify disallowed behavior, while non-real-time monitoring can be used to trace an attacker's activity.

c. Non-real-time monitoring is more effective in catching overt activity.

d. Real-time monitoring is more effective in catching covert activity.

13. Why is security monitoring necessary?

a. Because logging activity can show the steps an attacker used to modify or gain access to a system.

b. Log files can be correlated to form a timeline of events to be used in a forensic investigation.

c. Log files can show deviance from a security policy.

d. All of the above.

14. NIDS and HIDS generally employ the following techniques except:

a. Using a database of known attack signatures and comparing that to current traffic flow

b. Analyzing traffic flow to determine unusual activity

c. Monitoring for specific file changes by referencing known good file sets

d. Counterattacking a system to cut-off communication and prevent possible damage

15. Why are secure methods of logging system or device data important?

a. The hosts storing the log files are often easily compromised.

b. Common transport methods of log files are insecure and can be easily sniffed.

c. Unencrypted and unprotected log files are easily altered.

d. Both b and c.

Chapter 5

Networks and Telecommunications

Eric Waxvik and Samuel Chun

Contents

In today's global marketplace, the ability to communicate securely with others is a mandatory requirement. The networks and telecommunications domain encompasses the network structure, transmission methods, transport formats and security measures used to maintain the integrity, availability, authentication, and confidentiality of the transmitted information over both private and public communication networks.

The Systems Security Certified Practitioner (SSCP) candidate is expected to demonstrate an understanding of communications and network security as it relates to data and telecommunications in local area and wide area networks; remote access; Internet, intranet, and extranet configurations; use of firewalls, network equipment, and protocols such as TCP/IP, VPNs, and techniques for preventing and detecting network-based attacks. Key areas of knowledge include:

- Understand networks
  - OSI and TCP/IP models
  - Architecture and relationships (e.g., address translation, defense-in-depth, IP addressing)
  - Protocols
  - Admission control (e.g., NAC, remediation, quarantine)
- Understand telecommunications
  - Technology (e.g., VoIP, facsimile, PSTN)
  - Vulnerabilities

- Understand remote access
  - Methods
  - Technology (e.g., thin client, SSL/VPN)
  - Vulnerabilities
- Understand firewalls and proxies
  - Methods (e.g., application filtering, packet filtering)
  - Types (e.g., host based, stateful)
  - Vulnerabilities
- Understand wireless technology
  - Protocols (e.g., WPA, WPA2, TKIP)
  - Technology (e.g., Bluetooth, RFID, 802.11)
  - Vulnerabilities

Introduction to Networks and Telecommunications

This chapter is not intended to be a basic introduction in data communications; rather, we will be looking at all of the elements of a data network to see what security is, or is not, inherently provided (versus just another review of networking basics).

It is important to note that many organizations are pursuing a redundancy scenario for constant communications. More and more, an organization's livelihood rests on these networks and telecommunications, so it is important to know how that redundancy can affect the organization's security posture.

In the past, some of the people who needed their communication lines open all of the time would rather have their firewalls fail *open* and allow all traffic, good and bad, to pass, rather than fail *closed* and not pass any traffic. This decision was based on the company's risk acceptance policies. In today's communication arena, enhanced capabilities are available to allow firewalls to fail over from one firewall to another with times ranging from minutes to fractions of a second. There are also load-balancing technologies available that spread the load across many firewalls.

High availability and redundancy are not just limited to firewalls; internal and external network connections can also be set up in a redundant capacity. Another important redundancy option is having a completely redundant remote site, so in case of an emergency all of your network functionality and security are already in place. This capacity should be an integral part of your disaster recovery plans.

In this section, we will take a look at the following elements of a data communication network:

- OSI Model
- Network Topology
- Network Devices
- Network Access Methods

The Basic OSI Model: Its Security Strengths and Weaknesses

The International Organization for Standardization (ISO) set out to simplify communications by creating standards for networking protocol/hardware and software. The model they created—the Open System Interconnect (OSI) model—is actually a framework from which protocols can be created. Security was not built into the base model, although security recommendations were made for each of the layers. The OSI model defines how communication will work across the network with the intention of ensuring its success.

In reality, this model is used mainly as a reference model. While some OSI networks were created, most of today's common protocols are actually built against a different model such as the U.S. Department of Defense (DoD) TCP/IP model or the B-ISDN model. We will look at the TCP/IP model later.

Let us take a quick look at each of the layers of the OSI model. While looking at each layer of the model, be sure to consider its basic job and the security that is inherent at that layer or what can be added to enhance the security of your network.

The layers of the OSI model are:

■ Application
■ Presentation
■ Session
■ Transport
■ Network
■ Data Link
■ Physical

The OSI model is intended as a representation for how we build and use a network and its resources.

Application Layer

Basic Job: Manages program requests as needed to access a remote system.

Inherent Security: None

Added Security Features: Encryption, Digital Signature, Access Control, Authentication exchange, Traffic Padding, Routing control are all features that the ISO intended as possible add-ons for this layer.

Protocols: FTAM, X.400, Telnet, FTP, SMTP

FTAM—File Transfer and Access Management
FTP—File Transfer Protocol
SMTP—Simple Mail Transfer Protocol

Presentation Layer

Basic Job: Translates data from one format to another if necessary for a system to understand the received text (e.g., ASCII to EBCDIC).

Inherent Security: None

Added Security Features: Encryption and routing control can be added.

Protocols: ASN.1, SSL, and TLS

ASN.1—Abstract Syntax Notation One

SSL—Secure Socket Layer

TLS—Transport Layer Security

Session Layer

Basic Job: Establishes and maintains connection between the local and remote systems. This layer utilizes TCP/IP ports to coordinate communications between cooperating application processes.

Inherent Security: None

Added Security Features: Logins and passwords can be added at the layer.

Protocols: RADIUS, TACACS+

Transport Layer

Basic Job: Provides reliable, transparent data transfers between session entities. Assures end-to-end reliability and integrity through packet sequencing, detecting, and correcting errors and by regulating the data flow.

Inherent Security: Data Integrity

Added Security Features: Encryption, digital signature, authentication exchange, access control are all security features that can be added.

Protocols: TCP, UDP

TCP—Transmission Control Protocol

UDP—User Datagram Protocol

Network Layer

Basic Job: Defines network address and segmentation schemes.

Inherent Security: None

Added Security Features: The address provided at this layer can be utilized by routers, layer 3 switches, etc., to create inclusion or exclusion rules. Encryption, routing control, digital signature, access control, authentication exchange, and traffic padding are all security features that can be added at this layer.

Protocols: X.25, CLNP, IP, ICMP, IGMP

CLNP—Connectionless Network Service

IP—Internet Protocol
ICMP—Internet Control Message Protocol
IGMP—Internet Group Management Protocol

Data Link Layer

Basic Job: Transmits frames across the network links. Utilizes hardware or link layer addresses. This layer can also check data integrity through the use of frame checksums. This layer is commonly left unsecured by network administrators and one worth watching. Examples of layer 2 configurations commonly left unsecured include SNMP, STP, VLAN Trunks, VTP, and basic port-link configurations.

Inherent Security: None

Added Security Features: The address provided at this layer can be used by bridges, switches, and the like to create inclusion and exclusion rules. Encryption and routing control can be added at this layer as well.

Protocols: Frame Relay, 802.3, 802.2, FDDI, PPP, SMDS, HDLC, SLIP, ARP
FDDI—Fiber Distributed Data Interface
PPP—Point to Point Protocol
SMDS—Switched Multi-Megabit Data Service
HDLC —High-Level Data Link Control
SLIP—Serial Line Interface Protocol
ARP—Address Resolution Protocol

Physical Layer

Basic Job: Defines physical and electrical specifications for transmissions (e.g., connector, pin-outs, impedance, resistance). There are two strategies for communications over a physical link—asynchronous and synchronous. During an asynchronous communication, one side simply transmits and the other receives without any negotiations regarding the transmission. During a synchronous transmission, the two transmitting parties prenegotiate the connection at the data link level (one level above in the OSI model) before communications are initiated.

Inherent Security: None

Added Security Features: Encryption, data integrity, routing control, and traffic padding are all security features that can be added at this layer.

Protocols: ATM, SONET, T1, V.35
ATM—Asynchronous Transfer Mode
SONET—Synchronous Optical Network

DoD TCP/IP Model

The DoD TCP/IP protocol model is the basis of most of our LAN technologies today. This protocol stack was created for the DoD, although it has been carried around the world. This model is identical to the ISO OSI model in the lower four layers. The difference is in that layers 5 through 7 (Application, Presentation, and Session) of the OSI model are combined into the application layer (layer 5) in the DoD model.

The layers of the DoD TCP/IP Model are:

■ Application
■ Transport
■ Network
■ Data Link
■ Physical

Network Topologies and Their Security Issues

There are a few commonly implemented network topology schemes. Each scheme has its own native security level and security issues. We will take a look at the following network topologies:

■ Star
■ Bus
■ Ring
■ Point-to-point
■ Full Mesh

Star topology. A star topology, also known as a hub and spoke topology, has a device in the center, and PCs, servers, and such branch out from there. The center device will have a great deal to do with the transmission characteristics of the star topology. The progression of devices that have been used in center of the star topology has gone from hub and bridges to switches and routers.

A weakness of the standard star topology is that it is a single point of failure. If the device at the center of the star fails, then all communication in the star stops. In a modified star configuration, the device in the center of the star has been set up in a redundant configuration. This redundancy can be load balancing, failover, or hot-swapping the device. The last redundancy option requires human intervention to switch the device from the failed device to the backup device.

The fact that there is one device to protect may be either a potential strength or potential weakness of the star topology. If an intruder can get physical access to this device, they can monitor all communications on your network—an obvious weakness. Monitoring all of the communications does not require physical access to the device at the center of the star if the device is a simple hub. The nature of hubs is to rebroadcast all of the information they receive out to all ports. If an attacker has a device off of one of these ports, all of the information passing through the hub will be sent to him as well. This ability to monitor communications at one central point also benefits the security practitioner. It allows for a single point to monitor activity on the network or a single point to place an Intrusion Detection System (IDS) or an Intrusion Prevention System (IPS).

The modified star or the modified hub and spoke are the more common types of network topologies. In this modification, the points of various hubs are interconnected. If all points of all of the hubs are interconnected, this redundant configuration is called *fully meshed*. The fully meshed topology is probably the goal of most network architects. It is the most redundant of all the configurations.

To protect data transmissions from unauthorized viewers, encryption would be a valuable addition to this topology, although it is often considered impractical in most situations today.

Bus topology. Bus topologies have given way to star topologies over the years. The bus topology has the major disadvantage of passing all information down the wire to all connected users. This means that all transmitted traffic by all users is visible to all other users. Cable providers have used this type of bus architecture for their transmission of television signals for years; the result is the use of the same physical infrastructure for their Internet access as well. If you place a packet sniffer on a cable modem connection, you will see all of this data on this shared transmission media. Encryption would be a valuable addition to this topology for that reason, especially when connecting to a head office from a remote office.

Ring topology. A ring topology is similar in nature to the bus topology in that the distribution of information is sent to all users connected to the ring. A ring topology has the advantages of being deterministic (not prone to decreases in bandwidth due to excess traffic) and when deployed as multiple rings (generally in counter rotating fashion) offers decent redundancy. Consequently, they were widely deployed during the 1980s in financial markets especially in banking and ATM systems. Three of the most common types of ring topologies are Synchronous Optical Network (SONET), Fiber Distributed Data Interface (FDDI), and Token Ring. There have been some developments in this type of architecture with high-speed SONET rings. Some types of SONET rings can be self-healing and have some great redundancy features. While FDDI/CDDI (FDDI over copper) and Token Ring are older technologies, they may still be in use today.

Some ring topologies have the security disadvantage of not secluding a conversation to the two involved parties. Anyone connected to the ring can view all traffic on the ring. A security benefit can be gained using encryption. Adding encryption would protect the data transmissions from unauthorized viewers, but this is often considered impractical in most situations today. In a simple ring configuration, a single break in the link shuts down communication completely. Redundancy can be added by having a second ring.

Point-to-point topology. A point-to-point connection is the most secure of the aforementioned topologies. Only the sender and receiver are connected to the line. Although this method is still susceptible to eavesdropping, it is harder to listen in on than the shared media methods. While it may be more secure, it is not always fiscally practical to implement this type of topology to multiple remote sites. Again, it is also possible to increase the security with the use of encryption and firewalls.

If your overall network security is dependent on this point-to-point connection, you introduce several single points of failure. A backup connection that would failover in case of a disaster would solve this issue. A higher level of redundancy could be achieved by using a link through another provider whose initial connection goes through a different Point of Presence (POP) and runs over a completely different backbone. This higher-level solution is often cost prohibitive since most service providers will give you their backup link at a reduced cost. The backup link from the same service provider is also a good solution but not quite as redundant.

Full and partial mesh. A full-mesh network is one where a node in the network is connected to every other node on the same network. The full-mesh network topology offers the greatest level of redundancy and fault tolerance for a network (enhancing the all important availability aspect of the CIA triad). However, the nodes being connected to every other node offers some distinct disadvantages. In general, full-mesh networks are much more costly to deploy and manage due to their complexity. In addition, it can propagate threats much more quickly due to its mesh properties. Consequently, full-mesh networks are generally used for network backbones while endpoints are generally deployed as either point to point or partial mesh to reduce vulnerability, complexity, and cost.

WAN Access and Its Security Issues

Access to the outside world always carries security risks. The challenge is to have enough security to guard your network assets and still be able to maintain full functionality. The balance between security and functionality must be outlined by your risk analysis policy.

We will look at the physical access methods that can be used from the home or the remote office to gain access to the corporate network structure. With all of the connections, you should have a personal firewall and current antivirus on all computers that connect to the network directly. For higher-speed network access that may support multiple computers, a Small Office/Home Office (SOHO)-sized firewall may be a better fit. Many of the SOHO-sized firewalls have extra options available, such as high availability, antivirus scanning capability, wireless access points, or network print servers. While the last two may come with some of the home-based routing solutions, companies that use broadband access may be more concerned with the first two options and with a solution that will serve as a Virtual Private Network (VPN) back to their headquarters.

When dealing with computers that interact in a collision domain, there must be a way for the computers to communicate. A collision domain is like a large courtroom and the people in the courtroom are the computers. To understand someone, you must take your turn to speak. If two people start talking at the same time, neither one can be understood, and they will have to start again. Usually people wait for some period of time and start talking again if the other person has not started talking already. The same type of collision happens in the world of computers on a network. There are a couple of ways to deal with those conflicts to enable computers to communicate better in a collision domain, such as the Carrier Sense Multiple Access methods described below.

Carrier Sense Multiple Access (CSMA). CSMA is a Media Access protocol that simply makes sure that no one else is transmitting (talking in our example) before sending data. This approach is very basic and therefore prone to problems. If two devices try to broadcast and collide, they will often just try again and again with no intelligent way of solving the problem.

Carrier Sense Multiple Access with Collision Avoidance (CSMA/CA). CSMA/CA is a Media Access Control (MAC) protocol that is designed to make sure no other devices are transmitting on the wire at the same time by transmitting a notification of intent to send and then sending the data. If two intents are transmitted at the same time, the result is the same as CSMA. This has an increased degree of complexity and sophistication that will limit the number of collisions and retransmissions.

Carrier Sense Multiple Access with Collision Detection (CSMA/CD). CSMA/CD is another MAC protocol that is designed to detect the collision and stop the transmission for a random period of time before trying again. One hopes that if the wait times are random, then the likelihood of collision is reduced because transmission will probably not happen at the same time. This protocol is a little more complex and requires more sophisticated hardware to operate than the previous protocols. This protocol is commonly used today.

Carrier Sense Multiple Access with Bitwise Arbitration (CSMA/BA). CSMA/BA is an even more complex protocol in which priorities or identification values are provided. When a collision occurs, the device transmitting with the higher priority will be allowed to transmit first. This method is different than CSMA/CD because one can assign higher priorities to critical traffic nodes, without relying on randomness.

Dial-up access/narrowband access. Dial-up access allows a home- or small-office user with a PC and a modem to access the network. The modem bank could be maintained by the Internet Service Provider (ISP) or by the corporate office itself. While this was once seen as an economical, albeit slow, means of connection from the home, newer technologies can be more cost effective.

Anyone who gains access to the corporate phone number computer can call in and connect. If they do not have your phone number, a simple war dialer will eventually find these phone banks. Crackers then post the numbers they have found on Web sites and you will not remain hidden for long. Passwords and encryption can help to control these unwanted connections, and dial-back connections can also add a layer of security. The problem with these dial-back connections is that they are often preset, so users who are traveling may not be able to connect.

Broadband access. There are several additional WAN access protocols that are commonly found in the SOHO. These access methods include the most popular xDSL (where x represents the various forms of Digital Subscriber Lines (DSL), to include Asynchronous [ADSL], Synchronous [SDSL], etc.), Cable access, Integrated Service Digital Network (ISDN), and Point-to-Point Protocol over Ethernet (PPPoE).

DSL access. Digital Subscriber Line (DSL) has been a welcome addition to the access family for Internet use. It, along with cable, has increased overall performance for thousands of home users and small businesses.

DSL access is more secure than cable access. It has security issues similar to that of a T1 used for a larger corporation in that it is a dedicated connection to the DSL service provider. All data will flow over a Permanent Virtual Circuit (PVC) that is created from the user's home or small office to the Internet. A PVC is a circuit that is always up and available for your use. It is still recommended that you have a firewall to protect all computers connected to the DSL network and a VPN if connecting to a corporate network.

xDSL is a popular method of Internet access from the SOHO. The dedicated, always-on connection provides speeds up to 28 times faster than a 56 kbps modem. The most common xDSL method in use today is ADSL, with some SDSL in use. DSL is a physical layer technology that utilizes existing copper lines and is actually analog, not digital, in nature.

Cable internet access. Cable access utilizes the coaxial connection provided by the television cable company to access the Internet. As more and more homes are wired for cable TV, Internet access via cable access has surged over the past few years. The speed of Internet access combined with reasonable cost has made this a very attractive connection method. The unfortunate side to this access is that this is a shared media. As more users on your block connect simultaneously, your access speed will decrease.

The other major disadvantage is that it is possible for your neighbors to "listen in" on your network connection as all traffic passes by. This is the limitation of the bus topology used in the end-user portion of cable networks. A firewall solution along with a VPN should be used to access any critical resources such as the corporate network or banking information.

Integrated Services Digital Network (ISDN). ISDN was designed by the phone companies to create a method of bringing digital connections all the way down the last mile. The phone network was, for the most part, upgraded to digital a long time ago, but the last mile is still predominantly analog.

ISDN does not have any built-in encryption or authentication. This protocol is similar to SLIP in that its job is to send traffic across the interface. There is no security inherent in the ISDN protocol; any desired security would have to be added by some other means.

PPPoE access. When PPPoE is added to a connection such as DSL, a level of security has been added through the authentication of the user. The user's PC or router must be configured with the correct user name and password to gain access to the Internet. This makes it a little more difficult for someone to steal your access line from you or spoof your connection. This access method is growing as more and more communities are adding "Fiber to the Home" wiring.

VPN access. When configured correctly, a VPN creates an authenticated and encrypted channel across a network. The authentication and encryption adds some security to traffic traveling across an otherwise insecure network, such as the Internet. There is also some sense of data integrity when using a VPN. If the data cannot be decrypted, you know that it is possible that someone attempted to intercept the data and tried to change it. It is very difficult, although not impossible, to hijack a VPN session and take over the session with encryption. This hijacking attempt's greatest chance of success is with a very weak encryption scheme. It is still possible for the connection to be compromised through the end user's computer. If someone gains access to that computer, he will have access to the corporate network. This compromise can be eliminated by not allowing split tunneling on your VPN client. Split tunneling uses a connection to the secure or trusted network at the same time as allowing a connection to a nonsecure or untrusted network. For example, if an individual uses his work laptop from an unsecured home network, a compromise of the laptop in this unprotected home network would be an on-ramp for attackers to connect to the individual's corporate network.

This type of attack is a growing trend for crackers because it is easier to find unprotected home computers with little or no monitoring, or other defensive measures in place, than to attack a heavily monitored and defended corporate target. A nontechnical (and also unrealistic) example is as follows: someone wanting to get into a heavily defended fort could try attacking the fort—very difficult if not impossible—or he could attack the armored cars en route that carry all the supplies and daily needs for the fort (also very difficult) or he could go to the refueling station, get into the truck while it is unprotected, and ride it into the heavily protected fort. In this example, the heavily protected fort is the corporate network, the armored cars are the VPN, and the refueling station represents the unprotected home network. The attacker would choose the easiest way into the network: walking into the armored van.

Network Protocols and Security Characteristics

Network Protocols Introduction

This section looks at some of the network layer protocols currently in use, primarily Transmission Control Protocol/Internet Protocol (TCP/IP).

A protocol is a standard system used for the transmission of data across a network. A network protocol governs how various pieces of networking equipment interact with one another to deliver data across the network. For example, these protocols are used to manage the transfer of data from a server to a personal computer, from the beginning of the data transfer to the end. The protocol stack is made up of several layers that work together to accomplish the transmission of data.

TCP/IP overview. TCP/IP is the primary networking protocol in use at this time. TCP/IP is actually a suite of protocols that was developed for the Defense Advanced Research Project Agency (DARPA) to provide a highly available and fault-tolerant network infrastructure. The fourth and most widely deployed version of IP is version 4 (IPv4), and it will continue to be so for the foreseeable future, although IPv6 continues to be deployed in backbones (e.g., U.S. DoD) and geographic pockets (parts of Asia). Due to the dominance of IPv4 environments at the time of the writing of this chapter, the majority of the discussion in this section will revolve around IPv4.

IP addressing. One of the primary functions of the network layer protocols is to provide an addressing scheme. The addressing scheme in TCP/IP is found at the network layer. IPv4 addressing is a 4-byte address (32 bits long) while IPv6 has a much larger address space (128 bits long). The goal of IP addressing is to uniquely identify every device on the network.

Depending on the manner in which the addressing is implemented or protected, there may be security concerns. If an attacker knows your location and your address, it is much easier for him to break through your security barriers.

Some features to add to your network to protect your IP addressing scheme are Network Address Translation (NAT) and Port Address Translation (PAT). These options add a relatively minor level of security and could be considered "security by obscurity." A better solution would be to implement a firewall solution.

There are two ways that addresses are assigned to devices on a network: static assigned addresses and Dynamic Host Configuration Protocol (DHCP). The first method is often used for core pieces of a network infrastructure such as routers, switches, mail servers, and firewalls. DHCP is commonly used within a network to simplify the network configuration of each user's computer. This allows the computer to dynamically get its configuration information from a network device rather than the network administrator, who has to manually enter the configuration information into the computer. DHCP has simplified the configuration job of many network administrators.

DHCP has its own security issues. The DHCP server gives out IP addresses, default gateways, and DNS information freely to anyone who asks. With this information, it is possible for someone to physically connect a device to your network, receive a network configuration, and gain access to your LAN, which could leave computers, servers, and network devices vulnerable. A request for the DHCP address information can be sent through a connection such as a VPN, wireless access, or direct physical access within your building. A request through the VPN authentication process adds an extra level of security to the process because the user would have to be authenticated before the DHCP request would be forwarded. There are also some available products that require a user to authenticate before any information is pushed down to the user. These devices also record the IP address and at what time it was given. Having users authenticate before assigning addresses also assists in any future forensics investigation or violation of "proper usage policy."

NAT/PAT. NAT and PAT were not designed for security, but their addition to a network can add a small measure of security that would otherwise not exist.

NAT was designed to contend with the ever-shrinking number of available public IP addresses. It allows a set of computers to be represented on a public network, such as the Internet, as only one IP address. NAT will translate from a hidden internal (private) address to the known external (public) address.

When the network layer address translation of NAT is combined with TCP port number translation, you arrive at PAT. Due to the method of translation that is found with PAT, the added security is greater.

Other technologies that can be employed by network devices for security purposes are:

- NAT
- PAT
- Packet Filtering and Access Control Lists

As mentioned above, while NAT was implemented initially to compensate for our growing limitation of public IP addresses, today it also provides security by hiding the true IP address of a device. A computer will send a request bound for outside the network, and the device used for NATing the connection will translate the IP address from the internal/real address to another IP address, usually that of the external interface of the device used for NATing. The device can also assign an address from an external pool of addresses, to which the device will respond when the Address Resolution Protocol (ARP) request is issued. The device then logs the location from which the connection is coming and where it is going. When the return packet is sent back, the device compares the NATed source address to its table, then redirects the packet to the real internal address. The security features provided by NAT are usually considered security by obscurity, but they will significantly reduce your threat from less skilled crackers.

PAT increases the security by also monitoring the port numbers used. Multiple internal IP addresses may be NATed to one or multiple external addresses through the use of Port Address Translation.

Internet Control Message Protocol (ICMP). ICMP is a management and control protocol for IP. ICMP has the responsibility of delivering messages between hosts regarding the health of the network.

ICMP messages carry information regarding the accessibility of hosts in addition to routing information and updates. PING and Traceroute utilize ICMP messages to carry their information.

ICMP can be an open door for some would-be attackers, and you should consider how you use ICMP, the roles it plays in your network management schema, and how it traverses your network. Controlling how ICMP flows in and out of your network will reduce the amount of information that can be used against you.

ICMP can be used to create a denial of service (DoS) attack against a network. One example of this type of attack is known as a Smurf attack. The attack works by sending spoofed ICMP echo requests to a broadcast address on a network, hoping that the hosts on that network will all respond. If enough replies are sent, it is possible to bring down a T1 from an attack that was launched from a dial-up connection.

Simple Mail Transfer Protocol (SMTP). SMTP is used to send and receive e-mail. SMTP is used to control how two mail servers interact and the type of controls they use to transfer mail.

E-mail is one of the most commonly used services on the Internet today, and as a result, SMTP servers have been the largest target of crackers. Most sites may not have a Web server but they usually have a mail server. Because the protocol and the mail handling software have been so heavily scrutinized, many programming bugs and security vulnerabilities have been found. The following security risks may leave your organization vulnerable to several different types of attacks:

- The mail server's underlying operating system is vulnerable to "buffer overflows" and similar types of attacks. The most severe effects of these attacks will leave the cracker with the highest level permissions and in complete control of the mail server. With that control, the attacker could read all of the mail that is stored or passing through the mail server. The attacker could also use the mail server as a launching point to assail the rest of your network.
- For convenience, roaming users forward confidential business e-mail to public mail servers like Hotmail or Yahoo.
- Common viruses are propagated as e-mail attachments.
- Hackers can send executable Trojans disguised as legitimate e-mail attachments (e.g., "Nimda").
- E-mail travels in the clear, unless encryption is used, which may result in organizational sensitive information being exposed.
- The network administrator fails to install important security patches. This can easily happen due to the large number of patches and difficulty of installation, especially if multiple servers are involved.
- Hackers can target your server with SYN floods or other similar attacks.
- Hackers can flood your mail server with huge messages to exhaust resources.
- Default installation of some mail handling software results in an insecure installation.
- It is easy to spoof—pretend to be someone else—e-mail due to the open architecture and origins.

One security recommendation is to put your Mail Transfer Agent (MTA) in a DMZ. If the MTA is compromised, then the attacker will only have access to the DMZ, not your entire internal network. There are hardened security appliances that will act as an MTA, severely limiting the likelihood of a compromise. Some of these appliances will also block unauthorized e-mail content, spam, viruses, and other malicious code.

Trivial File Transfer Protocol (TFTP). TFTP is a simplified File Transfer Protocol (FTP). TFTP does not have any authentication or encryption capabilities. This lack of authentication and encryption leaves TFTP as a very insecure protocol.

A network administrator commonly uses TFTP inside a network to allow easy configuration of the network devices, and as a result, TFTP can be an open door into your network devices.

TFTP is used by network users to transfer files to and from a common, shared file server. TFTP servers are set up with anonymous logins, allowing anyone to connect and view the stored files. Depending on the server's mission and the files stored on the server, serious security concerns may arise from the use of a TFTP server on a corporate network. TFTP capabilities should be turned off on all networking devices unless it is necessary to have them enabled.

Syslog. The syslog of a router/firewall can provide valuable information as to how your network is working, as well as who is accessing the network, when, and how. If the syslog is maintained on the router itself, there may be space constraints. Redirecting the syslog to display on another device in the network can alleviate this problem.

One of the most critical elements of having a syslog is the periodic review of the information it contains. This may not be the most exciting part of a system administrator's job, but it is nonetheless an important one.

Syslog's protocol has been known to have its own security problems, as when its messages are unauthenticated and there is no mechanism to provide verified delivery and message integrity. If your security device is sending the syslog messages, this also presents a problem: since syslog messages are sent in clear text, an attacker or anyone else on the network can see the content of the logs. Therefore, what your security system does or does not capture should not be sent in the clear.

Network Level Security

Now that we have taken a look at some of the networking protocols that are responsible for delivery or maintenance of information across the network, let us take a look at a few weaknesses and vulnerabilities of this level. The purpose of presenting these threats is not to provide a canonical list of things to watch for but to demonstrate that network level security does not inherently exist with the commonly used protocols on the Internet.

SYN flood. A well-known attack that uses the repeated transmission of SYN request of a TCP three-way handshake to cause a DoS to a system. A SYN flood attack relies on the creation of numerous half-open connections that eventually leads to the system running out of resources.

Session hijacking. An attack that exploits a legitimate connection to gain unauthorized access. Typically, this occurs via "sniffing" of packets for Web session cookies. Free WiFi hotspots and environments that use hubs (rather than switches) are the most vulnerable.

TearDrop. This attack relies on the normal process of hosts taking fragmented packets and attempting to reassemble them when received. When packets are intentionally designed to overlap, it can cause poorly written operating systems to mishandle the reassembly and result in a system crash.

Smurf. A Smurf attack uses ping packets (ICMP echo requests) sent to broadcast addresses with the source address being the spoofed address of the intended victim. The ICMP echo replies (return of the ping) from the broadcast are sent directly to the victim resulting in DoS.

LAND. A LAND attack uses a specially crafted packet to cause a computer to crash. An example of a LAND attack is where a SYN request is sent to a computer with the target computer as both the source and destination address. LAND has been found effective in attacks against a wide variety of operating systems.

Ping of Death. Ping of Death attacks involve attacking a host with ping packets that are malformed. Typically a ping packet is 64 bytes in size, and many operating systems have trouble with ping packets that are extremely large or small (or worse, rotating between the two). A combination attack of a Ping flood combined with Ping of Death can cause a DoS against a whole range of IP addresses.

Redirection attack. Redirection attacks forward legitimate connection requests to malicious sites (i.e., phishing sites). Redirection attacks are generally mounted against vulnerable routers (manipulating the in memory routing tables) but can be used with attacks against a local computer's host files.

Port scanning. A fundamental, and arguably the most common, type of Internet attack, used specifically to probe for weaknesses in a network environment by sending a message to each port and "listening" for a response. There are numerous types of port scanning, including vanilla (connect to all ports), stealth (concealing source of request), ftp bounce (use of ftp servers for stealth), and sweep (multiple hosts, same port).

Clearly, these vulnerabilities demonstrate that there are numerous, complex threats with not much inherent security to be found at the network layer. One element that has been added to alleviate some of the security issues in the network layer is protocol tunneling. Tunneling allows you to encapsulate insecure payload protocols with delivery protocols that allow for encryption.

There are numerous tunneling protocols that are in use:

■ Layer 2 Forwarding (L2F)
  Developed by Cisco in the mid 1990s, L2F is one of the earliest tunneling protocols invented. It was designed exclusively for use in dial-up connections for Virtual Private Dialup Network Service and is typically seen in environments where broadband access is not available.

- Point to Point Tunneling Protocol (PPTP)
  Developed by Microsoft, PPTP saw widespread use due to it being the first VPN tunneling supported by Microsoft operating systems through its Dial Up Networking. PPTP connections were authenticated via MS-CHAP and optionally encrypted using Microsoft Point to Point Encryption (MPPE).
- Layer 2 Tunneling Protocol (L2TP)
  L2TP is a combination of Cisco's L2F and Microsoft's PPTP protocols. L2TP acts as a layer 2 protocol (even though it is actually a layer 5 session-based protocol) for tunneling traffic between two peers over the Internet. Unfortunately, L2TP does not have strong authentication or encryption capabilities so it is often used with IPSEC to provide confidentiality, integrity, and authentication.
- IPSec
  IPSEC is the de facto datagram-based tunneling protocol used today. IPSec provides the following security services: data origin authentication, replay protection, data confidentiality, limited traffic flow confidentiality, and key negotiation and management. These services are provided once a Security Association (SA) between two network peers is established. An SA defines the method for secure communication including key exchanges for cryptography and digital certificates for nonrepudiation. The IPSEC protocol suite uses the Internet Key Exchange (IKE) protocol in two separate phases (known as phase 1 and 2) to establish an association.

  IPSec has two methods it uses for security: Authentication Header (AH) and Encapsulated Security Payload (ESP). AH integrity authenticates only the payload, whereas ESP confidentiality authenticates and encrypts the payload. Therefore, ESP is considered a more secure option.

  The AH protocol uses a keyed-hashed function to ensure the integrity of a packet and provide data origin authentication. This is done by passing a portion of the packet through a hashing algorithm, which generates a message authentication code value and can be checked by the receiving device.

  ESP works in a similar fashion to AH, but it also adds on the encryption of the packet.

  IPSec also has two functional modes: tunnel and transport. Transport mode only protects the data payload, whereas tunnel mode protects the headers as well as the payload.

  One of the drawbacks to IPSec is that it could be incompatible with NAT. Many of the devices that support NAT allow for IPSEC traffic to pass through them. The feature of allowing the IPSEC packet to be transmitted through the device is called IPSEC pass-through.
- Point-to-Point Protocol (PPP)/Serial Line Internet Protocol (SLIP)
  PPP and SLIP are two protocols that are used over a serial line such as DSL, dedicated circuit, or a serial line between two routers. Both PPP and SLIP are considered data link layer protocols. SLIP will only carry a single protocol

(i.e., TCP/IP), whereas PPP can carry multiple protocols at the same time on the same connection (i.e., TCP/IP, Appletalk, IPX).

SLIP is the older of the two and is used to encapsulate data for transmission across the line. This unfortunately is about the extent of this protocol: it follows along with the link layer's basic job. SLIP delivers data across the link.

PPP is the more commonly used protocol of the two. It takes the basic function of SLIP and adds:
– Header and data compression for efficiency and better use of bandwidth
– Error detection and correction
– Support of different authentication methods
– Encapsulation of protocols other than IP
■ Password Authentication Protocol (PAP)
PAP is an authentication protocol used to identify a remote user before allowing access to a network. The method of authentication requires a user to enter a username and password for authentication purposes.

The unfortunate side to PAP is that the username and password are sent as clear text across the network, rendering this a very insecure method of authentication. The username and password are also static, allowing replay attacks or spoofing to occur.
■ Challenge Handshake Authentication Protocol (CHAP)
CHAP is a little more secure than PAP as an authentication method. CHAP uses a challenge/response mechanism to authenticate users. This replaces the sending of a password over the network.

CHAP uses an authentication server-generated random value challenge, which is encrypted for transfer across the network. The predefined password at the user's station is used as the encryption key and is then able to reply to the challenge.

CHAP is not as susceptible to man-in-the-middle (MITM) or replay attacks because the challenge or response process is repeated several times over the life of the connection.

Some things to watch out for in your configuration of CHAP authentication: some systems will fail back to PAP in the event of a CHAP authentication failure and the passwords must be stored in clear text on the machines. In a Microsoft environment, you can use MS-CHAP. MS-CHAP is an extension to the current RFC in which the passwords are not required to be stored in clear text.
■ Extensible Authentication Protocol (EAP)
EAP is a standardized protocol from the IETF (RFC 2284) and has a growing family of protocols that include LEAP, PEAP, EAP-TLS, etc. Unlike PAP and CHAP, it provides the facilities to create a more flexible, general purpose authentication protocol, and it can be extended as new authentication methods become available. For example, EAP is the first PPP authentication protocol to provide a standard way to support digital certificates.

The following steps are part of the authentication process using EAP:

1. The client connects to the Network Access Server and sets up a PPP link.
2. The server asks for the UserID
3. The server sends one or more challenges, including a nonce
4. The client sends the UserID in reply to the request in step 2.
5. The client sends a response to each of the challenges, using whichever authentication type the NAS requested. If using simple passwords, the challenge is for an MD5 hash of the password and the nonce, much like CHAP.
6. The server checks the credentials and either allows the connection or indicates failure.

There is replay protection because of the nonce.

Wide Area Network Protocols

Whenever you connect your network to networks other than your own, you open the possibility that someone will take advantage of that connection. Most often, organizations have their networks connected to the Internet to conduct day-to-day operations. These operations may include a Web site "public presence" or opportunity to exchange e-mail with customers and partners. Organizations can also take advantage of what the Internet offers, namely, the opportunity to connect to remote sites without paying for the long-haul costs. The caveat is that any access to the outside world can open your doors to an intruder. We are going to take a look at a few of the protocols used for these connections to see what level of security they add to the connection on their own. Before we look at some of the Wide Area Network (WAN) Protocols, it is worthwhile to address the two types of switched traffic commonly available for WAN connections:

1. *Circuit switched.* In circuit-switched networks, a fixed amount of bandwidth is preallocated or committed to the connection before communication begins. The preallocation (typically in channels) of dedicated paths allow for a constant rate of information—ideal for voice or multimedia communications. Examples of circuit-switched networks include ISDN, Public Switched Telephone Network (PSTN), and GSM in cellular networks.
2. *Packet switched.* In packed-switched networks, no bandwidth is preallocated, allowing for accommodation of burst traffic. There is also less waste in bandwidth that is not used. Some common packet-switched networks include MPLS, ATM, and Frame Relay used in Public Data Networks (PDN).

Integrated Services Digital Network (ISDN). ISDN is a type of circuit-switched telephone system that provides multiple types of data over a single circuit (i.e., voice, data, or video). This system and the protocols involved are designed to use the same copper wires that were previously used in the Plain Old Telephone System (POTS) to transmit the traffic digitally instead of via the old analog method. Transmitting digitally usually results in increased throughput and quality.

Digital Subscriber Lines (DSL). DSL is technology that provides for increased data over the normal telephone copper wires. The speed of the data is based on the technology, the gauge of the wire, and the distance the wire is run from the Central Office, taps loops, and other interference. Data throughput rates are usually higher than with ISDN. There are many types of DSL, including

Asymmetrical DSL (ADSL)—Traffic is downloaded faster than it is uploaded (used more for personal connections).

Symmetrical DSL (SDSL)—Traffic is the same speed in both directions (used more for businesses).

High data rate DSL (HDSL)—Capable of handling higher speeds of traffic but uses multiple phone lines instead of just one.

Symmetric high bit rate DSL (SHDSL)—Symmetric traffic handling using only one set of twisted pair.

T-Carriers (T1, T3). T-Carriers are signaling schemes that were originally designed by Bell Labs. A T1 can also be called a Digital Signal 1 (DS1), as the terms are often used interchangeably. The T1 actually refers to the physical piece, and the DS1 actually refers to the data riding over that physical connection. A T1 circuit consists of 24 8-bit channels that can handle 1.544 Mbits per second. A T3 is a circuit that consists of 28 T1s or 642 channels to create a connection that can handle 44.5 Mbits per second. In Europe the coding is slightly different and their circuits are labeled using the E designation; an E1 has 32 channels and an ability to handle 2.048 Mbits per second, and an E3 has 512 channels with the ability to handle 34.268 Mbits per second of traffic.

Optical Carriers (OC-x). Optical Carriers are usually used to describe the levels or categories of bandwidth on a Synchronous Optical Network (SONET) network. As a general rule, to calculate the bandwidth an OC carrier can handle, one can use the x from the OC-x and multiply it by 51.8 Mbits per second. An OC-1 would therefore be capable of handling 51.8 Mbits per second. An OC-3 would be approximately three times as fast.

Synchronous Data-Link Control (SDLC) and High-Level Data-Link Control (HDLC). SDLC/HDLC are two more data link layer protocols that are used to send data across a serial link. IBM designed SDLC. HDLC was the ISO's revision and standardization of the SDLC protocol. SDLC is used primarily in a mainframe environment or a point-to-point WAN connection with IBM equipment. HDLC is more commonly used than SDLC.

There is no authentication or encryption with HDLC. In fact, HDLC does not even include information regarding the type of network layer traffic it is carrying.

Frame Relay. Frame Relay is one of the most predominate WAN protocols in use today. Frame Relay is a link layer protocol that delivers traffic from one link to the next, spanning the entire Frame Relay network. Frame Relay was developed to replace the old X.25 network standard.

X.25 had the disadvantage of being designed for low-quality network connections, so it spent a lot of time checking and rechecking the user's traffic for errors. In the process of building a replacement for the slow X.25, the decision was made to remove all unnecessary functions from Frame Relay, essentially leaving them to the upper layer protocols.

Frame Relay does not include any authentication or encryption. The one advantage of Frame Relay is its use of Permanent Virtual Circuits (PVC). PVCs make it very difficult for someone to "connect" to your system through the Frame Relay network. Mistakes have happened at service providers' routers and nothing is guaranteed 100%, so it is always safer to have firewalls protect the network segment and VPNs encrypt any data running across them.

Asynchronous Transfer Mode (ATM). ATM was designed to replace Frame Relay. ATM is being used in the LAN for desktop connectivity. Again, in the design, ATM was scaled down to make it an even faster data transfer protocol. For this reason there are no authentication or encryption methods included in ATM.

At this time, most connections and networks are designed for Permanent Virtual Circuits (PVC), although ATM can and does support Switched Virtual Circuits (SVC). A PVC requires configuration on all routers and switches that the connection traverses. A SVC is created dynamically when an edge device such as a router places a call across the ATM network. To place a call, the edge device must know the address of the destination that it is trying to reach. The addressing system that is used in ATM is called the ATM End Station Address (AESA). The AESA was created based on the Network Service Access Point (NSAP) address system from OSI. Due to the static and manual configuration of a PVC, it is a more secure type of connection on an ATM network.

Multi-Protocol Label Switching (MPLS). MPLS is a newer packet switching networking service that is gaining momentum over ATM and Frame Relay. MPLS has major interoperability and performance advantages that will likely make it ubiquitous technology for WANs in the future. It is natively able to transport packets and frames in a single management footprint. This means that MPLS networks can potentially transport IP packets and ATM, SONET, and Ethernet frames simultaneously.

Transport Layer Security Protocols

Out of concern for our financial information, several secure protocols have been created to transmit banking and financial information across a network. These protocols can be used to secure any information being sent but are most commonly used for online banking and online purchases today.

Secure Socket Layer (SSL). SSL is another option for providing security that is often associated with HTTP browsers, although SSL can be used for telnet, FTP, or anything else. SSL operates at the session layer, just above the transport layer. SSL was originally published by Netscape to allow applications to have authenticated, encrypted communications across a nontrusted network.

SSL encrypts all data to be transported using one of a variety of encryption algorithms. SSL uses digital certificates to authenticate systems and distribute encryption keys. SSL provides RSA encryption using public/private key encryption. System authentication can be done in a one-way format, to verify that you have reached the correct destination, or as mutual authentication, which is rare.

If a user logs onto a Web site using SSL, say for online banking, the following steps must be followed to create a secure session:

1. The client establishes communication with a server.
2. The server sends the client a certificate to authenticate itself.
3. The client checks the trustworthiness of the server's certificate.
4. The client uses the certificate authority's public key to verify the server's digital signature.
5. The client computes a message digest of the certificate to compare to the message digest of the certificate to verify integrity.
6. The client checks validity dates and the URL in the certificate.
7. The client extracts the server's public key.
8. The client creates a session key.
9. The session key is encrypted with the server's public key and is then sent to the server.
10. The server decrypts the session key.
11. Secure communication has been established between the client and the server.

The Internet Engineering Task Force (IETF) has taken SSL and created Transport Layer Security (TLS). TLS is backward-compatible with SSL.

Secure Electronic Transmission (SET). SET was created as a form of protection against fraud. SET was created by Visa and MasterCard as a method of securing credit card transactions by using a public key infrastructure.

SET has not yet gained a lot of acceptance. Both the users and the companies they are communicating with must load special software for SET communications. This is complicated more by the financial institutions' need to buy more hardware and coordinate the effort with their customers.

SET takes a customer's entered credit card information and sends it in encrypted format to a merchant's Web server. The merchant's Web server forwards the encrypted information to a payment gateway with their own digital signature attached. The payment gateway sends this information on to the merchant's bank. The merchant's bank then checks with the issuer of the credit card to see if the necessary funds are in that account and available for this purchase. Once confirmed, the message goes back to the merchant, and the transaction is complete. Using this technology both the customer and the merchant are authenticated and there is no repudiation about the payment. This technology could reduce the amount of fraud and theft for electronic transactions over the Internet although newer technology like 3-D Secure from VISA will probably replace it.

Application Layer Security

Application Layer security, such as Secure Multipurpose Internet Mail Extensions (S/MIME), Privacy-Enhanced Mail (PEM), Public Key Infrastructure (PKI), Pretty Good Privacy (PGP), and Message Security Protocol (MSP), was designed to add security to the application itself rather than relying on some lower-layer protocol to secure network transmissions. Because e-mail is so widely used to transmit all kinds of traffic across the Internet, these protocols were developed to protect our traffic from attackers.

The basic steps that the sender must take with these protocols are:

1. Calculate a message digest on the e-mail message.
2. Use the session key to encrypt the e-mail message.
3. Use a private key (creating a digital signature) to encrypt the message digest.
4. Use the receiver's public key to encrypt the session key.

The basic steps for the receiver are:

1. Use the receiver's private key to decrypt the session key.
2. Use the sender's public key to decrypt the message digest.
3. Use the session key to decrypt the message.
4. Recalculate the message digest and compare with the sender's for authentication.

Secure/Multipurpose Internet Mail Extensions (S/MIME). S/MIME is a specification for secure e-mail transmission. MIME was created to allow e-mail users to attach binary messages to their e-mails in a standardized method. S/MIME is the security extension to MIME.

Cryptographic Security services were added to MIME to create S/MIME. The standardization provides interoperability for e-mail clients from a variety of vendors.

The following are components used within the S/MIME standard to ensure authentication, nonrepudiation, message integrity, and confidentiality:

- DES, 3DES, or RC4 for content encryption
- MD5 or SHA-1 for data integrity
- DSA or RSA for digital signatures
- Diffie–Hillman or RSA for symmetric key encryption
- X.509 for public key certificates

Privacy-Enhanced Mail (PEM). PEM is defined in RFC 1421, 1422, 1423, and 1424. PEM is rarely used because of its use of a proprietary form of RSA encryption. PEM is designed to provide authentication, message integrity, encryption, and key management. PEM operates in a hierarchical trust model, meaning all users and resources trust one entity. Through association, everyone is able to trust each other.

The following are components used within the PEM to ensure authentication, nonrepudiation, message integrity, and confidentiality:

- 3DES-CBC for content encryption
- MD2/5 for data integrity
- RSA for sender authenticity, key management, and nonrepudiation

Pretty Good Privacy (PGP), written by Phil Zimmerman, is an example of a public key/private key algorithm. While originally freeware, PGP has also branched off into a commercial product.

Message Security Protocol (MSP) is the military's version of PEM and was developed by NASA.

Data Communications and Network Infrastructure Components and Security Characteristics

We are now going to take a look at data communications and network infrastructure components and their security characteristics. To secure your corporate resources from an attacker, it is necessary to first look at the network, its components, their functions, configurations, and their security limitations and capabilities.

We will discover in this section that there may be much vulnerability in a network environment. The inherent security of our data communications and network infrastructure is only the first step in the process of securing our corporate resources. To complete this process, we must know where our network is vulnerable and take the steps necessary to prepare our defense against attacks.

Physical Transmission Media

Infrastructure is defined as the "underlying foundation or basic framework" in the Merriam-Webster dictionary. The key to network infrastructure is the wiring and cabling plant. There are several different types of cables, wires, and wireless network connections that are used in networks today. The type of cabling used in any given section of the network depends on the environmental requirements.

Local area networks (LANs) typically use one of three types of cabling: coaxial, unshielded twisted pair (UTP), or fiber. Recently, there has been the addition of wireless to the LAN connectivity options.

Different Transmission Media

The security limitations of physical media. We seldom look at our physical media as lending itself to being a cause of insecurity of our networks, but it may be. Each of the physical media types that we use has its own level of security or insecurity. For example, digital communication has a very predictable method of transmission. Certain combinations of pulses represent certain transmitted characters. One could take advantage of the predictability of digital communication, depending on the type of physical media selected for your network.

It is recommended that you protect your network cable. This includes the cable itself as well as unused connectors. Any intruder who can gain access to your network cables or a network port can cause a great deal of damage by either gaining access to your network or by disabling the network by cutting cables. Something to consider in this decision is how easy is it for someone to walk into your building, or do damage if already inside. For a high-security site, you may need to seal the cable conduits.

Coaxial cable. Thin-net or 10Base-2 networks use coaxial cabling with T-connectors to interconnect networking devices. Thick-net or 10Base-5 networks use coaxial cable with vampire tape and AUI transceivers to interconnect networking devices. Coaxial networks are connected in a bus configuration. A resistor (terminator) is placed at each end of the bus to stop the signal once it has passed the entire length of the connected cables. Due to the bus configuration, a single point of failure anywhere along the length of the cable will stop all communication on the network. The difficulty of locating and repairing a single point of failure renders this type of network difficult to manage and troubleshoot.

When using an electrical circuit running over media such as CAT5 or coaxial, the electrical pulses used to transmit characters expose your network to a potential security problem: electromagnetic interference (EMI).

Sophisticated monitoring devices can detect the EMI radiation from electrical circuits. This radiation can be converted into the actual transmitted characters by these monitoring devices. It is also very easy to tap into a coaxial cable undetected.

Unshielded twisted pair (UTP). UTP is the most common cabling type in use for today's networks. UTP is used for 10Base-T and 100Base-TX networks. The cabling specification for UTP is category 3, 4, 5, 5E, 6, and 7. The category of wire is determined by the number of wires, the number of twists in the wires, and the signal quality capability of the cable. The most widely used cable is category 5. Because UTP is not shielded, as the name states, it is very susceptible to outside electromagnetic interference such as fluorescent lights. UTP is configured in a star topology, resulting in a much easier- to-diagnose network.

Fiber optic. Fiber optic cable is predominantly used for backbone and network device interconnectivity. It consists of three layers: the inside core fiber, the surrounding cladding, and the outside buffer. The core fiber is used for light transmission, while the cladding reflects the light back as it tries to leave the core. The outside buffer or coating is usually made of PVC or plenum and is either in direct contact with the cladding or is separated with a layer of gel. Single Mode Fiber Optic cable is made of a cylindrical glass thread center core wrapped in cladding that protects the central core. This is encapsulated in a jacket of tough Kevlar®, and then the entire cable is sheathed in PVC or Plenum.

Multimode fiber optic cable is made of a plastic core wrapped in cladding. This is encapsulated in a jacket of tough Kevlar and then the entire cable is sheathed in PVC or Plenum. Fiber optic cable transmits light rather than electricity. Due to the light transmission, there is no EMI radiation with fiber optics and no susceptibility to the same kind of monitoring as electrical circuits. Single-mode fiber uses laser as the light source, whereas multimode fiber uses LED as a light source. Fiber optic cable is more delicate than UTP or coaxial and is more expensive, although the cost has dropped significantly over the past several years. The maximum transmission capability of fiber has not been reached at this time, but is at least well into the terabits per second.

Wireless. Wireless networks are quickly becoming a common way to connect network devices. This is especially true in small offices and home offices (SOHO). Most commonly, wireless networks use radio transmissions for data transfer. There are several standards available at this time with more to come (e.g., 802.11a, 802.11b, 802.11g, and Bluetooth). With wireless networks, one of the most critical considerations at this time is to be certain that all equipment you buy is compatible.

Wireless transmissions are not constrained by any formal boundaries so the atmospheric medium is referred to as an unbound medium. Unbound transmissions are more susceptible to interception and monitoring. Different wireless transmissions include:

- Light transmissions
- Radio waves
  - Fixed frequency signals
  - Spread spectrum signals

Inherent security vulnerabilities. There are inherent security vulnerabilities with all types of cabling. As we compare the different technologies, we will see that the severity of the risk is significantly different depending on the technology.

Coaxial cable is the least used of the media in a LAN environment. Thin-net and thick-net have given way to UTP, fiber optic, and now wireless. Possibly the most susceptible part of a coaxial network would be a DoS attack. It is so easy to cause a link failure on a coaxial network, resulting in a downed network that can take tremendous effort to troubleshoot.

UTP is now the most commonly used cable, although it is susceptible to eavesdropping. There are devices available that allow an attacker to listen in on the traffic being transmitted across the line. Another problem with UTP is a physical security issue—any person with a laptop and a cable can easily gain access to the network.

Fiber optic is the most secure of the transmission methods. First, fiber optic cable is not as easily susceptible to eavesdropping because the light does not escape the cladding or the outside buffer. Second, just about all attempts to cut through the cladding or buffer will result in too much bleed off of the light, and the link signal will fail. Third, a splitter could be inserted at one end of the fiber so a listening device could be attached, but to insert the splitters requires the fiber to be unplugged from one of the networking devices, and this will cause a link failure.

In a point-to-point, ring, or self-healing ring environment, the connected devices may be affected by the link failure but the attachment of the splitter would be a quick process, and the link will be back up. Such a short break in the availability of a link will not usually result in a physical inspection of the circuit. Unless the circuit is examined physically, the insertion of the splitter and listening device would probably never be discovered. If the networking devices are under lock and key, this is an even more difficult, but possible, attack to achieve. There are other devices coming about today that make it possible to intercept the traffic over a fiber cable without splicing or causing bleed off.

Wireless transmission is the least secure of the transmission methods. It is very difficult to control the direction and distance that the wireless signal will travel. This makes it very difficult to keep the signal away from any area that an attacker may enter. A safeguard to implement would be to secure the transmission using encryption, but the IEEE standard for encryption is susceptible to cracking. The use of a private encryption method and VPNs can create a more secure wireless signal.

Wiring and communication closets and data centers. Physical security may be the most critical element of the security plan when the communication closets, data centers, and wiring are considered. As discussed earlier, the wiring used in our networks today is susceptible only when an attacker gains access to the wires themselves or comes within the signal range of a wireless network.

Communication closets have a similar physical security risk. If an attacker gains access to the closet, the potential damage to a corporate network or the corporate resources is enormous. One often-forgotten element to a wiring closet is the lone modem-connected router used by the IT professional for connection and management purposes. An attacker doing war dialing may discover this modem and possibly use this unprotected or poorly protected access to gain entry to the rest of the corporate network and its resources.

Data centers are the same—if an attacker is able to walk around inside of the data center, all corporate resources are at risk.

The Enterprise Network Environment and Its Vulnerabilities

There is a common network scenario that exists within most enterprise environments. The types of equipment that are normally used are hubs, switches, and routers. These devices are usually connected in a star configuration utilizing the

Ethernet protocol. When connecting computers together, whether it is 2 or 200, those connected computers are called a Local Area Network (LAN). The local area network (LAN) is essential to our corporate environment as well as our homes at this point. The equipment and its topological configuration, as well as the protocols we place on top of them, have a great impact on the vulnerability of our network. LANs can spread across a wide area of a campus environment (sometimes referred to as a CAN—Campus Area Network) and are not generally limited to certain-size geographic space.

When a network grows to encompass a city, it is usually called a Metropolitan Area Network (MAN). A network that encompasses many LANs in different cities and countries is called a Wide Area Network (WAN). Currently efforts are underway to create a global network able to support communications via wireless and satellite regardless of location. This proposed network, which is still in development, has been referred to as a Global Area Network (GAN).

Local Area Networking. Earlier, we took a look at some of the protocols and topologies in use on the network. Now let us take a look at the equipment we use in the LAN.

Hubs

Basic Job: A hub is the center device in a star configuration. It is used to join media connections. Once the hub is connected, it will essentially act as a repeater to take in traffic from one port and forward it out all other ports.

Inherent Security: None

Added Security Features: None

Security Risks: Anyone who can connect to one of the attached cables will be able to see all of the traffic on that segment of the network. Also, anyone can plug in to any one of the empty ports on a hub and see all of the traffic that passes through that hub.

Bridges

Basic Job: A bridge will connect multiple network segments. The bridge will then listen to all network traffic that passes through it and build its bridging table based on the port through which the traffic arrived. The bridge table will contain the MAC addresses of all attached devices that are active. Bridges are mostly a waning technology, being replaced by switches.

Inherent Security: A bridge selectively forwards traffic to the correct destination.

Added Security Features: None

Security Risks: Broadcast traffic is still forwarded to all attached devices. A common error made by network professionals is the use of the TELNET protocol for management of infrastructure devices. Unfortunately TELNET does not encrypt any transmitted data or provide any protection against MITM attacks. Secure Shell (SSH) and SSHv2 are more appropriate protocols for management as they provide much more secure communications paths.

Switches

There are two layers at which switches can operate: layer 2 and layer 3.

Layer 2 switch. Layer 2 switches are a wonderful way to increase the transmission speed of a LAN. The networking device used to connect PCs, servers, and printers is changed from a hub or bridge to a layer 2 switch. Instead of processing the transmitted frame completely, the switch will read the least amount of information necessary to be able to send the frame on to its destination. Since a switch has a much higher throughput than a bridge, implementing switches throughout our network can increase the transmission speed of frames across the LAN.

Layer 3 switch. The layer 3 switch is used to increase the transmission speeds between network segments. The layer 3 switch will act as a router by reading the network layer address information and then sending the frame on to the correct destination. In fact, the layer 3 switch is often incorporated into a router, which increases the throughput capabilities of the router by reducing the amount of processing required per frame. A layer 3 switch also has the capability of falling back to layer 2 switch mode when necessary.

Basic Job: The switch will monitor each of the network interfaces and thereby learn the MAC addresses of all attached devices. The traffic that is destined for a device attached to that interface will be sent out that interface only.

Inherent Security: Traffic is only sent to the intended destination.

Added Security Features: Most smart switches have the ability to support 802.11q VLANs to create special purpose zones. These zones can be used for a variety of security purposes, including the creation of honeypots (traps), network quarantine areas, wireless zones, guest login network, virtual path isolation, and the creation of virtual compartments.

Security Risks: A switch port can be configured as a monitoring port and hear all traffic that passes through the switch. It is also possible to cause the switch to dump its MAC address table and fail to an open configuration, similar to a hub. A common error made by network professionals is the use of the TELNET protocol for management of infrastructure devices. Unfortunately TELNET does not encrypt any transmitted data or provide any protection against MITM attacks. Secure Shell (SSH) and SSHv2 are more appropriate protocols for management as they provide much more secure communications paths.

Access Points

Basic Job: An Access Point acts as a bridge for a wireless network between the wireless connected computer and the other devices whether they are wired or wireless.

Inherent Security: Most access points have little to no security, but some have firewalls integrated into the device.

Added Security Features: Service Set Identifier (SSID) and Wired Equivalent Privacy (WEP). While these methods are weak, they do provide some protection.

Security Risks: This uses an unbound medium, so it is possible for anyone in the area to listen in on the traffic.

Routers

Basic Job: A Router handles traffic in from multiple ports and then forwards the traffic out based on the network layer protocol and address. A port on a router could be dedicated to a single device, shared through the use of a switch or hub, or connected to another router.

Inherent Security: Broadcast traffic can be blocked.

Added Security Features: Packet filtering, stateful firewall features, NAT, VPN support.

Security Risks: Dynamic Routing

Firewalls

Basic Job: Enforce an access control policy at the access points of a network.

Inherent Security: Stateful Firewalling, static packet filtering, dynamic packet filtering, proxy, dynamic content inspection.

Added Security Features: Some of the new firewalls can serve as Intrusion Detection Systems (IDS), Intrusion Prevention Systems (IPS), and antivirus.

Security Risks: Improper installation or misconfiguration

VPN termination points. VPNs are a good way to increase the security of data that is transmitted across the public data network. Using a VPN for remote network access provides a cost-effective security solution, especially compared to the cost of a dedicated connection between the same two sites. Using a VPN over an already-in-place broadband connection could also provide substantial savings when compared to the cost of a modem bank and the dial-up, long distance, or toll-free charges. Many hotels and airport hotspots have connection points that could be used for a VPN.

The security added by the VPN can vary, depending on the configuration of the tunnel and the encryption level that is used. It is also important to have a strong authentication mechanism in place to make sure that the appropriate people are using the network.

One major disadvantage with a VPN is that it requires the use of your gateway equipment processing cycles to handle the encryption algorithms. This increased utilization can be off-loaded to another device through the use of another VPN endpoint rather than terminating the VPN on your router or firewall. The increased utilization may not be a factor if the firewall is designed to be a VPN as well and this capability is built into the product. Consult the manufacturers for more specifications on their products.

One other security consideration is the level of security on an end user's PC. Many security companies allow you to package their VPN software for remote users so they will not be able to have split tunneling available while connected over the VPN. Split tunneling—connecting to the outside world while also connected to another network (most commonly the Internet)—is a practice that should be avoided if your firewall/VPN software is not set up to handle the risks properly. The risks of not properly handling split tunneling include allowing a Trojan horse that is installed on the end user's computer to act as an ingress point into your network once your VPN has been established. A prior action, such as a previously installed Trojan horse, is not the only worry for split tunneling; a cracker could compromise your end users' computers while they are connected to the corporate network and take advantage of that tunnel.

Compromising a network is also possible via split tunneling when a computer that is connected to a LAN or a broadband connection is dialed up to the corporate network. Having a host-based firewall or a network-based firewall and a current antivirus solution would greatly minimize the risks of this potential vulnerability, especially when your network-based firewall acts as the VPN termination point.

Routers and routing protocols. Static routing, dynamic routing, and most commonly a combination of both routing methods are used in routers. Static routing requires a network administrator to have the knowledge of the other IP networks, how to reach them, and the backup means of reaching them to correctly configure the router. Dynamic routing allows for the routers to update the path on which traffic flows. These updates could redirect traffic around bottlenecks or link outages, allowing for the data to flow seamlessly.

If your router is not carefully controlled, all of your routing information could be sent back to an attacker or false routing information could be sent from the attacker to a corporate router. Getting the information from your routers would help the attacker map your network and enable him to better target segments for future compromise. False routing information that is injected into a router could create a black hole. A black hole is a way for routers to exclude/drop information that the administrator has deemed it should not forward. This exclusion could be to prevent routing loops, or to prevent other networks from using your network as a cheaper shortcut. If the router were misconfigured or intentionally changed by an attacker, the router could black hole all traffic that is passed to it, causing a DoS attack.

Another means of causing a DoS can be through false route injection. This DoS can also be caused through a carefully crafted update of a dynamic protocol. The false update would be used to send traffic away from the intended recipient and possibly flood some other network. The routing protocol used should also be carefully considered. Some routing protocols have the ability to use route authentication, which requires a secret password to be configured on a router. These routing protocols include RIPv2, OSPF, EIGRP, and BGP. It should be noted that RIPv1 and IGRP do not support route authentication.

Care should be taken to control dynamic routing updates on each router link. Access Control Lists (ACL) can also be used as a security defense. For example, an ACL can configure a router interface with the range of allowed or disallowed IP routing information.

Router placement. The placement of a router within the network architecture is critical since there are two basic locations of a router: as a border router and as an internal router.

A border router is directly subject to attack from an outside source. In planning the configuration of the router, it should be determined if the router is the lone defense or acts in conjunction with another device such as a firewall. The lone defense router can protect internal resources but is subject to attack itself. It is not normally recommended that you have a router as a lone defense, but instead use a defense in-depth technique where some of the harmful traffic can be dropped by the router and a finer in-depth look at the packets can be handled by a firewall. If an organization can only afford one device, then serious consideration should be given to a firewall appliance that has built-in routing functionality.

The internal router might be configured to allow all traffic to pass or it might be configured to protect some internal resources. Internally, more and more companies are using firewalls to segment off or protect in-depth their internal network. This technique is on the rise because it has been reported that a large percentage of the attacks occur from inside and because more companies are adopting a "need-to-know" posture. For example, this need-to-know posture would be used to keep the workings of Human Resources and Finance away from unauthorized viewers, much as it would protect a new project that is vital to the corporate future from industrial espionage or disgruntled employees.

Packet filtering is something that routers can do well. Packet filters can be configured for ACLs and may be used to increase the security of a router's defense; however, if done poorly, it only adds to the security vulnerabilities. Some of the ACLs can be difficult to configure and can give you a false sense of security.

Remote Access

With the growth of telecommuting and greater employee travel, remote access has become a common part of many corporate networks. There are many companies today that have employees who never or rarely come into the corporate office. In the United States, some states provide tax breaks for companies that have their employees telecommute 2–3 days a week. Federal programs are also in place that mandate that a certain percentage of federal employees telecommute.

Although these users are at home or on the road, they still need access to corporate resources. This means providing access to more corporate resources via the Internet, thus increasing potential security risks. The job of the security practitioner is to allow the necessary access that these traveling employees need, while reducing the exposure of all internal systems to outside compromise.

Clientless VPNs. As the workplace becomes more mobile and decision-making time decreases, there is a greater need for mobile access. Employees no longer have the luxury of leaving the office for long periods of time, like a weeklong training class or a conference, without checking their e-mail. Also, as more and more workers check their mail or need access to corporate resources from a home machine or Internet kiosk, the need to access these corporate resources securely also increases. Because most users do not have control over the computers at an Internet kiosk or at a large conference, and Information Technology departments do not want to maintain an end user's home machine, the ability for them to use an IPSEC solution decreases in these scenarios. Instead, many companies are opting to use a clientless VPN for these situations.

There are many benefits:

- There is no user end configuration necessary and no additional software to install.
- A clientless VPN usually uses the SSL/TLS-capable Internet browser that is already included in most systems.
- The clientless VPNs use the standard ports that people would use to surf the Net or conduct secure transactions, like ordering something from a Web site or checking their banking records.
- Clientless VPNs are mainly used for Web-based applications but many of them have the ability to allow non-Web-based applications (such as telnet, ftp, or file sharing) to ride over the encrypted tunnel via port forwarding.
- Clientless VPNs are also a benefit to some end users whose service providers block UDP port 500 to prevent them from using VPNs without paying for the "business" class of service. No service provider would dare block port 80 (HTTP) or port 443 (SSL), since even checking your Web-based mail requires these ports.

There are security risks:

- Using a public nontrusted machine to connect to your internal network could be risky.
- The machine may have viruses, Trojan horse applications, keystroke monitoring tools, or other common attack tools running in the background.
- Some of the clientless VPNs on the market today allow you to change the level of access or deny access to the corporate network based on the results of a scan of the machine being used to try to access the network.
- Some of the machines provide redundancy via high availability and session persistence. High availability comes in several forms, including having a second device on the same network segment that will share the load with the

other clientless VPN termination point or pick up connections when the first clientless VPN termination point goes off line. High availability can also be a distributed design. The distributed design fails over everything to hot or cold sites when a major catastrophe or impact happens to the main site.

Session persistence is a great security tool for the administrator and end user. If an end user walks away from the connection for a customizable period of time, the connection requires that the user re-authenticate. Upon reauthentication, the end user resumes his previous activity, such as typing a mail message, losing none of his work. These redundancies strengthen your network security architecture and provide continuity of operation.

Remote access servers. Microsoft's Terminal Server and Citrix's server solutions are very common in corporate networks. Both solutions are considered thin clients and allow remote users to log onto a server and operate as if they were sitting in the office. This gives them access to the corporate network, printers, and data. This would be no different than if they were using their computers within the corporate building. The risk is that if an attacker gains access to the Terminal or Citrix server, he may also have access to other corporate resources.

Identification and Authentication for Remote Users

RADIUS, TACACS+, LDAP, SecureID, and other two-factor authentication servers are common methods of authenticating remote users. These methods of authentication allow centralized management of user logins and passwords. When a client attempts to connect to the network, they are prompted for a user name and password combination that the server verifies. Digital Certificates are also a very useful means of authenticating the user.

Firewalls. Firewalls are a critical element of our networking security today, but they are just that, an element. Firewalls will not solve all of our security problems, but they do play a large part in our efforts to secure our networks.

Firewalls are designed to control the flow of traffic by preventing unauthorized traffic from entering or leaving a particular portion of the network. They can be used between a corporate network and the outside world, or within the corporate network, to allow only authorized access to corporate assets.

Firewalls can be configured in a local high-availability scenario or a distributed high-availability scenario. Within these scenarios, the firewalls can be configured in load balancing or load sharing, failover, or a less desirable stand-alone solution. Load balancing and load sharing are very similar, with the difference being that the first method more evenly distributes the load across the firewalls. The latter may share the load between the firewalls but it could be severely unbalanced. Failover is not quite as effective as load balancing, and may occur in seconds or as much as minutes. The stand-alone solution may leave you with a single point of failure on your network. Any single point of failure could be a liability to your operations. If that point failed, it could cause your data transmission to cease. You will have to compare the requirements of your risk analysis plan against your solution. These redundant configurations are critical to maintaining an organization's ability to conduct business across the Internet or other transmission medium.

Different types of firewalls. There are seven basic types of firewalls:

1. Stateful inspection—Stateful inspection firewalls monitor the state of all connections that pass through them. In other words, if a user were to send a request to a Web site, the firewall would allow the return information to pass because it knows that the user's connection is waiting for a response. The firewall is also aware of the established connection, and upon inspection of the packet to make sure that it is in fact part of the previously established connection, will allow the traffic to pass. Stateful inspection firewalls are the most popular type of firewall today.
2. Packet filtering—Packet filtering firewalls are very similar in nature to a router. They compare received packets against a set of rules that define which packet is permitted to pass through the firewall.
3. Dynamic packet filtering—Dynamic packet filtering firewalls function by queuing all of the connectionless packets that have crossed the firewall and, based on that, will allow responses to pass back through.
4. Application proxy—Application proxy firewalls read the entire packet up through the Application layer before making a decision as to whether the data are allowed to pass. The client is really communicating with an application proxy that in turn communicates with the destination service. This allows the application proxy to examine packets to protect against known application and data stream attacks. As a result these firewalls are slower but more effective than packet filtering firewalls.
5. Kernel proxy—Kernel proxy firewalls are specialized firewalls that are designed to function in the kernel mode of the operating system. This firewall technology is much older and is currently used in very few firewalls. Any new service that is introduced, such as Voice over IP (VoIP) or NetMeeting, would require changes to the kernel. These firewalls are often much slower.
6. Circuit level gateway—Circuit level firewalls relay TCP connections by reading and tracking header information such as source and destination addresses and ports. The caller connects to a TCP port on the firewall, which connects to some destination on the other side. During the call, the firewall's relay program copies the bytes back and forth, in essence acting as a wire. A circuit level gateway just checks the source and destination addresses before allowing connectivity. Once the connectivity is established, no further checking is done. This type of firewall is rarely used today. This firewall is one step more secure than a packet filter as it checks the actual connections before passing the traffic and traffic appears to be handled by the gateway. A disadvantage is it checks the initial connection but none of the subsequent packets.

7. Reverse proxy—Reverse proxies are generally deployed to "screen" inbound requests of Web servers. All traffic destined for the "screened" servers are routed to the reverse proxy, which are then in part or whole forwarded to the appropriate servers after inspection. Reverse proxies can also perform load balancing and fault tolerance functions for the screened servers as well.

Firewall configuration alternatives. There are two main examples of security configuration architectures:

1. Packet-filtering routers—Packet-filtering routers are designed to sit between an internal trusted network and an external nontrusted network. Security is maintained through an ACL, which may be time consuming to manage. These firewalls also lack authentication and usually have weak auditing capabilities.
2. Dual or multihomed host firewall—Dual or multihomed host firewall systems have the gateway connected to the internal network on one interface and the external network on another. (In the multihomed configuration, another network interface could be connected to a DMZ, partner network, extranet, or many other possibilities.) The security is maintained through the firewall rule set. This type of firewall is the most commonly used type of firewall today. The benefits of this type of firewall are that it can be less expensive because you can deploy only one firewall and protect many network segments and it simplifies your network configuration. A disadvantage of this type of firewall is that one incorrect or erroneous rule or filter may allow traffic into your network without a secondary security check. This potential is the reason to choose a firewall with an easy to understand and implement configuration tool or GUI.

A clarification of terms:

- Filters—A list of rules that allow or block traffic. These rules could be based on source, destination, service, time of day, port, day of the week, user, authentication type, combination, of any or all of these, and more.
- Gateway—A machine or a set of machines that enforce the policy or filters.
- DMZ—A network attached to a firewall or between two firewalls, which usually has limited permissions for some type of public traffic but often not as limited a set of permissions as traffic intended for the internal segment. In the past, the DMZ was placed between two routers with different ACLs, with more stringent controls on the internal router. With today's modern technology, the DMZ is usually just another interface off of the firewall with a rule set governing the access to and from the external network, to and from the internal network, and in some instances, to and from another DMZ or extranet.

- Bastion host—This terminology is outdated, and the roles of the bastion host are now incorporated into a gateway. It provides a single entry/exit point or gateway to your network.
- Proxy server—A client functioning as an intermediary device between an end device and a server, which acts on behalf of the end device to access the resources on the server.

Intrusion Detection Systems. Intrusion detection is critical to a corporate network defense because you can be sure that your systems will come under attack. When you come under attack, you will want to be alerted as soon as possible and have as much information as possible for the investigation. An IDS should alert you and log the critical information about the attack. It is estimated that any new system on the Internet will be attacked within 3 days. There are enough attackers out there, attacking for various reasons, to guarantee that the first attack will not be the last. The IDS has the ability to monitor incoming and outgoing traffic to determine if the passing traffic is a threat to your network.

A passive attack could be simple eavesdropping. In this attack, the attacker is just waiting for login and password information to pass or an e-mail with an attached financial file to be passed across the network. This type of attack requires that they have physical access to your network or have already compromised a device on your network.

An active attack could be one of many such as brute force, DoS, spoofing, or exploitation of a vulnerability. What must be remembered is that there is always a way into a system; it may take longer to breach a well-protected system, but there is always a way in.

Intrusion detection systems will not notify you of a passive attack since it generates little to no noise on the network. IDSs are mostly used to detect an active attack.

Auditing and monitoring. Auditing and monitoring are a critical part of intrusion detection. "Prevention is ideal, but detection is a must" is a key motto in security. As long as your network is connected to an external network, your system is subject to attack at any time. A well-setup system will be able to prevent most attacks from getting through, but will not prevent 100% of the attacks. Therefore, you must monitor your network systems to detect, and learn from, any attack that is launched at your system.

Different types of IDS solutions. There are two basic types of IDS solutions: host-based and network-based.

A host-based IDS requires loading software on the host machine. The IDS software then watches traffic coming into and exiting the host machine. To be truly effective, host-based IDS software should be loaded onto every host in the network. This software can also take advantage of information in the computer's logs and monitor the integrity of the file system for a broader picture of changes and attempted changes that might mean an intrusion attempt is or has happened.

If it is cost-prohibitive to place software on all machines on the network, then serious consideration should be given to monitoring devices deemed critical to your mission.

Network-based IDS devices monitor the traffic on the network. These devices can add some other helpful features such as network monitoring, traffic analysis, and statistical collection. Unlike routers or firewalls, the IDSs only monitor the traffic.

Ideally, network-based IDSs should be placed outside of your firewall, on your DMZ link, just inside your firewall, and on internal network segments or at least on any critical network segment or any network device (switch or hub) providing connectivity for that segment. The IDS outside your firewall will alert you to the types of attacks that intruders are trying to use against your system. Knowing what types of attacks an intruder is trying to use would help you make sure that you are patched and prepared for those types of attacks.

Having an IDS on your DMZ would enable you to see what types of attacks are allowed through your firewall rule set into your DMZ. Usually company Web servers and mail servers are kept in the DMZ. A compromise of one of these devices may allow for a follow-on attack to the internal part of your network or public embarrassment.

The IDS on the network segment inside the firewall may alert you to a misconfigured firewall policy or for the potential that an attack is coming from inside your network.

An IDS on the internal network segments could alert you to the possibility that a disgruntled employee, a saboteur, or spy (industrial or governmental) has gotten onto your network.

All IDS solutions should provide alerting, logging, and reporting capabilities.

Techniques for IDS monitoring. IDS solutions have two basic methods of intrusion detection available to them—signature matching and anomaly detection.

Signature matching is also called pattern matching. These IDS systems maintain a database of known attack signatures. The first obvious problem with this type of monitoring is that any unknown methods of attack will not be detected. The IDS database works in a similar fashion to that of virus detection software. You must continually update the signature database with the latest known methods of attack. The IDS then monitors traffic to see if it conforms to any known attack methods. The problem with this type of IDS is the amount of time between when an attack is released into the wild and the vendor has a pattern match or signature for that type of attack. Your system will not recognize and not flag that type of attack.

Anomaly detection is done by first determining the normal network traffic patterns and usage and then watching for traffic that does not fall within the normal patterns. The advantage to this is that both new and known methods of attack can be detected. The difficulty with this method of IDS is that what is normal can change over time for any given company or if where the device is located is under a heavy attack or already compromised while taking the baseline.

IDS audit logs can be very useful in computer forensics. The logs can show what systems were attacked and how the systems were attacked, as well as the possible source of the attack. With attacks that are spoofed, you most likely will not see the actual source.

Wide Area Networking. WAN is a critical element to every corporate network today. A corporation must be able to connect between their offices, their remote users, their customers, and perhaps to their competition on occasion. WAN allows access to the corporate resources from almost anywhere in the world. There are several different types of WAN protocols and configurations in use today. Each configuration has its advantages and disadvantages, like all other aspects of networking.

Circuit-switched versus packet-switched WANs. The first thing to consider is the different manner in which the WAN can operate. Public networks operate in either a circuit-switched or a packet-switched manner.

Circuit switched networks include the telephone network (POTS; modem access) and ISDN.

Packet switched networks include X.25, Frame Relay, SMDS, and ATM.

A circuit-switched network operates in a time division manner by allocating timeslots (DS0s) to each user's connection. The connection is established between two end points or between two corporate offices. This connection could be dynamically (SVC) created as in a telephone call or statically (PVC) created to permanently connect two locations/devices.

A packet-switched network operates in a similar fashion to the circuit-switched network in that it establishes either dynamic (SVC) or static (PVC) connections between two end points on the network. The difference is in the bandwidth that is allocated to the connection. The packet-switched connection works on a first-come, first-served basis, allowing users to share all of the available bandwidth.

In either scenario, there is a security risk with dynamically created connections. These connections are created by one end location dialing the address of the requested destination. The network then places the call across the network. The network is not designed to limit or filter connections for the users. Once the connection is established across the network, it is up to the receiving device to accept or decline the connection attempt.

Common WAN infrastructures used in enterprise networks. The most common WAN infrastructure used at this time in enterprise networks is a PVC-based Frame Relay network. X.25 has given way to Frame Relay, and ATM is still a growing network.

The Permanent Virtual Circuit (PVC) used in Frame Relay adds to the security of the network. Frame Relay networks do not support SVC at this time even though the standard does exist. A PVC is manually configured by the IT department for the corporation, utilizing the Frame Relay network at the router and the carrier at the network switches. This manually intensive process makes it harder for an attacker to create an illegal connection to a corporate router.

As with all configurations, there is a possible way in for an attacker. If an attacker were to gain access to one of the networks in a corporate office, then the Frame Relay PVC will not protect corporate resources. Remember, the modem connected to the router in the wiring closet or the unprotected wireless network will let an attacker right in. There is also a remote possibility that an attacker could gain access to the carrier's switches and reconfigure the PVC.

Wireless Local Area Networking

Wireless networks have become very popular for connecting devices within the home, small office, or even large office buildings. They are used to connect laptops, desktops, PDAs, and so much more. Wireless has added a true feeling of mobility to laptops and freedom with a PDA in hand.

Configuring a wireless network has proved to be fairly easy with a wide variety of products on the market and interoperability at work. The question then becomes: What does wireless do to the security of my network? If it is so easy for an employee to connect to the network, does that mean that others can connect as well?

Some of the biggest blunders with wireless networks so far are:

■ Encryption not enabled.
■ Forgetting that a wireless network can extend outside the perimeter of the building.
■ Broadcasting your wireless network's presence (SSID).
■ Treating the wireless network as an integral part of the wired network, rather than a perimeter to the wired network.
■ Setting up a secure wireless network (at least as secure as any of our wired networks) is possible, but it must be done with careful planning, execution, and testing.

IEEE 802.11 standard. The IEEE committee for Local and Metropolitan Area Network Standards began the 802.11-working group in 1990. The first wireless standard was completed in 1997. 802.11 standards define the interface between wireless clients and their network access points; this includes both the physical and the MAC layers of the OSI model. These standards also define how roaming between access points and the WEP security mechanism works.

There are three transmission types that are defined within the 802.11 standard: diffuse infrared, DSSS radio, and FHSS radio.

The MAC layer has two main standards of operation: a distributed mode (CSMA/CD) and a coordinated mode.

IEEE 802.11a specification. The 802.11a specification was begun before 802.11b as the letter "a" suggests, although it was completed afterward. 802.11a uses the 5 GHz band and is designed to pump through 54 Mbps worth of information using the new modulation scheme known as Orthogonal Frequency Division Multiplexing (OFDM).

Due to the different band used than 802.11b, these two standards are not compatible, although vendors are making equipment that supports both standards. Using the 5 GHz range should provide cleaner transmissions. Other wireless devices such as cordless phones, microwave ovens, baby monitors, and Bluetooth devices use the 2.4 GHz band. This standard is also referred to as WiFi5.

IEEE 802.11b specification. 802.11b is the most widely recognized standard currently in use. This standard was approved in September 1999 allowing for transmission rates of up to 11 Mbps using the 2.4 GHz radio band. Due to MAC overhead, errors, and collision, the actual data transfer rate is about 6 Mbps.

802.11b uses Complimentary Code Keying (CCK) and direct sequence spread spectrum (DSSS), which allows it to be fully backward compatible with DSSS implementations of 802.11. This standard is also referred to as WiFi.

IEEE 802.11g. 802.11g was approved by IEEE on June 12, 2003, although vendors began shipping products well before this date. This is another high-speed extension of the standard that is similar to 802.11b. 802.11g uses DSSS (like 802.11b). The changes that exist in this version of the 802.11 standard allow for transmission rates up to 54 Mbps.

802.11g is designed to have backwards compatibility and interoperability with 802.11b DSSS-based products.

One of the drawbacks with 802.11g is that it uses the same radiofrequency as other devices such as wireless phones, microwaves, and Bluetooth devices, which could cause some interference with the transmission.

802.11h is an amendment to the existing 802.11a standard to help reduce interference between 5Ghz 802.11a networks with military radars and satellite communications, which also happen to use the same frequency. 802.11h standards allow 802.11a networks to coexist using dynamic frequency selection and transmit power control harmoniously with potentially conflicting signals.

802.11n is a proposed amendment to existing 802.11 standards that support multiple-input multiple-output (MIMO), channel bonding, and other features to achieve bandwidths much higher than the current 54 Mbps achieved by 802.11g. Although the final version of 802.11n is not anticipated to be approved until late 2009, many manufacturers are already producing 802.11n wireless access points, easily identifiable by their numerous antennas, based on draft versions of the 802.11 standard.

IEEE 802.11i. 802.11i, also known as WPA2, is an amendment to the original 802.11 standard to include security mechanisms for wireless networks. This amendment was the result of the security features lacking in Wired Equivalent Privacy and the original Wi-Fi Protected Access (WPA). There were two main developments: WPA security improvements and Robust Security Networks (RSN). The WPA uses the Temporal Key Integrity Protocol (TKIP) to exchange keys. This protocol strengthens and changes the way keys are created and changed. It also adds a message-integrity-check function to prevent forged packet playbacks from occurring. RSN takes advantage of Extensible Authentication Protocol (EAP) and Advanced Encryption Standard (AES). RSN allows for dynamic negotiation of authentication and encryption protocols. This flexibility allows the protocol to adapt to the new threats and new advancements in the encryption schemes. RSN will likely not run very well on legacy hardware since the encryption and security computations require more processing power. Until devices, both the mobile device and the wireless access point, are given more processing power or specific hardware accelerators to handle this processing, RSN will likely have a slow acceptance.

IEEE 802.11 wireless LAN equipment and components. To install a wireless LAN, there are a few pieces of equipment that are required. First, the computer must have a wireless network interface card (NIC) installed. The wireless NICs can be built in to the computer or the NIC can be connected through a PCI slot, a USB port, or PCMCIA slot. Second, there must be a wireless access point for the NIC to communicate with or an additional NIC that can accept connections. Optionally, there can also be additional antennas for added distance.

IEEE 802.15. The IEEE 802.15 is broken down into four task groups: The first task group is targeted toward Wireless Personal Area Networks (WPANs). This technology focuses around Bluetooth. It has derived the Media Access controls and physical layer stipulations from Bluetooth 1.1. The second task group is focused on the interaction between WPANs and 802.11 standards. The third task group is broken into two subgroups dealing with WPAN high rate and WPAN alternate higher rate. Both of these groups deal with a WPAN with data connection speeds in excess of 20 Mbits per second. The fourth task group deals with a very low rate WPAN but with an extremely long battery life.

IEEE 802.16. IEEE 802.16 is also known as WiMAX. WiMAX is derived from the Worldwide Interoperability for Microwave Access. It was targeted to set the standards for Broadband Wireless Access to Metropolitan Area Networks (MANs). This standard varies from the traditional WiFi MAC. In the standard WiFi MAC, every device wishing to talk with the Access Point interrupts the access point while contacting it. Higher-priority services like Voice over IP and video may get dropped or severely interrupted in this type of environment. In the WiMAX environment, devices compete for the initial entry into the network and from then on the device is allocated a time slot from the base station or access point. This allows for more efficient use of bandwidth and does not suffer under a heavy load or possible oversubscription.

Wireless access points. Wireless access points (AP) are the connection points between the wired and wireless networks. As a result, if they are not secured properly they can provide easy entry into your wired network. The single biggest threat associated with APs is their low cost and ease of deployment in enterprise environments. APs are almost always configured to be "plug and play" out of the box so that the instant they are plugged into a wired jack, they are ready to use by anyone without restriction. These unsecured APs, often referred to as being "rogue," can pose serious risk to a network. The search for these rogue access points and marking their locations have been referred to as "war driving" and "war chalking."

With these serious risks in mind, there are several recommended actions that you take to begin securing the APs when you are deploying them.

One of the first recommended actions is to change the Service Set Identifier (SSID) from the factory default. The SSID identifies the AP by name on your network. If the name is known or discoverable, then an attacker is one step closer to gaining access to the network. Therefore, the second action is to disable the broadcasting of the SSID from the AP.

The third recommended security practice for your AP is to enable MAC address filtering. When MAC address filtering is enabled, only the MAC addresses that were previously specified to the AP will be allowed to connect. While it is possible to spoof a MAC address, you are increasing the level of difficulty for the attacker to compromise your network. The fourth recommended security practice is to set up logging on the AP. This will allow you to monitor the activity of your AP.

The fifth recommended security practice is to disable all unnecessary services such as SNMP. If you neglect to disable unused services, you may be inadvertently providing an open door to your wired network through the AP.

The sixth recommended security practice is to limit the broadcast power output of your AP if possible. You might find that the coverage area of your AP as configured from the factory extends beyond your building limits.

The seventh recommended security practice is to enable encryption whether it is WPA, WPA2, or the lowest security level—Wired Equivalent Privacy (WEP) encryption. WEP has known vulnerabilities and there are tools available to exploit these vulnerabilities, but nevertheless you should enable WEP encryption at a minimum. When doing so, consider that the longer your WEP key is and the less traffic you send on your wireless network, the more security WEP provides. If the AP supports WPA or WPA2, one of these should be configured instead of WEP.

The final recommendation would be to design your architecture so that behind your wireless access point you would have a firewall/VPN that would prohibit any traffic that is not encrypted and authenticated. The firewall should be set to drop and log all other traffic. Placing an IDS solution between the firewall/VPN and the access point is also another good idea. While it may not tell you who is passively listening on your network, it may alert you to attacks or probes against your network.

Antennas. When creating a wireless network for the purpose of a point-to-point connection between two buildings, antennas must be considered. There are two basic types of antennas: omnidirectional and directional.

Omnidirectional antennas are more of a security concern due to the nature of the horizontal beam width covering a full 360 degrees. If you are using omnidirectional antennas consider terrain masking, or blocking the transmission of the signal in the unwanted direction with a "backstop" such as a roof, stairwell, or a heavily constructed wall.

Directional antennas contain the beam within a limited spread and allow for finer control of the area that they cover.

Antenna configuration and placement. Once you choose either an omnidirectional or directional antenna, the real work begins. Obstructions and signal attenuation are two concerns to be addressed when placing and configuring your antenna.

The following are considerations when planning your antenna placement:

- Trees
- Buildings
- Weather
- Curvature of the earth (with connections with distances exceeding 7 miles)

These items can work with you or against you. Consider how they will affect the intended wireless users as well as the attackers.

When using a site-to-site wireless connection, there is no reason not to use a VPN to add an extra layer of security for the data. The VPN termination points can also be set up to disregard all traffic not being sent via the other termination point, therefore limiting the external access for an intruder.

Wireless network interface cards and adapters. The wireless NIC or adapter for your mobile device needs little configuration. The first configuration might be the SSID that you want this device to attach to. If you have disabled the SSID broadcast capability in your AP, then you must configure the SSID in the NIC. Also, if there are multiple APs available, you may wish to configure the NIC for the SSID that you want it to connect to.

The second configuration is for authentication, encryption, and integrity parameters. When you have enabled WEP, the key usually needs to be entered into the NIC configuration as well as the AP configuration.

If you have increased security on your wireless network, you may also have to change or set up your WPA2 or WPA settings. Other settings may include how you will authenticate to the network—either PSK or 802.1X.

Inherent security vulnerabilities with IEEE 802.11x. There are many inherent security vulnerabilities with IEEE 802.11x. The nature of a wireless network alone can leave a WLAN subject to attacks. Wireless is not bound by the same physical principles as a wired network and is accessible from any location within the antenna's signal beam.

The security included with 802.11x has been discovered to be vulnerable to attacks. The first common problem with wireless networks is that, by default, security mechanisms are disabled and are often not enabled by network administrators. This leaves a wireless network susceptible to both passive and active attacks, which includes everything from simple eavesdropping to WLAN jacking.

Over the next several pages, we will take a look at these vulnerabilities and attack techniques.

802.11 authentication and its weaknesses. The authentication options with 802.11 are few. 802.11b includes an option called "open authentication." Open authentication is basically no authentication at all. This authentication is not appropriate for corporate environments but might be suitable for public access points, such as libraries or coffee shops.

If a company is relying on 802.11b authentication for security, they have missed the boat. The way that authentication is accomplished is with the SSID in the following way:

1. The user's station will send out a probe frame (active scanning) with the desired Service Set ID (SSID).
2. The AP with that SSID will send back a probe response frame.
3. The user's station will accept the SSID, Timing Sync Function (TSF), timer value, and physical setup values from the AP frame.

Since the SSID is often broadcasted from the AP, there is little security in this approach.

WEP encryption and its weaknesses. WEP allows for a standards-based form of encryption on a wireless network. WEP relies on the RC4 encryption algorithm created by RSA. WEP can be used in either a 64- or 128-bit form. Some vendors will advertise a 40- or 104-bit WEP encryption method. The 40- and 64-bit formats are identical to each other, it is just a matter of linguistics. WEP 64-bit uses 40 bits for the private key and 24 bits for the Initialization Vector (IV).

There are a couple of inherent weaknesses with WEP encryption. The first is the authentication is not mutual. The client never has the opportunity to authenticate the AP so it is subject to MITM attacks.

The second weakness with WEP is that the key can be recovered if the attacker gathers enough of the transmission. There are tools available on the Internet that allow an attacker to listen to your wireless transmission, gather the data, and then recover your WEP key within a few hours of beginning. The WEP key will only slow down an attacker; it will not stop the attack. Relying on WEP alone for security would be a mistake.

Passive network attacks. Passive network attacks are relatively easy to implement and are very difficult to detect. The most common problem with wireless technology is that any anonymous attacker could be listening in. Anyone could set up a laptop with relatively little extra time and equipment, and start listening in to wireless communications. These attacks could be simple eavesdropping or MITM attacks.

The equipment needed to listen in on a wireless connection is a computer (laptop, PDA, etc.), a wireless card, and some downloadable software to detect and then eavesdrop on any unsecured wireless network. A WLAN with security enabled could take a little more work, but is still vulnerable to attacks. The MITM attacks require a little more work because the attacker will intercept the user's transmission and then forward it on to the actual network device. The goals of MITM attacks include injecting data, modifying communications, or simply eavesdropping on a network or its clients.

Active network attacks. Active network attacks can take the form of:

- Rogue client
- Rogue network access point
- Client-to-client attacks
- Infrastructure equipment attacks
- Denial of service attacks
  - Client jamming
  - Base station jamming

There are many actions that an attacker can do to gain access to a WLAN. First, an attacker can mimic the identity of a known WLAN client. The attacker could steal an access point or set up a rogue access point to impersonate a valid network resource. They can attack another unprotected client on the WLAN to gain authentication information for some other part of the network. The attacker could gain access to your APs through a default login and password or a guessed password such as your company name. It is also possible to attack a switch by using a MAC or ARP table flood causing the switch to fail open.

War driving. The term *war driving* derives from the term *war dialing*, and refers to the practice of dialing different phone numbers to locate an open and available modem to connect to. This can also be used to dial numbers looking for an open PBX that allows the attacker to place long distance or international calls. The war driving attacker drives around in a car equipped with everything that they need to connect to your WLAN—a laptop or PDA with a wireless card, a network discovery tool such as NetStumbler, and a homemade antenna. As an addition to their configuration, they can add a GPS to record the locations of the networks that they discover.

WLAN jacking. Once a network has been discovered, the attacker can exploit it. Many attackers are only looking for a way to connect to the Internet, although some are looking for information or resources on your network that they can exploit. Caution needs to be taken in setting up a wireless network, or any network for that matter, to avoid potential fines or lawsuits in the event that your network is used for malicious intent.

WLAN jacking is easy for an attacker if there is no security turned on at the AP. All the attacker needs is a laptop or PDA, a wireless card, a network discovery tool such as NetStumbler, and optionally a GPS and an antenna to acquire the signal of the target network. Once the network is discovered, the attacker can connect. Once connected to your network, he has access to your network resources and your Internet access.

The current legal argument is that looking for unsecured WLANs is not a crime; however, a crime is committed if the perpetrator then uses the network for illegal activity.

There is also an argument that if there is no security turned on at the AP, then how does the attacker know that this is not just a public access network, like you can find at coffeehouses and such, and, therefore, is not breaking the law by using your network?

If there is any form of security turned on at the AP, then it may take the attacker a little more work to crack through the WEP or to try guessing your SSID or intercepting a transmission from a user and "stealing" their connection. There are enough tools available on the Internet to exploit WLANs to make this all possible.

Securing 802.11 wireless LANs. It is possible to secure your wireless network (relatively speaking) from outside attack. You should not rely on one method alone to secure your wireless network though. Actions to consider implementing include:

■ MAC address filtering
■ Authentication
■ Authentication Servers
■ WEP Keys
■ VPN
■ Firewalls

MAC address filtering. MAC address filtering can be enabled on most APs today. MAC filtering allows you to control which MAC addresses are allowed to connect to your AP. For a small network, this is relatively easy to manage. As your network reaches 100 wireless users and beyond, this becomes a little more difficult to manage. In a large network, the wireless user would be restricted to the AP that her or his MAC address has been programmed into. This may or may not be considered a limitation for your network.

There is still a way around this security mechanism though. With the network discovery tools and listening capabilities that are on the market, an attacker with the right wireless NIC could discover an active MAC on your network and then change their NIC to use a valid MAC.

The second way around this security mechanism is our weak password habits. An AP with default or easy-to-guess passwords is easy prey for attackers. The attacker can gain access to your AP and then add their MAC to the list.

Authentication. As stated earlier in this chapter, the authentication that comes with 802.11b might as well be considered no authentication at all. There are other authentication methods that can be added to your wireless network to increase the security. The authentication methods include EAP-TLS, EAP-TTLS, or proprietary methods such as Cisco's LEAP. It is necessary for a Security Practitioner to be constantly vigilant. Security vulnerabilities in LEAP have been found and the vendor recommends users quickly upgrade to EAP.

Extensible Authentication Protocol (EAP) provides an authentication method that allows an administrator to centrally manage access to the wireless network and is, therefore, more robust than the authentication found with 802.11b. This method allows the administrator to enable per-user, per-session keys (EAP-TLS). This requires the user to enter a username and password to gain access to the wireless network.

As an example, a username and password are authenticated by a RADIUS server. Once authentication is completed, the RADIUS server sends the session key to the client. This process greatly improves the security of the wireless connection over static WEP keys and open authentication. The TLS portion of the authentication continues the process of authenticating between the client and the RADIUS server.

It is also recommended to use either WPA or WPA2 instead of simple WEP.

Authentication servers. Adding a Remote Authentication Dial-In User Service (RADIUS), two-factor tokens, or other two factor authentication Server, or Digital Certificates to your WLAN has many advantages:

- Reduction or elimination of WEP vulnerabilities
- Centralized MAC address management
- Centralized user management
- Domain/directory authentication
- Accounting reports
- Interoperability

There are many other types of authentication server that could be used. We have listed a few for example purposes. The most important idea is that you should have a strong method of authentication before you allow anyone on your network, especially through a wireless LAN connection.

WEP keys. Due to the weaknesses with WEP keys if used alone, your network is susceptible to attack, as discussed earlier in this chapter. There are many additions and changes that are being made to the standard to enhance the effectiveness of this element of security. They include:

- Temporal Key Integrity Protocol (TKIP) implements key hashing to prevent attacks on the WEP key.
- Message Integrity Control (MIC) appends a unique identifier to each packet to enable verification in both transmission directions to prevent MITM attacks.
- Extensible Authentication Protocol (EAP), as previously discussed, adds a per-user, per-session key to enhance security.
- IEEE 802.1X standard is a refinement of the current authentication mechanism for WEP.

IEEE 802.1X standard. 802.1X was approved in June 2001 as an authentication method that can be used on wireless and wired networks. This standard uses existing protocols for user authentication, such as EAP and RADIUS. Windows XP as well as some wireless equipment already has the capability of 802.1X built-in.

The basic purpose of 802.1X is to authenticate users, although it can be used to optionally establish encryption keys. The authentication can be performed by any means the vendor chooses, such as RADIUS or KERBEROS. Until authentication is complete, traffic is not allowed to pass onto the network. The 802.1X standard includes the mandatory use of 128-bit keys for RC4 data encryption and encryption key rotation.

With 802.1X, the user device is referred to as the supplicant. For wireless purposes, the access point is referred to as the authenticator system. The RADIUS server is referred to as the authentication server.

VPN in a wireless network. A VPN is a valuable addition to a wireless LAN. A useful point of view to take about your WLAN is that it is an external part of your network and VPNs and firewalls are good measures to add to protect this entry into your network. A common trap with WLANs is to consider them an internal part of the network. Since they are so hard to secure, if an attacker compromises your WLAN, your entire network is potentially compromised.

A WLAN secured with a VPN has the following benefits:

- The VPN increases the security of the WLAN well beyond the capabilities of WEP.
- Security tools, such as two-factor tokens increases the strength of the authentication used.

Wireless LAN policy, standard, and procedures. A network security policy must be amended to include wireless networking and devices. This should be the case even if a network does not include a wireless segment. It is possible for a user to add wireless capability to their network-connected desktop for the purpose of file sharing from their laptop. Their desktop could and probably does allow access to the wired network. If an attacker were to discover this unprotected wireless AP, then the network would be compromised.

The network policy should include a policy prohibiting a user to add wireless equipment unless they have the express permission of the IT department. PDAs and handheld computers should also be included in the network security policy. If these devices offer either Bluetooth or 802.11 connections, they may be subject to attack.

New Network and Telecommunications Frontiers

The continual advances in network and telecommunications technologies have led to an explosive growth in available bandwidth for just about everyone that uses a computer. In just a few short decades, the typical data transmitted over the network have gone from a string of simple ASCII characters to remarkable high-definition multimedia. Security practitioners now need to be knowledgeable in areas that have been traditionally outside of the normal scope of control. Some examples include:

Voice-over IP (VoIP). VoIP has converged the traditional analog telephony services with that of the Internet. This technology was initially adopted by large corporations to reduce long distance costs, now VoIP has matured into consumer phone services available through providers such as Vonage and Skype. The increasing popularity of VoIP has led to new threats and nuisances such as Vishing (a form of phishing using VoIP phone calls) and VoIP Spam (prerecorded phone messages through VoIP).

Instant messaging (IM). Although predominantly introduced as a social networking tool, there has been widespread acceptance of the use of IMs as an enterprise collaboration tool. Typical uses of IM in the enterprise include the ability to "ask quick questions," perform ad hoc meetings, and enhance telepresence (con call+). Unfortunately, IM technologies introduce potential vulnerabilities, including SPIM (spam over IM), phishing attacks, file sharing, information leakage, inappropriate use (reduction of productivity), and compliance to organizations. Consequently many enterprises have made the decision to either prohibit the use of IM (via technological controls such as port blocking) or introduce business-driven IM technologies such as Microsoft LCS (Live Communications Server). Enterprises should consider treating IM as another other disruptive technology, balancing risks with business value before making the decision to invest in either encouraging the use of IM or eliminating it.

Peer-to-Peer (P2P) and file sharing: The maturation of the PC from a "green screen" text-based editor in the DOS years to a multimedia platform today is also leading to new complexities and challenges for the security practitioner. The ability to create, edit, share, and play pictures, movies, and music on the PC is fueling the market for potentially disruptive technologies. For example, the nefarious peer-to-peer file-sharing programs such as KaZaa, eDonkey, and Morpheus not only allow viruses and malware to be spread globally but also serves as a primary engine for innovation of applications that will enable illegal digital reproduction of movies and music (mp3, mpeg, etc.).

These technologies and others have in turn sparked a technology arms race, which has created an entirely new technology domain called Digital Rights Management (DRM), which has the sole goal of intellectual property and copyright protection via file level encryption. While the use of DRM technologies have been a regular staple in the entertainment industry in protecting copyright restricts for nearly a decade, the controversy regarding the legality of imposing technological restrictions on software (especially derivatives of open source), music, publications, and entertainment persists.

To bifurcate the issues of protecting enterprise content (protection of documents, industrial intellectual property, etc.) versus the growing controversy in the multimedia industry, a new term, Information Rights Management (IRM), has gained acceptance. Technologies such as Microsoft Windows Rights Management Services and Liquid Machines are some of the leaders in the area of enterprise IRM who develop solutions specifically for IRM. Other technologies and approaches such as watermarking (visual cues for users) and MetaData Tagging (no discernable cues to users of ownership) are beginning to gain attention for IRM. The single biggest issue for all IRM (DRM also) technologies is the lack of a common standard for implementing the base technologies, which means that each technology will require the use of a separate PC client to enforce the IRM policies. This lack of commonality and standardization means that multiple clients must be used between different organizations deploying different technologies. This singular issue of interoperability between IRM systems will likely need to be resolved before the widespread implementation of IRM.

With advances in networking and telecommunications technologies not expected to slow anytime soon, the security practitioner should be on constant guard for emerging threats from the increasing volume of multimedia being transmitted and used and technologies that are being used to protect the content on the local network and Internet.

Need for Security Policies, Standards, and Procedures for the IT Infrastructure

The need for security policies, standards, and procedures becomes readily apparent when one recognizes that an IT infrastructure is only as secure as the weakest link in the chain of security responsibility. For example, one could secure data resources and maintain the confidentiality by storing it in an encrypted database stored on a server positioned on a LAN behind a firewall. However, if that same server is not installed in a data center or hosting center with proper physical security measures where access is limited to authorized personnel, is that IT resource secure? It is safe to say no, and, unfortunately, it has been shown to be a frequent scenario.

Securing the IT Infrastructure

The roles and responsibilities for maintaining confidentiality, integrity, and availability of a company's information technology infrastructure require defining. Until people are held responsible for each and every aspect of the IT infrastructure, there is sure to be a weakness that can be exploited by an attacker.

To secure your network and assets requires thought and planning. The following 10 tips for creating a network security policy are from http://www.windowsecurity .com:

1. Identify and locate your assets.
2. Perform a threat risk assessment.
3. Adopt a "need-to-know" philosophy.
4. Perform an informal site survey of your organization.
5. Institute a standard for classifying all information.
6. Ascertain who needs access to external resources.
7. Create a disaster recovery plan.

8. Appoint someone to be responsible for security policy enforcement.
9. Review the impact of any intended procedural changes on your employees.
10. Understand that the implementation of any security policy needs regular validation.

Domains of IT Security Responsibility

When identifying and locating your corporate assets, the entire IT infrastructure must be examined. For a logical breakdown of your assets, the IT infrastructure can be broken down into seven domains:

1. User domain
2. Workstation domain
3. LAN domain
4. Remote Access domain
5. LAN-to-WAN domain
6. WAN domain
7. System/Application domain

User domain. The user domain defines the roles, responsibilities, and accountability for employees and nonemployees that will be accessing corporate owned resources and systems. The policies and standards that apply to the user domain must be reviewed, signed, and executed by all users, employee or not, before they have access to the network and its resources. This policy should include the Acceptable Use Policy (AUP) for Internet access, e-mail access, and system access.

An audit is necessary to verify that the end user is indeed who they claim to be; this should be done for both employees and nonemployees that will be accessing the corporate systems and resources.

Workstation domain. The workstation domain defines the roles and responsibilities for the workstation device (thin client, Windows workstation, UNIX workstation, etc.) that resides on the user's desktop. This domain pertains to maintaining and updating the user workstations and devices (e.g., hardware, software, firmware, operating systems, memory, etc.) that are authorized and approved for access and connectivity to company owned resources and systems.

This domain includes the following hardware:

■ Desktop computers
■ Laptop computers
■ Smartphones
■ Printers/scanners
■ Handheld computers
■ Wireless equipment (access points)
■ Modems

This domain's specifications for the workstation operating systems, antivirus software updates, and other workstation configuration state that standards must be kept current and validated to maintain the integrity of the workstation domain. Workstation client software used for remote access and security is also part of this domain. An audit is necessary to verify that the workstation has the appropriate "hardening" completed. This would include appropriate and up-to-date antivirus protection software.

LAN domain. The LAN domain defines the roles and responsibilities for the local area network physical connection (e.g., LAN hub/switch setup and configuration) as well as the logical connection to corporate file servers from the workstation devices on the user's desktop.

The physical connection for the LAN includes infrastructure elements, wiring, switches, and the physical connection to the departmental or building local area network systems. The logical connection from the desktop includes the authorized logon UserIDs and passwords for access to the LAN server.

An audit and assessment would need to check and verify that the local area network server, operating system, and access control methods are implemented as per the appropriate data classification level. A review and "hardening" of the LAN components both physically and logically is typical for the LAN domain. This would include an assessment of the location of the server (e.g., LAN server hosted in a data center with secured access, UPS electric power, behind VPN termination point on server farm, behind firewall when WAN connectivity is required, etc.).

In addition, more stringent back-up procedures are required for a server; thus, audit and assessment of the CD-ROM or disk storage devices and procedures are necessary. Logical "hardening" will typically occur on the operating system of the server and the client. This "hardening" may include more secure system administration and access control procedures, stricter user login and password changing requirements, or system audit entries that are triggered when access to certain folders, applications, or data is needed.

LAN-to-WAN domain. The LAN-to-WAN domain defines the roles and responsibilities for the End Site Router and firewall providing interconnectivity between the LAN and the WAN domain.

Router configuration, firewall configuration, system monitoring, intrusion detection monitoring, and on-going system administration for the router, firewall, and intrusion detection system are part of this domain.

An audit is necessary to verify that the LAN-WAN domain is configured to permit only authorized access between these two domains. This domain is also where session monitoring and intrusion detection monitoring systems are best utilized when access to data of a sensitive nature is required.

WAN domain. The WAN domain defines the roles and responsibilities for the WAN that provides end-to-end connectivity for all company end-site locations.

This domain is composed of backbone circuits, POP switches, routers, firewalls, intrusion detection systems, and end-site devices, such as routers, CSU/DSUs, and codecs that will be installed at identified end-site locations.

An audit is necessary to verify that the WAN domain is properly configured to permit traffic flows between it and the end-user workstation and LAN. This is especially important if tunnels or VPNs are utilized between end points.

Remote access domain. The remote access domain defines the roles and responsibilities of authorized users who access corporate resources remotely (e.g., secured and authenticated remote access).

This domain applies to both company-owned and user-owned systems that provide remote access (e.g., authorized users from home or other remote locations) to corporate-owned resources and systems through the public Internet (e.g., dial-up, DSL, or cable modem Internet access) or a dedicated connection to outside entities or value added services. In addition, this domain pertains to the logical workstation-to-network connection via an authorized logon UserID and password for access to company-owned resources and systems. Remote workstations that require client software for VPN or thin client support or intrusion detection monitoring are also part of this domain.

An audit is necessary to verify that any remote access to data conforms to the level of data classification assigned. This is important because remote access to sensitive data or applications typically requires VPN technology between client and server or an additional level of authentication as part of the access control procedures.

System/application domain. The system/application domain defines the roles and responsibilities of the systems and applications that are to be accessed by the users from their desktop workstation device (e.g., mainframe, departmental LAN servers, application servers, Web servers).

This domain includes the configuration and "hardening" of the operating systems software as well as application security implementations and data base security measures. This domain encompasses all server platforms: Mainframe, UNIX, and Windows.

An audit is necessary to verify that the systems and applications include embedded security elements for access control, data storage, data encryption, and such. This includes systems and applications that reside on mainframes, departmental LAN servers, application servers, or Web servers, and the like.

Defining Standard and Enhanced Security Requirements

Defining standard and enhanced security requirements includes the following categories:

- Data sensitivity to attack
- Insertion of malicious code
- Loss of critical business functions

- Disaster recovery planning
- Confidentiality of sensitive information
- Physical security
- Security policies
- Response of personnel to security policies

Implementing Standard and Enhanced Security Solutions

There are many security countermeasures that can be implemented and deployed throughout a LAN and WAN network environment. Some of the tools, requirements, and items to incorporate into a security counter measure strategy are:

- Internet-facing systems should run the vendor's most stable and secure operating systems and have any necessary patches applied.
- Network-based intrusion detection systems (IDS) should monitor the outside perimeter segment to provide details on outside system attacks taking place before their entry into the firewall. These IDS should report activity back to the security information management system.
- As budgets allow, key network devices should be deployed in pairs with automatic fail over capability to increase overall network availability.
- VPN clients with built-in software firewalls should be used to prevent tunneling attacks. Incoming remote access data streams should be decrypted outside of or at the corporate firewall, optionally analyzed by an IDS system, run through the firewall rule base, and analyzed by an IDS system once inside the system.
- Key network devices should employ the use of out-of-band management channels that only allow a minimum of management communication from a dedicated management segment to the devices. Devices that are remotely located and cannot be connected to the management segment should employ VPN tunnels for their management. Other out-of-band management techniques (e.g., asynchronous terminal servers) should be considered.
- The organization's servers and workstations should employ the use of centrally managed and updated antivirus systems.
- Network-based IDS should monitor key segments for post-firewall data traffic intrusions and internal intrusions. These IDS should report activity back to the security information management system.
- Host-based IDS should be utilized on key hosts, if not all hosts, and be configured to report back to the security information management system.
- Internal WAN data traffic should be encrypted over private links if the data's value is sufficiently high and risk of exposure exists.
- Make sure that your remote VPN connections and internal network users are authenticated using one or more types of authentication servers.

Sample Questions

1. Match the topology with the appropriate description and vulnerabilities:
   a. Star
   b. Bus
   c. Ring
   d. Point to point
      i. In its most basic setup, the traffic flows in one direction. A break in the link and all traffic flow is severely limited.
      ii. One of the more secure topologies due to the limited opportunities to intercept the traffic.
      iii. The type of topology used in older networks or by cable companies. It is easy to listen to all of the traffic being broadcast on the wire.
      iv. If the center point fails or is compromised, the traffic can be completely stopped.
2. Match the following protocols with their descriptions:
   a. SMTP
   b. ICMP
   c. TFTP
   d. DHCP
      i. This protocol is used as an unauthenticated protocol to transfer data.
      ii. This protocol is used between two mail servers to determine how they will communicate.
      iii. This protocol is used to transmit the health and status of a network.
      iv. This protocol is used in assigning IP addresses, default gateways, and DNS information.
3. True or False—It is not important to look at the syslog files because they are being backed up and can be reviewed at any time.
4. Choose the best description for the following protocols:
   a. SSL
   b. IPSEC AH
   c. IPSEC ESP
   d. NAT
      i. Message confidentiality is provided by encrypting the payload.
      ii. Originally designed to compensate for a decreased number of IP addresses; has been used for security purpose of hiding IP addresses.
      iii. Message integrity is performed by authenticating the payload and the origin of the information.
      iv. Operates at the session layer and is often used with Digital Certificates.
5. Which of these protocols is not normally used to help make e-mail more secure?
   a. PGP
   b. S/MIME

     c. PEM

     d. MSP

     e. SNMP

6. Match the network equipment with its most common PRIMARY function:

     a. Firewall

     b. Router

     c. Switches

     d. VPN Termination Points

         i. Will pass traffic from one network to another network based on IP address.

         ii. Will pass traffic to the appropriate network segment based on the MAC address.

         iii. Enforced access control policy at given points of the network.

         iv. Terminates encrypted communications and forwards them to the internal network.

7. Choose the descriptions and benefits or risks that best match the following Remote Access Solutions:

     a. RAS

     b. VPN

     c. Clientless VPN

         i. Allows the user to access the network without necessarily having to have his own device with him. Using a third-party device might increase the network vulnerability by the use of hidden Trojans or keystroke monitoring tools.

         ii. Does not require Internet access and can be secured by other means like two-factor authentication; is not easily sniffed. Usually requires a large phone bank to receive calls, can be expensive for long distance bills, and subject to discovery by War dialing.

         iii. Allows for the user to have a strong means of authentication and verification. Often requires the IT department to touch and maintain every device, and the device is required to connect to the network.

8. Choose which of the following actions will help secure a wireless access point:

     a. Choosing WPA2 over WEP

     b. Hiding the SSID

     c. Activate MAC address filtering

     d. Having an access control technology with authentication capability built into the device or having this access control product immediately behind the access point.

     e. All of the above

9. Which of the following is true?

     a. Full-mesh topology is less expensive to deploy than other topologies.

     b. Full-mesh topology is just as expensive to deploy as other topologies.

    c. Full-mesh topology is typically used in local area networks.

    d. Full-mesh topology is the less fault tolerant than other topologies.

    e. None of the above is true.

10. Which of the following is typically deployed as a screening proxy for Web servers?

    a. State inspect firewalls

    b. Packet filters

    c. Reverse Proxies

    d. Intrusion Prevention Devices

    e. Kernel Proxy

11. Which of the following 802.11 specifications support MIMO?

    a. 802.11b

    b. 802.11n

    c. 802.11g

    d. 802.11a

    e. 802.11h

12. Which of these attacks use an intentionally malformed packet to cause DoS?

    a. LAND

    b. SYN Flood

    c. Session Hijacking

    d. Redirection

    e. Port Scan

13. Which of these is not true?

    a. MPLS differs from ATM in that it supports IP natively.

    b. MPLS supports both cell- and frame-based traffic.

    c. MPLS is packet switching technology.

    d. MPLS is a OSI Layer 4 technology.

    e. MPLS is expected to gain popularity.

14. What is the difference between DRM and IRM?

    a. DRM is completely supported by common law.

    b. DRM's best feature is its interoperability.

    c. IRM is intended to be used on multimedia only.

    d. IRM generally refers to DRM for enterprise content.

15. True or False: IRM technologies strictly deal with the encryption of protected content.

16. Which of the following is true?

    a. NAT "hides" private IP addresses behind a single public IP address.

    b. PAT "hides" private IP addresses behind a single public IP address.

    c. NAT and PAT cannot be used simultaneously.

    d. None are true.

17. Select the most correct statement:

    a. Derivative copies of content of documents is best prevented by using metadata tagging.

     b. Derivative copies of content of documents is best prevented by using file-level rights.

     c. Derivative copies of content of documents is best prevented by using encryption and IRM technologies.

     d. None are true.

18. True or False: Disabling of IM should be part of routine operations in an enterprise.

19. What is the primary advantage of a fully meshed network?

     a. It has the lowest operating cost to the end customer.

     b. It has the highest operating cost to the end customer.

     c. It has the lowest fault tolerance.

     d. It has the highest fault tolerance.

20. Which of the following is a common network configuration error?

     a. Using Telnet instead of SSH

     b. Leaving default, factory settings.

     c. Copying and using "sample" configurations from technical support Web sites.

     d. All of the above.

Chapter 6

Security Operations and Administration

C. Karen Stopford

Contents

Security operations and administration entails the identification of an organization's information assets and the documentation required for the implementations of policies, standards, procedures, and guidelines that ensure confidentiality, integrity, and availability. Working with management information owners, custodians and users, the appropriate data classification scheme is defined for proper handling of both hardcopy and electronic information.

A Systems Security Certified Practitioner (SSCP) candidate is expected to demonstrate knowledge in privacy issues, data classification, data integrity, audit, organization roles and responsibilities, policies, standards, guidelines, procedures, security awareness, configuration controls, and the application of accepted industry practices. Keys areas of knowledge include:

- Implement security administration
  a. Maintain adherence to security policies, baselines, standards, and procedures
  b. Validate security controls
  c. Data classification (e.g., control, handling, categorization)
- Participate in change management
  a. Participate in the implementation of configuration management plan
  b. Review the impact of changes to the environment
  c. Test patches, fixes, and updates
- Provide security evaluation and assistance to the organization (e.g., product evaluation, data flow management)

- Participate in security awareness education
- Adhere to Code of Ethics
  a. Understand and comply with (ISC)² Code of Ethics
  b. Understand and comply with the organizational code of ethics
- Assess the infrastructure using appropriate tools
- Understand concepts of endpoint device security

The terms *security administration* and *security operations* are often used interchangeably by organizations to refer to the set of activities performed by the security practitioner to implement, maintain, and monitor effective safeguards to meet the objectives of an organization's information security program. In many organizations, security administrators are responsible for configuring, managing, and participating in the design of technical and administrative security controls for one or more operating system platforms or business applications, while security operations personnel primarily focus on configuring and maintaining security-specific systems such as firewalls, intrusion detection and prevention systems, and antivirus software. Placing knowledgeable practitioners in operations and administration roles is critical to security program effectiveness. This chapter focuses on the knowledge and skills needed to become an effective security administrator.

Security Program Objectives: The C-I-A Triad

The essential mission of any information security program is to protect the confidentiality, integrity, and availability of an organization's information systems assets. Effective security controls, whether they are physical, technical, or administrative, are designed and operated to meet one or more of these three requirements.

Confidentiality

Confidentiality refers to the property of information in which it is only made available to those who have a legitimate need to know. Those with a need to know may be employees, contractors and business partners, customers, or the public. Information may be grouped into a logical series of hierarchical "classes" based on the attributes of the information itself; the parties authorized to access, reproduce, or disclose the information; and the potential consequences of unauthorized access or disclosure. The level of confidentiality may also be dictated by an organization's of conduct and operating principles, its need for secrecy, its unique operating requirements, and its contractual obligations. Each level of confidentiality is associated with a particular protection class; that is, differing levels of confidentiality require different levels of protection from unauthorized or unintended disclosure. In some cases, the required level of protection—and thus the protection class or confidentiality level—is specified by laws and regulations governing the organization's conduct.

It is important to distinguish between confidentiality and privacy. Many states have privacy laws that dictate how and for what purpose personal, nonpublic information may be accessed. However, privacy also refers to an individual's ownership of his or her information, and includes not only the need to maintain confidentiality on a strict "need to know" basis, but also the individual's right to exercise discretionary control over how his or her information is collected, the accuracy of the information, and how, by whom, and for what purpose the information is used.

Authorization, identity and access management, and encryption and disclosure controls are some methods of maintaining an appropriate level of confidentiality. Detective controls such as data leakage prevention tools may be used to monitor when, how, and by whom information is accessed, copied, or transmitted.

The consequences of a breach in confidentiality may include legal and regulatory fines and sanctions, loss of customer and investor confidence, loss of competitive advantage, and civil litigation. These consequences can have a damaging effect on the reputation and economic stability of an organization. When certain types of an individual consumer's information such as personally identifying data, health records, or financial information are disclosed to unauthorized parties, consequence such as identity and monetary theft, fraud, extortion, and personal injury may result. Information central to the protection of government interests may have serious public safety and national security consequences if disclosed.

Integrity

Integrity is the property of information whereby it is recorded, used, and maintained in a way that ensures its completeness, accuracy, internal consistency, and usefulness for a stated purpose. Systems integrity, on the other hand, refers to the maintenance of a known good configuration and expected operational function. Integrity is a key factor in the reliability of information and systems.

Integrity controls include system edits and data validation routines invoked during data entry and update; system, file, and data access permissions; change and commitment control procedures; and secure hashing algorithms. Detective controls include system and application audit trails, balancing reports and procedures, antivirus software, and file integrity checkers.

The need to safeguard information and system integrity may be dictated by laws and regulations, such as the Sarbanes–Oxley Act of 2002, which mandates certain controls over the integrity of financial reporting. More often, it is dictated by the needs of the organization to access and use reliable, accurate information. Integrity controls such as digital signatures used to guarantee the authenticity of messages, documents, and transactions play an important role in non-repudiation (in which a sending or signing party cannot deny their action) and verifying receipt of messages. Finally, the integrity of system logs and audit trails and other types of forensic data is essential to the legal interests of an organization.

Consequences of integrity failure include an inability to read or access critical files, errors and failures in information processing, calculation errors, and uninformed decision making by business leaders. Integrity failures may also result in inaccuracies in reporting, resulting in the levying of fines and sanctions, and in inadmissibility of evidence when making certain legal claims or prosecuting crime.

Availability

Availability refers to the ability to access and use information systems when and as needed to support an organization's operations. Systems availability requirements are often defined in Service Level Agreements (SLAs), which specify percentage of uptime as well as support procedures and communication for planned outages. In disaster recovery planning, system Recovery Time Objectives (RTOs) specify the acceptable duration of an unplanned outage due to catastrophic system nonavailability. When designing safeguards, security practitioners must balance security requirements with the need for availability of infrastructure services and business applications.

Availability controls include hardware and software RAID (Redundant Array of Independent Disks) controllers, UPS (uninterruptable power supply), backup and recovery software and procedures, mirroring and journaling, load balancing and failover, and business continuity plans.

Consequences of availability failures include interruption in services and revenue streams, fines and sanctions for failure to provide timely information to regulatory bodies or those to whom an organization is obliged under contract, and errors in transaction processing and decision making.

Code of Ethics

All (ISC)²-certified security practitioners must comply with the Code of Ethics, which sets forth standards of conduct and professionalism that characterize our dealings with our employers, business associates, customers, and the community at large. There are four mandatory tenets of the Code of Ethics:

- Protect society, the commonwealth, and the infrastructure.
- Act honorably, honestly, justly, responsibly, and legally.
- Provide diligent and competent service to principals.
- Advance and protect the profession.

Additional guidelines for performing your role in a professional manner are also provided in the Code of Conduct.

Violations of the (ISC)² Code of Conduct are a serious matter, and may be subject to disciplinary action pursuant to a fair hearing by the Ethics Committee established by the (ISC)² Board of Directors. The complete Code of Conduct is available at the (ISC)² Web site.

Security Best Practices

When designing and implementing a security program, the security practitioner seeks to combine the needs of the organization with industry best practices. Best practices are defined as processes and methods that have been proven by thorough testing and real-world experience to consistently lead to desired results. A best practice may set the standard for performing a particular process such as managing system access or configuring a specific type of security device, or it may be broader in scope, covering one or more aspects of a security program such as risk management or personnel security. Security practitioners should refer to best practices where available to make use of the industry knowledge and experience that has gone into their creation and avoid "reinventing the wheel." Be mindful, however, that citing best practices is rarely, in itself, a sufficient argument for adopting a particular strategy for your organization. The technologies and practices you implement should first and foremost address the specific risks, objectives, and culture of your organization. Most best practices documents are designed with sufficient flexibility to allow you to readily adapt their principles into the specific set of practices that best meet the unique needs of your organization.

Designing a Security Architecture

Security architecture is the practice of designing a framework for the structure and function of information security systems and practices in the organization. When developing security architecture—whether at the enterprise, business unit, or system level—security best practices should be referenced for guidance when setting design objectives. Essential best practice considerations include:

- Defense-in-depth
- Risk-based controls
- Least privilege
- Authorization and accountability
- Separation of duties

Defense-in-Depth

There is no such thing as perfect security. Preventive measures designed to safeguard an organization's assets can and do fail due to the presence of unknown vulnerabilities, hardware or software failures, human error, weaknesses in dependent processes, and the efforts of external attackers and malicious insiders. Reliance on a single safeguard to protect any critical asset is an invitation to a security breach. Security practitioners understand this and avoid single points of failure by designing safeguards using a layered approach.

Designing for defense-in-depth requires an understanding of the specific threats to the target asset, and the anatomy of potential attacks or "attack vectors"; that is, the specific means by which a particular attack can occur. Defenses may be designed to prevent or deter attack using an outside-in or inside-out approach. By placing safeguards at two or more points along the access path to the asset, failure of one safeguard can be counteracted by the function of another safeguard further along the access path. For example, a firewall protecting an organization's Web server may be designed to only allow Web browsing (Http or Https) to the server from the external network. An attacker may either circumvent the firewall policy by following an indirect path, for example, accessing a Web server via a compromised host or user account with access to the server; by exploiting vulnerabilities in the firewall itself; or by using the allowed ports and protocols for purposes other than that for which they were intended. A defense-in-depth strategy might go beyond perimeter defenses, adding safeguards to the Web server and hosted Web applications, for example by disabling unnecessary services such as FTP (file transfer protocol), TELNET (terminal emulation), and remote procedure calls, requiring use of a unique identifier and strong authentication method to gain access to services, implementing protections against brute force of passwords, etc. If the actual target lies downstream from the interface, further protection along the access path is advisable. For example, if the Web server uses a database to store data, it can be protected by using stored procedures, using strong input validation, requiring additional authentication for people and applications, or installing a host-based intrusion prevention system on the database server. It is important to note that a true defense-in-depth strategy requires that safeguards not share a common mechanism or be dependent on one another for proper operation. This is because failure of a common mechanism causes failure of all safeguards that rely on that mechanism.

Network segmentation is also an effective way to achieve defense-in-depth for distributed or multitiered applications. The use of a demilitarized zone (DMZ), for example, is a common practice in security architecture. Host systems that are accessible through the firewall are physically separated from the internal network by means of secured switches, or by using an additional firewall (or multihomed firewall) to control traffic between the Web server and the internal network. Application DMZs are more frequently used today to limit access to application servers to those networks or systems that have a legitimate need to connect.

Although preventive controls are usually the first and primary design elements in a security architecture, no preventive mechanism is 100% foolproof. Furthermore, not all attacks can be prevented even by layering preventive safeguards along the access path to an asset without interfering with legitimate activity. For that reason, defense-in-depth design also includes detective and corrective controls along the attack path. Detective controls are designed to inform security practitioners when a preventive control fails or is bypassed. Activity logs, audit trails, accounting and balancing procedures, and intrusion detection systems (IDSes) are typical detective controls. Intrusion detection systems, which operate in real-time or near real-time, are the best choice for critical assets. Signature-based intrusion detection systems are designed to flag activity that the security practitioner has identified as suspicious or malicious. Such systems are useful for known attack scenarios. However, the so-called zero-day attacks for which no signature is yet available can evade these systems. Anomaly-based IDS have the advantage of identifying new attacks, but they must be constantly tuned as new applications or functions are introduced to avoid alarming on legitimate activity.

Finally, corrective controls seek to minimize extent or impact of damage from an attack and return compromised systems and data to a known good state. Furthermore, they seek to prevent similar attacks in the future. Corrective controls are usually manual in nature, but recent advances in intrusion detection and prevention technology have allowed security practitioners to place these systems in-line along the access path where they can automatically close ports, correct vulnerabilities, restore previous configurations, and redirect traffic as a result of a detected intrusion. Caution must be taken when implementing these systems to avoid interfering with legitimate activity, particularly when detective controls are set to automatically trigger corrective action.

Risk-Based Controls

Security has traditionally been considered "overhead" in many organizations, but this attitude is changing as more security practitioners enter the field armed with an understanding of business practices and the concept of risk-based security controls. All organizations face some degree of risk. Information security risk can be thought of as the likelihood of loss due to threats exploiting vulnerabilities, that is:

$$RISK = THREAT + VULNERABILITY + IMPACT$$

The degree of risk tells the organization what losses can be expected if security controls are absent or ineffective. The consequences or impact to assets may be tangible, as when computer equipment is lost or stolen, operations are interrupted, or fraudulent activity occurs. They may also be intangible, such as damage to an organization's reputation, decreased motivation of staff, or loss of customer and investor confidence. A "reasonable" expectation of loss may or may not be a result of a known probability or frequency of occurrence; for critical assets, large losses could result from a single security incident and, therefore, the risk may be high even if the probability of an incident occurring is low. Conversely, highly probable events that incur minimal losses may be considered acceptable as a "cost of doing business" depending on your organization's risk tolerance.

The concept of risk-based controls states that the total costs to implement and maintain a security measure should be commensurate with the degree to which risks to the confidentiality, integrity, and availability of the assets protected by the security measure must be reduced to acceptable levels. Safeguards that address multiple risks can and should be implemented to provide economies of scale wherever possible, as long as they are a part of an overall defense-in-depth strategy. The cost of safeguards includes not only capital expenses for software and equipment but also the use of resources to implement and maintain the safeguard and the impact, if any, on current business processes and productivity levels. An objective presentation of risk, including the likelihood and anticipated impact of adverse events, will help you gain needed support from financial decision makers and line staff. Risk treatment decisions—that is, whether and to what extent to transfer, mitigate, or accept a certain level of risk—are management decisions that should be founded in an objective view of the facts. Similarly, the prioritization and selection of safeguards is guided by the extent and nature of the risks uncovered in the risk assessment.

Using a standard process for assessing and documenting risk provides consistent and repeatable results that can be readily compared, trended, and understood by decision makers. Methodologies such as the Carnegie Mellon Software Engineering Institute's OCTAVE (Operationally Critical Threat, Asset, and Vulnerability Assessment) and COBRA (Consultative, Objective and Bi-Functional Risk Analysis), and guidance from industry best practices such as National Institute of Standards and Technology (NIST) Special Publication 800-30: Risk Management Guide for Information Technology Systems, enhance the credibility of your results and promote more efficient and effective use of time and resources.

A risk assessment may be qualitative or quantitative in nature; whenever possible, use quantitative data to document incident probability and impact. Data for the risk assessment may be based on internal events and historical data, surveys, interviews and questionnaires, and industry experience available through various publications and industry forums. The use of metrics and cost/benefit analyses are key success factors in gaining your organization's buy-in for security measures. Transparency of process, open communication, and a willingness to include non-technical management and line staff as participants in the risk assessment process make the risk assessment a collaborative effort and promote effective adoption of risk treatment recommendations.

Least Privilege

The least privilege concept is the analog of "need to know." Under least privilege, access rights are permissions are granted based on the need of a user or process to access and use information and resources. Only those rights and privileges needed to perform a specific function are granted. Eliminating unnecessary privileges reduces the potential for errors committed by users who may not have the knowledge or skills necessary to perform certain functions, and protects against random errors such as unintentional deletion of files. Limiting the number of privileged users on critical systems and auditing the activities of those who have a high privilege level also reduces the likelihood of authorized users performing unauthorized functions. On the desktop, least privilege or least user access (LUA) is often implemented to prevent casual users from installing software, modifying system settings, or falling prey to malicious code operating in the context of the logged-in user. Some organizations assign administrators two logins, one with administrative privileges and one with ordinary user privileges, to reduce the impact of mistakes when performing routine activities that do not require administrative authority. As an alternative, some systems provide temporary augmentation of privileges under "run as" or privilege adoption schemes in which additional privileges are granted for a specific task or session, then removed when the task is complete.

Least privilege can be implemented at the operating system, application, process, file, data element, or physical security layers. Unfortunately, many COTS (commercial, off-the-shelf) applications are developed in environments that have not adopted least privilege principles and, as a result, these products often require elevated privilege to run. For desktop applications, the use of Microsoft's FILEMON and REGMON utilities and similar tools can identify system files, registry keys, and other protected resources accessed by the application so that policy configuration can be modified to provide specific permissions as needed. However, this is time consuming and only useful in certain operating environments. When a full implementation of least privilege is not feasible or possible, adopting a defense-in-depth strategy using such things as audit logs, event monitoring, and periodic audits can be used as a compensating control strategy.

In practice, privileges are typically set by associating specific roles or groups with an access control entry. Maintaining role- or group-based privileges is much more efficient than granting these rights at an individual level, which requires frequent modifications across multiple access entries to accommodate changes in each individual's status and job function. The groups "Everyone," "Public," "Authenticated Users," and the like, which contain all authorized users of a system, should be associated with access control entries that grant only the minimum privileges needed to authenticate to the system.

Authorization and Accountability

Access control systems are designed with the assumption that there is an appropriate process in place to authorize individuals to specific access privileges. The decision of which privileges to grant to which individuals or groups should not be made by the security practitioner, but rather by the owners of the data or system to be accessed. A system or data owner is the individual who has the most vested interest in maintaining the confidentiality, integrity, or availability of a particular system or data set and is typically a business line manager or above. A record of authorizations should be kept to support access control system validation testing, in which actual access is compared to authorized access to determine whether the process of assigning access entitlements is working as intended and is aligned with the stated policy. Testing also helps to catch errors in assigning access privileges before a breach can occur. Documented authorizations are also used in forensic work when determining whether an incident occurred at the hands of a legitimate or illegitimate user.

Accountability is a principle that ties authorized users to their actions. Accountability is enforced through assigning individual access accounts and by generating audit trails and activity logs that link identifying information about the actor (person, system, or application) with specific events. Audit data should be protected against unintentional or malicious modification or destruction, as it is an important forensic tool. It should be backed up regularly and retained for a sufficient period to support investigations and reporting. Some regulations require a specific retention period for audit trail data. Individuals should be cautioned never to share their access with others and to protect their credentials from unauthorized use. They should be informed that any information recorded under their unique access accounts will be attributed to them; that is, they will be held accountable for any activity that occurs through use of the access privileges assigned to them.

Separation of Duties

Separation of duties is an operational security mechanism for preventing fraud and unauthorized use that requires two or more individuals to complete a task or perform a specific function. (Note: Separation of duties does not necessarily require two people to perform a task, but requires that the person performing is not the person checking on the task.) Separation of duties is a key concept of internal control and is commonly seen in financial applications that assign separate individuals to the functions of approving, performing, and auditing or balancing a transaction. This ensures that no single person operating alone can perform a fraudulent act without detection. Most COTS financial software packages have built-in mechanisms for enforcing appropriate separation of duties, using transaction segmentation and role-based access control. In nonfinancial systems, separation of duties may be implemented in any system subject to abuse or critical error to reduce the impact of a single person's actions. For example, most program change control processes separate development, testing, quality assurance (QA), and production release functions.

Dual control is similar to a separation of duties in that it requires two or more people operating at the same time to perform a single function. Examples of dual control include use of signature plates for printing, supervisor overrides for certain transactions and adjustments, and some encryption key recovery applications.

Separation of duties does not prevent collusion; that is, cases where two or more persons cooperate to perpetuate a fraudulent act. Careful transaction balancing and review of suspicious activity and output captured in logs, transaction registers, and reports are the best methods of detecting collusion. In some organizations, additional operational security practices such as *mandatory vacation* periods or *job rotations* are enforced to provide management with an opportunity to prevent and detect collusion.

Security Program Frameworks

An organization's security program should be tailored to the specific needs of the business, taking into consideration its overall mission, business objectives, operating climate, and strategic and tactical plans. It should incorporate the practices described in the above sections, as well as the results of an organization's risk and vulnerability assessments that identify the need for specific safeguards. Several reference *frameworks* (systems of organization) are available to guide the practitioner in planning, organizing, and documenting a program that covers all bases and meets generally accepted standards of due care. The most popular frameworks are the ISO/IEC 27000 information security standards series and the NIST Special Publications 800 series.

ISO/IEC 27002 Code of Practice for Information Security Management— This international standard, jointly issued by the International Organization for Standardization (ISO) and the International Electrotechnical Commission (IEC) provides a best practices framework for implementing and managing an information security program. First released in 2000 and later in 2005 as ISO/IEC 17799, it has since been republished as ISO/IEC 27002—part of the 27000 series of information security standards. The standard defines how information security is structured and organized, presents guidelines for implementing an information security management system (ISMS), and contains control objectives designed to protect the confidentiality, integrity, and availability of information assets. The standard treats information itself as an asset and thus extends beyond IT systems into any area where information in all forms is acquired, stored, used, processed and communicated. There is a strong emphasis on the role of risk management. Its comprehensive menu of implementation choices can be adopted as needed based on the unique needs and risks of your operating environment and thus the standard has broad applicability to any industry and type and size of organization.

ISO/IEC 27002's 133 control objectives are organized into 11 categories of practice that define the scope of an information security program. These categories are:

- Security Policy
- Security Organization
- Asset Management
- Human Resources Security
- Physical and Environmental Security

- Communications and Operations Management
- Access Control
- Information Systems Acquisition, Development, and Maintenance
- Incident Management
- Business Continuity Management
- Compliance

Because it is a code of practice (as opposed to a configuration standard), organizations cannot be certified against ISO/IEC 27002. The ISO/IEC 27001 provides more detailed implementation guidance for the security practitioner, and defines the requirements for a formal specification of an Information Security Management System (ISMS) that can be independently certified. The ISMS is a comprehensive, documented security program framework that is designed, built, monitored, and managed using a Plan–Do–Check–Act (PDCA) continuous improvement cycle (see Figure 6.1). Each component of the process has an associated set of activities and documentation deliverables. These four phases form a continuous cycle designed to adapt security practices to accommodate changes affecting an organization over time.

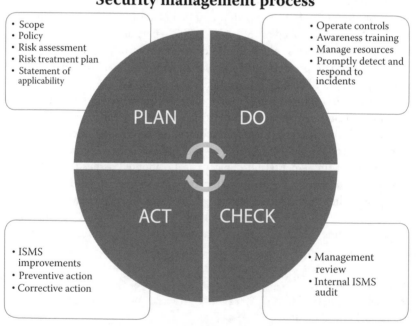

Figure 6.1 Security management process.

Plan—An effective ISMS has a well-defined, documented scope that is established up front. Scoping the ISMS involves defining the assets requiring protection; setting objectives for confidentiality, integrity, and availability; determining the levels of risk in each of these areas that the organization is willing to accept; and identifying any constraints such as laws and regulations or technical or cultural limitations under which the ISMS must operate. Security program scope is defined in a high-level security policy document that describes the assets, risk management objectives, and roles and responsibilities covered by the ISMS. The actual level of risk to the organization's assets is then ascertained by performing a thorough risk assessment. Protection goals and risk assessment results are used as inputs to a concrete risk treatment plan, which includes mechanisms to mitigate, accept, or transfer the risk. The risk treatment plan will include control objectives that can be selected from the list in ISO/IEC 27001, although you may need to adopt additional controls depending on your environment. Finally, the Statement of Applicability shows, for each ISO/IEC 27001 control, whether or not it was selected and why. Your justification for using or not using individual controls should tie clearly back to the risk assessment and, in some cases, the ISMS policy

Do—This is the phase in which you implement and operate the controls selected in the planning phase. Operational procedures are developed and executed. Allocation and training of resources and awareness training are important components of an effective operational environment. Prompt detection and response to incidents (i.e., control failures) is an important aspect of operations addressed in this phase.

Check—In this phase, activities are performed to ensure that the planned-for controls are in place and operating effectively. There are a number of ways to validate control effectiveness. ISO/IEC 27001 mandates that, at a minimum, the organization conduct internal ISMS audits and management reviews. Generating, collecting, and analyzing key metrics and performing security testing are examples of other important activities in this phase.

Act—Checking activities often produce actionable results. Where control deficiencies are found, *corrective action* must be taken to bring controls in line with stated objectives. *Preventive action* often goes hand-in-hand with corrective action to ensure that deficiencies do not resurface. Finally, even those controls that are in place and operating as designed may have room for improvement of efficiency, effectiveness, or scope of application.

NIST is an arm of the U.S. Department of Commerce that is charged with developing U.S. government technology standards. The NIST 800 series contains standards, guidelines, and procedures for federal computing information security. These standards are applicable to the private sector as well, and many organizations have adopted the 800 series as a basis for security planning and management. Unlike the ISO/IEC standards, which are available for purchase by individuals and organizations, NIST has made its material freely available in a series of Special Publications. NIST SP 800-30, Risk Management Guide for Information

Technology Systems, is the most widely used NIST document for designing and planning information security strategies.

The National Industrial Security Program Operating Manual (NISPOM), a combined governmental agency directive for government contractors who access and handle classified information, sets forth multiple security requirements for information classification and security practices. NISPOM provides a framework for developing security strategies in defense and related industries.

Aligning Business, IT, and Security

The best practices frameworks described above are useful guides to security planning only when used within the context of the organization's mission, scope, and nature of operations, and the environment in which it operates. Security strategies are designed to support the organization's goals, protect critical assets, and meet legal and regulatory obligations. Alignment of IT and security plans to business strategies is achieved by involving system and information owners in the planning process, understanding the laws and regulations affecting systems and information, and assessing the risks to confidentiality, integrity, and availability within the scope of operation.

The security practitioner participates in risk assessments, and in designing and implementing security plans and mechanisms to address risks and business requirements. As compliance liaison, he or she monitors logs and other sources of security event data to ensure that policies and procedures are followed, and that security systems are operating effectively. Measurements of security effectiveness are then used to further improve the security posture of the organization.

Security Architecture and Models

Security architects often use established security models as points of reference in design work. Established, tested models identify the major components in a security solution and how they interact. Chief among these models are the Bell–LaPadula confidentiality model, and the Biba and Clark–Wilson integrity models.

Bell–LaPadula Confidentiality Model

The Bell–LaPadula model was designed as an architectural reference for controlling access to sensitive data in government and military applications. The components of the model are subjects, objects, and an access control matrix. *Objects* (access targets) are classified into a hierarchy of security levels based on sensitivity, from low to high. If information has been previously classified (Top Secret, Secret, etc.) then classification levels corresponding to the organization's policy are used.

Subjects (actors)—which may be human actors, application programs, or system processes—are assigned security levels called *clearance* levels. The relation between the sensitivity level of objects and the clearance level of subjects is defined in the *access control matrix*. The access control matrix defines permissions (read-only, read/write, append, execute) for each clearance level and object classification. Each access operation is defined within the matrix by a subject, object, access permission triple. The matrix provides assurance that the confidentiality of the system will remain stable despite transitions in state; that is, a system that is in a secure state before an operation will be in the same secure state at the conclusion of the operation.

The basic tenet of Bell–LaPadula is that a given subject can read objects at the same or lower sensitivity level, but not those at a higher sensitivity level; this is called the simple security property and can be remembered as "no read up." The simple property is usually sufficient for implementing systems that control access to classified documents and files when the files have corresponding read-only attributes. However, it does not take into consideration the possibility that a subject may add, append, or transmit sensitive information to an area of lower sensitivity, and thus create a channel that defeats the access control mechanism. Bell–LaPadula adds another property to counteract this called the star "*" property. The * property blocks the channel between areas of different sensitivities such that when a subject has accessed an object for a read operation, then objects at a lower sensitivity level cannot be accessed for create and modify operations ("no write down"). Covert channels, such as backup and monitoring channels and image capture utilities, still present a risk for systems designed using Bell–LaPadula confidentiality models as these processes may be used for legitimate as well as illegitimate purposes.

Biba and Clark–Wilson Integrity Models

The Biba security model also describes a set of access control rules; in this case, rules that maintain the integrity of information and systems during state transitions. Biba is most easily thought of as the reverse of Bell–LaPadula, that is:

> The simple integrity property asserts that a subject at a given level of integrity cannot read an object at a lower level of integrity (no read down).
> The * (star) property asserts that a subject at a given level of integrity cannot write up to a level of higher integrity (no write up).

David D. Clark and David R. Wilson developed their Clark–Wilson integrity model to address what they viewed as shortcomings in the Bell–LaPadula and Biba models. While these models were useful for protecting classified information from unauthorized access or leakage to unclassified systems, they did not provide any framework to prevent corruption of data (either maliciously or unintentionally) during processing of the data. Clark–Wilson's addresses this risk using the idea of a well-formed *transaction* operating on the data. The components of this model also form a triple: authenticated principals (users), programs acting on data (transaction processes), and the data items themselves. Each triple or *relation* between user, transaction, and data item must be maintained in the system.

Systems designed to enforce Clark–Wilson integrity policy consist of well-formed transactions; that is, transactions that maintain a consistent level of integrity between the initial and end state. Integrity verification processes ensure the integrity of data items before, during, and after a transaction. Clark–Wilson also protects against malicious users by requiring separation of duties between people who can create relations used in a process and those who can execute the process.

Bell–LaPadula, Biba, and Clark–Wilson are all useful frameworks for designing so-called multilevel security (MLS) systems, in which information with various sensitivities or integrity requirements can be processed concurrently in a single system by users or actors with multiple levels of clearance or need to know.

Access Control Models

Discretionary access control (DAC) applies access restrictions to objects based on the identity or group membership of subjects. Subjects with a given level of access permissions can pass permissions to other subjects. DAC may be implemented on any type of object, but is not suitable as an access control mechanism for highly sensitive information. Most operating system implementations support DAC.

Mandatory access control (MAC) applies access restrictions to objects based on an object's sensitivity level and the subject's clearance level. Traditionally, MAC has been applied to *Multilevel security (MLS)* systems, in which information at different levels of classification reside and can be accessed by users with different clearance levels. MAC requires labeling of both subjects and objects. MAC is currently implemented in operating systems such as Secure Linux (SELinux), Trusted BSD, and Trusted Solaris, or by use of the Linux Security Modules (LSM) interface in other UNIX/Linux distributions.

Role-based access control (RBAC) assigns users to roles based on their functions within the organization, and specifies the operations that can be performed by each role. Operations are units of control that can be as simple as read/write/execute file permissions, or as complex as a fully executed business transaction. RBAC promises to reduce complexity in security administration for large networked operations and provide a means for enforcing least privilege; however, in practice, RBAC is often difficult to implement and maintain because of the sheer number and variety of roles that must be specified and maintained in the face of organizational changes. RBAC also supports a distributed security administration model using central and distributed protection domains, in which centralized administrators can define policies that apply to all operational units, and local administrators can define and manage roles that apply at their specific local level. NIST introduced a model for

RBAC in 2004, which is now an ANSI (American National Standards Institute) standard.

Identity and Access Management

Identity and access management describes a comprehensive set of security services that encompass the disciplines of authorization management, user identification and account provisioning, authentication services, entitlements or privilege management, and audit. Traditionally, these disciplines have been managed by security administrators and operations staff as separate activities, although in the past decade there have been major advances in systems that integrate and at least partially automate one or more of these services. Collectively, these are known as Identity and Access Management (IAM) systems. In the wake of tougher regulatory and attestation requirements, increases in identity theft, and the burgeoning costs of managing these services in large, distributed organizations, more software vendors and integrators are offering services that promise a silver bullet that will solve IAM woes for both internal and externally facing systems.

Whether you have a partially or fully automated solution, or are administering user identity and access manually, your IAM "system" must address the following components:

■ *Request management*
Request management refers to the processes and underlying workflow used to submit, route, approve, monitor, and deliver services. Requests to add, modify, and delete user accounts may be submitted via electronic or paper forms, or may be generated automatically by a process such as a new employee enrollment in an HR database. All user accounts and associated privileges must be authorized by the system Owner, or a delegate. Authorizations may be obtained through electronic or paper forms. Alternatively, manual or automated RBAC models may allow for some degree of preauthorization based on a user's role or group membership; for example, all new hires in the group, "Financial Accounting" may be granted access to a specific application or shared file system.

■ *Authorization*
Each user account must be authorized by the system Owner, or a delegate, to access specific systems and exercise the privileges associated with the account. Authorizations should be periodically reviewed and updated as changes in management, organizational structure, and individual job status and function may require changes to an account that may have been overlooked.

■ *Identity management*
Identity management links an identifier (name, user ID, etc.) with a subject, and optionally assigns one or more attributes (characteristics) to the identity. Each authenticating subject—whether a person, application, or process—that

is authorized to access and use nonpublic system resources must be assigned a unique identifier for accountability purposes. Ideally, the identifier should not be modeled after a dynamic attribute such as surname, which can change with changes in marital status, as this produces additional administrative overhead and makes it difficult to maintain historical data.

■ *Provisioning and deprovisioning services*
Manage the creation, modification, disabling, and deletion of accounts across the life cycle of the individual. This may be an entirely manual process, or may be partially or fully automated for efficiency and quality purposes. Provisioning services are usually accompanied by an SLA specifying committed turnaround times from request to account creation. Your policy may specify that accounts will be disabled after a period of inactivity, during authorized leaves of absence and, of course, on termination of employment or association with the organization. Disabled accounts that are no longer required should be deleted after a reasonable period to ensure that they are not reactivated or reused without appropriate authorization. Automated provisioning services for major operating systems and application packages are available in most vendor solutions, along with APIs and software development kits that allow you to script your own provisioning logic.

■ *Entitlements*
Most automated IAM systems provide some ability to establish group membership or assign accounts to roles that have been preestablished in access control entries. In the absence of automated solutions, some organizations have created templates that may be copied to create new accounts that are automatically assigned to specific groups and roles.

■ *Auditing*
A full audit trail of authorizations and account management activity must be preserved to detect unauthorized activity and to demonstrate adherence to account management policies and standards. Audit trails are also useful for troubleshooting and for documenting performance against SLAs.

Managing Privileged User Accounts

Privileged users are those individuals that have access to perform restricted functions such as systems and security configuration, backup and recovery, database administration, and other powerful functions. Included in this category are the built-in generic accounts supplied with operating system platforms (such as Windows Administrator, Root on UNIX, and Cisco Enable) and some applications, and accounts created with administrative or superuser privileges. These accounts often provide unrestricted access to system files and processes, and the data residing on the systems they operate. Many such accounts have the ability to enable and disable auditing and event monitoring, or modify or delete system logs.

The risk of intentional or inadvertent data destruction, modification, disclosure, or deletion and changes to critical processes such as system clocks, routing tables, and service parameters is compounded by this ability to bypass normal access controls and detection mechanisms.

Powerful generic accounts should never be used with default or static passwords, and they should only be used to perform administrative tasks when required by the specific platform. Complex passwords at a minimum should be required to access these accounts and, if possible, two-factor or other strong authentication mechanisms should be used. Accounts and passwords with powerful authority should never be hardcoded into scripts or programs where they may be read by unauthorized individuals. Instead of using privileged generic accounts, unique accounts with comparable privileges should be assigned to administrators, and activity on these accounts should be actively audited (not just logged for posterity). The number of these accounts should be kept to a minimum, and authorizations should be reviewed periodically. Some platforms such as UNIX and its variants provide the option of adopting the authority of a privileged generic account using a "switch user" or "run as" command while preserving a record of the session associated with the unique identifier that initiated the command.

Some organizations establish so-called "firecall" accounts, which may be maintained in a physically secured location and manually distributed to authorized users. While this is better than no control at all, there are still risks associated with access to passwords by the person or persons responsible for securing the firecall accounts, and failures to establish authorization or change passwords once the account is no longer needed for a specific use. As an alternative, privileged accounts can be centrally managed through third-party software designed to address the risks of privileged user access. Password vaults, for example, provide a request broker function that allows authorized administrators, using their unique credentials, to "check out" passwords for accounts they are authorized to use. The vault allows separation of duties among vault administrators, IT and security administrators, and auditors, so that an individual responsible for configuring access to the account passwords cannot view or manage audit logs and cannot view the data in the vault (passwords).

Outsourcing Security and Managed Security Service Providers

Outsourcing security operations and administration tasks is still a controversial topic for many organizations. The main reason given for outsourcing all or part of a security operation is the expected financial savings from recouping costs associated with staff acquisition, training, and retention, and by leveraging a service provider's infrastructure. Possible other benefits of outsourcing include the ability to rely on the expertise of professional security providers, the ability to use newer technology without additional administrative burden, and the ability to reallocate existing security staff to more strategic efforts by offloading routine operational tasks.

Managed security services may be provided by traditional network or system integrators that have added security services to their portfolio, by infrastructure, application and data center hosting providers, or by specialty firms that provide a range of services from consulting to full-blown infrastructure build and management. Services may be provided on-site, at the vendor's site, or co-located in a third-party facility using an organization's equipment, the vendor's equipment, or a combination of both.

Services most often considered for outsourcing include:

- Managed firewall and VPN
- Vulnerability scanning and management
- Network or security log monitoring
- Incident detection and response
- Security testing
- Content security services—antivirus management, content scanning, and URL blocking
- Identity and access management

Despite the promised benefits, security outsourcing is not for everyone. Depending on the organization and the type of services under consideration, the risks inherent in delegating security services management to a third party may outweigh the benefits. Hidden costs, loss of control over infrastructure, operations and personnel, reduced visibility into internal events, and a loss of internal expertise are some arguments against outsourcing. Any decision to outsource should include a full cost/benefit analysis and a careful examination of benefits and risks.

If a decision is made to outsource, it is best to start small—that is, with a limited range of services that are not considered of strategic importance to the organization or its security posture. This will allow time to assess the effectiveness and cost savings of the decision as well as the capabilities of specific vendors, without putting critical operations unnecessarily at risk.

No matter what the scope of the outsourcing arrangement, overall responsibility for security cannot be delegated. Organizations must provide appropriate oversight and management of managed security service providers (MSSPs) to ensure compliance with applicable laws and regulations, security policies, and risk management goals. A disciplined approach is needed across phases of evaluation, selection, contracting, implementation, management, and termination of MSSP relationships.

Evaluation—Two or more MSSPs should be compared based on their ability to meet specific requirements and provide the best mix of services, cost savings, and reduction in risk. Typically, an organization will issue a formal Request for Proposal (RFP) that provides a description of the organization and services sought, policy requirements and other service parameters, and the process and timeline by which vendors will be evaluated. Responses to the RFP should provide an overview of the MSSP's business, markets served, and scope of services offered. Attributes of services such as architecture, hardware and software, asset ownership, financial statements, and a copy of the provider's annual report, together with any significant recent or pending changes in organizational structure (such as mergers, acquisitions, and divestitures), should be included. Sources of capital and number of active contracts and renewal rates should be listed as well as any additional information that will help you assess the viability of the business. The MSSP should describe its security program, including risk and vulnerability management processes, compliance with control objectives, personnel, and operational procedures. If external assessments are performed, the most recent results should be included. A detailed response to each requirement showing how it is met or, if it cannot be met, alternatives offered, should follow.

Selection—A side-by-side comparison may be made by constructing a detailed matrix, rating vendor responses by their ability to meet each specific requirement. Requirements may be categorized as essential, important, and optional to make it easier to narrow the playing field. This process usually results in one or two finalists who may be subject to further evaluation that may include demonstrations, site visits, and feedback from existing customers. Respondents should be notified of their status in writing and thanked for their participation at the end of the selection process.

Contracting—The MSSP contract sets forth the rights and obligations of both parties and is usually accompanied by a statement of work (SOW), service and equipment schedule, price quotes, and other supporting documents. Hours of availability and schedule of services, service level agreements (SLAs) and warrantees, limitations of liability, reporting requirements, and termination clauses are all essential components of the contract. Ramifications for poor performance and a process for settling disputes when either party fails to meet its obligations should be clearly spelled out. Terms of service and renewal timelines should be specified. During contract negotiation, it is often possible to negotiate a better price for a longer commitment.

Implementation—An implementation plan should be spelled out and agreed to before signing the contract. The implementation plan is often included in the SOW attached to the contract as an addendum. Implementation may involve provisioning new hardware and software, rerouting network traffic, moving equipment, configuring controls, and establishing communication links and access accounts. The organization should allocate a dedicated project manager to oversee implementation to ensure that all obligations outlined in the SOW have been met, that schedules are adhered to and any issues are identified and addressed, and that information on progress is made available to management.

Management—An account manager should be assigned by each party to oversee the ongoing relationship and performance of the other party over the life of the contract. Periodic reporting using established metrics should be spelled out in the contract and used as a basis for review of MSSP performance. Procedures for change management, notification of planned and unplanned outages, and incident response and reporting should be documented and followed. Establishing vendor management practices helps maintain an effective working relationship with your MSSP, in which any performance gaps can be easily identified and quickly corrected.

Termination—MSSP contracts may automatically renew unless they are cancelled within a certain time period before the renewal date. Renewals should not be automatic, but should be used as an occasion to review performance over time, make any changes or adjustments to services, and negotiate better pricing. If an MSSP at any time fails to meet performance requirements, details should be documented for further use in case termination is warranted. Termination clauses in the contract specify the conditions under which either party can terminate the contract and the processes required to establish cause, settle outstanding obligations, notify affected parties, and account for movement of systems and data as needed.

Business Partner Security Controls

Most organizations work with one or more business partners who develop, market, or service portions of IT or business products. For example, a typical insurance company might work with one company to develop a new business application, another for claims settlement, and yet another to provide payment processing services. These business relationships often involve sharing confidential or proprietary data among affiliates, and may require network connections and other extensions of access across organizational boundaries.

Just as with its MSSP relationships, an organization cannot delegate accountability for protection of customer data and other information systems assets to its business partners; therefore, a careful review of partner security practices should be performed to ensure compliance with all legal, regulatory, and policy requirements. It is good practice to prepare these requirements in advance, and spell them out in third-party agreements. Depending on the nature of the relationship and the type and extent of access to protected assets that is to be provided, organizations may require independent verification of partner security controls through an external audit report or attestation. The SAS70 (Statement on Auditing Services No. 70) is a widely recognized independent review of internal controls that many service organizations use to demonstrate their ability to maintain appropriate levels of protection for business partner and customer assets. ISO27001 certification has yet to reach SAS70's popularity, but is an excellent indicator of the strength of an organization's information security program.

Where network connectivity between organizations is required, a third-party connection agreement is a type of contract frequently used to assure that business partner security controls are in place to minimize the risks of connecting to an organization's systems. The agreement spells out how the partner is to access and use network resources, and what measures must be taken to prevent the introduction of new security risks and vulnerabilities. The right to audit third-party security controls is an important element in all third-party agreements.

Security Policies, Standards, Guidelines, and Procedures

Security policies are formal, written documents that set the expectations for how security will be implemented and managed in an organization. Security policies may be specific, setting forth the rules or expectations for administering or managing one aspect of the security program or a particular type of technology, or they may be more general, defining the types of practices the organization will adopt to safeguard information systems assets. Policies are relatively static, and typically do not reference specific technology platforms or protocols. Because of this, policies remain current in the face of technical changes. Examples of general security policies are security program policies, which set forth the operating principles of the security program, and acceptable usage policies, which prescribe the authorized uses of information systems assets. General policies, especially those governing acceptable usage of e-mail, Internet, and other assets, may require employee signatures indicating that they have read, understood the policy, and agree to comply with it.

Subject-specific security policies typically address a limited area of risk related to a particular class of assets, type of technology, or business function. Examples of specific security policies include:

- E-Mail and Internet Usage Policies
- Antivirus Policy
- Remote Access Policy
- Information Classification Policy
- Encryption Policies

Policy Document Format

The security practitioner should understand the basic elements of an information security policy that define and enforce the organization's security practices. Typical policy elements include:

Objective: This statement provides the policy's context. It gives background information and states the purpose for writing the policy, including the risk or threat the policy addresses and the benefits to be achieved by policy adherence.

Policy Statement: A succinct statement of management's expectations for what must be done to meet policy objectives.

Applicability: This lists the people to whom the policy applies, the situations in which it applies, and any specific conditions under which the policy is to be in effect.

Enforcement: How compliance with the policy will be enforced using technical and administrative means. This includes consequences for noncompliance.

Roles and Responsibilities: States who is responsible for reviewing and approving, monitoring compliance, enforcing, and adhering to the policy.

Review: Specifies a frequency of review, or the next review date on which the policy will be assessed for currency and updated if needed.

To be effective, security policies must be endorsed by senior management, communicated to all affected parties, and enforced throughout the organization. When policy violations occur, disciplinary action commensurate with the nature of the offense must be taken quickly and consistently.

Policy Life Cycle

Security policies are living documents that communicate management expectations for behavior. Policy development begins with determining the need. The need for a policy may arise due to a regulatory obligation, in response to an operational risk, or a desire to enforce a particular set of behaviors that facilitate a safe, productive work environment. Impacted parties, such as human resources, legal, audit, and business line management, should be identified so that they can participate throughout the development process. Once the need is determined and the team assembled, the security practitioner should address the following areas:

State the objective. A clear statement of policy objectives answers the question, "Why are we developing this policy?" The statement of objective will guide development of the specific points in the policy statement and will help keep team discussions in scope and focused.

Draft the policy specifics. The policy statement should be drafted in simple, clear language that will be easily understood by those who must comply with the policy. Avoid vague statements that could be open to multiple interpretations, and be sure to define all technical terms used in the policy document.

Identify methods for measurement and enforcement. Policy enforcement mechanisms may include technical controls such as access management systems, content blocking, and other preventive measures as well as administrative controls such as management oversight and supervision. Compliance with policy expectations can be measured through audit trails, automated monitoring systems, random or routine audits, or management supervision. The means of monitoring or measuring compliance should be clearly understood, as well as the logistics of enforcement. The logistics of taking and documenting disciplinary action should be established at this time to ensure that the organization is willing and able to enforce policy, and prepared to apply corrective action quickly and consistently.

Communication. The timing, frequency, and mechanism by which the policy will be communicated to employees and others should be established before final policy approval. Expectations must be clearly communicated and regularly enforced so that everyone remains apprised of the appropriate conduct is considered to be. Whenever disciplinary action may be taken in response to policy violations, it is especially important that management make every effort to ensure that employees are made aware of the policy and what they must do to comply. Some organizations require employees to sign a form acknowledging their receipt and understanding of key policies and agreeing to comply with expectations.

Periodic review. Policies should be reviewed at least annually to ensure that they continue to reflect management's expectations, current legal and regulatory obligations, and any changes to the organization's operations. Policy violations that have occurred since the last review should be analyzed to determine whether adjustments to policy or associated procedures, or enhancements to communication and enforcement mechanisms may be needed.

Standards and Guidelines

A standard is a formal, documented requirement that sets uniform criteria for a specific technology, configuration, nomenclature, or method. Standards that are followed as common practice but are not formally documented or enforced are so-called de facto standards; such standards often become formalized as an organization matures. Some examples of security standards include account naming conventions, desktop and server antivirus settings, encryption key lengths, and router ACL (access control list) configurations. Standards provide a basis for measuring technical and operational safeguards for accuracy and consistency. A *baseline* is a detailed configuration standard that includes specific security settings. Baselines can be used as a checklist for configuring security parameters and for measurement and comparison of current systems to a standard configuration set.

Guidelines, on the other hand, are recommended practices to be followed to achieve a desired result. They are not mandatory and provide room for flexibility in how they are interpreted and implemented; therefore, they are rarely enforced except through an organization's culture and norms. Guidelines are often instructional in nature. They are useful for cases where an organization wishes to provide enough structure to achieve an acceptable level of performance while allowing room for innovation and individual discretion. Some examples of security guidelines include methods for selecting a strong password, criteria for evaluating new security technology, and suggested training curricula for security staff.

Standards, baselines, procedures and, to a lesser extent, guidelines, help organizations maintain consistency in the way security risks are addressed, and thus provide assurance that a desirable level of security will be maintained. For example, a desktop antivirus standard might specify that all desktops be maintained at the current version of software, configured to receive automatic updates, and set to scan all executable files and templates whenever a file is opened or modified. By consistently applying the same criteria across the board, all desktops are equally protected from virus threats and this can be assured through periodic scanning or auditing. In addition, unlike guidelines, standards specify repeatable configurations. This enhances productivity by allowing practitioners to develop reusable templates that can be applied quickly and easily either manually, or through automated configuration management tools. Similarly, programmers can create standard security logic for functions such as login sequences, input validation, and authority checks, and store this logic in a central repository as reusable components that can be compiled into new business applications. This saves time and effort, reduces errors, and assures enforcement of application security rules during the development life cycle.

Standards differ from policies in that they are typically more technical in nature, are more limited in scope and impact, do not require approval from executive management, are more likely than policies to change over time. Standards are often developed to implement the details of a particular policy. Because of their more detailed technical nature, security practitioners responsible for administering security systems, applications and network components typically play a more active role in the development of standards than in policy development, which largely occurs at management levels in an organization. Many organizations have formal standards and procedures review committees composed of IT practitioners, whose role is to assist in the development of standards documents, review documents for clarity, accuracy, and completeness, identify impacts, and often implement approved standards.

A *baseline* is a special type of standard that specifies the minimum set of security controls that must be applied to a particular system or practice area in order to achieve an acceptable level of assurance. Baselines may be derived from best practices frameworks and further developed according to your organization's unique needs. They are often documented in the form of checklists that can be used by teams to specify the minimum security requirements for new and enhanced systems.

Standards should be reviewed at specified intervals, at a minimum annually, to ensure they remain current. Standards must often be modified in response to:

- Introduction of new technology
- Addition of configurable features to a system
- Change in business operations
- Need for additional controls in response to new threats or vulnerabilities

External to the organization, the term "standards" is used in two special contexts: industry standards and open standards. *Industry standards* are generally accepted formats, protocols, or practices developed within the framework of a specific industrial segment, such as engineering, computer programming, or telecommunications. Industry standards may be developed by leading manufacturers, such as IBM's ISA (Industry Standard Architecture) PC bus standard, for use in their equipment and compatible equipment developed by other vendors. They may also be developed by special interest groups such as the Institute of Electrical and Electronic Engineers (IEEE), American National Standards Institute (ANSI), or International Telecommunications Union (ITU). For example, standards set for electrical interfaces, such as the RS-232C serial communication standard used in PC mice, display terminals, modems, and other devices, were developed by IEEE and are adopted by most manufacturers to meet the need for consistency and interoperability across individual implementations of technology. Industry standards are not always formally developed and accepted, but may be so widely adopted by organizations across industries that they become necessary for the industry to incorporate them in products and services in order to serve their customers needs. Examples of these de facto industry standards include the PCL print control language developed by Hewlett-Packard and the Postscript laser printer page description language developed by Adobe.

In contrast to industry standards, *open standards* are specifications that are developed by standards bodies or consortia and made available for public use without restrictions. They are designed to promote free competition, portability, and interoperability among different implementations. The standards themselves are platform independent, and are published as source code or as a set of detailed specification documents that can be used to develop new products and services that can be integrated into existing, standards-based products.

Development of open standards follows due process and is a collaborative venture. Typically, an expert committee or working group develops a draft and publishes it for peer review and open comment before formalizing the results in a standards document. Some bodies such as the Internet Engineering Task Force (IETF) produce documents called RFCs (Request for Comment) for this purpose. Formal approval completes the process of codifying a standard for final publication. The Internet and many of its protocols and services are based on open standards. For example, TCP/IP (Transmission Control Protocol/Internet Protocol) is an open standard that is implemented in every operating system and network device. You can imagine what would happen if every vendor decided to implement their own version of TCP/IP—the Internet would simply cease to function.

Organizations choosing to adopt open standards find that they are not as locked in to specific vendor solutions and proprietary interoperability requirements, and may be able to streamline their approach to securing and managing distributed systems. Open standards allow such organizations to adopted a "best of breed" strategy when selecting security and other technologies—that is, where individual solutions are selected for depth of functionality and ability to meet most requirements—rather than a uniform, single-vendor strategy that may be comprehensive yet not provide all the functionality desired in individual components. When all components of a security system are implemented according to open standards, they can work together without cumbersome manual intervention to provide a comprehensive security solution.

A list of standards-setting bodies and samples of the standards they have produced that are relevant to the security practitioner is provided in Table 6.1.

Note that the term "open standards" should never be confused with *open source*. Open source is software that is freely distributed and available for modification and use at little or no cost. To be considered open source, software must be distributed in source code and compiled form; must allow for derivative works; must not discriminate against any person, group, or use; and must not be tied to any specific product or restrict distribution of any associated software with the license. Licensing is covered by public agreement, which typically includes "copyleft" provisions requiring that any derived works be redistributed to the community as open source. A popular example of open source licensing is the GPL (Gnu Public License).

While many organizations have begun to adopt open source, others are more cautious. Some drawbacks to using open source are lack of vendor support, incompatibility with proprietary platforms, and inability to protect the organization's intellectual property rights to systems built on open source. Because of these limitations, many organizations prefer to limit use of open source to noncritical systems.

Procedures

Procedures are step-by-step instructions for performing a specific task or set of tasks. Like standards, procedures are often implemented to enforce policies or meet quality goals. Despite the fact that writing documentation can be one of a technical person's least favorite activities, the importance of documenting security procedures cannot be overemphasized. When followed as written, procedures ensure consistent and repeatable results, provide instruction to those who are unfamiliar with how to perform a specific process, and provide assurance for management and auditors that policies are being enforced in practice. In addition, clear procedures often allow organizations to delegate routine functions to entry-level staff, or develop programs to automate these functions, freeing up more experienced practitioners to perform higher-level work. For example, account provisioning software has been implemented in many organizations to automate procedures that contain multiple steps such as establishing login credentials, home directories, assigning users to groups and roles, and the like. This software can be used by junior staff who lack the depth of knowledge and understanding of the systems configuration behind these procedures. Organizations justify the cost based on savings in salaries,

Table 6.1   List of Standards Organizations

Organization	Material Produced	Web Site
NIST – National Institute of Standards and Technology	FIPS (Federal Information Processing Standards) NIST Special Publication Series	http://csrc.nist.gov/
ISO – International Organization for Standardization and IEC – International Electrotechnical Commission	More than 17000 international standards and guidelines., including specific information security standards	http://www.iso.org/iso/home.htm http://www.iec.ch/
ANSI – American National Standards Institute	Voluntary standards for US private sector. Includes standards for information technology and panels on homeland security and identity theft.	http://www.ansi.org/
CIS – Center for Internet Security	Security configuration standards (benchmarks)	http://www.cisecurity.org/
IETF – Internet Engineering Task Force	Internet Drafts and Requests for Comments (RFCs) covering detailed Internet-related engineering standards	http://www.ietf.org/
W3C – World Wide Web Consortium	International standards for the Web (XML, HTML, SOAP, etc.)	http://www.w3.org/
ITU – International Telecommunication Union	Network and telecommunication standards	http://www.itu.int/net/home/index.aspx
ICT Standards Board – Information Communications and Technologies Consortium	European standardization for industry. Covers topics such as data protection, privacy, digital signature and other standardization efforts	http://www.ictsb.org/
OASIS - Organization for the Advancement of Structured Information Standards	Open standards for Web services, security, ebusiness, etc.	http://www.oasis-open.org/home/index.php
ASIS International – American Society for Industrial Security	Asset protection, risk assessment, physical, etc.	http://www.asisonline.org

an ability to free up senior staff to perform more complex activities, improvements in consistency and quality by reducing human error, and eliminating the manual effort needed to create an audit trail of account management activity.

When developing procedures, you should not take the reader's level of knowledge or skill for granted; instead, each step in the process should be explained in sufficient detail for someone who is unfamiliar with the process to be able to perform it independently. All technical terms should be defined, and acronyms should be spelled out. A procedure, like a good novel, has a beginning, middle, and an end. Typical components of a procedure are:

Purpose: The reason for performing the procedure, usually the desired outcome.
Applicability: Who is responsible for following the procedure, and in what circumstances the procedure is followed.
Steps: The detailed steps taken to perform the procedure.
Figures: Illustrations, diagrams, or tables used to depict a workflow, values to enter in specific fields, or display screen shots to show formats and to enhance ease of use.
Decision points: Yes–no questions whose answer results in branching to a different step in the procedure. These may be written as steps in the procedure or included in a workflow diagram or decision tree.

System Security Plans

A system security plan is a comprehensive document that details the security requirements for a specific system, the controls established to meet those requirements, and the responsibilities and expected behaviors of those administering and accessing the system. It is developed with input from system and information owners, individuals with responsibility for the operation of the system, and the system security officer. The system security plan and its supporting documents are living documents that are periodically reviewed and updated to reflect changes in security requirements and in the design, function, and operation of the system. Security plans are developed and reviewed before system certification and accreditation; during these later stages of preproduction review, system security plans are analyzed, updated, and finally accepted.

Roles and responsibilities in the system security planning process include:

■ *System owner*—Responsible for decisions regarding system procurement or development, implementation and integration, and operation and ongoing maintenance. The System Owner has overall responsibility for system security plan development in collaboration with the information owner, system security officer, and users of the system, and for maintaining current plans. In addition, he/she is responsible for ensuring that the controls specified in the plan are operating as intended.

- *Information owner*—Has overall authority for the information stored, processed, or transmitted by the system. The information owner is responsible for specifying policies for appropriate use of information, and security requirements for protecting information in the system. He/she determines who can access the system and the privileges that will be granted to system users.
- *Security officer*—Responsible for coordinating development, review and acceptance of security plans and for identification, implementation, administration and assessment of security controls.
- *Authorizing official or approver*—A senior executive or manager with the authority to assume full responsibility for the system covered in the system security plan. This is the person empowered to authorize operation of the system, and accept any residual risk that remains after security controls have been implemented.

The system security plan scope is determined by performing a boundary analysis to identify the information, hardware, system and application software, facilities, and personnel included in the overall system's function. Typically, the resources constituting a "system" are under the same management control and work together to perform a discrete function or set of functions. If scoping is difficult, it may be helpful to start with the specific type or set of information assets in question, and define the hardware, software, and personnel involved in its storage, processing, and use. Larger systems may be subdivided into subsystems that perform one or more specific functions. The controls documented in the system security plan should consist of administrative, technical, and physical mechanisms to achieve the desired level of confidentiality, integrity, and availability of system assets.

The system security plan should include the following information:

- System name and a unique ID—An ID is assigned to the system to aid in inventory, measurement, and configuration management.
- System categorization—The system should be categorized low, medium, or high (or some other relative ranking) for each element of the C-I-A triad.
- System owner—Identify the name, title, and organization of the system owner.
- Authorizing official—The name, title, and organization of the authorizing official.
- Technical and administrative contacts—Contact information for personnel who have knowledge of the configuration and operation of the system.
- Security requirements—Security requirements for confidentiality, integrity, and availability of system resources.
- Security controls—Administrative, physical, and technical controls applied to meet security requirements.
- Review and maintenance procedures—Roles, responsibilities, and procedures for reviewing and maintaining the system security plan.

Additional Documentation

In addition to the documentation described above, the security practitioner maintains associated documentation such as security recommendations, technical specifications, design documents, and implementation checklists to support administration and troubleshooting. General information documents may be created to provide an overview of specific security systems for new employees, or for those performing backup functions.

Security recommendations are developed to address specific issues that are identified as a result of a risk, vulnerability, or threat assessment. Recommendations may be presented as a section in a formal risk assessment report; may be presented to management as follow up to an incident report; or may be published as guidelines for developers, administrators, or users of a system. Recommendations are not mandatory actions but instead are suggested steps that, if taken, can achieve a specific security outcome.

Disaster recovery documentation is created and maintained for any critical system that must be restored onsite or offsite in the event of system interruption. System restoration does not always follow the same steps as building a new system; for example, policy and other configuration files and application data may need to be backed up and restored to bring systems back to the state they were in when the interruption occurred. A copy of disaster recovery documentation should be maintained at a sufficient distance from the organization's offices to support restoration activities in the event of local or regionalized disaster.

Another type of documentation maintained by the security practitioner is the collection of audit and event logs, incident data, and other information captured during the course of operating the organization's security systems. These data are necessary for system tuning, troubleshooting and problem resolution, forensics investigations, reporting, and validation of security controls. It may also be used to validate compliance with applicable policies, procedures, and regulations. Audit and event data should be protected from unauthorized access and modification, and retained for a predetermined period. Most security systems are self-documenting, although you may be required to document procedures for collecting, reviewing, and securing the data.

Considerations for Safeguarding Confidentiality

Regulations and Contractual Obligations

Organizations have an obligation to protect the confidentiality of certain types of information that they collect, use, and maintain. These may be legal obligations dictated by statute or industry regulations, or by contractual agreement. Failure to comply with legal obligations may result in fines, sanctions, and expensive litigation as well as damage to an organization's reputation. Organizations also have a duty to maintain the confidentiality of certain types of information to protect the interests of shareholders, employees, business partners, customers, and the public. Getting a clear understanding of the unique legal, regulatory, contractual, and strategic imperatives that drive an organization's need for confidentiality is a first step in developing an effective protection strategy. Common types of information that are protected by federal statute or contract include:

Personally identifiable information. Many national and international laws and regulations, such as the United States Health Insurance Portability and Accountability Act (HIPAA), the European Union Directive 95/46/EC, the Gramm–Leach–Bliley Act (GLBA), and others are designed to protect the privacy and integrity of consumer health, financial, educational, and other data that can be used to identify individuals and their affiliations. These laws are designed to uphold individuals' privacy rights and to guard against identity theft, which is a growing international concern. Most if not all privacy laws also contain integrity protection provisions to ensure accuracy of data that are maintained about individuals, including an individual's right to examine and correct data held in systems of record.

Cardholder data. The Payment Card Industry Data Security Standard (PCI DSS) is a comprehensive set of safeguards intended to protect credit and debit cardholder data from fraudulent access and use. The standard is a product of the industry's Security Standards Council, made up of executives from the major card issuers. All merchants who accept debit and credit card payments must comply with the standard, with varying degrees of rigor based on transaction or dollar volumes processed. Penalties for noncompliance include fines and breach fees (levied in the event cardholder data in a noncompliant organization is lost, stolen, or disclosed to unauthorized parties), and possible denial of participation in card issuer programs. Loss of credit card revenue resulting from even short periods of suspension can be substantial. In addition, noncompliant organizations run the risk of losing customers ("runoff"), and shareholder and investor confidence.

Intellectual property. Intellectual property (IP) refers to creations of the mind— inventions, methods, designs, documents conveying original ideas, and artistic works. Intellectual property is an important asset to any business and is a source of competitive advantage.

There are two basic types of intellectual property: copyright and industrial property.

Copyright

If your organization develops or produces music, video, written publications, or software, its works should be protected by copyright. Federal copyright laws and international treaties such as the Berne convention grant the copyright holder with authority to determine who may copy, distribute, and use their works and under what circumstances. Software copyright is typically protected by legal contracts called licensing agreements. While confidentiality per se is not an issue with copyright, it is important for you to be aware of the risks of unauthorized use and distribution of your organization's copyrighted materials, as well as copyrighted materials used by your organization (e.g., commercial application software and technical manuals). Most software licensing agreements prohibit reverse engineering or otherwise incorporating licensed code into an organization's applications, and place limits on the number of copies that may be distributed or the number of simultaneous uses of a copy of the software are allowed. These licensing agreements typically include provisions for backup copies of software for disaster recovery purposes. However, other types of licensing do not have such prohibitions. Under permissive licensing agreements, for example, original code can be reused as long as the copyright statement is preserved. Under the open-source GNU Public License, or GPL, code may be used for any purpose with the expectation that enhancements to the code will also be offered without restriction to the open source community for further development.

Software and other digital media is also protected under the U.S. Digital Millennium Copyright Act (DMCA) and under the auspices of the United Nations' World Intellectual Property Organization (WIPO). Digital rights management (DRM) technology has been used with varying degrees of success to provide access control and copy protection solutions for digital media, particularly audio and video and can be used to enforce digital copyright laws such as the DMCA. However, application of this technology creates a myriad of interoperability issues. For this reason, its use was abandoned in digital music recordings, and its continued use in operating systems software has been the subject of protest by some organizations. Copy protection for Web pages can also be achieved through JavaScript coding (freely available on the Web) or by using commercial copy protection software. Internally, most organizations integrate software metering with their asset or configuration management facilities to protect the rights of software copyright holders and prevent and detect unauthorized proliferation and use of digital media. Several software distribution management systems also offer metering as a function. Metering solutions may track the number of accesses to server-based software and deny access to users once the maximum limit specified in the licensing agreement is reached. They may also include desktop agents that provide inventorying and audit capability and track usage to allow administrators to eliminate unnecessary licensing fees by removing software that is not being used. One drawback of many metering solutions is that many currently available products allow administrators to manually configure usage limits and license counts, and there may be temptation to temporarily increase thresholds or install additional, unlicensed copies of software in response to calls from frustrated users. Protection of licensing keys and periodic audits for adherence to licensing agreements should be performed to protect the organization from these well-meaning but noncompliant administrators.

Most commercial software requires a licensing key to activate installed software for initial use, or for continued use after a brief trial period. The key is typically a long sequence of letters and numbers that is provided with the packaged media or downloaded from the vendor's Web site by authorized administrators. The key is usually entered manually during software installation and configuration. Software licensing keys must be secured to prevent unauthorized software installations and software piracy by placing paper copies in locked cabinets, storing electronic copies of license keys on removable media or in secured locations such as within a configuration management database, and limiting access to software configuration files containing license key information. License keys must also be available for disaster recovery purposes, and copies may be stored offsite in an organization's DR facility. In 2007, Microsoft released its Software Licensing Protection (SLP) service, which allows software developers to incorporate license creation, tracking, and enforcement into products developed for use with the Microsoft operating system. However, such facilities are still in their infancy, and software piracy remains an international problem costing developers an estimated US$35 billion annually.

Industrial Property

Industrial property is another form of intellectual property that refers to objects created for commercial use; this would apply to most network devices, for example. Industrial property is typically protected by patent or trademark. Patents are granted for original, non-obvious inventions to protect the patent holder's right to exclusively manufacture and market their product. A trademark (or service mark) is a visible sign such as a logo or other indicator that uniquely identifies a product or service an organization provides. Patents, trademarks, and service marks are usually protected through the legal system. Another form of industrial property, trade secret, refers to any nonpublic information that a business possesses and that confers competitive advantage, such as the formula for Coca-Cola®. A trade secret can be any formula, design, process, pattern, or practice that has these characteristics. Trade secrets should be protected under the umbrella of an organization's information handling policy and treated as highly confidential by applying restrictive access controls, auditing, and monitoring.

Privacy and Monitoring

In the United States, individual's right to privacy in digital communication is governed by the Electronic Communications Privacy Act (ECPA) of 1986. However, an important *business exception* exists that allows employers to monitor employee communications as a routine operational procedure. It is important that employees be made aware that regular monitoring of e-mail, telephone, Internet and Intranet chat, and other forms of communication that make use of company-supplied facilities is sanctioned by law, and, therefore, no reasonable expectation of privacy exists in the workplace. Outside of the United States, particularly in the European Union, employee privacy considerations may outweigh an organization's desire to monitor communications. Security professionals should understand the applicable privacy laws and business case when developing a policy on monitoring.

Information Life Cycle

Information may be subject to unauthorized disclosure at any stage in its life cycle. An established tenet of information security states that the security of a system or process is only as strong as the weakest link in the chain. That being the case, the security practitioner must consider the risk to information assets during each stage of the life cycle, and ensure that a consistent level of controls is maintained during:

- Acquisition
- Entry
- Storage and Archival (Backup and Recovery)
- Access
- Modification
- Transmission/Disclosure
- Disposal

Protecting Confidentiality and Information Classification

Information classification is an important tool in determining the level of protection required for different types of information on the basis of the information's value to the organization and the potential impact of compromise.

Traditional information classification schemes primarily deal with the confidentiality side of the C-I-A triad, although information may be classified based on criticality for disaster recovery purposes as discussed elsewhere in this text. Different types of information are assigned different levels of sensitivity based on the "need to know" and the impact of unintended or malicious disclosure to unauthorized parties. Each classification level has unique protection requirements, with the highest level of sensitivity warranting the greatest degree of protection.

Organizations that devote time and resources to developing and maintaining an information classification scheme benefit in several ways:

- Information protection standards can be developed by class level.
- Information may be labeled according to its classification to improve compliance with policy in both manual and automated information handling processes.

- The necessary safeguards for any given type of information can be readily determined by referring to the classification scheme.
- Practitioners can assess effectiveness of current disclosure controls against agreed-upon requirements, perform gap analysis, and recommend and implement improvements.
- Application development and infrastructure groups can incorporate protection requirements into new and enhanced systems.
- Organizations can demonstrate compliance with laws, regulations, and contractual obligations.

Classification Schemes

An effective information classification scheme clearly distinguishes between different levels of sensitivity and effectively links classification levels to protection requirements. Remember to keep it simple—the more complex the scheme, the more difficult and time-consuming it will be to administer. Organizations will differ as to the number of classification levels assigned and the nomenclature used to describe each level of sensitivity. Most organizations find that three to five levels are sufficient to assign unique protection requirements. More than five levels add overhead and make it difficult to assure compliance.

The U.S. DoD classifies information according to the extent to which unauthorized disclosure would damage national security interests using the following levels:

Top Secret—Disclosure could result in exceptionally grave damage to national or international security. Examples include vital military intelligence data, cryptographic keys used to protect communications, and detailed weapons design.

Secret—Disclosure could seriously damage national security. Examples include significant intelligence and military plans and information, technical developments, and diplomatic strategies.

Confidential—Disclosure could cause damage to national security. Examples include tests of military strength, performance data, and technical training and operations documents.

Sensitive but Unclassified—Information that is not classified top secret, secret, or confidential but whose dissemination is still restricted to protect national interests.

Unclassified—In general, this information is publicly available through the Freedom of Information Act, although special classifications such as "Unclassified—For Law Enforcement Only" may be assigned to restrict disclosure to certain organizations with a need to know.

Governments outside of the United States use similar classification schemes to protect their national interests. One commonly used category outside of the United States is "Restricted." Restricted information provided to the U.S. government by other countries is treated as Confidential.

In the private sector, it is more common to see classifications such as Personal Confidential, Management Confidential, Proprietary, and Internal Use Only. The terminology you use is less important than the ability of your classification scheme to map to your organization's data access needs and information protection obligations.

Marking and Labeling

Marking or labeling information with its classification provides a mechanism to indicate any special handling procedures that must be performed. Marking or labeling may be as simple as using a rubber stamp on paper documents circulated within the company. Watermarking is another form of labeling in which classification information, typically text, is embedded in a digital file. The watermark is automatically reproduced when the file is copied. Watermarks may be visible or invisible. Visible watermarks can be produced by most word processing software applications, and are most often used in conjunction with administrative safeguards such as policies and procedures for handling sensitive information. Invisible watermarking has been in use for many years to provide copyright protection for video and music files. Digital watermarking software for PDF and other file types is now available that can be used with network or host-based watermark detection systems to provide both copy protection and disclosure control.

Information Classification Process

To achieve the appropriate level of support for information classification, a formal process should be followed to identify and document classification levels for the organization's data. This process should include the following steps:

1. Identify and document information assets by type of information—Information types should be based on the mission or function supported by the information.
2. Determine ownership of information—Information owners are individuals responsible for using the information to support a particular mission or function of the organization. These individuals must be of sufficient authority to make decisions regarding the management and use of information assets they own.
3. Determine sensitivity levels—Based on impacts, should the information become compromised.

Role of Classification in Business Continuity Planning Risk

Information and information systems should be classified according to their degree of criticality in carrying out the organization's mission, including necessary operations in support of that mission. Criticality classifications are usually made during the Business Impact Analysis (BIA) phase of business continuity planning. Systems and data owners are responsible for determining the classification levels and recovery time objectives needed to minimize the impact to the organization should data and automated functions become unavailable or corrupted. Continuity plans are then developed to meet these objectives. This process is discussed in more detail in the chapter on Risk, Response, and Recovery.

Information Handling Policy

An organization's information handling policy specifies the practices for collection, storage, management, use, and destruction of information that are designed to maintain the degrees of confidentiality and integrity specified by information owners. Some policy implementation and enforcement considerations for information handling at each stage in the life cycle are discussed in the sections on Information Collection, Secure Information Storage, and Record Retention and Disposal. The security practitioner plays a key role in establishing safeguards for information throughout its life cycle, including access control mechanisms and monitoring and audit trails to ensure policy compliance.

Information Collection

Information should be collected lawfully and, typically, only with the full knowledge and consent of affected parties. Web site privacy policies are often used to inform Web site visitors about data that are routinely collected through mechanisms such as cookies and Web-based forms. Only information necessary for the stated purpose should be collected. If any personally identifiable information that is collected is to be retained, procedures for individuals to verify the information and correct any errors should be established to maintain integrity. In some cases, sensitive data such as credit and debit card validation codes may be used in processing but must not be collected and stored.

Secure Information Storage

Data security breaches in which stored confidential information is lost or stolen are becoming commonplace and widely publicized. Most organizations are now considering encryption of data stored in databases, on local hard drives of laptops and other devices, and on backup tapes to reduce their exposure to breaches of confidentiality. Many storage vendors are now including encryption capabilities in their systems. Alternatively, third-party software may be purchased to encrypt a variety of devices and media.

Laptops and other mobile devices are at significant risk of being lost or stolen. Sensitive mobile data may be encrypted at the file or folder level, or the entire disk may be encrypted. File/folder encryption is simpler and faster to implement, but presents exposures if the operating system or user of the machine writes data to an unencrypted location. Full disk encryption protects the entire contents of a laptop's hard drive, including the boot sector, operating system, swap files, and user data. Since it does not rely on user discretion to determine what information to encrypt, it is typically the preferred method of protecting sensitive mobile data from unintended disclosure. There are some drawbacks; full disk encryption comes at the cost of a more complicated setup process that includes changes to the drive's boot sequence, and it may take hours during initial implementation to encrypt the hard drive (subsequently, new data are encrypted on the fly).

Typically, disk encryption products use software-generated symmetric keys to encrypt and decrypt the contents of the drive. Keys are stored locally and protected by a password or passphrase or other authentication mechanism that is invoked at boot time to provide access to the decryption key. Devices containing a TPM (Trusted Platform Module) chip contain a unique, secret RSA key burned into the chip during manufacture to securely generate derivative keys. Using hardware encryption in conjunction with software-based encryption products is a more secure approach to protecting highly sensitive mobile data. In addition, TPM chips provide additional security features such as platform authentication and *remote attestation*, a form of integrity protection that makes use of a hashed copy of hardware and software configuration to verify that configurations have not been altered.

Authentication may be integrated with a network directory service such as LDAP or Active Directory, or other external authentication service or two-factor authentication method such as smart cards, hardware tokens, and biometric devices.

Encrypted data can be irrevocably lost when a disk crashes or a user forgets his or her password, unless there is a mechanism in place to recover from such events. Some software allows for a master key or passphrase that can access the data without knowledge of the user password. Recovery disks containing backed-up data and boot information can be created during the initial installation; however, for ease of administration, it is best to combine disk encryption with a network-based backup solution.

Before implementing an encryption solution, care must be taken to thoroughly test all laptop software for compatibility, particularly software that interacts directly with operating system processes. Applications used for asset tracking, desktop intrusion prevention, patch management, and desktop administration may not be able to access encrypted information. If the organization uses other mobile devices such as PDAs, encryption software should support these devices as well for ease of integration, support, and maintenance.

Some free encryption solutions are available for common client operating systems. While the price is attractive, such solutions do not have the management features that are available with most commercial products and, therefore, do not scale well and may have a higher total cost of ownership for all but very small-scale implementations.

Encryption is a relatively straightforward and cost-effective means of protecting mobile data, but it is not a silver bullet. Encryption keys are vulnerable to discovery during encryption/decryption operations while the key data are stored in system memory, and users may inadvertently or knowingly reveal the password to unlock the decryption key. Personal firewalls, antivirus software, and appropriate physical and personnel security are essential elements of an overall mobile data protection program.

Backup tapes lost or diverted during transport and offsite storage have been another source of security breaches. Backup tapes can be encrypted during the backup operation using software built into or integrated with your backup management solution. In many implementations, the server containing the backup software acts as a client to the key management server whose function is to create, store, manage, and distribute encryption keys. Special encrypting tape drives or libraries must be used to encrypt and decrypt the tapes. When implementing a backup tape encryption solution, you may need to update internal hardware as well as hardware specified in disaster recovery equipment schedules. Thorough planning and testing should be performed to ensure that data on encrypted backup tapes will be accessible when needed.

Data residing on a storage area network (SAN) can be encrypted at various levels. Both internal and external disk array controllers offer encryption capabilities. Alternatively, data may be encrypted on the host system or at the individual disk level, offering the possibility of encrypting individual files and directories. SAN encryption implementations typically make use of a key management server, a corresponding client, and an encryption processing device integrated into the SAN infrastructure.

In an enterprise environment, sensitive data are often stored in centralized databases for access by a variety of applications. Database encryption is used to protect these data from unauthorized access by human and software agents. Database encryption has the distinct advantage of protecting sensitive data from the eyes of even the most privileged system and database administrators (except, of course, those with access to the key management system). Encryption mechanisms may be built into the database management system itself, or those provided by third-party software compatible with the database and operating system platform may be employed. Database encryption may occur at the file, database, or column/field level. It is not necessary and, in fact, it is detrimental to encrypt an entire database when only one data element is confidential. Database encryption solutions are available for most common database management systems. Implementing these solutions presents a number of challenges. When selecting a solution, you should understand how each candidate addresses the following:

Database size—Encryption may increase the size of data elements in your database by padding smaller chunks of data to produce fixed block sizes. If the database is not sized to accommodate these changes, it may need to be altered.

Performance—Performance degradation, particularly when encrypting indexed or frequently accessed fields, may be noticeable. If application performance is a concern, databases may need to be reorganized and reindexed to accommodate the additional overhead of decrypting fields.

Application compatibility—While some newer, integrated encryption solutions provide transparent decryption services to applications, most communicate through APIs, which must be compiled into business applications that access encrypted data. A thorough inventory of such applications is needed to prevent unanticipated failures, and resources will be required to modify impacted applications.

Data Scrubbing

An organization wishing to avoid the effort and expense of implementing encryption on large-scale production systems may choose to implement strong access controls, database segmentation, and other measures to restrict sensitive data access to those with a need to know. If so, it must still address issues of data replication to test environments. Wholesale replication of data from production to test is a common practice. Wholesale replication of security controls from production to test is not. There is a practical reason for this; if developers do not have access to accurate representations of data to work with, test results cannot be a reliable indicator of application performance in the production environment. Organizations that outsource development or testing are especially at risk of unauthorized access to sensitive production data because of difficulties in supervising and monitoring third-party account activity. One method of addressing this issue is to sanitize the data; that is, to mask, scramble, or overwrite sensitive data values with meaningless data, which nonetheless conform to data format and size restrictions. Data sanitization is also known as scrubbing or de-identification. It is not to be confused with encryption, which implies that data can be decrypted and viewed in its original form. The goal of data sanitization is to obfuscate sensitive data in such a way that the actual data values cannot be deduced or derived from the sanitized data itself, or through inference by comparing the sanitized data values with values of other data elements (the so-called inferential disclosure). For example, if a sanitization routine transposes characters on a one-for-one basis, substituting Q for A and W for S, and so on, original values for each character of a data element may be easily guessed.

Merely replacing data with null values is not an effective way to sanitize data, as most developers require a fairly accurate representation of the actual data element to interpret test results. Masking replaces characters in specified fields with a mask character, such as an X; for example, the masked credit card number 0828 2295 2828 5447 may be represented as 0828 XXXX XXXX 5447. Since the values of particular fields (such as those containing card issuer details) may need to remain intact for adequate testing, masking data in this manner requires coordination with the development teams. Another sanitization technique is substitution, wherein certain field values are replaced with randomly generated values that have no relationship to the original value. For example, substituting salary information in a payroll database with values randomly selected from a table of salaries. This technique produces data that is true to the original format, but it may be difficult to generate and maintain tables containing the large variety and amount of random data needed to meet data sanitization requirements for large systems. Shuffling and other techniques that merely rearrange existing data—for example, reorganizing the salary column so that salaries are associated with different employees—are fast and efficient, but are only effective on large databases and do not address all the needs of de-identification, particularly if the operation is not entirely random.

One concern with applying data sanitization is the maintenance of referential integrity within the database or file system. That is, relationships between files and tables cannot be altered or broken when data are sanitized; for example, if an account number used as a primary key in one table is used as a foreign key in another table, the relationship will be broken if the account number is converted to different values in each table. Data sanitization solutions should thus allow the administrator to define all critical relationships during configuration so that consistent values are produced across database tables. Sanitization is typically a batch operation that is run when production data are copied or refreshed into the test environment. It should be performed by an administrator who is not part of the development group who maintains the test environment.

Managing Encryption Keys

Because encryption keys control access to sensitive data, the effectiveness of any encryption strategy hinges on an organization's ability to securely manage these keys. Key management refers to the set of systems and procedures used to securely generate, store, distribute, use, archive, revoke, and delete keys. Defining a key management policy that identifies roles, responsibilities, and security requirements is a critical yet often overlooked component of any successful encryption strategy. Few organizations have tackled the key management problem at an enterprise level, and it remains the most difficult component in any encryption strategy to manage. In the absence of platform-independent standards, most applications and storage systems use isolated, proprietary key management systems, making key management more complex and inefficient even when the same type of encryption is used across multiple platforms.

The key management policy and associated documentation should be part of the organization's overall systems security plan. Considerations for key management policy and for selecting and deploying an effective key management system include the following:

- *Roles and responsibilities.* Responsibilities for generation, approval, and maintenance of the key management system and its associated processes should be clearly articulated in the policy document. The key management system access control mechanism must operate at sufficient level of granularity to support the policy, including any provisions for separation of duties or dual control required by the organization's security plan.

- *Key generation and storage.* Random number generators are used to generate keys. The key generation process should produce keys of the desired length and be sufficiently random and contain sufficient entropy so that keys cannot be easily guessed. Some systems generate entropy to seed keys by collecting timing data from random system events. The server used to generate and store keys may be a software application running on a standard server operating system, or may be a purpose-built, hardened platform dedicated to key management. One advantage of using a purpose-built system is that common operating system vulnerabilities that might be exploited to compromise encryption keys can be avoided. Another is that key management roles can be separated from database and server administration roles, reducing the risk of data compromised by privileged administrator accounts. The keys themselves, key control material (such as the unique key identifier or GUID created during key generation that uniquely identifies the key within a particular name space), and key server event logs must be protected from unauthorized access.

- *Distribution.* The key distribution center or facility should be capable of authenticating and checking authorization for key requests. The authentication mechanism should be sufficiently robust and protected from compromise. The client should have an integrity mechanism to validate the authenticity of the issuer and proper format of the keying material before accepting a key, and verifying receipt once the key has been accepted.

- *Expiration.* Encryption keys are assigned a cryptoperiod, or time span in which they are authorized for use. In general, shorter cryptoperiods are more secure, but create logistical issues for rekeying and updating keys, especially for enterprise applications in which the cost of rekeying and re-encrypting large amounts of data can be prohibitively high. Typically, keys generated to secure stored data have longer cryptoperiods than those used to secure communications. Strong keys combined with other forms of access control can compensate for longer cryptoperiods.

- *Revocation and destruction.* The key management system should support timely revocation of expired and compromised keys, and secure destruction of key material that is no longer valid.
- *Audit and tracking.* All key management operations should be fully audited, and event logs or audit records should be protected from unauthorized access and modification. Facilities must be available to track keying material throughout its life cycle, and should include mechanisms to detect and report on key compromise. Key labeling may be used to identify attributes of keys such as its identity, cryptoperiod, key type, and the like; labels should be stored with the key for identification purposes.
- *Emergency management.* The key management policy should specify the requirements for emergency replacement and revocation of encryption keys. Availability should be protected by storing backup or archive copies of keys in a separate location. The appropriate disaster recovery procedures must be created to address both key recovery and recovery of the key management system itself.

Secure Output

Many print processing functions send output to printers in the form of print spooler files, which contain human-readable copies of data to be printed. Securing spooled files is necessary to preserving confidentiality. One way to accomplish this would be to direct certain sensitive output to a secure document or print server for processing. If this is not possible, you should limit the number of individuals who have print operator authority or who are otherwise able to view, redirect, or manage output files and control functions. Printers receiving sensitive output should be located in secured areas or, in some cases, in individual offices. Users should be instructed to monitor their print jobs and pick up their output as soon as it is produced.

Some printers support encrypted file transfer and storage, which should be considered for highly sensitive documents.

Record Retention and Disposal

A business record is defined as data or information that has been fixed on some medium and that has content, structure, and context regarding its creation, receipt, storage, and use. Records are not just physical documents, but any information used by the organization to support operations and accountability. Operational needs or regulatory requirements may specify certain types of records that must be retained for a designated time period, after which time it should be discarded or destroyed. A record retention policy and schedule (list of records, owners, retention periods, and destruction methods) is an important component of an organization's information handling procedures. Information owners are responsible for designating retention periods and assigning custodial duties, typically in IT, to ensure that record integrity is preserved for the specified retention period. Audits may be performed to ensure policy compliance. Many organizations use a commercial document management system to organize and automate aspects of their record retention policy.

Handling procedures for confidential information must include provisions for secure destruction of records containing sensitive information. For private industry in the United States, such procedures may be required by U.S. privacy regulations such as the Fair and Accurate Credit Transactions Act of 2003 (FACTA), HIPAA, and GLBA. Additional mandates apply to government entities and contractors working with national interest information. Records destruction should be authorized, appropriate to the level of sensitivity of the record, secure, timely, and documented. The goal of secure destruction is to assure the appropriate sanitization of sensitive information so that it is no longer legible and so that insufficient data remains to be pieced together to derive protected data elements. Secure destruction methods are designed to combat the problem of data *remanence*, which is generally used to refer to the information left in a record or file after the original data has been deleted, or moved to another location. Secure destruction methods include burning, shredding, disk cleaning or reformatting, and tape degaussing.

Due to environmental concerns, it is typically not considered appropriate to burn paper records or disks. Instead, paper documents and CD/DVD media should be shredded using special equipment designed for this purpose. Paper shredders typically cut documents into thin strips or small fragments. They come in a variety of capacities, from personal shredders to industrial-strength models. Several types of shredders are available, such as:

Strip-cut shredders—cut paper in long, thin strips
Cross-cut shredders—preferable to strip-cut, these cut paper into small rectangular fragments
Particle-cut shredders—similar to cross-cut; creates tiny square or circular fragments
Hammermills—pound paper through a screen
Granulators (or disintegrators)—repeatedly cut paper into fine, mesh-size particles

DIN 32757, a shredding standard developed by the German Institute for Standardization, is the de facto standard used by the shredding industry to classify equipment into hierarchical security levels based on the residue produced by shredding. Government and certain private applications may require use of shredders certified and labeled at a specific maximum security level for paper documents containing classified information. Security levels (with general applicability) are:

Level 1—Least secure, cuts paper into 12-mm strips. Not suitable for classified information.
Level 2—Cuts paper into 6-mm strips. Not suitable for classified information.

Level 3—Cuts paper into 2-mm strips. Limited suitability for confidential information.

Level 4—Cuts paper into particles 2 × 15 mm particles. Suitable for Sensitive but Unclassified or Business Proprietary information.

Level 5—Cuts paper into 0.8 × 12 mm particles. Suitable for Classified information.

Level 6—Cuts paper into 0.8 × 4 mm particles. Suitable for Top Secret information.

Shredding services can be contracted to process large volumes of information, either onsite using mobile equipment, or at a specially designed facility. Depending on the application, such companies may require a security clearance and may only be suitable for some classification levels. For typical applications, such clearance may not be necessary, but it is wise to request a *certificate of destruction*, which most companies will supply on request.

Magnetic media, including diskettes, CD/DVDs, disk drives, and tapes, may be destroyed using a number of methods. Often, however, these methods are not environmentally friendly, require excessive manual effort, and are not suitable for high-volume enterprise application. CD/DVD shredders are available at nominal cost and are practical for small business units. Fixed disk shredders are also available, but they are mainly geared to the consumer market and may not produce consistent results with data in disparate formats. When disk shredders are used, they should produce fragments that contain less than one (512k) block of data. Many organizations may wish to preserve the media for reuse or redeployment to another location. For example, many organizations donate used PCs to schools or charitable organizations. Even when media is redeployed within an organization, care should be taken to remove sensitive information before the media is reused.

Methods of destroying data contained on magnetic media include various techniques for *clearing* or *sanitizing* data. Clearing refers to any operation that removes or obscures stored data such that it cannot be reconstructed using operating system or third-party utilities. Sanitizing or purging removes data in such a way that it cannot be reconstructed at all. While disk clearing may be acceptable protection against accidental or random disclosure, it is not adequate to prevent someone with intent and commonly available tools from restoring data.

Erasure or reformatting. Conventional magnetic recording heads do not operate at sufficient density to totally erase the contents of disk and tape; therefore, merely erasing or reformatting magnetic media using conventional drives will not eliminate all the stored information. Furthermore, most operating system file management utilities do not delete the data itself, but instead remove the entry in the system directory or address table so that it cannot be immediately accessed. The data itself will typically remain on disk until the sector it occupies is overwritten with new data. Metadata, or schema information, usually remains intact as well.

Even when metadata is erased or overwritten, forensic software that performs direct reads on the disk sectors is available to retrieve the information.

Formatting, repartitioning, or reimaging a disk drive is only slightly more secure than erasing the data. Modern disk drives cannot be reformatted by older, low-level methods that skew sector or track numbers or interleave sectors, as certain data are necessary for the servo mechanism in the drive to locate a desired track. Instead, many reformatting utilities (such as UNIX dd utility) write a zero byte to each sector on the disk (also known as *zero filling*) in a single pass. High-level reformatting methods operate by creating a file system on disk and installing a boot sector. Although space is marked as available on disk and data appear to be erased, data are not actually deleted or overwritten in the reformatting process.

Disk wiping, or *overwriting*, is a method of writing over existing data—typically with a stream of zeroes, ones, or a random pattern of both. Special procedures may be required, such as using certain combinations of patterns or making a certain number of passes over the disk, each time writing a different pattern. Overwriting is acceptable for clearing media for reuse, but is not a sufficient method of sanitizing disk or tape. Overwriting before reformatting is a much more effective technique than reformatting alone and can be a suitable means of clearing less sensitive content from disk.

Degaussing is a technique of erasing data on disk or tape (including video tapes) that, when performed properly, ensures that there is insufficient magnetic remanence to reconstruct data. This is performed with a machine called a degausser, which applies a magnetic field to the media and then removes it, eliminating the residual magnetic signals on the media. Media can be classified in terms of coercivity, or the intensity of the magnetic energy a disk or tape can store, measured in a unit called Oersteds. To perform properly, the degausser must be capable of creating a magnetic field with two to three times the intensity of the capacity of the media. Magnetic tape may be classified by coercivity as type I, II, or III, and must be degaussed with a machine rated for the type of tape employed. Type I degaussers can erase media having a maximum coercivity of 350 Oersteds, whereas type II degaussers are rated for media up to 750 Oersteds. Degaussers that handle media up to 1700 Oersteds (type III magnetic tape) are not yet approved by the U.S. government.

Degaussers may be operated manually, or be automatic using a conveyor belt assembly. Because of the strength of the magnetic field generated, not all media can be successfully degaussed without destroying the information needed by the servo mechanism used to read the disk or tape, which would render the media unusable. This is particularly true of some disk and tape cartridges used in midrange and mainframe systems. Therefore, manufacturer's specifications should be consulted before planning a degaussing strategy.

The U.S. Defense Security Service provides a matrix (shown in Figure 6.2) for determining requirements for clearing and sanitizing media at various classification levels.

Media	Clear			Sanitize			
Magnetic Tape							
Type I	a		b			m	
Type II	a		b			m	
Type III	a		b			m	
Magnetic Disk							
Bernoullis	a	c	b			m	
Floppy	a	c	b			m	
Non-Removable Rigid Disk		c	a	d		m	
Removable Rigid Disk	a	c	a	d		m	
Optical Disk							
Read Many, Write Many		c				m	
Read Only						m	n
Write Once, Read Many (Worm)						m	n

Figure 6.2   Clearing and sanitization matrix.

Memory											
Dynamic Random Access Memory (DRAM)	c	h			c		h		m		
Electronically Alterable PROM (EAPROM)			i					j	m		
Electronically Erasable PROM (EEPROM)			i				g		m		
Erasable Programmable ROM (EPROM)			k		c				m	l	l then c
Flash EPROM (FEPROM)			i		c			i	m		c then i
Programmable ROM (PROM)	c								m		
Magnetic Bubble Memory	c		a		c				m		
Magnetic Core Memory	c		a	e					m		
Magnetic Plated Wire	c			f	c				m		c and f
Magnetic Resistive Memory	c								m		
Non-Volatile RAM (NOVRAM)	c	h			c		h		m		

Figure 6.2 (Continued)

Read Only Memory (ROM)							m
Synchronous DRAM (SDRAM)	c	h		c	h		m
Static Random Access Memory (SRAM)	c	h		c	f	h	m
							c and f
Equipment							
Monitor	h						q
Impact Printer	h				p	h	p then h
Laser Printer	h				o	h	o then h

a Degauss with type I, II, or III degausser.

b Degauss with same type (I, II, or III) degausser.

c Overwrite all addressable locations with a single character.

d This method is not approved for sanitizing media that contains top secret information. 1) Before any sanitization product is acquired, careful analysis to the overall costs associated with overwrite/sanitization should be made. Depending on the contractor's environment, the size of the drive and the differences in the individual products time to perform the sanitization, destruction of the media might be the preferred (i.e., economical) sanitization method. 2) Overwrite all addressable locations with a character, then its complement. Verify "complement" character was written successfully to all addressable locations, then overwrite all addressable locations with random characters; or verify third overwrite of random characters. Overwrite utility must write/read to "growth" defect list/sectors or disk must be mapped before initial classified use and remapped before sanitization. Difference in the comparison lists must be discussed with the DSS Industrial Security Representative (IS Rep) and/or Information System Security Professional (ISSP) before declassification. *Note:* Overwrite utilities must be authorized by DSS before use.

Figure 6.2 (Continued)

e   Overwrite all addressable locations with a character, its complement, then a random character.

f   Each overwrite must reside in memory for a period longer than the classified data resided.

g   Overwrite all locations with a random pattern, then with binary zeros, and finally with binary ones.

h   Remove all power to include battery power.

i   Perform a full chip erase as per manufacturer's data sheets.

j   Perform i above, then c above, a total of three times.

k   Perform an ultraviolet erase according to manufacturer's recommendation.

l   Perform k above, but increase time by a factor of 3.

m   Destruction see items 1) and 2) below.

n   Destruction required only if classified information is contained.

o   Run 1 page (font test acceptable) when print cycle not completed (e.g., paper jam or power failure). Dispose of output as unclassified if visual examination does not reveal any classified information.

p   Ribbons must be destroyed. Platens must be cleaned.

q   Inspect and/or test screen surface for evidence of burn-in information. If present, screen must be destroyed.

Figure 6.2   (Continued)

Disclosure Controls: Data Leakage Prevention

While encryption and proper disposal of sensitive data are necessary components of a confidentiality strategy, sensitive data may "leak" out of an organization in a variety of ways based on intentional or unintentional acts of people who have a legitimate reason for accessing and using the data to support the organization's functions.

Data leakage or loss prevention (DLP) technology has surfaced relatively recently in the marketplace in response to regulatory requirements to protect confidential data from such unintentional or malicious loss or disclosure. Various implementations of DLP systems exist; the two most common are those that protect transfer of sensitive data to mobile storage devices such as USB keys and Smart Phones, and those that prevent data leakage via Web and e-mail at an organization's Internet gateway. Less prevalent are those solutions that tackle confidentiality of data at rest in files, databases, and mass storage facilities. An effective data leakage prevention strategy includes use of both host- and network-based components that perform the following functions:

Data Discovery—The process of "crawling" distributed files and databases to locate sensitive data is the first step in implementing data leakage prevention tools. The discovery process has intrinsic value, even without implementing loss prevention tools, in that organizations can use it to pinpoint exactly where their sensitive data are stored and design additional safeguards, such as policies and access control mechanisms, to protect the data. One may uncover, for example, cases where users run queries over sensitive data that are stored in a secured database and then save the results to their desktops or to an unsecured public file, where access control safeguards may be weaker. Note that this violates the "*" property of the Bell–LaPadula model!

Labeling—Data may be labeled or "tagged" with an identifier that can be used to subsequently monitor movement of that data across the network. This is particularly useful in identifying documents and files containing sensitive information. Labels used may correspond to the sensitivity levels defined in the organization's information classification policy, or may identify specific types of data such as PHI (Private Health Information).

Policy Creation—Content monitoring and usage policies specify which data are sensitive, and define rules for copying or transmitting that data, typically using a combination of predefined labels, keywords, and regular expressions (e.g., nnn-nn-nnnn to identify a social security number) to identify unique data elements.

Content Detection/Monitoring—Data communications over local and wide area networks, data traversing perimeter gateway devices, and data leaving host computers via USB or serial connections are monitored by inspecting the contents of the communication at the file, document, and packet level. At the network layer, packet-level monitoring can be used to identify and intercept transmission of sensitive data through FTP, SSL, and posting to blogs and chat rooms among other things. Documents transferred as attachments to e-mail and instant messages can also be monitored and blocked at gateways if they contain sensitive content. To identify data transferred to removable storage, software agents are typically employed on target machines to monitor traffic over USB, wireless, and Firewire ports.

Prevention or Blocking—When policy violations are detected, user actions may be prevented or network traffic may be dropped, depending on the location of the violation. Alternatively, encryption may be enforced before a write operation to CD, USB, or other removable media.

Reporting—Violations of data disclosure policies are reported, typically showing the policy that was violated, the source IP address, and the login account under which the violation occurred.

While an integrated approach to data leakage prevention is desirable, currently available solutions may be too cost-prohibitive or considered too disruptive for some organizations to implement. It is possible for the creative security practitioner to launch a grassroots effort to detect, and even prevent, some forms of data leakage using technology already available in his or her security toolkit. For example, most content filtering technologies such as those installed on Web and e-mail proxies allow the administrator to set up regular expressions or keywords to audit and block sensitive data sent via e-mail, instant messaging, and via Web forms and even file transfers. A network IDS can also be configured to detect "signatures" within the payload of network traffic, including labels on sensitive documents if your organization has instituted a data classification and labeling scheme.

Regardless of the method used to detect and prevent data leakage, it should be supplemented with traditional safeguards such as physical and logical access controls, encryption, and auditing. It must also be kept current to accommodate changes in applications, business processes and relationships, and infrastructure.

Secure Application Development

Software applications have become targets of an increasing number of malicious attacks in recent years. Web-based applications that are exposed over public networks are a natural choice for criminal hackers seeking entry points to an organization's data and internal network infrastructure. Internal applications are also at risk due to internal fraud and abuse, logical processing errors, and simple human mistakes. While firewalls and other network security devices offer a great degree of protection, they are often bypassed by legitimate users, attackers using stolen login credentials or hijacked user sessions, and unauthorized activity conducted over allowed ports and protocols. Indirect access through a remote access gateway or compromised internal host can also bypass perimeter protections. Safeguards built into applications early in systems design are needed to counteract these threats, thwart application-level attacks, and maintain data and system integrity in the face of human error.

The security practitioner will be better able to build security into his or her organization's application systems by actively participating through all phases of the development process. Rather than becoming an impediment to productivity, secure design and development practices introduce efficiencies and enhance quality if they are applied consistently throughout the development life cycle. This process of building security in requires an understanding of commonly used application software development methods, common threats and vulnerabilities, and application-level safeguards.

Most organizations adhere to a standard methodology to specify, design, develop, and implement software applications. Various models exist for developing software applications. Some of the more prevalent are described below.

Waterfall Model

The waterfall model consists of a linear sequence of seven steps. Steps are taken in order, and as each step in the process is completed, the development team moves on to the next step. Steps in the waterfall model are:

- *Feasibility or concept development phase*
  A feasibility analysis usually precedes approval of any development project. In this stage, the business problem and a recommended approach are documented in the project charter. The project charter also includes a preliminary plan, resource estimates and budget, and constraints. The person designated as the project *sponsor* typically signs off on the charter, giving the go-ahead to proceed. Additional stakeholders may be named to participate in review and approval at key milestone points. The security practitioner who is fully hooked in to the development process will ideally be asked to participate in charter development and review.
- *Requirements definition*
  Functional and nonfunctional requirements are documented in this phase. Functional requirements specify user interactions and system processing steps, and are often documented in the form of sequences of action called *use cases,* documented using Unified Modeling Language (UML). Nonfunctional requirements, such as those for performance and quality, or those imposed by design or environmental constraints, are documented using narratives and diagrams. Security requirements may be incorporated within the nonfunctional requirements specification. Examples of this type of security requirement include user and process authentication, maintaining access logs and

audit trails, secure session management, and encryption of passwords and sensitive data. Functional security requirements, such as how an application responds to incorrect passwords, malformed input, or unauthorized access attempts, can be documented in the form of "abuse" or "misuse" case diagrams. Security requirements are typically derived through a risk or threat assessment conducted during this stage of development.

The project sponsor and stakeholders sign off on the completed requirements before the team begins solution development.

■ *Design*

Software design activities are typically performed by architects or programmer analysts who are well versed in both the business process to be developed and the environment in which the application will operate. Specifications elicited during the requirements phase are documented into application events using a set of flow charts and narratives. Design may first be laid out in a *general design document*, which is then refined to produce specifications for the *detailed design*. Design walkthroughs are often held to review the design before construction to ensure that all of the requirements have been accounted for in the application design. A security architect or administrator should participate in the design phase to ensure that security design requirements are integrated with the overall application design.

■ *Construction*

Software programming is completed in this phase. Functional design specifications, typically created by analysts, are translated into executable processes using one or more programming languages. The usual scenario has multiple programmers working concurrently on discrete functional units or modules that comprise the whole application. Each capability is separately tested by the developer before being rolled up, or integrated, with other functions.

■ *Integration*

Integration occurs when multiple functional units of code, or modules, that form the application are compiled and run together. This ensures, for example, that outputs produced by one process are received as expected by a downstream process.

■ *Testing*

Testing is not a separate phase of waterfall development projects; instead, different types of testing and debugging occur from construction to installation and beyond. Programmers perform unit testing to validate proper functioning of code at the lowest level of functionality, which can be a process, function, program, or method in the case of object-oriented programming. Automated tools built into the developer's programming environment are often used for unit testing.

Integration testing is the next phase, in which individually tested units are assembled in functional groups and retested as a whole, following a test script or plan. Use and abuse cases generated during requirements gathering may form the basis of functional testing at this stage. The purpose of integration testing is to ensure that major application functions specified in the design are working together. All interactions, such as program calls, messages, etc., are tested in this phase.

System testing is performed on a complete, integrated system to ensure that all requirements and approved changes have been incorporated into the application. Some organizations create separate environments, such as servers, databases, files, and utilities, for the purpose of system testing. Objects in the system test environment should be secured in the same manner as in production to avoid "breaking" the application once it is released.

■ *Installation*

When the application has been system tested, it is installed into a controlled environment for quality assurance and user acceptance testing. At this stage, the application is considered to be in its final form, installation and operational documentation has been developed, and changes are tightly controlled. Typically, a separate QA team performs quality testing before releasing the application to end users for the final acceptance testing phase. User acceptance testing requires formal signoff from the project sponsor to indicate that the application has met all requirements. Certification and accreditation may also be required before an application project can be closed. Release management, discussed in a later section, is a set of controlled processes used to implement the final, approved application into the production environment.

■ *Maintenance*

Applications rarely remain in the form in which they were originally released to production. Changes in business needs and practices, newly discovered bugs and vulnerabilities, and changes in the technical environment all necessitate changes to production applications.

The waterfall model described above is the oldest and most widely used formal development model; it is common practice in defense applications and in large, established organizations. Key differentiators of the waterfall model are its adherence to a highly structured linear sequence of steps or phases, an emphasis on completeness of up-front requirements and design, and the use of documentation and formal approvals between phases as primary control mechanisms. Major benefits of using the waterfall method are its ease of use and management (even with large teams), and the broad scope and detailed specificity of systems documentation that is available to certification, accreditation, and application maintenance and enhancement teams. A major drawback of the waterfall model is that it assumes a static set of requirements captured before design and coding phases begin. Thus, errors may not be noticed until later testing phases, where they are more costly to address. Even in the absence of errors, new requirements may surface during development due to regulatory and operational changes and emergence of new threats that impact the automated process. To correct for this, project managers must establish rigorous change management processes to reduce the disruption, delays, and cost overruns that can occur as a result of having to retrofit new requirements into the application. The later in development requirements surface, the more potentially disruptive they are, and the more likely they are to be shelved for future development. For this reason, security practitioners are urged to actively contribute to requirements gathering and documentation, and maintain awareness of the change management process to address any functional changes that may introduce new security requirements.

Additional Application Development Methods

Spiral Model

The spiral model is based on the waterfall development life cycle, but adds a repeated PDCA (Plan–Do–Check–Act) sequence at each stage of the waterfall progression. A first pass through the steps of the waterfall model is taken using a subset or high-level view of overall requirements, which are used as a basis for an initial *prototype* (working model) of the application. The spiral model assumes that requirements are naturally flushed out in a hierarchical way, with high-level or basic requirements giving rise to more detailed functional requirements.

Extreme Programming and Rapid Application Development

Rapid Application Development (RAD) was designed to fully leverage modern development environments that make it possible to quickly build user interface components as requirements are gathered. Application users are intimately involved in RAD projects, working with the screen flows as they are being built and providing feedback to the developers. The advantages of RAD include high error detection rates early in development, bypassing the need for extensive retrofitting and regression testing. RAD projects thus require less project change management overhead. This very fact can be a downside, however; RAD projects may suffer fatal "scope creep," as new requirements are continually added and teams lose sight of the end goal while cycling through an unending series of prototypes.

Agile Development

Agile is a fairly new phenomenon built on the example of iterative development models. Agile development methods rely on feedback from application users and development teams as their primary control mechanism. Software development is seen as a continuous evolution, where results from continuous release testing are evaluated and used to enhance subsequent releases of the developing code. Enhanced team productivity, increased development speed, and a reduction in production defects are all stated benefits of agile development. IT personnel who are well versed in traditional development methods take some time to get used to agile development, and performance gains in the first year are expected to double—or better—in the second year after adopting agile methods.

Component Development and Reuse

The idea of component-based development is based on the reuse of proven design solutions to address new problems. This is not really a new concept; traditional utility programs such as date conversion routines are an example of components that have been in existence for decades. Components may be retained as design patterns, common modules, or architectural models in a component library that is searchable by developers looking to incorporate them in their applications. Component reuse reduces development and testing time and cost, increases quality and reliability, and promotes consistency and ease of maintenance among applications.

User and application authentication sequences, authorization checks, and encryption and decryption methods are examples of security functions that can be developed for reuse across applications. Some development platforms, such as J2EE (Java 2 Enterprise Edition), incorporate security methods in their programming libraries. Using prepackaged components is encouraged whenever possible to avoid vulnerabilities that can easily be introduced into homegrown security logic.

Web Application Vulnerabilities and Secure Development Practices

Exposing applications, infrastructure, and information to external users via the Internet creates an opportunity for compromise by individuals and groups wishing to steal customer data and proprietary information, interfere with operations and system availability, or damage an organization's reputation. Vulnerabilities within Web-facing applications provide opportunities for malicious attack by unauthorized users, authorized but malicious users, and malicious code executing locally or on a compromised machine connected to the application. Internal development projects should combine secure coding practices, appropriate program and infrastructure change control, and proactive vulnerability management to reduce vulnerabilities.

The Open Web Application Security Project (OWASP) provides a freely available listing of the top vulnerabilities found in Web applications; in reality, the list contains a mix of vulnerabilities and exploits that frequently occur as a result of compromised Web browsers and, in some cases, Web servers. Most of these attacks are platform independent, although specific platforms have been targeted by variants. At a minimum, coding standards and guidelines should be developed to protect applications against the OWASP Top Ten, which are currently as follows:

A1. *Cross-site scripting (XSS)*—Vulnerabilities to cross-site scripting attacks are found on all Web development platforms. The basic attack injects code, typically Javascript, into the HTTP (Hypertext Transfer Protocol) request sent to the Web server. In a reflected cross-site scripting attack, the Web server echoes the request data back to the browser, which will execute the script or command. Stored attacks are also possible, where the injected code is written to a file or database that the Web server has access to; alternatively, the attack can target the Javascript in the application itself. The best way to prevent XSS attacks is to include code that validates all user-supplied input to the application.

A2. *Injection Flaws*—Injection flaws occur when user-supplied data are sent to a command or query interpreter for processing. The attacker alters the query or inserts a command in the input stream, tricking the interpreter to execute commands or queries to reveal unauthorized data, or create, modify, or delete data in any area the application has access to. SQL injection is the most common form of injection attack. Recently, it has been gaining momentum in the form of a worm that uses SQL injection to attack ASP (Active Server Pages) and ASP. NET applications. The best protection against injection flaws is to avoid use of dynamic queries, and use strongly parameterized APIs that restrict what will be accepted as input.

A3. *Malicious File Execution*—These attacks affect any application that accepts files or filenames as input, or that allow external object references such as URL names. Platforms most commonly affected are those that use PHP server-side scripting or those that consume XML (Extended Markup Language) messages. Web applications vulnerable to malicious file execution may process content or invoke code provided by the attacker, potentially leading to a total compromise of the system (local file server access is possible on Microsoft Windows platforms). When combined with XSS attacks, the remote code provided by the attacker may be sent to the user's browser for execution. The best protection against malicious file execution is to design applications that make use of indirect object reference maps and parameter bounds checking. Securing the PHP execution environment and implementing basic egress filtering on perimeter firewalls to prevent Web servers from initiating outbound connections provides defense-in-depth.

A4. *Insecure Direct Object References*—A direct object reference is made whenever forms or URLs used in the application expose references or links to objects used internally to the application, such as files and database or directory entries or keys. These references can be exploited by attackers who modify parameters to gain unauthorized access to system objects. Whenever possible, applications should not display or expose any references to internal objects in URL strings. In addition, all references and object accesses should be validated by the application before processing.

A5. *Cross-Site Request Forgery (CSRF)*—A cross-site request forgery works by forcing a compromised client's browser to send a request to the Web server on behalf of the attacker. If the Web server does not authenticate individual requests once the user logs in to the application, it can be susceptible to the attack. The best defenses against such attacks are to use custom tokens in forms and URLs that would not be automatically submitted by the browser, and to correct XSS vulnerabilities that can be exploited to bypass CSRF protections. Additional safeguards include using form POST methods (instead of GET), and using out-of-band verification for transactions (such as sending an electronic or paper mail confirmation of transactions).

A6. *Information Leakage/Improper Error Handling*—This refers to a number of vulnerabilities involving unintentional disclosure of system configuration, application logic, transaction state, or sensitive data used by the application. Many of these issues are caused by improper error handling on the part of the application, the application environment, or both. The best defense against unintentional disclosure is to create a default error handler to catch and translate exceptions from all application layers (database, Web server, operating system, application) into sanitized versions that do not disclose information that could be exploited by an attacker.

A7. *Broken Authentication and Session Management*—Most of these flaws result from a failure to properly protect authentication credentials and artifacts such as session tokens used to verify user identity during use of the application. The best protection against these flaws is to perform a risk or threat assessment, and design all identity and authentication management functions to mitigate threats, covering all aspects of the user life cycle (from enrollment, through usage, to deprovisioning users).

A8. *Insecure Cryptographic Storage*—Weaknesses in, or lack of, encryption used to protect user credentials and sensitive application data can be exploited by attackers to steal sensitive data, including user accounts and passwords. The best protection against these flaws is to encrypt sensitive data using strong, industry-standard (not home grown) encryption algorithms, and ensure that processes are in place to adequately protect and manage encryption keys.

A9. *Insecure Communications*—A failure to encrypt sensitive data transmitted over networks can result in compromise, often by way of software sniffers installed on compromised machines in the network. At a minimum, SSL should be used to encrypt all connections where authentication credentials and sensitive data are sent.

A10. *Failure to Restrict URL Access*—This vulnerability arises when applications do not limit access to URLs and files that are not intended for access by non-administrative users. Exploits can lead to de facto privilege escalation and execution of unauthorized system changes or application transactions. The best protection is to set strong access control permissions on files and paths not intended for ordinary user consumption. These and other vulnerabilities can be largely avoided by active security participation in the application development process. Ideally, the security practitioner is a member of the enterprise architecture team, and works with developers to promote awareness of security vulnerabilities and their consequences, create standards for design and construction of secure applications, and promote reuse of secure components. As the vulnerabilities described in this chapter have illustrated, guidelines for developers should include the following areas:

- *Authentication*: Use standard, secure authentication mechanisms for users and applications, including mechanisms for forgotten passwords and password changes (require the old password be entered first), secure encrypted storage of authentication credentials, and enforcement of strong passwords not susceptible to dictionary attacks.
- *Authorization*: Perform authorization checks to requested objects such as files, URLs, and database entries. Secure objects from unauthorized access.
- *Session management*: Most Web application platforms include session management functions that link individual requests to an authenticated user account, so that the user does not need to manually reauthenticate to each Web page. Custom cookies should be avoided for authentication (user and session) where possible. Proper session management includes timing out inactive sessions, deleting session information after timeout, not passing credentials in URL strings, and using salted hashes to protect session IDs.
- *Encryption of sensitive data*: Encryption of data at rest may not be feasible for your organization, with the exception of authentication credentials, which should always be encrypted. Encryption of sensitive data in transit is simple and inexpensive to configure and should be required of all applications. Avoid homegrown encryption methods wherever possible.
- *Input validation*: Applications should never assume that data sent to them in the form of HTTP requests, form field input, or parameters are benign and in the proper format. User input should be validated using an "accepted known good" approach wherever possible (matching input to a set or range of acceptable values). String length or field size limits, data types, syntax, and business rules should be enforced on all input fields.
- *Disallow dynamic queries*: Dynamic queries and direct database access should not be allowed within Web applications. Stored procedures (routines precompiled in the database, or callable as program code) should be used wherever possible. Use strongly typed, parameterized APIs for queries and stored procedure calls.
- *Out-of-band confirmations*: Consider sending confirmations out of band when there has been a password change, or significant business transaction performed via the Web site.
- *Avoid exposing system information*: Avoid exposing references to private application objects in URL strings, cookies, or user messages.

- *Error handling*: Avoid exposing information about the system or process, such as path information, stack trace and debugging information, and standard platform error messages in response to errors and consider setting a low debug level for general use. Instead, consider using a standard default error handling routine for all application components, including those in the application environment (server operating system, application system, etc.). Ensure that error messages do not expose any information that could be exploited by hackers; for example, a return "incorrect password" indicates that the supplied UserID is valid, while "login failed" does not expose any such information. Timing attacks can be avoided by enforcing a consistent wait time on certain transactions.

Protecting against Buffer Overflows

Buffer overflow vulnerabilities are still common in many applications, whether or not they are exposed to the Web. These vulnerabilities arise when systems allow information to be written beyond the bounds of computer memory that has been allocated to hold the program stack, or that the program has allocated to certain items such as pointers, strings, and arrays. Overflow vulnerabilities may be present in a host Web or application server, or in developed program code.

In the best-case scenario, overrunning the bounds of a buffer results in a program crash, which may lead to failure of subordinate processes or systems. However, if an attacker is able to control what is written to the buffer, he or she can force execution of instructions supplied by the attacker. Buffer overflow attacks may be classified as stack attacks (where the return address after a function is executed or overwritten) and variable attacks (where variables supplied to a program function are overwritten).

Some programming languages and development kits provide automated bounds checking but others, such as Assembler, C, and C++, do not—leaving it to the programmer to include this logic when allocating buffer storage. Techniques for preventing buffer overflow attacks include use of appropriate bounds checking and input validation logic; avoidance of certain program functions such as strcpy, which do not allow for bounds checking; and use of compilers that protect buffers from overwrites. Many source code analyzers and vulnerability checkers now include functions for detecting buffer overflow vulnerabilities.

Implementation and Release Management

Release management is a software engineering discipline that controls the release of applications, updates, and patches to the production environment. The goal of release management is to provide assurance that only tested and approved application code is promoted to production or distributed for use. Release management also seeks to meet timeliness goals, minimize disruption to users during releases, and ensure that all associated communication and documentation is issued with new releases of software. The most important role is that of the release manager. The release manager is responsible for planning, coordination, implementation, and communication of all application releases. This function may be situated within a unit of a quality assurance or operational group, or may be part of a separate organization responsible for overall change and configuration management. The decision of where to locate release management functions should be based on the need to achieve separation of duties and rigorous process oversight during application installation or distribution and ongoing maintenance. This is essential to mitigate risks and impacts of unplanned and malicious changes, which could introduce new vulnerabilities into the production environment or user community.

Release management policy specifies the conditions that must be met for an application or component to be released to production, roles and responsibilities for packaging, approving, moving and testing code releases, and approval and documentation requirements.

The release management process actually begins with the QA testing environment. It is important to ensure that any defects found and corrected in QA are incorporated back into the system test environment, or previously corrected bugs may resurface. An organization may have separate user acceptance and preproduction or staging environments that are subject to release management before code is released to production. Typically the configuration and movement of objects into these environments are controlled by the release management team. Once user acceptance testing is complete, the application is packaged for deployment to the production or preproduction environment and the final package is verified. Automated build tools are typically used to ensure that the right versions of source code are retrieved from the repository and compiled into the application. In organizations that use automated deployment tools, builds are packaged together with automated installers (such as Windows MSI service for desktop operating systems) and other necessary components such as XML configuration and application policy files.

To ensure integrity of the source code or application package and to protect production libraries from release of unauthorized code, applications may be hashed and signed with a digital signature created with a public key algorithm. *Code signing*, which is typically used for Web applications such as those based on Java and ActiveX to assist users in validating that the application was issued by a trusted source, also has an application in release management. For example, Sun provides a jarsigner tool for Java JAR (Java Archive) and EAR (Enterprise Archive) files that allows an authorized holder of a private key to sign individual JAR files, record signed entries into a file called a Manifest, and convert the Manifest into a signature file containing the digest of the entire Manifest. This prevents any modifications to the archive file once it has been approved and signed. The public key used to verify the signature is packaged along with the archive file so that the person responsible for deploying the file can verify the integrity of the release, also using the jarsigner tool.

Release management tools aid in automating application deployments and enforcing an organization's release policy. Such features include role-based access control to enforce separation of duties; approval checking and rejection of unapproved packages; component verification tools to ensure that all required application components, documentation, etc., are included in the release; rollback and demotion facilities to protect against incomplete deployments; and auditing and reporting tools to track all aspects of the release process. Automated tools may also be capable of verifying integrity by interrogating a digital signature.

Applications deployed into preproduction or production environments may be smoke tested as part of the release process. Smoke testing is high-level, scripted testing of the major application components and interfaces to validate the integrity of the application before making it publicly available.

The release manager assures that all documentation and communication regarding the release are prepared and distributed before going "live" with a new or modified application. Any planned outages or other impacts should be communicated in advance, and contacts for assistance with the application should be made available. Following the release, a "burn in" period may be instituted in which special problem resolution and support procedures are in effect.

Release management policy is typically enforced through access control mechanisms that prevent developers from modifying production programs and data. Sensitive system utilities should reside in their own libraries and should only be executed by authorized personnel and processes. Utility programs such as compilers and assemblers should never be executed in production environments.

Systems Assurance and Controls Validation

Systems assurance is the process of validating that existing security controls are configured and functioning as expected, both during initial implementation and on an ongoing basis. Security controls should never be assumed to be functioning as intended. Human error, design issues, component failures, and unknown dependencies and vulnerabilities can impact the initial configuration of security controls. Even once properly implemented, controls can lose effectiveness over time. Changes in the control environment itself, in the infrastructure that supports the control, in the systems which the control was designed to protect, or in the nature of threats that seek to bypass controls all contribute to reduced control effectiveness. Even in the absence of known changes, a "set it and forget it" mentality can expose an organization to risk. Therefore, controls should be tested on a periodic basis against a set of security requirements.

Certification and Accreditation

Certification is a process of reviewing the security features of an information system against a set of requirements to determine whether, and to what extent, the systems design and configuration meet specifications. Both technical and nontechnical safeguards are reviewed during the certification process. When conducting a certification review, the practitioner must not only verify the existence of required safeguards, but test those safeguards to ensure they are functioning as intended.

Accreditation is the process of obtaining an official signoff on the decision to implement an information system in a specific environment, based on input from the certification process asserting that technical and administrative safeguards are sufficient to reduce risk to acceptable levels.

In internal application development projects, review and signoff on the project charter and requirements, design, risk assessment, and user acceptance testing may substitute for formal certification and accreditation of the system.

Certification and Accreditation Roles

Program manager—This individual has overall responsibility for acquisition or development, function, operation, and performance of the system.

Certifier—This individual, typically a security specialist, should have sufficient knowledge of the system to assess the security configuration and secure operation of the system against requirements. The certifier should be independent of the organization responsible for developing the system.

Designated Approving Authority (DAA)—This individual is the person who determines the acceptable level of residual risk for the system in light of organizational mission, system costs and benefits, and constraints. He/she is typically at the executive level within the organization.

User Representative—Represents the functional requirements for using the system.

The certification process centers on the development and signoff of the Systems Security Authorization Agreement (SSAA), which documents the scope, security architecture and environment, security requirements necessary for accreditation, and security testing plans for the system. The SSAA is drafted during requirements gathering and is updated during system design, construction, and testing to yield the final certification. Once the results of certification are approved by the DAA, the completed document becomes the baseline security configuration for the system and is used as an operational and change control reference throughout the system life cycle. The SSAA is a living document, in that outputs from change control are used to maintain a record of the current security state of the system.

The certification and accreditation process is conducted in four phases:

1. **Definition**—The system scope and boundaries are defined, and security requirements are documented. The scope and plan for certification activities are prepared. Activities include assessing risks and threats from external sources and the internal operating environment, and developing mitigation strategies that can be stated as requirements.
2. **Verification**—Initial certification analysis is performed to verify that security requirements have been incorporated into system design and development. Activities include conducting design and code reviews, assessing the operational platform, environment, network connectivity and interfaces (including integrated third-party software and systems), performing vulnerability analysis, reviewing proposed maintenance processes, and test planning for Phase 3.
3. **Validation**—The system is tested against security requirements once it is installed in the production environment, and all associated physical, administrative, and technical controls are validated through active vulnerability assessment and penetration testing. This phase includes a review of configuration and change management, operational procedures, incident and contingency plans, and training. Results of these assessments are documented in the SSAA with the certifier's recommendation and statement of residual risk. The certification is then handed over to the DAA for accreditation.
4. **Post-Accreditation**—Secure operation of the system is periodically validated. Outputs from configuration and change management processes are used to update the SSAA and set a new security baseline.

Security Assurance Rating: Common Criteria

Shortly after publication of the Trusted Computer Systems Evaluation Criteria (TCSEC), the European community published the ITSEC (Information Technology Security Evaluation Criteria). These requirements have now been replaced by the Common Criteria.

Common Criteria refers to an internationally agreed-upon collection of security properties that form the basis of evaluating an information system for certification and accreditation, and methods used in the evaluation process. The Common Criteria evolved from the European ITSEC and the original U.S. Department of Defense (DoD) Trusted Computer Systems Evaluation Criteria (TCSEC), better known as the *Orange Book*, and officially replaced the DoD standard shortly after publication in 2005. The Common Criteria are now published as international standard ISO15408. Practitioners will find the Common Criteria useful in evaluating technical confidentiality, integrity, and availability safeguards in both internally developed and commercially acquired systems and in individual hardware, software, and firmware components.

A Protection Profile (PP) is an integrated set of security requirements for a specific type of system, which forms the basis for systems certification. The system described in the PP is known as the Target of Evaluation (TOE). The U.S. government has validated a number of protection profiles, including those for operating systems, database management systems, firewalls, antivirus software, and key management systems. The PP describes security objectives, requirements, assumptions, and rationales within a given policy framework and threat environment, but does not specify how these requirements are to be implemented.

Common Criteria defines a hierarchically ordered set of Evaluation Assurance Levels (EALs), each containing a baseline set of security requirements that must be met by the TOE. Each TOE is evaluated against the desired assurance level. The higher the level of assurance, the greater the scope, depth of detail, and rigor required in assurance testing. Each level includes criteria from lower levels. The seven Common Criteria EALs are:

EAL1—Functionally Tested: Independent testing of TOE security functions against functional requirements and operational documentation validates that the security system is functioning as documented, and provides protection against stated threats. EAL1 provides more assurance than an unevaluated system, but it is minimal; therefore, EAL1 is not sufficient in the face of significant security threats.

EAL2—Structurally Tested: Security testing is performed against functional requirements, operational documentation, and high-level design. EAL2 requires evidence of developer testing against functional design and searching for vulnerabilities, and is sufficient in cases where a low to moderate level of assurance is required.

EAL3—Methodically Tested and Checked: In addition to the criteria above, EAL3 provides validation of development environment controls, and configuration and deployment management to assure that the TOE is not tampered with during development. EAL3 provides a moderate level of assurance.

EAL4—Methodically Tested, Designed, and Reviewed: EAL4 provides a moderate to high level of assurance based on the above criteria plus additional verification through independent low-level penetration testing, more in-depth design reviews including interfaces and TOE security policy, and improved (often automated) change and configuration management procedures.

EAL5—Semiformally Designed and Tested: A modular design, with informally reviewed, documented general design and functional specification, comprehensive configuration management, and evidence of covert channel analysis are all required at this level. This is the first level at which the implementation of the design specification is reviewed in its entirety, and is sufficient for cases where a high level of assurance is required, and where formal, rigorous development processes are used.

EAL6—Semiformally Verified Design and Tested: EAL6 provides a high level of assurance and requires much greater rigor in development and testing. In addition to the above criteria, EAL6 requires a modular and layered design, a general and detailed design and functional specification informally reviewed for consistency, improved configuration management and environmental controls, and a more comprehensive independent vulnerability analysis.

EAL7—Formally Verified Designed and Tested: This is the highest level of assurance and is suitable for high-risk situations. It requires more formal system specifications and reviews, and more comprehensive testing for vulnerabilities. EAL7 is generally reserved for security-specific systems design reviews.

Products may be evaluated against their protection profiles by independent certification laboratories and be certified at a specific assurance level. Certificates issued by these independent laboratories are recognized under the international Common Criteria Recognition Agreement (CCRA). These certificates are currently the most widely accepted means of assurance that a specific product or technology component lives up to the security claims of its manufacturer.

Change Control

Change control refers to the formal procedures adopted by an organization to ensure that all changes to system and application software are subject to the appropriate level of management control. Change control seeks to eliminate unauthorized changes, and reduce defects and problems related to poor planning and communication of changes. Change control is often enforced through use of a Change Control Board, who reviews changes for impact, assures that the appropriate implementation and backout plans have been prepared, and follows changes through approval and post-implementation review.

The change control policy document covers the following aspects of the change process under management control:

- Request submission—A request for change is submitted to the Change Control Board for review, prioritization, and approval. Included in the request should be a description of the change and rationale or objectives for the request, a change implementation plan, impact assessment, and a backout plan to be exercised in the event of a change failure or unanticipated outcome.
- Recording—Details of the request are recorded for review, communication, and tracking purposes.
- Analysis/impact assessment—Changes are typically subject to peer review for accuracy and completeness, and to identify any impacts on other systems or processes that may arise as a result of the change.
- Decision making and prioritization—The team reviews the request, implementation and backout plans, and impacts and determines whether the change should be approved, denied, or put on hold. Changes are scheduled and prioritized, and any communication plans are put in place.

- Approval—Formal approval for the change is granted and recorded.
- Status tracking—The change is tracked through completion. A post-implementation review may be performed.

Configuration Management

In the security certification and accreditation process, the SSCA documents the baseline security configuration of a system having a specific set of boundaries and operating within a specific environment. Throughout the system life cycle, changes made to the system, its individual components, or its operating environment can introduce new vulnerabilities and thus impact this security baseline. Configuration management (CM) is a discipline that seeks to manage configuration changes so that they are appropriately approved and documented, so that the integrity of the security state is maintained, and so that disruptions to performance and availability are minimized. Unlike change control, which refers to the formal processes used to ensure that all software changes are managed, configuration management refers to the technical and administrative processes that maintain integrity of hardware and system software components across versions or releases.

Typical steps in the configuration management process are: change request, approval, documentation, testing, implementation, and reporting. A configuration management system consisting of a set of automated tools, documentation, and procedures is typically used to implement CM in an organization. The system should identify and maintain:

- Baseline hardware, software, and firmware configurations
- Design, installation, and operational documentation
- Changes to the system since the last baseline
- Software test plans and results

The configuration management system implements the four operational aspects of CM: identification, control, accounting, and auditing.

Identification

Identification captures and maintains information about the structure of the system, usually in a configuration management database (CMDB). Each component of the system configuration should be separately identified and maintained as a configuration item (CI) within the CMDB using a unique identifier (name), number (such as a software or hardware serial number), and version identifier. The CMDB may be a series of spreadsheets or documents, or may be maintained within a structured database management system (DBMS). Use of structured databases is preferred to enforce consistency and maintain the integrity of information (such as preventing duplicate entries and preserving associations between CIs) and to safeguard against unauthorized modifications and deletions.

Within the CMDB, changes are tracked by comparing the differences between a CI before and after the change in a change set or *delta*. The CMDB thus is capable of storing the baseline configuration plus a sequence of deltas showing a history of changes.

In addition, the system must maintain a consistent mapping among components so that changes are appropriately propagated through the system. Dependencies between components are identified so that the impacts of logical changes to any one component are known.

In addition, automated tools able to generate the new baseline configuration are required for highly sensitive government systems (TCSEC Level A1) and are good practice for any system to promote efficiency and reduce human error.

Control

All configuration changes and releases must be controlled through the life cycle. Control mechanisms are implemented to govern change requests, approvals, change propagation, impact analysis, bug tracking, and propagation of changes. Control begins early in systems design, and continues throughout the system life cycle. Before changes are implemented, they should be carefully planned and subjected to peer review. Implementation and rollback plans (in case of change failure) should accompany the change request. Technical controls to enforce this aspect of CM include access control for development, test and production environments, as well as to the CMDB itself.

Accounting

Accounting captures, tracks, and reports on the status of CIs, change requests, configurations, and change history.

Auditing

Auditing is a process of logging, reviewing, and validating the state of CIs in the CMDB, ensuring that all changes are appropriately documented and that a clear history of changes is retained in such a way that they can be traced back to the person making the change and provide detail on the delta (difference) between the baseline and the current state of the system. Auditing also compares the information in the CMDB to the actual system configuration to ensure that the representation of the system is complete and accurate, and association between components is maintained.

Change Management Roles

Change Manager—Individual in charge of CM policies and procedures, including mechanisms for requesting, approving, controlling, and testing changes.

Change Control Board—Responsible for approving system changes.

Project Manager—Manages budgets, timelines, resources, tasks, and risk for systems development, implementation, and maintenance.

Architects—Develop and maintain the functional and security context and technical systems design.

Engineers and analysts—Develop, build, and test system changes, and document the rationale for and details of the change.

Customer—Requests changes and approves functional changes in the design and execution of a system.

Automated Configuration Management Tools

Many in-house software development teams use automated tools for software version change control and other aspects of configuration management. Most development platforms include features such as source code comparators, comment generators, and version checkers. When linked to a central repository, these tools use check in/check out functions to copy code from the repository into a development library or desktop environment, make and test modifications, and place the modified code back into the repository. Branching and merging tools help resolve concurrency conflicts when two or more individuals modify the same component. Standalone or add-on tools are available commercially or as open source, and typically contain more robust functionality suited to teams of developers. Tool vendors do not always distinguish between features that manage the CM process, and those that manage actual configurations. Datacenter CM tools, for example, range from standalone CMDBs to full suites that include workflow engines, access control, policy enforcement, and reporting capabilities.

Patch Management

The application of software and firmware patches to correct vulnerabilities is a critical component of vulnerability and configuration management practices. Most security breaches that have occurred over the past decade are not the result of the so-called zero-day attacks, but rather were perpetrated by attackers exploiting known vulnerabilities. The SQL Slammer worm, which exploited a buffer overflow vulnerability in Microsoft's SQL server and desktop engines, cost between $950 million and $1.2 billion in lost productivity and denial of service during its first 5 days in the wild. Yet not 7 months later, Blaster arrived on the scene to wreck similar havoc. These attacks could have been prevented by timely and effective application of patches that were already available to administrators—so why did not the affected organizations keep up to date on patches? The answer is that patching, and patching distributed desktop and laptop systems in particular, is not a straightforward process. Vulnerabilities can target a number of systems, including desktop and server operating systems; database management systems; client software such as browsers and office productivity software; and network devices such as routers, switches, and firewalls. The sheer volume of vendor patches to be deployed across these disparate systems necessitates an automated solution that accommodates an organization's core platforms. The patches themselves must be acquired, tested, distributed, and verified in a coordinated and controlled manner, which means processes must be designed and followed religiously to ensure effectiveness. Application of patches can be disruptive to operations, slowing down systems or making them unavailable during the installation window, and often requiring reboot or restart after installation, and some can be "bad," meaning that they introduce new vulnerabilities, create downstream impacts, or do not deploy correctly on all target systems. Not all patches are of equal criticality to an organization, meaning that someone must make a decision regarding when and why to deploy patches as they are made available. This is typically done through the organization's change control system.

Despite these obstacles, an organization must adopt some form of patch management discipline to mitigate vulnerabilities. Decisions regarding when, what, and how to patch should not be left up to individual administrators, but should be backed by a formal patch management policy or process and carried out by a specifically designated team or committee. The policy should identify roles and responsibilities, criteria for determining whether and how to deploy patches, and service-level objectives for fully deploying patches at each criticality level. The patch management process includes the following steps:

Acquisition—Patches are most often supplied via download from the vendor's Web site. Some patch distribution and management systems may automatically scan these sites for available patches and initiate downloads to a centralized, internal site.

Testing—Patches must be tested to ensure that they can be correctly distributed and installed, and that they do not interfere with normal system or application functioning. Despite a vendor's best efforts, patches are often created under pressure to fix critical vulnerabilities and may not be thoroughly regression tested. Furthermore, each organization's operating environment is unique, and it is impossible to test these myriad variations, so impacts on dependent services and applications and compatibility with all possible configurations are not always identified during vendor testing. Patches should initially be tested in a laboratory environment that contains replicas of standard target machine configurations. A limited pilot deployment may then be used for further testing in the production environment.

Approval—Not all patches will be immediately approved for deployment. Noncritical patches and patches that are not applicable to the platforms and services used in the organization may be deferred to a later date, or to a time when they are included in a more comprehensive vendor update. Patches that cannot be deployed via standard means or those that cause issues on test machines may require further planning and testing before they are approved. The approval process should include provisions for emergency deployments of critical security patches.

Packaging—Patches must be packaged or configured for distribution and installation on target systems. Depending on how patches are deployed, packaging can take several forms. Some platforms such as Windows provide installation software or scripts that are bundled with the patch and automatically invoked when distributed. Custom scripts can also be written to execute a series of installation actions. Patch management software typically includes facilities to package as well as deploy patches.

Deployment—Having an accurate inventory of machines and their current patch levels is critical to successful deployment of patches. Automated patch management and software deployment tools may maintain an independent inventory or CMDB, or may integrate with third-party configuration and asset management software. Deployment features include scheduling, user notification of patch and reboot (with or without a "snooze" option), and ordering options for multiple-patch deployments.

Verification—Automated patch management tools should be able to verify correct application of patches and report all successful and unsuccessful deployments back to a centralized console or reporting engine.

To minimize user disruption during the workday, organizations can purchase Wake-on-LAN (WOL) compliant network cards, now standard on most end-user computers and servers. These cards respond to wake-up transmissions (called "magic packets") from a centralized configuration management server that are sent before distributing the patch. The server will send the transmission only to those systems that require the scheduled patch updates.

Monitoring System Integrity

A comprehensive configuration and change management program should include a mechanism to monitor or periodically validate changes to system configuration. Sophisticated integrity monitors such as Tripwire integrate with the organization's CMDB to produce a detailed history of system changes. Integrity checkers work by taking a "snapshot" of the approved system configuration, including UNIX object properties and Windows registry keys, access control lists, and contents of system configuration files. This snapshot is then hashed and cryptographically signed to protect against modification. Periodically, the snapshot is compared to a hash of the current configuration, and any changes are reported back to the administrator or noted directly in the CMDB, if an automated interface exists.

Integrity checkers such as Tripwire do not necessarily record who made the change, or prevent unauthorized changes from occurring. Use of additional protections such as host-based IPS and log collection and correlation is recommended to supplement integrity checking functions.

Endpoint Protection

The emergence of end-user computing devices as the weak link in enterprise security may come as no surprise to those who have followed the evolution of enterprise threats and countermeasures. Traditional perimeter controls such as firewalls, IDS, and IPS have been almost universally adopted as effective means of preventing and detecting external network-based attacks. Thwarted by these safeguards, attackers turned to weaknesses in externally facing host and application systems, and in response, organizations increased their focus on configuration and patch management and secure development practices. End-user computing devices—desktops, laptops, PDAs, and similar systems—have now emerged as the newest challenge for the security practitioner. Solutions to address these challenges generally fall under the heading of "endpoint security."

Endpoint security refers to the measures taken to protect confidentiality and integrity of data stored on devices, defend against malicious code and direct attack, address vulnerabilities, and maintain system integrity and availability. It also refers to the measures taken to protect the organization's network and internal systems from these devices, as well as the operation and administration of these security measures. These measures are taken in light of an increasing number of threats targeting endpoints. Examples of these threats include:

Viruses, worms, and other malicious codes: Viruses and worms spread through e-mail, Web sites, downloads, and networks to which endpoints may be connected—including home computer networks—threaten not only the endpoints, but the internal network itself. Mobile devices in particular are subject to these threats when not protected by network security defenses, and may introduce viruses and worms to the internal network when they connect as local or remote hosts. Instant messaging, increasingly popular for business and personal use, can also introduce these threats on- and off-network.

Trojan horses and other malicious code: Keystroke-loggers, backdoor Trojans, spyware, and other malicious codes may be used by attackers to target endpoints directly to steal data including login accounts and passwords, to run software, or hijack operating system functionality.

Vulnerabilities such as *buffer overruns, Web browser vulnerabilities, and unpatched operating system and application software* may be targeted for a variety of purposes, including session hijacking and, using endpoints as Zombie or remote control hosts, to carry out distributed network attacks.

A number of endpoint security tools are available to combat these threats, including:

- Client antivirus and antispyware software
- Personal firewalls
- Host intrusion prevention for desktop systems
- Encryption
- Patch management systems
- Network access control (NAC) systems, which may include endpoint vulnerability or compliance analysis and quarantine

In practice, implementing and maintaining endpoint security solutions offers special logistical challenges. Hosts that are only intermittently connected to the network require security solutions that operate independently from central configuration and management systems. Regular patching and software and firmware updates may be difficult to achieve and monitor for compliance, and distribution of large update files over slow networks is prone to failure. End users may install software or make configuration changes that cannot be centrally managed, and they may be reluctant to endure the interruptions in processing for patches and updates, making routine maintenance difficult to schedule. Finally, special defenses such as access control systems and vulnerability detection and remediation require additional hardware, software, and skill sets to maintain.

When designing an endpoint security strategy, the practitioner must not overlook the culture of the organization and its unique business needs, which may vary from department to department. While a policy of complete centralized control, locking down endpoint devices to known good configurations and approved software and services, and disallowing use of personal devices or software for organization use can be very effective, many organizations view this as a draconian approach that interferes with its business needs. Some flexibility may be necessary, as well as acceptance of a greater degree of risk. A risk assessment that incorporates business needs, philosophy, and risk tolerance is a critical first step in successful endpoint security design. Incorporating design principles such as risk-based controls, least privilege, authorization and accountability, and defense-in-depth can help you design a solution that is more consistent with your organization's overall security strategy.

Endpoint security technology is most manageable when incorporated into the overall security technology framework. Whenever possible, the selected technology should be an extension of the solutions already in place for enterprise protection, or should be well integrated on a technical and procedural level. Centralized management and integration with enterprise directory services is now a commodity feature in endpoint protection solutions, and can significantly lower administrative costs. Local event logging at the operating system and security software level should be enabled and configured to send log data to a centralized collection point such as a log server or security information or event management (SIM or SEM) system on a periodic basis, or when the user connects to the network. Some options specific to endpoint security systems are discussed below.

Endpoint Antivirus Solutions

Antivirus solutions are available for a variety of endpoints, such as laptops, PDAs, and Smart Phones, and are compatible with a number of host and mobile device operating systems. Enterprise antivirus software vendors offer endpoint solutions that allow administrators to create and distribute a centralized policy to scan specific file types based on scheduled intervals or system events such as opening or modifying files. The policy can be locked down to prevent end users from modifying scanning parameters. When combined with least privilege, administrators can also prevent end users from stopping or disabling the antivirus service. For mobile devices that may be intermittently connected, local logging should be enabled and configured to send events such as virus detection, cleaning, and quarantine to a centralized collection point at specified intervals when a user connects to the network. Software updates and new versions of virus signature files may be obtained when the user connects to the network; alternatively, "auto-update" features may be configured to retrieve updates from the vendor's distribution server when the client is operating remotely.

Antispyware

Antispyware software scans file systems and downloaded files for spyware, adware, and other threats distributed via the Internet. Antispyware typically operates on a signature- or pattern-matching basis, and, similar to signature-based antivirus, it must be updated frequently as new threats emerge. These updates may be performed via a centralized management console or via an auto-update feature. Many antivirus software vendors now include antispyware features in their products, so there is no need for additional software to protect against this threat.

Personal Firewalls and Host Intrusion Prevention Systems

Personal firewall systems protect endpoints from network attacks whether connected to the enterprise as an internal node or remote node, or operating as a single, unconnected host. Firewalls are rule-based, typically configured to deny by default any sources, ports, or protocols that are not specifically needed for end-user applications. Most firewalls can be configured to block certain network protocols such as

NetBEUI, Ethernet, and IPX/SPC unless the endpoint is connected to the enterprise network by combining source/destination and port/protocol rule attributes. Rules may be configured separately for different network adaptors as well. Rulesets are typically configured centrally, and pushed out to endpoints from the management console. Logging may be consolidated at the management console, or sent directly to a SIM or SEM. Standalone personal firewalls (not integrated with other security software) are not considered adequate protection for endpoints as many attacks occur over port 80 and 443 (HTTP and SSL), and attack vectors such as e-mail and mobile storage devices often bypass firewall protection.

Traditional host intrusion prevention systems (IPS) detect and prevent known exploits targeting published operating system vulnerabilities. These systems are also useful in combating the so-called zero-day attacks; that is, attacks that target vulnerabilities that have been identified but for which no vendor patch is yet available. Their effectiveness against these attacks is contingent on the speed with which the IPS vendor can release signatures to identify the attack; therefore, contractual service levels and historical data are important considerations when selecting an IPS vendor. More effective than signature-based IPSes are those that operate on a "default deny" basis, much like a firewall. These IPSes allow administrators to configure policy that allows all approved processes, and by default denies any process or application that is not approved. This approach is much more successful in protecting endpoints against attacks that are released before the IPS vendor can create a signature, including variants of known attacks that are modified just enough to bypass the signature triggers of the original attack. However, increased effectiveness comes at an additional administrative cost. Configuring policies requires that all approved software and processes are profiled and allowed via a policy rule. The more variation in endpoint configuration, the greater the number of policies that need to be created and maintained. Processes for policy maintenance must be closely linked with the organization's change and configuration management practices, as new software, version upgrades, patches, and changes in usage patterns may all necessitate IPS policy changes. When selecting a type of endpoint IPS, then, the practitioner must balance a realistic capacity to maintain effective policy implementation with the risk of zero-day exploits. Mobility of end-user devices, the frequency with which they connect for updates, and the pace of change in the technical environment are all considerations when selecting an endpoint IPS.

Thin Client Implementations

Maintaining secure, reliable, and up-to-date systems in distributed, client/server environments is costly and time-consuming. The more functionality and computing power that is pushed down to the desktop, the greater the risk of new vulnerabilities, malicious code, software incompatibilities, and unauthorized configuration changes and software installations. Organizations spend millions of dollars annually in endpoint security software, configuration, and patch management tools, remote management facilities, and other technology to manage distributed systems. One solution to this dilemma is to adopt a *thin client* architecture. A thin client is basically a scaled-down version of a desktop or laptop machine containing only an operating system and communication software. The operating system may be Windows- or UNIX-based. Thin clients run software applications remotely using terminal emulation or virtual desktop, such as Citrix, Windows Remote Desktop, and VMWare. The client acts essentially as the interface, while the network server performs all of the application functions and acts as a repository for client data. Client machines may be diskless, or have small hard drives installed; diskless clients can boot from USB or CD/ROM. An organization's existing machines can be converted to thin clients, eliminating the need to purchase new hardware.

One of the greatest advantages of thin clients is the ability to centrally maintain a limited number of images or desktop configurations (in the case of virtualization) or copies of software programs to be maintained and verified. This not only simplifies configuration and vulnerability management but also enables administrators to quickly respond to vulnerabilities and issues and seamlessly "push" fixes to client machines. Another huge advantage is that, by eliminating end users' ability to store data and install application software, data leakage protection and policy compliance are simplified. However, thin client architectures are not suitable for all organizations, particularly those with a wide variety of end-user applications and configurations. Since operation of the client is entirely dependent on the availability of the centralized server, thin clients are extremely sensitive to network interruptions and server failures and may require an organization to implement redundancy and failover to meet service levels. Processor-intensive and rich multimedia applications are poor candidates for a thin client deployment. Initial start-up costs can be extensive.

Metrics

Metrics is the discipline of measuring security performance. Long used in other areas of the organization, metrics are now becoming increasingly important to justify security budgets, to measure the success of specific security implementations, to report on service levels, and to gauge the overall effectiveness of a security program. The need to answer management questions such as "how secure are we?" and "what am I getting for my security investment?" has led security practitioners to adopt a variety of tools and techniques for measuring performance. The processes involved include specification, collection, analysis, reporting, and remediation. These processes form a continuous improvement loop much like the Plan–Do–Check–Act cycle used in ISO27002 and, in fact, constitute an important aspect of an organization's ISMS.

Getting started with security metrics can be a daunting proposition to an organization that has historically relied on subjective or purely qualitative measures of risk and control effectiveness. Just what to measure, when to measure, and how to present data in a meaningful way, are some of the questions that the metrics program should answer. NIST SP800-55, Performance Measurement Guide for Information Security, provides comprehensive guidance on building and sustaining a metrics program.

Some organizations choose a top-down approach that begins by setting a *context* within which the metrics will be generated. The context might be a regulation, best practice, or particular area of risk, or it might be a specific product or program. For example, if PCI compliance is a concern, the initial context of the metrics program would be those things that measure the degree of compliance with the PCI standard. Each PCI requirement that has a corresponding security solution is an item that can potentially be measured. The requirement to maintain a vulnerability management program, for instance, is addressed by safeguards such as patch management and antivirus software deployment and maintenance. To specify the metrics to collect for vulnerability management, then, the practitioner can list those areas in the patch and antivirus management systems that can be measured—that is, that can produce quantitative data. Such things might be:

- Number of systems patched during a typical patch cycle
- Number and percentage of unpatched systems
- Mean time from issuance to application of patches
- Number of systems with current antivirus definitions
- Number of out-of-date systems
- Number of viruses detected, cleaned, and quarantined
- Number of virus outbreaks

Once meaningful data have been specified—that is, you have defined what to measure—you must determine how and when it is to be collected. In our example, most antivirus and automated patch management systems produce event or activity statistics from the management console. Alternatively, data may be ported to a SIM or SEM for measuring. Even if you do not have an automated means of collecting the data, it is possible to collect it manually, preferably by including data collection procedures in the process you are measuring. The degree of manual effort needed to collect and assemble your metrics data should not exceed the meaningfulness of the information you produce. In some cases, when you collect the data may not be important. However, if you are tracking certain measurements tied to some cyclical process, such as patch management, the results may differ dramatically depending on when you take your measurements. For instance, if patches are performed on the 15th of every month, data collected on the 14th will be vastly different than data collected on the 16th. Once collection schedules have been identified, they should remain consistent for your results to be meaningful.

Once data are collected, they can be analyzed and organized into reports. For analysis, you may find that numbers alone are relatively meaningless as a measure of performance. For example, suppose you find that during a given month, 78% of systems have current virus definition files. Is that good or bad? Setting benchmarks and performance targets or standards are ways to add meaning to the numbers you collect. Benchmarks are useful in measuring positive (improvement) or negative (decline) over time. By setting the initial measurement as a starting point or *benchmark* measurement, and measuring the same thing over successive intervals, statistical trends in the difference from the benchmark can be noted. Such trend analysis is essential to planning and measuring continuous improvement efforts and can assist you in pinpointing the effects of changes in the environment. Performance targets or standards are useful in measuring compliance. Setting targets for the level of compliance you wish to achieve, individual measurements become meaningful relative to that standard. For example, you may set a standard of 95% as the desired percentage of systems with current antivirus definitions at any given point in time. When data are analyzed, their deviation from the standard is noted. If 95% or more of the systems measured are current, you can be said to be in compliance with the standard.

Standard analysis and reporting tools can be used with the metrics you collect to create a number of views into the data for different audiences. Security analysts may need detailed or drill-down views, while senior management may prefer simple charts or graphs. In general, those responsible for administering security systems need the greatest detail, while higher levels of management prefer general, "big picture" views. A number of tools are available to produce reports, from simple spreadsheets to complicated statistical analysis and reporting tools. Popular forms of management reporting are the *scorecard* and the *dashboard*. The scorecard is a tabular or graphic representation of key metrics arranged in categories which support general organizational performance objectives. The original Balanced Scorecard uses the categories of Financial, Customer, Internal Operations, and Learning and Growth to measure performance against specific, quantifiable goals; if your organization already uses this tool, security metrics may be incorporated in the Internal Operations sector or may be distributed across all four categories. A dashboard is a visual display summarizing key metrics using graphical displays such as graphs, pie charts, and tables, typically accessed through a Web browser. Some dashboards have drill-down and historical trending capabilities and customizable displays, so that different views can be generated based on the user's interests. The dashboard has the feel of real time or "just in time" reporting and dashboard generators are available in a number of commercial reporting packages.

In addition to supporting management decision-making and validation of security program performance, metrics also serve as a call to action for improving an organization's security posture. Results that consistently fall below target performance levels should be addressed through a resolution process. This is where detailed views of your metrics data become important. The security practitioner who notices, for example, that a consistently high percentage of systems have out-of-date virus pattern files, may need to reorganize or drill down into the data to determine the root cause. It may be that certain systems are configured improperly, or entire network segments or classes of devices may be affected. Alternatively, there may be flaws in the mechanisms used to collect and report on the data. By including specific remedial actions in your metrics program, it can become an important part of security performance management.

Not all organizations begin with a top-down approach to metrics. Less formally structured organizations, or those who are comfortable with taking a highly iterative or learn-as-you-go approach may begin by collecting and examining the entire universe of the data generated by security systems and processes. Many organizations start this way to begin generating data immediately, and then go on to refine their processes based on initial results. The most commonly used metrics in organizations today are readily available for extraction from traditional security software and operating systems, and include:

- Virus detection statistics
- Invalid logins
- Intrusion attempts
- Unauthorized access attempts
- Unauthorized changes
- SPAM detection rates

However, you need not limit your imagination to the data that you have at your fingertips every day. Other sources of data, such as vulnerability scans, software security defects, awareness training attendance sheets, and audit resolution reports, can be reviewed for meaningful input.

Security Awareness and Training

Common sense tells us that the security posture of any organization is only as strong as its weakest link. Increased focus on technical and administrative safeguards in the wake of data security breaches, international terrorism, and large-scale fraud and abuse have improved the situation, but many organizations still fail to consider the human element. Basel II defines operational risk, of which information security risk is a component, as "the risk of direct or indirect loss resulting from inadequate or failed internal processes, people, and systems or from external events." Security awareness seeks to reduce the risk related to human error, misjudgment, and ignorance by educating people about the risks and threats to confidentiality, integrity, and availability, and how they can help the organization be more resistant to threats in the performance of their daily job functions. Many national and international regulatory and standards bodies recognize the importance of security awareness and awareness training by making them security program requirements.

Critical success factors for any security awareness program are:

Senior management support—Security success stories happen when individuals begin to treat security as part of their job function. Too many security programs fail because senior management does not buy in to the security team's mission and message. To get this buy-in, start your awareness program at the top. Involve senior management in the design and oversight of the program, and tie awareness program goals to business goals.

Cultural awareness—There is no such thing as a "one size fits all" awareness program. Is your organization a large, established, hierarchical institution or an agile, high-tech, entrepreneurial firm? Are workers unionized, or independent professionals? Does your organization value customer service, operational efficiency, or personal achievement? These and other questions help define your target audience and deliver a message whose content, style, and format are designed to have impact on your specific audience.

Set communication goals and build a strategy to meet these goals—Perform a needs assessment to identify gaps in security awareness and develop objectives to close these gaps. Be as specific as you can when stating your goals. Do you intend to alert users to social engineering threats? Communicate policy? Teach people how to spot and report incidents? Your objectives will dictate how your awareness program is delivered.

Taking a change management approach—The end goal of awareness programs is to produce changes in behavior in your target audience. Understanding barriers to change and methods that successfully stimulate people to change will help you reach this goal. People change because they are motivated to change. Motivators include small prizes and awards, financial incentives, time off, peer recognition, feelings of personal pride and accomplishment, feelings of job competency, and just plain fun. Organizations that tie security awareness to their formal system of salary and performance management are the most likely to foster interest in security issues and compliance with expectations. Promoting awareness that "hits home" by spotlighting issues such as identity theft, spyware and malicious code, online shopping safety, and protection of children on the Internet and tying these to workplace issues is an effective way to capture employee interest.

Measurement—Measuring success against stated objectives not only helps justify the awareness program to senior management, but will allow you to identify gaps and continuously improve on your delivery.

General security awareness differs from awareness training, in that awareness is designed to get people's attention while training instructs people on practices they can adopt to identify, respond to, and protect against security threats. Some specific vehicles for delivering general security awareness include:

- Threat alerts distributed by e-mail
- Security-specific newsletters or articles in your company's newsletter
- Security awareness Intranet sites
- Screen savers and computer wallpaper
- Posters and notices in prominent locations
- Brochures or pamphlets

Awareness efforts should also focus on user responsibilities for promoting ethical practices and a productive work environment. RFC 1087, "Ethics and the Internet," promotes personal responsibility and provides sound general principles for behavior when using computing resources. These include prohibitions against unauthorized access, wasteful use of resources, and violations of confidentiality, integrity, and availability of information and systems.

Awareness training is typically more formal in nature and produces more directly measurable results. It is a good idea to make security awareness training a mandatory annual or semiannual event by partnering with Human Resources or training areas. Some organizations require specific training on security policies and procedures and appropriate use of information systems, and may maintain a record of attendance and formal, signed acknowledgment that training has been received. Training can be general or it can focus on specific areas such as:

- Labeling and handling of sensitive information
- Appropriate use policies for e-mail, Internet, and other services
- Customer privacy laws, policies, and procedures
- Detecting and reporting security incidents
- Protecting intellectual property and copyright

Training typically addresses issues that are specific to the work environment and provides explicit instruction on policies, standards, and procedures. Training should be required for employees, contractors, and third parties that use or manage the organization's information systems assets. Instructors providing security awareness training should be well versed in the security domain as well as related policies and procedures.

To measure the effectiveness of security awareness training, consider using surveys or quizzes that test knowledge of key issues before and after training. Other tests for improved awareness include password analyzers or crackers that test the strength of user-selected passwords, number of incidents reported by personnel using established procedures, number of security policy violations, or number of help desk calls or system-related issues due to malicious code, social engineering attacks, etc. You should determine what metrics you will use when designing your awareness program. Results should be reported to senior management to ensure their continued support.

Security Staff Training

Personnel with specific security job responsibilities must have specialized knowledge and skills in traditional security domains as well as the specific tools, technologies, and practices used on the job. Training should begin by identifying roles and responsibilities and determining the specific knowledge and skills needed to perform security functions. Training should cover the basics of the seven SSCP domains, and offer continuing advancement in each of these specialized areas:

- Access controls
- Analysis and monitoring
- Cryptography
- Malicious code
- Networks and telecommunications
- Risk, response, and recovery
- Security operations and administration

In addition, training in the specific industry regulations, laws, and standards applicable to the security practitioner's role in the organization should be included in the curriculum.

Most organizations do not have the capacity to provide specialized professional training in these areas, and must look outside the organization for assistance. When selecting a security training provider, take care to ensure that the company employs only highly qualified, experienced trainers who will be prepared to explore topics in depth and provide answers to technical questions. A number of organizations provide security training and training programs and general and advanced security certifications. Some of them (this is by no means an all-inclusive list) are:

(ISC)² SSCP, CISSP, and CAP review seminars conducted by (ISC)² and Authorized Education Affiliates (see http://www.isc2.org for more details).
CPP—ASIS International offers the Certified Protection Professional (CPP), Professional Certified Investigator (PCI), and Physical Security Professional (PSP) credentials. Information on certification review courses and domain-specific classroom and e-learning courses are available at http://www.asisonline.org/education/index.xml.
CISA, CISM—Certified Information Systems Auditor and Certified Information Security Manager certifications are offered by ISACA (Information Systems

Audit and Control Association), as well as security courses and conference programs. More information can be found at: http://www.isaca.org/Template .cfm?Section=Education_and_Conferences2&Template=/ContentManagement/ ContentDisplay.cfm&ContentID=36582.

SANS GIAC—SANS (Systems Administration and Network Security) offers a number of technical and professional security training programs, many leading to the GIAC (Global Information Assurance Certification) offering in a number of technical security areas. See the site at http://www.sans.org for more information.

Review Questions

1. Security awareness training aims to educate users on:
   a. The work performed by the information security organization
   b. How attackers defeat security safeguards
   c. What they can do to maintain the organization's security posture
   d. How to secure their home computer systems
2. The following are operational aspects of Configuration Management (CM):
   a. Documentation, Control, Accounting, and Auditing
   b. Identification, Control, Accounting, and Auditing
   c. Identification, Documentation, Control, and Auditing
   d. Control, Accounting, Auditing, and Reporting
3. An access control model that supports assignment of privileges based on job function is called:
   a. Discretionary Access Control
   b. Distributed Access Control
   c. Role-Based Access Control
   d. Mandatory Access Control
4. The security management cycle described by ISO/IEC 27002 contains the steps:
   a. Plan, Check, Document, Act
   b. Document, Plan, Act, Check
   c. Plan, Organize, Check, Act
   d. Plan, Do, Check, Act
5. The systems certification process can best be described as a:
   a. Method of testing a system to assure that vulnerabilities have been addressed
   b. Means of documenting adherence to security standards
   c. Process for obtaining stakeholder signoff on system configuration
   d. Method of validating adherence to security requirements

6. A degausser is a device used to:
   a. Reformat a disk or tape for subsequent reuse
   b. Eliminate magnetic data remanence on a disk or tape
   c. Render media that contains sensitive data unusable
   d. Overwrite sensitive data with zeros so that it is unreadable

7. A protection profile is:
   a. A set of security requirements for a specific type of system
   b. A documented security configuration for a specific system
   c. A hierarchical classification denoting a system's assurance level
   d. A description of how security requirements must be implemented on a system

8. A Web application software vulnerability that allows an attacker to extract sensitive information from a backend database is known as a:
   a. Cross-site scripting vulnerability
   b. Malicious file execution vulnerability
   c. Injection flaw
   d. Input validation failure

9. The security practice that restricts user access based on need to know is called:
   a. Mandatory access control
   b. Default deny configuration
   c. Role-based access control
   d. Least privilege

10. A security guideline is a:
    a. Statement of senior management expectations for managing the security program
    b. Recommended security practice
    c. Set of criteria that must be met to address security requirements
    d. Tool for measuring the effectiveness of security safeguards

11. A security baseline is a:
    a. Measurement of security effectiveness when a control is first implemented
    b. Recommended security practice
    c. Minimum set of security requirements for a system
    d. Measurement used to determine trends in security activity

12. An antifraud measure that requires two people to complete a transaction is an example of the principle of:
    a. Separation of duties
    b. Dual control
    c. Role-based access control
    d. Defense-in-depth

13. The waterfall model is a:
    a. Development method that follows a linear sequence of steps
    b. Iterative process used to develop secure applications

c. Development method that uses rapid prototyping
d. Extreme programming model used to develop Web applications

14. A buffer overflow attack:
    I.   Can be used to execute code supplied by the attacker
    II. Can be used to escalate privileges on a target server
    III. Can be prevented by appropriate bounds checking
    IV. Can be prevented by appropriate error handling
       a. I, II, and III
       b. I, II, and IV
       c. II, III, and IV
       d. I, III, and IV

15. Code signing is a technique used to:
    a. Ensure that software is appropriately licensed for use
    b. Prevent source code tampering
    c. Identify source code modules in a release package
    d. Support verification of source code authenticity

16. Advantages of using thin client architecture include:
    I.   Ability to support a wide variety of applications
    II. Ease of maintaining a limited number of configurations
    III. Rapid deployment of security patches
    IV. Simplified policy enforcement
       a. I, II, and III
       b. I, II, and IV
       c. I, III, and IV
       d. II, III, and IV

17. Most security breaches that have occurred in the past decade are a result of:
    a. Attackers exploiting zero-day vulnerabilities
    b. Poor password management
    c. Attackers exploiting known vulnerabilities
    d. Poor configuration management

18. A firecall account is used to:
    a. Grant administrator privileges to production programs
    b. Confer authority using the "run as" command
    c. Administer critical systems
    d. Provide temporary access to production systems

19. The Common Criteria security assurance level EAL4 is awarded to systems that have been:
    a. Structurally tested
    b. Semiformally designed and tested
    c. Methodically tested and checked
    d. Methodically tested, designed, and reviewed

20. The role of information owner in the system security plan includes:
    a. Determining privileges that will be assigned to users of the system
    b. Maintaining the system security plan
    c. Authorizing the system for operation
    d. Assessing the effectiveness of security controls

References

The complete Code of Conduct for the security practitioner is available at the (ISC)² Web site at https://www.isc2.org/cgi-bin/content.cgi?page=11378.

Risk assessment methodologies and guidance can be found on the following Web sites:
COBRA—http://www.security-risk-analysis.com/introcob.htm.
OCTAVE—http://www.sei.cmu.edu/publications/documents/99.reports/99tr017/99tr017abstract.html.
NIST SP 800-30—http://csrc.nist.gov/publications/nistpubs/800-30/sp800-30.pdf.

Information on the Open Web Application Security Project (OWASP) can be found at http://www.owasp.org (The complete OWASP Guide to secure development is available free of charge at http://www.owasp.org/index.php/OWASP_Guide_Project.).

National Information Assurance Certification and Accreditation Process (NIACAP) can be found on the U.S. Committee on National Security Systems Web site: http://www.cnss.gov/Assets/pdf/nstissi_1000.pdf.

Validated security system protection profiles can be found at the National Information Assurance Partnership's Web site: http://www.niap-ccevs.org/cc-scheme/pp/.

The Common Criteria, CC assurance testing methodology, and associated documentation can be found at http://www.commoncriteriaportal.org/thecc.html.

The Basel II Accord in its entirety can be found at http://www.bis.org/publ/bcbsca.htm.

More information on security and the systems development life cycle can be found in NIST Special Publication 800-64 at http://csrc.nist.gov/publications/nistpubs/800-64/NIST-SP800-64.pdf.

Information for building and managing a metrics program can be found in NIST Special Publication 800-55, Performance Measurement Guide for Information Security, found at http://csrc.nist.gov/publications/nistpubs/800-55-Rev1/SP800-55-rev1.pdf.

Advice for creating security awareness programs can be found in NIST special publication 800-50 at http://searchsoftwarequality.techtarget.com/news/article/0,289142,sid92_gci1216994,00.html.

The Rainbow Series of security standards and guidelines can be found on the NIST publications site at http://csrc.nist.gov/publications/secpubs/rainbow/.

A portal for ISO/IEC standardization efforts and documentation can be found at the ISO/IEC information center at http://www.standardsinfo.net/info/livelink/fetch/2000/148478/6301438/index.html.

A list of ISO Standards for information security management, IT security management, IT network security and others with links to relevant documents can be found at http://www.iso27001security.com/html/others.html.

Industry standards for engineering including computing and telecommunications industries can be found at the IEEE Standards Association Web page at http://www.ieee.org/web/standards/home/index.html.

ANSI (The American National Standards Institute) has specialized groups for information technology standards in areas such as health care, national security, and identity management that can be accessed through their Web site at http://www.ansi.org.

Resources for storage security information can be found at the Storage Security Forum Web site at http://www.snia.org/forums/ssif/.

Guidance for classifying information systems according to impact level can be found in NIST Special Publication 800-60 Volume 1, "Guide for Mapping Types of Information and Information Systems to Security Categories" at http://csrc.nist.gov/publications/nistpubs/800-60-rev1/SP800-60_Vol1-Rev1.pdf.

The NISPOM and related documents are available for download at the U.S. Defense Security Service Web site at https://www.dss.mil/GW/ShowBinary/DSS/isp/fac_clear/download_nispom.html.

The Canadian Public Works and Government Services Policy on Destruction of Sensitive Information can be found at the department's Web site: http://www.tpsgc-pwgsc.gc.ca/acquisitions/text/pns/pn40-e.html.

Information on copyright laws can be found at the World Intellectual Property Organization's Web site at http://www.wipo.int/portal/index.html.en.

A complete list of open source licenses governed by the Open Source Initiative can be found on the OSI Web site at http://opensource.org/licenses/alphabetical.

NIST key management pages can be found at http://csrc.nist.gov/groups/ST/toolkit/key_management.html.

The Internet Activities Board's RFC 1087—Ethics and the Internet can be found at http://www.faqs.org/rfcs/rfc1087.html.

Chapter 7

Risk, Response, and Recovery

Chris Trautwein

Contents

Organizations face a wide range of challenges today, including ever-expanding risks to organizational assets, intellectual property, and customer data. Understanding and managing these risks is an integral component of organizational success. In your role as a security practitioner, you will be expected to participate in your organizational risk management process, to assist in identifying risks to information systems, and to develop and implement controls to mitigate identified risks. As a result, you must have a firm understanding of risk, response, and recovery concepts and best practices.

Effective incident response allows organizations to respond to threats that attempt to exploit vulnerabilities to compromise the confidentiality, integrity, and availability of organizational assets. As a Systems Security Certified Practitioner (SSCP) you will play an integral role in incident response at your organization. You must understand your organization's incident response policy and procedures and be able to effectively execute your role in the incident response process. Key areas of knowledge include:

- Understand risk management process
    - Understand concepts such as threats, vulnerabilities, etc.
    - Participate in risk assessment
    - Support mitigation activity
- Participate in security assessments
    - Scan for vulnerabilities
    - Participate in penetration testing
    - Review security configurations of infrastructure
    - Address audit findings
- Participate in incident handling analysis
    - Understand the concepts of incident handling (e.g., discovery, escalation, reporting)
    - Understand the concept of evidence handling (e.g., chain of custody)
    - Participate in the implementation of countermeasures
    - Understand forensic investigation techniques
- Differentiate between a business continuity plan (BCP) and a disaster recovery plan (DRP)
    - Components of a BCP
    - Components of a DRP

Finally, organizations must be able to effectively recover their information technology assets after a disruption in system availability or data integrity. The disruption may result from a security breach, hardware failure, or as a result of an unintentional error by an administrator or end user. Regardless of the cause, organizations must be able to effectively recover to limit the damage caused by disruptions to availability and integrity.

The sections below discuss risk, response, and recovery concepts and best practices. Along with best practices, we will provide practical recommendations based on real-world experience.

Introduction to Risk Management

As an SSCP you will be expected to be a key participant in your organizational risk management process. As a result, it is imperative that you have a strong understanding of your responsibilities in the risk management process. To obtain this understanding, we will define key risk management concepts and then present an overview of the risk management process. We will then present real-world examples to reinforce key risk management concepts.

Risk Management Concepts

While reviewing risk management concepts, it is critical to remember that the ultimate purpose of information security is to reduce risks to organizational assets to levels that are deemed acceptable by senior management. Information security should not be performed using a "secure at any cost" approach. The cost of controls should never exceed the loss that would result if the confidentiality, integrity, or availability of a system was compromised. Risks, threats, vulnerabilities, and potential impacts should be assessed. Only after assessing these factors can cost-effective information security controls be selected and implemented that eliminate or reduce risks to acceptable levels.

We will use the National Institute of Standards and Technology (NIST) Special Publication 800-30 "Risk Management Guide for Information Systems" as a baseline document for establishing definitions of key risk management concepts.

Risk—A risk is a function of the likelihood of a given threat source's exercising a potential vulnerability, and the resulting impact of that adverse event on the organization.

Likelihood—The probability that a potential vulnerability may be exercised within the construct of the associated threat environment.

Threat Source—Either intent and method targeted at the intentional exploitation of a vulnerability or a situation or method that may accidentally trigger a vulnerability.

Threat—The potential for a threat source to exercise (accidentally trigger or intentionally exploit) a specific vulnerability.

Vulnerability—A flaw or weakness in system security procedures, design, implementation, or internal controls that could be exercised (accidentally triggered or intentionally exploited) and result in a security breach or a violation of the system's security policy.

Impact—The magnitude of harm that could be caused by a threat's exercise of a vulnerability.

Asset—Anything of value that is owned by an organization. Assets include both tangible items such as information systems and physical property and intangible assets such as intellectual property.

Now that we have established definitions for basic risk management concepts, we can proceed with an explanation of the risk management process. It is important to keep these definitions in mind when reviewing the risk management process as these concepts will be continually referenced.

Risk Management Process

Risk management is the process of identifying risks, assessing their potential impacts to the organization, determining the likelihood of their occurrence, communicating findings to management and other affected parties, and developing and implementing risk mitigation strategies to reduce risks to levels that are acceptable to the organization. The first step in the risk management process is conducting a risk assessment.

Risk Assessment

Risk assessments assess threats to information systems, system vulnerabilities and weaknesses, and the likelihood that threats will exploit these vulnerabilities and weaknesses to cause adverse effects. For example, a risk assessment could be conducted to determine the likelihood that an un-patched system connected directly to the Internet would be compromised. Obviously the risk assessment would determine that there is almost 100% likelihood that the system would be completely compromised by a number of potential threats such as casual hackers and automated programs. Although this is an extreme example, it helps to illustrate the purpose of conducting risk assessments.

As an SSCP you will be expected to be a key participant in the risk assessment process. Your responsibilities may include identifying system, application, and network vulnerabilities or researching potential threats to information systems. Regardless of your role, it is important that you understand the risk assessment process and how it relates to implementing controls, safeguards, and countermeasures to reduce risk exposure to acceptable levels.

When performing a risk assessment an organization should use a methodology that uses repeatable steps to produce reliable results. Consistency is vital in the risk assessment process, as failure to follow an established methodology can result in inconsistent results. Inconsistent results prevent organizations from accurately assessing risks to organizational assets and can result in ineffective risk mitigation, risk transference, and risk acceptance decisions.

Although a number of risk assessment methodologies exist, they generally follow a similar approach. NIST Special Publication 800-30 "Risk Management Guide for Information Technology Systems" details a nine-step risk assessment methodology. The risk assessment methodology described by NIST is composed of the following steps:

- Step 1—System Characterization
- Step 2—Threat Identification
- Step 3—Vulnerability Identification
- Step 4—Control Analysis
- Step 5—Likelihood Determination
- Step 6—Impact Analysis
- Step 7—Risk Determination
- Step 8—Control Recommendations
- Step 9—Results Documentation

Although a complete discussion of each step described within the NIST Risk Assessment Methodology (Figure 7.1) is outside the scope of this text, we will use the methodology as a guideline to explain the typical risk assessment process. A brief description of each step is be provided below to help you understand the methodology and functions related to this methodology that you will be expected to perform as an SSCP.

Step 1. System Characterization

Before risk can be accurately assessed, a system must be characterized to determine the system's role within an organization. The system must be categorized in terms of:

- Technical settings (hardware, software, and network placement); in terms of the data it stores (type of data, sensitivity of data)
- Organizational role (business functions supported, system criticality, departments, and personnel using the system)
- Security controls (controls protecting the availability of the system, and the confidentiality and integrity of data stored by the system)

Characterizing a system ensures that all relevant information related to the system has been gathered. System characterization also permits identification of threats and vulnerabilities.

Step 2. Threat Identification

As mentioned previously, a threat is the potential for a particular threat source to successfully exercise a specific vulnerability. During the threat identification stage, potential threats to information resources are identified. Threat sources can originate from natural threats, human threats, or environmental threats. Natural threats include earthquakes, floods, tornadoes, hurricanes, tsunamis, and the like. Human threats are events that are either caused though employee error or negligence or are events that are caused intentionally by humans via malicious attacks that attempt to compromise the confidentiality, integrity, and/or availability of IT systems and

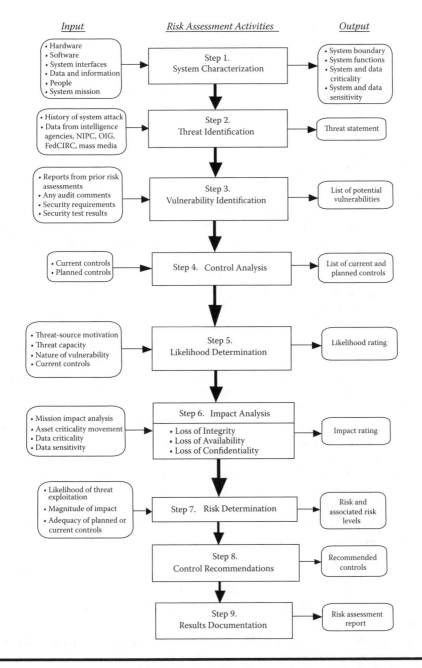

Input	*Risk Assessment Activities*	*Output*
• Hardware • Software • System interfaces • Data and information • People • System mission	**Step 1.** **System Characterization**	• System boundary • System functions • System and data criticality • System and data sensitivity
• History of system attack • Data from intelligence agencies, NIPC, OIG, FedCIRC, mass media	**Step 2.** **Threat Identification**	Threat statement
• Reports from prior risk assessments • Any audit comments • Security requirements • Security test results	**Step 3.** **Vulnerability Identification**	List of potential vulnerabilities
• Current controls • Planned controls	**Step 4. Control Analysis**	List of current and planned controls
• Threat-source motivation • Threat capacity • Nature of vulnerability • Current controls	**Step 5.** **Likelihood Determination**	Likelihood rating
• Mission impact analysis • Asset criticality movement • Data criticality • Data sensitivity	**Step 6. Impact Analysis** • Loss of Integrity • Loss of Availability • Loss of Confidentiality	Impact rating
• Likelihood of threat exploitation • Magnitude of impact • Adequacy of planned or current controls	**Step 7. Risk Determination**	Risk and associated risk levels
	Step 8. **Control Recommendations**	Recommended controls
	Step 9. **Results Documentation**	Risk assessment report

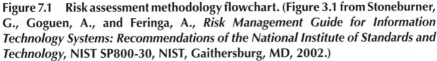

Figure 7.1   Risk assessment methodology flowchart. (Figure 3.1 from Stoneburner, G., Goguen, A., and Feringa, A., *Risk Management Guide for Information Technology Systems: Recommendations of the National Institute of Standards and Technology,* **NIST SP800-30, NIST, Gaithersburg, MD, 2002.)**

data. Environmental threats are those issues that arise as a result of environmental conditions such as power failure, HVAC failure, or electrical fire.

After the threat identification process has been completed, a threat statement should be generated. A threat statement lists potential threat sources that could exploit system vulnerabilities. Successfully identifying threats coupled with vulnerability identification are prerequisites for selecting and implementing information security controls.

Step 3. Vulnerability Identification

Identifying vulnerabilities is an important step in the risk assessment process. The step allows for the identification of both technical and nontechnical vulnerabilities that, if exploited, could result in a compromise of system or data confidentiality, integrity, and/or availability. A review of existing documentation and reports is a good starting point for the vulnerability identification process. This review can include the results of previous risk assessments. It can also include a review of audit reports from compliance assessments, a review of security bulletins and advisories provided by vendors, and data made available via personal and social networking.

Vulnerability identification and assessment can be performed via a combination of automated and manual techniques. Automated techniques such as system scanning allow a security practitioner to identify technical vulnerabilities present in assessed IT systems. These technical vulnerabilities may result from failure to apply operating system and application patches in a timely manner, architecture design problems, or configuration errors. By using automated tools, systems can be rapidly assessed and vulnerabilities can be quickly identified.

Although a comprehensive list of vulnerability assessment tools is outside the scope of this text, an SSCP should spend a significant amount of time becoming familiar with the various tools that could be used to perform automated assessments. Keep in mind that although there are many commercial tools available, there are also many open-source tools that are very effective in performing automated vulnerability assessments. Figure 7.2 is a screenshot of policy configuration using Nessus, a widely used vulnerability assessment tool.

Manual vulnerability assessment techniques may require more time to perform when compared to automated techniques. Typically automated tools will initially be used to identify vulnerabilities. Manual techniques can then be used to validate automated findings. By performing manual techniques, false positives can be eliminated. False positives are potential vulnerabilities identified by automated tools that are not actual vulnerabilities.

Manual techniques may involve attempts to actually exploit vulnerabilities. When approved personnel attempt to exploit vulnerabilities to gain access to systems and data, it is referred to as penetration testing. Although vulnerability assessments merely attempt to identify vulnerabilities, penetration testing actually attempts to

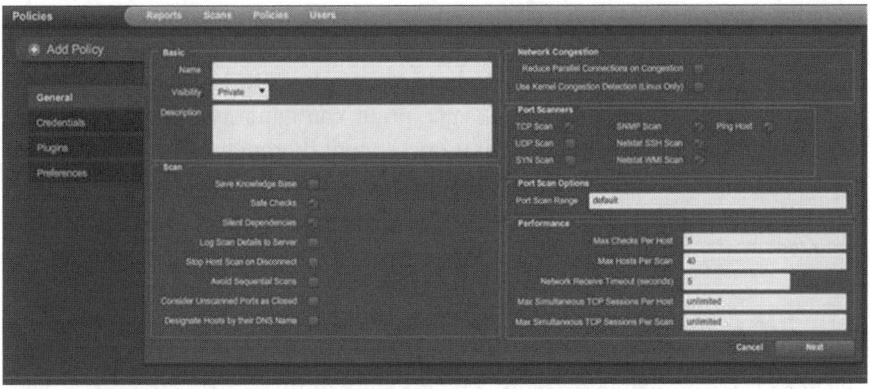

Figure 7.2   Screenshot of Nessus policy configuration.

exploit vulnerabilities. Penetration testing is performed to assess security controls and to determine if vulnerabilities can be successfully exploited. Figure 7.3 is a screenshot of the Metasploit console, a widely used penetration testing tool.

Step 4. Control Analysis

In the Control Analysis step of the risk assessment process, controls are assessed to evaluate their effectiveness in reducing the likelihood that a given threat can exploit a specific system vulnerability. Controls are technical, administrative, and

Figure 7.3   Screenshot of Metasploit console used in conjunction with the Metasploit penetration testing framework.

operational methods for controlling system functionality and restricting personnel actions and activities. As an SSCP, you will primarily be involved with the implementation and evaluation of technical controls such as user authentication requirements, password constraints, encryption configuration, and firewall and intrusion prevention system configuration. A more thorough explanation of controls will be provided in Risk Mitigation. Once controls have been assessed, a determination can be made related to the likelihood that a vulnerability will be exploited.

Step 5. Likelihood Determination

Likelihood determination attempts to define the likelihood that a given vulnerability could be successfully exploited within the current environment. Factors that must be considered when assessing the likelihood of a successful exploit include:

- The nature of the vulnerability, including factors such as:
  - The operating system, application, database, or device affected by the vulnerability
  - Whether local or remote access required is required to exploit the vulnerability
  - The skills and tools required to exploit the vulnerability
- The threat source's motivation and capability, including factors such as:
  - Threat source motivational factors (i.e., financial gain, political motivation, revenge)
  - Capability (skills, tools, and knowledge required to exploit a given vulnerability)
- The effectiveness of controls deployed to prevent exploit of the given vulnerability

Step 6. Impact Analysis

An impact analysis defines the impact to an organization that would result if a vulnerability was successfully exploited. An impact analysis cannot be performed until system mission, system and data criticality, and system and data sensitivity have been obtained and assessed. The system mission refers to the functionality provided by the system in terms of business or IT processes supported. System and data criticality refer to the system's importance to supporting the organizational mission. System and data sensitivity refer to requirements for data confidentiality and integrity.

In many cases, system and data criticality and system and data sensitivity can be assessed by determining the adverse impact to the organization that would result from a loss of system and data confidentiality, integrity, or availability. Remember that confidentiality refers to the importance of restricting access to data so that they are not disclosed to unauthorized parties. Integrity refers to the importance that unauthorized modification of data is prevented. Availability refers to the importance that systems and data are available when needed to support business and technical requirements. By assessing each of these factors individually and aggregating the individual impacts resulting from a loss of confidentiality integrity and availability, the overall adverse impact from a system compromise can be assessed.

Impact can be assessed in either quantitative or qualitative terms. A quantitative impact analysis assigns a dollar value to the impact. The dollar value can be calculated based on an assessment of the likelihood of a threat source exploiting a vulnerability, the loss resulting from a successful exploit, and an approximation of the number of times that a threat source will exploit a vulnerability over a defined period of time. To understand how a dollar value can be assigned to an adverse impact, some fundamental concepts must be explained. An explanation of each of these concepts is provided below.

Single Loss Expectancy (SLE). SLE represents the expected monetary loss to an organization from a threat to an asset. SLE is calculated by determining the value of a particular asset (AV) and the approximated exposure factor (EF). EF represents the portion of an asset that would be lost if a risk to the asset was realized. EF is expressed as a percentage value where 0% represents no damage to the asset and 100% represents complete destruction of the asset.

SLE is calculated by multiplying the AV by the EF as indicated by the formula:

$$\text{Single Loss Expectancy} = \text{Asset Value} \times \text{Exposure Factor}$$

Annualized Loss Expectancy (ALE). ALE represents the expected annual loss as a result of a risk to a specific asset. ALE is calculated by determining the SLE and then multiplying it by the Annualized Rate of Occurrence (ARO) as indicated by the formula:

$$\text{Annual Loss Expectancy} = \text{Single Loss Expectancy} \times \text{Annualized Rate} \\ \text{of Occurrence}$$

Annualized Rate of Occurrence. ARO represents the expected number of exploitations by a specific threat of a vulnerability to an asset in a given year.

Organizations can use the results of annual loss expectancy calculations to determine the quantitative impact to an organization if an exploitation of a specific vulnerability was successful. In addition to the results of quantitative impact analysis, organizations should evaluate the results of qualitative impact analysis.

A qualitative impact analysis assesses impact in relative terms such as high impact, medium impact, and low impact without assigning a dollar value to the impact. A qualitative assessment is often used when it is difficult or impossible to accurately define loss in terms of dollars. For example, a qualitative assessment may be used to assess the impact resulting from a loss of customer confidence, from negative public relations, or from brand devaluation.

Organizations generally find it most helpful to use a blended approach to impact analysis. By evaluating both the quantitative and qualitative impacts to an organization, a complete picture of impacts can be obtained. The results of these impact assessments provide required data for the risk determination process.

Step 7. Risk Determination

In the risk determination step, the overall risk to an IT system is assessed. Risk determination uses the outputs from previous steps in the risk assessment process to assess overall risk. Risk determination results from the combination of:

- The likelihood of a threat source attempting to exploit a specific vulnerability
- The magnitude of the impact that would result if an attempted exploit was successful
- The effectiveness of existing and planned security controls in reducing risk

A risk-level matrix can be created that analyzes the combined impact of these factors to assess the overall risk to a given IT system. The exact process for creating a risk-level matrix is outside the scope of this text. For additional information, refer to NIST Special Publication 800-30 "Risk Management Guide for Information Technology Systems."

The result of creating a risk-level matrix is that overall risk level may be expressed in relative terms of high, medium, and low risk. A description of each risk level and recommended actions is provided below:

- High Risk—Significant risk to the organization and to the organizational mission exists. There is a strong need for corrective actions that include reevaluation of existing controls and implementation of additional controls. Corrective actions should be implemented as soon as possible to reduce risk to an acceptable level.
- Medium Risk—A moderate risk to the organization and to the organizational mission exists. There is a need for corrective actions that include revaluation of existing controls and may include implementation of additional controls. Corrective actions should be implemented within a reasonable time frame to reduce risk to an acceptable level.
- Low Risk—A low risk to the organization exists. An evaluation should be performed to determine if the risk should be reduced or if it will be accepted. If it is determined that the risk should be reduced, corrective actions should be performed to reduce risk to an acceptable level.

Step 8. Control Recommendation

During the control recommendation phase of the risk assessment process, controls are recommended, which, if implemented, will reduce risks to the confidentiality, integrity, and availability to levels that are acceptable to the organization. Control recommendation should result from the analysis of current controls as well as from the risk determination process. Controls that are recommended during this step will be evaluated and implemented during the risk mitigation phase of the risk management process.

Step 9. Results Documentation

Results documentation is the final step in the risk assessment process. Results from the risk assessment process are documented so that they may be presented to senior management. Risk assessment results help senior management understand the risks that are present and provide much needed data for making decisions related to security budgeting, policies and procedures, and risk mitigation strategies.

Risk Mitigation

Risk mitigation is the next step in the risk assessment process. The goal of risk mitigation is to reduce risk exposure to levels that are acceptable to the organization. Risk mitigation can be performed using a number of different strategies. These strategies include:

- Risk reduction and limitation
- Risk transference
- Risk avoidance
- Risk acceptance

Risk Reduction and Limitation

Risk reduction, also known as risk limitation, reduces risks to organizational assets by implementing technical, administrative, and operational controls. Controls should be selected and implemented to reduce risk to acceptable levels. When controls are selected, they should be selected based on their cost, effectiveness, and ability to reduce risk. Controls restrict or constrain behavior to acceptable actions. To help understand controls, it may be easiest to look at some examples of security controls.

A simple control is the requirement for a password to access a critical system. By implementing a password control, unauthorized users would theoretically be prevented from accessing a system. The key to selecting controls is to select controls that are appropriate based on the risk to the organization. Although we noted that a password is an example of a control, we did not discuss the length of the password.

If we determine that we will implement a password that is one character long that must be changed on an annual basis, we have implemented a control; however, the control will have almost no effect on reducing the risk to the organization as the password could be easily cracked. If the password is cracked, unauthorized users could access the system and, as a result, the control has not effectively reduced the risk to the organization.

On the other hand, if we determine that we will implement a password that is 200 characters long that must be changed on an hourly basis, we have implemented a control that will effectively prevent unauthorized access. The issue in this case is that a password with those requirements will have an unacceptably high cost to the organization. End users would experience a significant productivity loss as they would be constantly changing their passwords.

The key to control selection is to implement cost-effective controls that reduce or mitigate risks to levels that are acceptable to the organization. By implementing controls based on this concept, risk will be reduced but not totally eliminated.

Controls can be categorized in technical, administrative, or operational control categories. Administrative controls are controls that dictate how activities should be performed. Policies, procedures, standards, and guidelines are examples of administrative controls. These controls provide a framework for managing personnel and operations. They also can establish requirements for systems operations. An example of an administrative control is the requirement that information security policies should be reviewed on an annual basis and updated as necessary to ensure that they accurately reflect the environment and remain valid.

Technical controls are designed to control end-user and system actions. They can exist within operating systems, applications, database, and network devices. Examples of technical controls include password constraints, access control lists, firewalls, data encryption, antivirus software, and intrusion prevention systems.

Technical controls help to enforce requirements specified within administrative controls. For example, an organization could have implemented a malicious code policy as an administrative control. The policy could require that all end users system have antivirus software installed. Installation of the antivirus software would be the technical control that provides support to the administrative control.

In addition to being categorized as technical, administrative, or operational, controls can be simultaneously categorized as either preventative or detective. Preventive controls attempt to prevent adverse behavior and actions from occurring. Examples of preventative controls include firewalls, intrusion prevention systems, and segregation of duties. Detective controls are used to detect actual or attempted violations of system security. Examples of detective controls include intrusion detection systems and audit logging.

Although implementing controls will reduce risk, some amount of risk will remain even after controls have been selected and implemented. The risk that remains after risk reduction and mitigation efforts are complete is referred to as residual risk. Organizations must determine how to treat this residual risk. Residual risk can be treated either by risk transference, risk avoidance, or risk acceptance.

Risk Transference

Risk transference transfers risk from an organization to a third party. Risk can be reduced by transferring it to a third party via a number of methods. The most common risk transference method is insurance. An organization can transfer its risk to a third party by purchasing insurance. When an organization purchases insurance, it effectively sells its risk to a third party. The insurer agrees to accept the risk in exchange for premium payments made by the insured. If the risk is realized, the insurer compensates the insured party for any incurred losses.

Organizations can also transfer their risk to a third party by outsourcing functions. For example, if an organization was unwilling to accept the risk with shipping hazardous material between facilities, the organization could outsource that function to a shipping company. Any damage associated with shipping would be incurred by the shipping company, which effectively shields the outsourcing organization from the risk.

Risk Avoidance

Another alternative to mitigate risk is to avoid the risk. Risk can be avoided by eliminating the cause of the risk. This could involve disabling system functionality or preventing risky activities when risk cannot be adequately reduced.

Risk Acceptance

Residual risk can also be accepted by an organization. A risk acceptance strategy indicates that an organization is willing to accept the risk associated with the potential occurrence of a specific event. It is important that when an organization chooses risk acceptance, it clearly understands the risk that is present, the probability that the loss related to the risk will occur, and the cost that would be incurred if the loss is realized. Organizations may determine that risk acceptance is appropriate when the cost of implementing controls exceeds the anticipated losses.

Risk Management Summary

Effectively managing risk is a critical factor to the success of an organization. By understanding the risk assessment process as well as risk mitigation alternatives, you can ensure that you are a valuable team member in the risk management process. As an SSCP and a professional security practitioner, it is critical that you remember that every action you perform affects the security posture of your organization.

You should be able to identify opportunities to reduce organizational risk and be prepared to present these opportunities to the appropriate parties.

Incident Response

Incident response is the process of responding in an organized manner to a compromise or attempted compromise of organizational information technology assets. As an SSCP, you will be actively involved with the incident response process. You may be the first person to indentify that an incident has occurred or you may identify an active attempt to compromise system security. In any case, it is important that you understand incident response best practices so that you can react in a timely manner. It is equally important that you do not perform any activities that may make the situation worse or that may compromise evidence that may be required to investigate the incident.

The incident response process generally follows a phased approach as shown in Figure 7.4. Phases of the incident response process include:

1. Preparation
2. Detection and analysis
3. Containment, eradication, and recovery
4. Post-incident activity

Before explaining the phases of the incident response process, some definitions should be established. NIST Special Publication 800-61 "Computer Security Incident Handling Guide" provides an excellent source of guidance in this area. Per SP 800-61:

"An *event* is any observable occurrence in a system or network. Events include a user connecting to a file share, a server receiving a request for a Web page, a user sending electronic mail (e-mail), and a firewall blocking a connection attempt."

Figure 7.4 Incident response life cycle. (Figure 3-1 from Scarfone, K., Grance, T., and Masone, K., *Computer Security Incident Handling Guide: Recommendations of the National Institute of Standards and Technology*, NIST SP800-61 Rev. 1, NIST, Gaithersburg, MD, 2008.)

"*Adverse events* are events with a negative consequence, such as system crashes, network packet floods, unauthorized use of system privileges, defacement of a Web page, and execution of malicious code that destroys data."

"The definition of a computer security incident has evolved. In the past, a computer security incident was thought of as a security-related adverse event in which there was a loss of confidentiality, disruption of data or system integrity, or disruption or denial of availability. New types of computer security incidents have emerged since then, necessitating an expanded definition of an incident. An incident can be thought of as a violation or imminent threat of violation of computer security policies, acceptable use policies, or standard security practices."

Now that we have established definitions for an event, an adverse event and a computer security incident, we have the background necessary to explore each phase of the incident response process. Remember that incident response is focused on dealing with a subset of all adverse effects that could occur within the organization.

Preparation

It is important to note that the key to successful incident response is to have an established incident response policy. The incident response policy and related incident response procedures should clearly indicate who the members of the incident response team are and should define incident response responsibilities for each team member. The incident response policy should establish a phased approach to incident response, which mirrors, or is similar to, the process detailed above. Incident response procedures should describe the exact steps that should be performed during each phase of incident response.

Once an incident response policy and related procedures have been documented, reviewed, and approved, it is important that all personnel receive training related to their responsibilities. All personnel should understand the activities that they must perform. Of equal importance, personnel should understand activities that they must not perform. Training should include simulations to ensure that all personnel are prepared to act. Simulations also help to validate that the incident response procedures are effective and not missing vital details that will be needed when an incident occurs.

In addition to ensuring that the incident response policy and procedure are well documented, organizations must ensure that incident response tools have been acquired. Specific software may be needed for incident handling activities such as forensics analysis. This type of software should be evaluated and purchased so that it is available when needed. Preparation is the key to incident response.

Detection and Analysis

An SSCP will be presented with a myriad of events during the course of normal business operations. Many events occur normally as a result of business operations.

Examples of these events are authorized logon events, authorized access to files, and normal network usage. The SSCP should be able to identify normal events and realize that these events have no adverse affect on the environment.

Of the many events that occur on a daily basis, some of the events will be adverse. That is, the events will adversely affect the operation of information technology systems, network devices, applications, and services. Although these events may have a negative impact, they will not necessarily be classified as security incidents. For example, although a system may crash due to a hardware failure, this would not be considered a security incident because the failure was related to hardware and was not the result of a malicious activity that violated security policies.

Only a subset of all adverse events will be classified as security incidents. It is the responsibility of the SSCP to review adverse events and determine if the event is actually a security incident. Making this determination and acting appropriately is one of the SSCP's key responsibilities.

When an issue is identified, identification may result from a preventative control, but generally results from a detective control. Preventative controls are security controls that are designed to prevent an incident from occurring. Examples of preventative controls include firewalls, access control lists, and intrusion prevention systems. Detective controls are controls that help detect when an incident has occurred. Examples of detective controls include intrusion detection systems, network monitoring systems, and event logging.

Reports from end users also provide an important method for identifying security incidents. End users may submit complaints to a helpdesk about virus warnings, poor system performance, or suspect results from standard business processes and related data outputs. Subsequent research into issues reported by end users may identify issues that would have been otherwise undiscovered.

Once a determination has been made that a security incident has occurred, the incident must be triaged to determine systems and data affected. An analysis of the incident must be performed to determine the overall impact. Impact can vary depending on both the number of systems affected as well as the sensitivity of the data affected. The assessed impact level of the incident will dictate the actions that should be taken as detailed within the incident response policy.

After a security incident has been identified and triaged, a determination must be made regarding whom, if anyone, should be notified. Notification requirements may be explicitly stated within the incident response policy or you may be required to provide notification based on your best judgment. Generally, notification requirements will be based on the severity of the security event. For example, identification and correction of a virus affecting a single host may not require you to provide notification to anyone. On the other hand, if an incident affects a significant number of hosts, affects a critical system, exposes critical data, or could result in revenue loss, immediate notification should be provided.

When in doubt, the best course of action is to escalate the security incident. You may escalate the incident to a senior technical staff member, your manager, or the Information Security Officer depending on your position and the structure of your organization. Regardless, it is critical that timely notification is provided to all parties who should be aware of the incident or are directly involved in the incident response process.

Containment, Eradication, and Recovery

Once notification has been provided, a decision should be made regarding whether the incident should be contained or eradicated. Normally the SSCP will not make this decision directly, but rather will receive guidance from a manager or executive within the organization. Based on the magnitude of the incident, a decision from legal counsel may be required.

The goal of containment is to limit the damage caused by the security incident. Containment is required for most types of security incidents, including those that spread naturally. Some types of incidents, such as worms, spread rapidly and must be contained quickly to prevent affecting other systems. Other events, such as successful hacking attempts, should be contained by restricting access to the affected system or by ensuring that the affected system is unable to connect to additional systems or network resources that may not be compromised.

It is important that incident response procedures include containment instructions. Responders need to know the exact steps that they should perform to contain security incidents. If containment instructions are not included within incident response procedures, responders will either be forced to respond rapidly using a "best guess" approach or wait for containment instructions to be provided to them. In either case, critical steps in the containment process are likely to be missed. Missing steps will result in increased response and recovery times.

The steps taken during the containment process will vary depending on the type of security incident. For example, the steps taken when containing a virus outbreak would be different from the steps taken if credit card data were compromised. Incident response procedures should include a variety of containment strategies based on the type of security incident being contained.

Although a variety of containment strategies could be utilized based on the nature of the incident, some containment activities are commonly performed regardless of the strategy employed. Keep in mind that a complete system backup should be taken before altering the system. Forensics will be discussed later within this chapter, but it must be noted that if a complete system backup is not taken, valuable forensic data may be lost during the containment process.

Common containment activities include:

- Backing up the affected system for subsequent forensic analysis
- Disconnecting the affected system from the network
- Changing system, application, and user passwords

- Analyzing network traffic with packet sniffers or network monitoring tools to identify the source of security incidents
- Modifying firewall rules to restrict access to affected systems
- Reviewing system, application, and security logs for additional data that may be useful in the containment process

Once a security incident has been contained, the next step is to eradicate the incident. Eradication is performed to remove malicious code such as viruses, worms, and Trojan horses. Eradication can also be performed to remove tools and backdoors that may have been used to compromise affected hosts.

Antivirus software is generally effective in removing malicious code from affected systems. Keep in mind that antivirus software signature definition files must be routinely updated. Antivirus signature files are used by antivirus software to identify malicious code infections. Routine updates ensure that antivirus software is able to identify and remove newly released malicious code.

In many cases, eradication will not be required. This is true when systems are rebuilt from an image or restored from backup. Reimaging end-user workstations may prove to be a quicker and more reliable option for recovering from a security incident than trying to eradicate the incident. By reimaging the system, it can be restored to a known good configuration with minimal downtime. As an SSCP, you may be required to determine if eradication or reimaging is the more appropriate solution based on the nature of the incident. This decision may also be made by the system administrator of the affected system.

Administrators may decide that they prefer to restore affected systems from backup rather than attempting to eradicate the security incident. If it is not possible to validate that a security incident has been fully eradicated, restoration is the only viable choice. The system may either be rebuilt from scratch or restored from backup based on the nature of the system, the amount of time required, and the complexity of the process.

Post-Incident Activity

Once security incident recovery has been completed, post-incident activities should be performed. A post-incident report should be prepared that documents the security incident and all activities performed to recover from the incident. The report should include a technical section that details the root cause of the security incident that can generally be determined via a forensic analysis, actions taken to contain the incident, eradication and recovery steps, and the final restoration or recovery point that data were restored to. The report should also contain a management section that summarizes losses to the organization, residuals risks, lessons learned, and methods for improving security incident response. Post-incident reports should be distributed to appropriate parties and collaboratively reviewed.

The incident response policy and related procedures should be updated, as necessary, based on lessons learned during the incident response process. By updating these documents, organizations can continually improve their incident response process. This will result in reduced recovery times and thus provide financial savings to the organization.

Incident Response Summary

Effective incident response is a critical security function that an SSCP should be able to perform. To perform this function, the SSCP must be aware of incident response policies and procedure and be prepared to act immediately. An SSCP must be able to analyze potential security incidents and determine if an actual security incident has transpired. Once a security incident has been confirmed, it is imperative that the SSCP follows the defined procedure to ensure that incidents are contained and eradicated in accordance with organizational requirements. It is equally important that while recovering from an incident, evidence is handled appropriately and that a chain of custody is maintained. Finally, post-incident activities must be performed, incident reports finalized, and procedures and policies updated where appropriate to reflect lessons learned from the incident response process.

Forensics

Once containment and eradication activities have been completed, a number of post-incident activities should be completed. Obviously one of the most important activities to perform is to identify the root cause of the security incident. Root cause analysis is a critical step in the process of determining how a security incident occurred. A security incident may have occurred due to the exploitation of an unpatched application vulnerability, as a result of a malicious internal user, by an inadvertent visit to a Web site containing drive-by malware, or through a myriad of other possibilities. Performing a forensic investigation helps to determine the root cause of security incidents.

Evidence Gathering

Evidence gathering is a critical component of the incident response process and forensic analysis. During the course of investigating a security incident, evidence related to the incident will be discovered and accumulated. This evidence may exist in many different formats such as a disk image, log files, memory contents, or physical evidence. When evidence is gathered, it must be done in a method that does not compromise data. Data gathering must be done using industry-accepted tools that are widely recognized and that have been independently evaluated and validated to produce consistent results.

When evidence is gathered, steps should be performed to ensure that data cannot be subsequently altered. If evidence exists on disk, a disk image should be taken. The imaging tool should ensure that no additional data can be written to the compromised device nor should the tool change any data on the compromised device. After the image is taken, a cryptographic hash should be calculated and recorded. By calculating a hash, any alterations to data that occur after imaging can be easily detected.

Hash algorithms take a file or disk image as input and then use mathematical computations to produce a unique value of a fixed length which is referred to as a message digest. Examples of hash algorithms include MD5, SHA-1, and SHA-2. The MD5 hash algorithm produces a 128-bit message digest, while the SHA-1 hash algorithm produces a 160-bit message digest. Hash algorithms are one-way functions which mean that a message digest cannot be reversed to determine the original input.

To ensure that no changes have been made to the original disk image, a practitioner can calculate the hash value for an image and compare it to the original hash value. If the two values match, the practitioner can validate that no changes have been made to the image. On the other hand, if a different hash value result is produced, the practitioner will know that changes have been made to the disk image since the image was originally taken. Even a minor change to an image or file such as a change to a single character within a file would cause a different hash value to be produced.

Evidence Handling

Some security incidents will be severe enough that criminal charges may be filed against the incident perpetrator. For the evidence collected during the investigation to be admissible in a prosecution, the evidence must be handled properly.

A chain of custody must be established that clearly details how evidence was obtained and handled so that evidence maintains its admissibility. If any action is taken that taints the evidence, it will no longer be admissible and thus cannot be used during prosecution. To establish a chain of custody for evidence, documentation must be maintained throughout the evidence handling process.

The documentation must include, at a minimum, the following information:

■ What is the evidence?
■ How was the evidence obtained?
■ When was the evidence obtained?
■ Who obtained the evidence?
■ Who has handled the evidence since it was obtained?
■ Why was the evidence handled by anyone that handled it after it was obtained?
■ Where has the evidence traveled since it was obtained?

Recovery

As an SSCP, you will be expected to play a key role in business continuity and disaster recovery operations performed by your organization. You may be involved either directly in strategic planning efforts related to business continuity and disaster recovery or you may serve as a team member responsible for executing specific recovery tasks. As a result, it is important that you have a firm understanding of both business continuity planning and disaster recovery planning. You must understand both of these activities, how they are related, and how to professionally perform your responsibilities.

Organizations are threatened by a myriad of issues that could potentially impact the continuity of business operations. These issues include natural disasters such as hurricanes, tornadoes, floods and earthquakes; man-made disasters such as fires, chemical spills, and airplane crashes; health-related issues such as pandemic flu; loss of key personnel or vendors; and miscellaneous other issues that may be unique to your organization's location or business operations.

No matter what type of issue affects your organization, it is critical that you have plans in place to recover and restore operations. These plans must be developed with the input of key representatives from business units within your organization and must have the support of executive management. Key personnel must receive training related to their business continuity and disaster recovery responsibilities. Plans must be tested to ensure that they can be effectively executed. Finally, plans must be constantly reviewed and updated to maintain their effectiveness.

Although business continuity planning and disaster recovery planning are related, there are some key differences between the two. Disaster recovery planning is focused on recovery of information technology infrastructure, applications, communications equipment, and data after a disaster. Business continuity planning focuses on the continuity and recovery of critical business functions during and after a disaster. Both disaster recovery planning and business continuity planning will be discussed in detail.

Developing a BCP requires a significant organizational commitment in terms of both personnel and financial resources. To gain this commitment, organizational support for business continuity planning efforts must be provided by executive management or an executive sponsor. Without the proper support, business continuity planning efforts have only a minimal chance of success.

Business continuity planning is the proactive development of a plan that can be executed to restore business operations within predetermined times after a disaster or other significant disruption to the organization. To gain a thorough understanding of business continuity planning, it is first necessary to explain some key continuity planning concepts. After we have defined these concepts, we will then have a proper foundation of knowledge on which to build our BCP.

The first step in developing a BCP is to establish the business continuity program and the directly related business continuity policy. When a business continuity program is developed, a strategy is defined and overall responsibility for BCP development is formally assigned to a specific individual or department. Key participants from various business units are identified and program goals are established.

The business continuity policy normally includes a policy statement that sets program expectations and establishes management support for the program. The policy also documents BCP participant roles and responsibilities, program objectives, and key metrics. The policy should be reviewed and updated on an annual basis to ensure that it remains accurate.

The second step in developing a BCP is conducting a business impact analysis (BIA). BIA, shown in Figure 7.5, is performed to assess the financial and nonfinancial impacts to an organization that would result from a business disruption. Conducting a BIA aids in the identification of critical organizational functions and helps determine recovery time objectives, which are both prerequisites for developing the business continuity strategy and related DRP.

Before the process of performing a BIA is detailed, some key concepts should be defined. Once you have a clear understanding of important BIA concepts, it will be easy to understand the inputs required for the BIA process and the resulting outputs that allow us to develop an appropriate continuity and recovery strategy.

All organizations perform critical business functions as well as numerous support functions. Critical business functions are those functions that are integral to the success of an organization, without which the organization is incapable of operating. Critical functions vary depending on the nature of the organization as well as the types of goods or services provided by the organization. When constructing a BCP, it is imperative that each organizational function is identified. A criticality level should then be assigned to each function based on the impact to organization that would result if the function was unavailable.

A function's criticality level helps to determine the function's maximum tolerable downtime (MTD), also referred to as the maximum tolerable period of disruption (MTPOD). The MTD is the maximum amount of time that a business

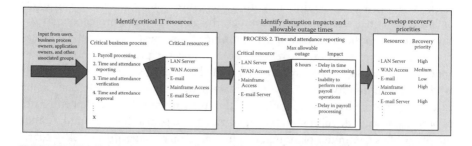

Figure 7.5 Business impact analysis process for a hypothetical government agency. (Figure 3.2 from Swanson, M., Bowen, P., Wohl Phillips, A., Gallup, D., and Lynes, D., *Contingency Planning Guide for Federal Information Systems*, NIST SP800-34 Rev. 1, NIST, Gaithersburg, MD, 2010.)

function can be unavailable before the organization is harmed to a degree that puts the survivability of the organization at risk. When a business function is unavailable for longer than the MTD, the organization may suffer irreparable damages, as either a direct financial result or as an indirect result from loss of customer confidence or damage to organizational reputation.

Related to the concept of MTD is the "recovery time objective" concept. Recovery time objectives can be specified for business functions as well as information systems and supporting infrastructure and communications components. The recovery time objective indicates the period of time within which a business function or information system must be restored after a disruption. Recovery time objectives may be expressed in terms of hours, days, or weeks depending on the criticality of the affected business function or supporting information system. The recovery time objective is set less than MTD/MTPOD.

Another related concept is that of the recovery point objective. During a disaster, there will typically be a loss of data. The recovery point objective specifies the point in time to which data could be restored in the event of a business continuity disruption. Recovery point objectives will vary depending on data backup and system availability strategies utilized. For example, if your organization takes daily backups at the end of each business day, your recovery point objective would be the end of the previous day. If your organization uses real-time data mirroring to an alternate location, your recovery point objective could be to restore data to the exact state it was in before the business continuity event.

Although it should be quite evident, it goes without saying that recovery time objectives for specific functions, services, and systems must be less than the related MTD. An organization must not consider any recovery strategy with a length that exceeds the MTD as the results to the organization would be catastrophic. All effort should be focused on selecting a recovery strategy that allows functions and related information systems to be recovered to defined recovery point objectives and within recovery time objectives.

As mentioned previously, a BIA is performed to assess the financial and nonfinancial impacts to an organization that would result from a business disruption. By assessing the organizational impact that would result from a disruption in various business functions and related information systems, business continuity and disaster recovery strategies can be evaluated, selected, and implemented.

When conducting a BIA, it is important that stakeholders understand that their responses serve as vital input into the development of business continuity and recovery strategies. Stakeholders must understand that the BCP can only be successful if they provide accurate and timely information to the BIA process. Stakeholders must also understand that failure to provide comprehensive information may result in either an extended delay or complete inability to recover business functions.

Conducting a BIA requires participation from stakeholders in all organizational business units. As a result, executive sponsorship is normally necessary to ensure that stakeholders are involved throughout the process. Without participation from stakeholders, it is difficult to validate that all business functions have been identified and properly categorized according to relative criticality levels.

Many approaches should be considered when determining how to obtain BIA information from stakeholders. Popular choices for obtaining this information include direct interviews with stakeholders, BIA questionnaires, review of organizational policies and procedures, and reviews of organizational contractual requirements and service level agreements.

An approach used by many practitioners is to initially review documentation, including policies, procedures, contracts, and service level agreements. The initial review provides an understanding of business functions and assists in defining recovery time objectives. The review also helps to define questions that should be asked to business unit personnel via questionnaires or via interview.

The documentation review is generally followed up by providing BIA questionnaires to project stakeholders. Stakeholders should complete BIA questionnaires related to functions in their areas of responsibility. Once completed, stakeholders should submit their completed questionnaires to the BIA coordinator. The coordinator should review the forms for completeness.

Note: As a security practitioner, you may find that conducting a business impact analysis (BIA) is an easier process if you actively assist stakeholders in completing their responsibilities related to the analysis. Most stakeholders will have little to no experience with either BIAs or business continuity planning. As a result, they may be hesitant to provide you with required information in a timely manner. This hesitation may occur because stakeholders do not understand their responsibilities or because they are uncomfortable or unfamiliar with the process. By providing assistance to stakeholders, you cannot only ensure that you receive timely and accurate information but you may also gain a deeper understanding of functions performed within your organization and show stakeholders your commitment to the success of the project.

When performing a BIA, a defined process should be followed that ensures consistency throughout the analysis. For example, the National Institute of Standards and Technology (NIST) suggests that when conducting a BIA as part of contingency planning for information technology systems, project stages should include:

1. Identification of critical IT resources
2. Identification of disruption impacts and allowable outage times
3. Development of recovery priorities

To support the identification of critical IT resources, it is first necessary to identify critical business functions. Once each critical business function is identified, it should then be relatively easy to identify the critical IT resources that are required to support each business function. Critical IT resources include IT systems and the applications residing on those systems, as well as supporting network connectivity and security devices and applications.

> **Note**: When identifying critical IT resources, it is imperative that interconnected systems and those systems providing supporting functionality are also identified. For example, while no critical business process may be provided directly by an LDAP (Lightweight Directory Access Protocol) server, if users are unable to authenticate to the network or directly to an underlying application, they will be unable to access the resource and thus, the resource will still remain unavailable.
>
> Business unit stakeholders may not be aware of underlying technologies and applications that support critical IT resources they rely on. As a result, it is important that IT personnel carefully review the list of critical IT resources generated by stakeholders and ensure that supporting resources are also identified and included when defining recovery time objectives and recovery priorities.

Once critical business functions and related information technology resources have been identified, the next step is to determine the potential impacts that could result if the functions or supporting resources were unavailable as a result of a business disruption. When identifying disruption impacts, it is important to identify the potential range of impacts that could result from a disruption.

Business disruption impacts may have tangible or intangible results to the organization. Tangible results from a business disruption are those results that can be measured and that can have a direct cost to the organization assigned. Examples of tangible results include increased processing time, loss of revenue, decreased employee productivity, and potential financial losses resulting from a failure to meet established service level agreements. Intangible results are those results that, although not easily measured, have a negative impact to the organization. Examples of intangible impact results include loss of customer confidence, effects to employee morale, and negative public relations.

Only by carefully evaluating the potential range of tangible and intangible results can allowable outage times be accurately established. Allowable outage time indicates the amount of time that an IT system can be unavailable before there is a significant or critical impact to business functions that rely on the system. When conducting a BIA, an allowable outage time should be established for each IT system.

Allowable outage times are directly related to the MTD of critical business functions. As business functions rely on IT systems, IT practitioners must ensure that outage times do not exceed MTD thresholds. In most cases, allowable outage times should be established that are well below the MTD of related business functions. This helps ensure that systems can be recovered and related business functions can be resumed before approaching the MTD threshold. This also helps to create a time buffer, which may be necessary if unforeseen circumstances that delay recovery efforts arise.

The establishment of allowable outage times for all information systems and related resources is required to prioritize the recovery of these systems. Assigning recovery priorities to systems allows an organization to determine the order that systems should be restored or recovered after a business disruption event. By setting recovery priority levels for systems, organizations can ensure that information systems supporting critical business functions are restored before systems that support less critical functions.

Establishing recovery priorities, recovery time objectives, and recovery point objectives allows an organization to evaluate alternative recovery strategies and select an appropriate recovery strategy. When selecting a recovery strategy, it is imperative to select one that meets organizational requirements.

Disaster Recovery Planning

While business continuity planning focuses on providing continuity of critical business operations, disaster recovery planning focuses on the restoration of IT functions after a business disruption event. A DRP is a document that details the steps that should be performed to restore critical IT systems in the event of a disaster. As an SSCP, you will be expected to be a participant in disaster recovery planning efforts. You will also be a valuable participant in the disaster recovery process in the event that a disaster occurs and the plan is activated.

Due to the heavy reliance on information technology, it is critical that a well-defined DRP exists to allow the organization to continue or resume operations in acceptable time frames and with minimal impact. As mentioned previously, critical IT systems will be identified during the BIA. The information technology group must ensure that a DRP is developed, which allows for the restoration of these systems to defined recovery point objectives and within established recovery time objectives.

When creating a DRP, it is important to identify different types of disasters that could threaten the organization and then try to assess the likelihood of each event occurring. Many different types of disasters could affect the organization, including natural disasters such as hurricanes, floods, earthquakes, and tornadoes; health- and wellness-related disasters such as the avian flu and swine flu; intentional acts of sabotage such as arson and hacking; as well as an untold number of potential threats that could result from geographic, industrial, political, and personnel factors that apply to your organization. By identifying potential threats and assessing the likelihood of their occurrence, business continuity and recovery solutions can be implemented that reduce organizational risk to acceptable levels.

As a result of the variety of threats an organization faces and the resulting losses that may occur, DRPs need to account for the potential loss of a variety of assets. These assets include:

- Data
- Information systems
- Network devices
- Telecommunications equipment
- Facilities
- Personnel
- Other assets unique to your organization

In subsequent sections of this chapter, we discuss recovery strategies for many of these assets, including data backup strategies and alternative processing facilities. Regardless of the strategy that is selected, the strategy should be documented within the DRP.

Although it is important to document data recovery and alternate facility strategies, it is equally important to ensure the organization can recover from the loss of key IT personnel. Personnel may have unique skills or knowledge that is not widely available within the organization. To mitigate the risk associated with the loss of key personnel, backup personnel should be assigned within the DRP. Cross-training should be performed to ensure that backup personnel are prepared to complete their responsibilities should they be called upon.

DRPs can either directly include or reference additional policies, procedures, and other related documents. By referencing these documents within the DRP, they can be located quickly in the event of a disaster. Personnel will be able to easily determine actions that should be performed and can avoid wasting critical time that could be used to perform recovery activities. Referencing related documents is especially important if key personnel are unavailable and recovery tasks must be performed by backup personnel or third parties.

Procedures are documents that list a series of steps that should be taken to perform a task. For example, a backup restoration procedure may be included in the DRP that indicates the steps that must be taken to restore a specific system from backup. It is critical that procedures for the backup and restoration of IT systems are well documented, reviewed on a periodic basis, and updated as needed based on technological or procedural changes.

Examples of other documents that may be included or referenced within the DRP include documents such as network topology maps, third-party contracts, and vendor contact lists. Although stated previously, the importance of including or referencing relevant information cannot be stressed enough as it is imperative that time is not wasted performing unnecessary tasks or searching for documentation when a disaster strikes.

Recovery Strategy Alternatives

Many recovery strategy alternatives exist, which vary in cost and complexity. These alternatives support different recovery time objectives and allow organizations to restore data to various recovery point objectives. The SSCP should have knowledge of these recovery alternatives and be able to assist in selecting an appropriate alternative based on organizational requirements. Remember when selecting a recovery strategy that the cost of the recovery strategy (Figure 7.6) should never exceed the loss that an organization would incur if a business disruption occurred.

Recovery alternatives include:

- Cold site
- Warm site
- Hot site
- Multiple processing sites
- Mobile sites

Cold Site

A cold site is a facility that could be utilized as an alternative processing site for recovering IT operations. The cold site is generally preconfigured with necessary infrastructure components such as electrical, water, and communications access. The cold site does not contain any provisional equipment such as computer hardware, telecommunications, and network devices. The site is merely available such that equipment could be acquired and installed at the location in the event of disaster.

The cold site recovery alternative has a longer recovery time than any other recovery alternative. This is because the cold site requires that equipment is provisioned,

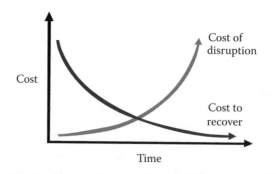

Figure 7.6 Recovery cost balancing. (Figure 3.3 from Swanson, M., Bowen, P., Wohl Phillips, A., Gallup, D., and Lynes, D., *Contingency Planning Guide for Federal Information Systems*, NIST SP800-34 Rev. 1, NIST, Gaithersburg, MD, 2010.)

installed, and configured at the cold site after the disaster has occurred. Once equipment and communications have been installed and configured, data must be restored from backup. Testing must then be performed to validate that systems and equipment operate as expected.

As no inventory of hardware or communications equipment is maintained at the cold site, the cold site alternative is far less costly than that of either the warm or hot site. The cold site should be considered when recovery time objectives do not require the immediate availability of information systems and related data housed on those systems. Cold site recovery normally requires days or weeks of recovery time to restore business operations. The cold site alternative is not an appropriate recovery strategy when immediate recovery is required.

Warm Site

A warm site recovery alternative is similar to the cold site alternative; however, at a warm site, computer hardware and related communications and networking equipment is available. Generally, at a warm site, equipment has been installed and configured but systems do not have current data. Restoration of data from backup is required before the warm site can function as a processing alterative. Depending on the recovery strategy selected, data backups may be stored at the warm site or may need to be recalled from an off-site data storage provider.

The warm site is a more expensive alternative than the cold site as equipment must be installed and configured at the warm site to ensure its availability during a disaster. As equipment has already been provisioned, installed, and configured, the warm site supports faster recovery of operations than the cold site alternative.

Hot Site

The hot site alternative provides a redundant processing environment that closely matches the production environment. The hot site contains all of the hardware and related communications and networking equipment required to provide continuity of operations. Data are maintained at the hot site, which is either a mirror of data at the production environment or a very close replica to that which is maintained at the production site. Technical solutions are utilized to provide real-time mirroring or synchronization of data between the production environment and the test environment. As a result, business operations can be transitioned from the production site to the hot site while minimizing downtime.

The hot site recovery alternative provides a shorter recovery time window than the warm site recovery strategy alternative. Although the hot site provides a shorter recovery time window, it is more expensive than the warm site recovery alternative. This results from the duplication of equipment and the real-time mirroring of data from the production environment to the hot site.

Multiple Processing Sites

A multiple processing site supports 100% availability because data are processed simultaneously at the alternate site. The alternate site is a redundant configuration of the primary facility and is fully operational at all times. Data are constantly synchronized between the primary facility and the multiple processing facility using data mirroring or synchronization technologies. This type of site is always staffed by organizational personnel and is always under organizational control. The multiple processing site provides the shortest recovery time alternative.

Because multiple processing sites permanently house organizational personnel, determining the costs allocation associated with this alternative may become complicated. These complications may arise if the personnel or equipment are used to perform support functions for the organization in addition to their business continuity responsibilities. It then becomes more complex to determine costs associated with business continuity when compared to costs associated with functions performed by personnel as part of normal day-to-day business operations.

Mobile Sites

Mobile recovery sites vary from traditional recovery alternatives in that a mobile recovery site can be deployed to any location based on the circumstances of the disaster. Traditional recovery alternatives exist in brick-and-mortar facilities and require that personnel are deployed from the disaster site to the alternate location. A mobile recovery site is a self-contained data processing facility. The mobile facility may be transported to an appropriate location by truck after a disaster situation. Due to the limited size of the mobile facility, this recovery alternative is most appropriate for recovery of individual departments within an organization.

For the mobile site alternative to be effective, the mobile site must be configured with necessary equipment and supplies. Mobile site alternatives are generally provided by a third party that specializes in this service. Therefore, it is important when considering this alternative to validate that any contract established between your organization and a mobile site provider includes a service level agreement that ensures that the mobile site will be available when needed.

Plan Testing

Once BCPs and DRPs have been developed, they must be tested to validate that they are accurate. They must also be tested to ensure that critical business functions can be recovered within defined recovery time objectives to established recovery point objectives. Several types of tests exist, which vary in complexity and thoroughness. Each test type will be detailed and a comparison of each type will be provided.

Test types include:

- Checklist test
- Structured walkthrough test
- Simulation test
- Parallel test
- Full interruption test

Checklist Test

A checklist test should be routinely performed by the business continuity coordinator and appropriate business unit personnel. In a checklist test, each participant reviews his or her section of the plan to validate that it still contains accurate information. Specifically, participants review the plan to ensure that the contact information for each participant in their area of responsibility is still correct and that the criticality levels assigned to various business functions described within the plan are still appropriate. Participants also validate that new business functions are accounted for within the plan and that business functions that no longer exist are removed from the plan.

Structured Walkthrough Test

In a structured walkthrough test, representatives from each business unit gather together to review the BCP. Each team presents their section of the BCP to the group. The participants validate that the plan is correct and that the responsibilities of each participant are understood. Additionally, the scope of the plan and plan assumptions are reviewed to ensure that they are still correct.

The walkthrough should be conducted before more in-depth testing is performed. By performing the walkthrough first, plan deficiencies can be identified and corrected early in the testing process. It is not uncommon for multiple walkthroughs to be performed before advancing to more thorough testing techniques. This is especially true with the initial development of BCPs as multiple iterations of design, documentation, and testing are common with new BCPs.

Simulation testing is a more in-depth testing technique than either checklist or structured walkthrough testing. In a simulation test, an actual disaster situation is simulated. The disaster is simulated so that business operations are not actually interrupted. Participant's responses to the simulated disaster are measured to evaluate the accuracy of response actions as well as response times.

While previous test techniques, including checklist testing and structured walkthrough testing, are paper-based tests, the simulation test is the first testing technique that may involve testing actual recovery techniques such as file restoration from backup or failover from primary to secondary systems. As simulation testing is an advanced testing technique compared to previously discussed test types, it is important that simulation testing is not performed until the results of checklist and walkthrough tests have been validated and resulting modifications have been incorporated into the plan.

Simulation testing involves more personnel than the checklist or walkthrough testing techniques and may be the first exposure that new personnel have to the BCP. As a result, it is likely that new issues will be encountered when executing simulation testing. These issues and any resulting plan modifications should be documented and reviewed at the conclusion of testing. Although issues may be encountered, testing should continue until the simulation has been completed. Simulation testing should only be ended prematurely if it becomes impossible to continue.

Parallel Testing

Parallel testing involves performing processing at an alternate site. Parallel testing is an operational test and generally does not include representatives from departments that do not have direct involvement in operations such as human resources, public relations, or marketing. Although processing is performed at an alternate site, processing at production facilities is not interrupted or otherwise disrupted.

Because parallel testing is performed at an alternate site, this type of testing generally involves a significant cost to the organization. Due to the cost involved, senior management approval must be obtained before considering this testing approach. It is critical that parallel testing scenarios and desired outcomes are clearly defined and communicated to all participants.

During parallel testing, historical transactions are processed against data backups that have been restored at the alternate site. Transaction results are compared against results from the production facility to validate accuracy. Results may be compared by running typical business reports and validating that report output is consistent between data at the production facility and data restored at the alternate site.

External auditors or designated observers are often present during parallel test execution. This allows an independent party to observe parallel test execution, document observations, and generate a report of test results. The report can then used by the BCP team to create a gap analysis, identify plan deficiencies, and implement plan corrections and improvements.

Full Interruption Testing

Full interruption testing is performed when business operations are actually interrupted at the primary processing facility. Processing is performed at the alternate site and processing is ceased at the primary facility for the duration of the test. This type of testing is highly disruptive and may result in an actual disaster if processing cannot be returned to the original status after testing.

Therefore, it is critical that this type of testing is only performed after all previous testing techniques have been executed successfully. Senior management must be fully informed of the risks of full interruption testing. Executive approval must be obtained before executing this testing. Executives should be provided with real-time updates throughout full interruption testing and must be immediately notified of test results and issues arising from the testing process.

During the BCP testing process, the SSCP will be expected to fulfill a number of important roles, including providing technical support during the process as well as ensuring that appropriate security controls are enabled. SSCP participation is particularly important when performing simulation, parallel, and full interruption testing as these tests involve the actual restoration of processing at an alternate site.

Although the SSCP understands the importance of implementing security controls at the alternate processing site, the organization's primary focus is restoring business operations within defined recovery time objectives. When possible, the SSCP should validate that security controls are in place and operational, which provide an equivalent level of security as that which exists at the primary processing facility.

Though security controls should be implemented, the controls implemented at the alternate site may not mirror those that exist in the primary processing facility due to financial resource constraints. When an equivalent level is not possible due to resource constraints, the SSCP should assist in defining and implementing additional manual controls. Additional controls could include increased monitoring and logging so that unusual activities can be identified and investigated.

Plan Review and Maintenance

Both BCPs and DRPs should be reviewed on an annual basis, at a minimum, or after significant changes to business operations or information technology infrastructure. This review is important to ensure that the plan is continually up-to-date and that it can be relied upon if disaster strikes. Just like initial plan development, plan review should involve participants from all business units.

When making modifications to the BCP, all modifications should be tracked and approved, as appropriate, by the business continuity team. A summary of changes made to the BCP should be provided to all participants. This ensures that all participants are aware of changes to the plan and prepared to fulfill their responsibilities.

The BCP should contain a section that documents important version control data. Data tracked within the version control section should include the current BCP version number, a summary of changes made to the BCP, the review date, and the approver or approvers. Tracking BCP version information allows BCP participants to verify they have the most recent version of the plan, which is vital to successful execution of the plan. A periodic review of the BCP is also a requirement of many compliance regulations. By tracking the review and approval dates within the BCP, evidence of periodic review can easily be provided to internal and external auditors.

Data Backup and Restoration

Many approaches exist to perform both data backup and restoration. Backup solutions vary in cost and complexity and allow data recovery within a wide array of time frames. An SSCP should be familiar with various alternatives for data backup and restoration and be able to recommend appropriate solutions based on recovery time objectives and recovery point objectives. In some cases, the SSCP will also be expected to utilize data backup and restoration procedures to restore data in the event of disaster. In other cases, data backup and restoration functions may be performed by a server or database administration team.

When evaluating backup solutions, it is important to remember that you must first evaluate what needs to be backed up. Solutions may vary depending on whether operating systems, file data, databases, applications, or utilities are to be backed up and subsequently restored. You should take time to familiarize yourself with available alternatives. Selecting the appropriate data backup solution is a critical component of implementing successful business continuity and DRPs. Only by understanding available alternatives can you ensure that you are selecting the most appropriate choice.

Several backup alternatives exist when selecting the frequency and amount of data to backup. These backup alternatives include full backups, incremental backups, and differential backups. Data are normally backed up to tape but can be backed up to other media, including CD, DVD, and disk. An explanation of each backup type is presented below.

Full Backup

When a full backup is performed, the entire system is copied to backup media. This is the slowest type of backup to perform as more data is copied to backup media when compared to incremental or differential backups. Due to this fact, full system backups are generally performed on an infrequent basis, normally weekly.

Differential Backup

Differential backups record differences in data since the most recent full backup. For example, if a full backup was performed on the weekend, a differential backup may be performed each day of the week. The differential backup records all differences between the current system configuration and the system configuration taken at the time of full data backup.

Incremental Backup

Incremental backups record changes that are made to the system on a daily basis. Each day when the incremental backup is performed, changes from the previous day are recorded on the incremental backup. Incremental backups generally complete faster than any other type of backup as only daily changes are recorded by the backup process.

When evaluating backup alternatives, it is important to note that although it is faster to perform incremental backups when compared to performing differential backups, there is an offsetting cost when restoring from backup. When restoring a differential backup, the full backup is restored initially and then only the most recent differential backup is restored. When restoring incremental backups, each incremental backup taken after the most recent full backup must be restored before the system restoration process can be completed. This is due to the fact that differential backups store all changes since the most recent full backup while incremental backups only record daily changes.

Backup Type	Data Backed Up	Time to Complete
Full Backup	All data are copied to backup media	The full system backup takes the longest time to complete
Differential Backup	All data that are different between the current system configuration and the system configuration at the time of the last full backup	The differential backup takes less time than the full system backup but more time than an incremental backup
Incremental Backup	Each incremental backup records changes in data from the previous incremental backup	The incremental backup is the fastest backup type to perform when compared to full and differential backups

Off-Site Storage

When at all possible, backup tapes should be stored off-site at a secure location. By storing backups off-site, we can ensure that they are available for restoration at an alternate location should the primary facility become unavailable. If backups are stored at the primary facility and a disaster strikes, the backup will likely also be damaged by the same event and thus will be useless for disaster recovery purposes.

Strong consideration should be given to using a secure, bonded courier service for transporting backup media to an off-site storage vendor. By using a bonded courier and a secure storage service, organizations can guarantee that data are stored at an off-site location that provides equivalent security controls to their own.

Any time that data are stored off-site, strong controls should be in place related to access to backup media. Access to backup media should be restricted to authorized personnel. Transfer of backup media to a third party should be tracked via an inventory control system that records barcodes of tapes entering and exiting the facility. Data backups should be encrypted to prevent access to data by unauthorized parties in the event that backup media is lost, misplaced, or stolen.

It is important to note that when data backups are encrypted and stored off-site, encryption key management procedures must be implemented to ensure that data can be accessed and restored should access to the original keys become unavailable. The keys should not be stored directly with the data backups, but rather should be stored separately in a secure manner. Access to encryption keys should be restricted to appropriate personnel. As key rotation occurs, it is important to ensure that off-site keys are updated to match those in use in the production environment. In addition to performing backups locally and then transferring them off-site, data backup can be performed directly to an off-site location. Backups to an offsite location can either be performed directly to another site that is owned by your organization or they can be performed to a vendor location. By backing up directly to an offsite location, data loss can be reduced in the event that there is a disaster that renders the primary facility unavailable. Electronic vaulting and remote journaling are methods for performing data backup to an offsite location.

Electronic Vaulting

Electronic vaulting is another method of performing data backup. This method allows data backup across a WAN connection or the Internet to an offsite location. With many electronic vaulting solutions, an appliance sits at the source location, which collects data backups from individual systems and then transmits them to the vendor location. The backup is encrypted in transit to preserve confidentiality and eliminate the risk of data being intercepted in transit. Data backups may be restored directly from the electronic vault to the source system should data be lost as a result of human or technical error.

Remote Journaling

Remote journaling is a similar concept to electronic vaulting. In remote journaling, journals and database transaction logs are transmitted electronically to an offsite location. Transaction logs can then be applied against a copy of the database at the offsite location. In the event of a processing interruption at the primary site, the offsite copy can be restored quickly from the offsite location to the primary site.

System and Data Availability

Although we have discussed a number of different methods for backing up and restoring critical systems, we have not discussed any methods for preventing system downtime. In addition to the numerous methods that we have discussed for recovering data, there are also numerous methods available to enhance system and data redundancy and resiliency. Redundant configurations can be established for both individual system components as well as complete systems. Examples of redundant system components include redundant hard drives, power supplies, and network interfaces. Redundant system configuration options include standby servers and clusters.

Clustering

Clustering refers to a method of configuring multiple computers so that they effectively operate as a single system. Clustering can be performed for several reasons, including high availability, load balancing, increasing computational performance, and grid computing. For purposes of our discussion, we will focus on high availability clusters and load-balancing clusters, which are the clustering methods that provide redundancy to the information technology environment.

High-Availability Clustering

High availability clustering is a clustering method that uses multiple systems to reduce the risk associated with a single point of failure. In a high availability cluster, systems may be configured in an active/passive configuration. In this configuration, there is a primary system that is considered the active system and a secondary system with an identical configuration that operates as a passive server. The passive system does not process any transactions, but rather stands by in case it must take over processing for the primary system.

Failure monitoring is implemented through a heartbeat, which is a communications link between the active and passive server. The secondary server is configured to monitor the "health" of the active server via the heartbeat. In the event that the secondary server detects an issue with the primary server, automatic failover occurs. When failover occurs, the secondary system begins performing all processing activities in place of the primary server.

Automatic failover provides service redundancy and allows system administrators to investigate and correct issues with the primary server. After the issues have been corrected, the primary system can be reactivated. Once the primary system has been reactivated, the secondary system returns to its passive state and continues to monitor the heartbeat for additional issues.

IT systems that provide support for critical business functions are prime candidates for high-availability clustering if clustering is supported by the operating system and application. When evaluating high-availability clustering, you should determine the overall cost of implementing high availability and then compare the cost to the cost associated with system downtime. Performing this comparison will allow you to determine if the costs associated with implementing high availability can be justified.

Load-Balancing Clustering

In addition to the active/passive high availability configuration, an active/active configuration is also available. This configuration is referred to as a load-balancing configuration. In a load-balancing cluster, all cluster nodes are active. Load balancing provides redundancy because multiple systems are simultaneously active. If a single system fails, the remaining systems continue to provide the service.

Load balancing can be implemented through a number of algorithms that determine how to allocate processing and network traffic. The "round-robin" algorithm allocates service requests by distributing them to each server based on a rotation regardless of processing load. For example, in a three-server configuration, the first request would be processed by the first server, the second request by the second server, the third request by the third server, and the fourth request would be directed back to the first server.

Other load-balancing algorithms exist that allocate service requests based on server load, geographic location, ping response times, and a number of other factors. Although a description of these algorithms is outside the scope of this text, the SSCP should be aware that implementing load balancing is an effective method for improving system redundancy that should be evaluated when designing a redundancy and recovery strategy.

Redundant Array of Independent Disks

A method that may be used to provide data redundancy is via a RAID (Redundant Array of Independent Disks) implementation. In a RAID implementation, data are written across a series of disks. RAID can be implemented via either software or hardware. Although multiple disks are used in the RAID array, they are seen as a single disk by the operating system and by the end user. Also, RAID provides disk redundancy; it does not provide for redundancy of other system components.

RAID is based on three different data redundancy techniques that can be applied in multiple combinations to achieve varying results. Different RAID levels exist, which are used to describe each combination. The data redundancy techniques employed by RAID include parity, striping, and mirroring. The following excerpt from NIST Special Publication 800-34 "Contingency Planning Guide for Information Technology Systems" provides a thorough explanation of the concepts of parity, striping, and mirroring.

■ *Mirroring.* With this technique, the system writes data simultaneously to separate hard drives or drive arrays. The advantages of mirroring are minimal downtime, simple data recovery, and increased performance reading from disk. If one hard drive or disk array fails, the system can operate from the working hard drive or disk array, or the system can use one disk to process a read request and another disk for a different processing request. The disadvantage of mirroring is that both drives or disk arrays are processing in the writing-to-disks function, which can hinder system performance. Mirroring has a high fault tolerance and can be implemented through a hardware RAID controller or through the operating system.

■ *Parity.* Parity refers to a technique of determining whether data had been lost or overwritten. Parity has a lower fault tolerance than mirroring. The advantage of parity is that data can be protected without having to store a copy of the data, as is required with mirroring.

■ *Striping.* Striping improves the performance of the hardware array controller by distributing data across all drives. In striping, a data element is broken into multiple pieces, and a piece is distributed to each hard drive. Data transfer performance is increased using striping because the drives may access each data piece simultaneously. Striping can be implemented in bytes or blocks. Byte-level striping breaks the data into bytes and stores the bytes sequentially across the hard drives. Block-level striping breaks the data into a given-size block, and each block is distributed to a disk.

RAID uses a numeric-level system to represent different data redundancy techniques. It is important to note that although some RAID levels provide data redundancy, not all do. An SSCP should be familiar with available RAID configuration choices and be able to recommend and configure an appropriate RAID configuration based on the needs of the organization.

RAID Levels

■ **RAID 0**—A RAID 0 configuration, also known as a striped set, is a configuration that relies on striping data across multiple disks. In a RAID 0 configuration, data are striped across multiple disks but no parity information is included. As a result, although performance is improved, RAID 0 provides no data redundancy. Because no redundancy is provided by a RAID 0 configuration, it is not a viable solution for disaster recovery.

■ **RAID 1**—In a RAID 1 configuration, data mirroring is used. Identical copies of data are stored on two separate drives. In the event that one disk fails, an exact duplicate of the data resides on the other disk. RAID 1 is a simple solution to implement; however, 50% of total disk space is lost because all data are duplicated on both disks.

■ **RAID 2**—In a RAID 2 configuration, striping is performed at the bit level. RAID 2 configuration is costly, difficult to implement and, therefore, not used in practice.

■ **RAID 3**—In a RAID 3 configuration, striping is performed at the byte level and uses a dedicated parity disk. RAID 3 is not used in practice.

■ **RAID 4**—RAID 4 configurations implement striping at the block level and uses a dedicated parity disk. RAID 4 is not used in practice.

- **RAID 5**—RAID 5 uses block level striping with parity information that is distributed across multiple disks. In the event that a single disk fails, the data on the disk can be recreated based on the data that are stored on the remaining disks.

In addition to the RAID levels detailed above, RAID levels can be combined to gain the benefits of both levels. For example, a RAID 10 (1+0) configuration would be a configuration with mirrored disks, which are then striped. In a RAID 01 (0+1) configuration, a striped data set exists, which is then mirrored.

Summary

An information security practitioner must have a thorough understanding of fundamental risk, response, and recovery concepts. By understanding each of these concepts, you will have the knowledge required to protect your organization and professionally execute your job responsibilities.

Sample Questions

1. Which of the following terms refers to a function of the likelihood of a given threat source's exercising a potential vulnerability, and the resulting impact of that adverse event on the organization?
   a. Threat
   b. Risk
   c. Vulnerability
   d. Asset
2. The process of an authorized user analyzing system security by attempting to exploit vulnerabilities to gain access to systems and data is referred to as:
   a. Vulnerability assessment
   b. Intrusion detection
   c. Risk management
   d. Penetration testing
3. The process for assigning a dollar value to anticipated losses resulting from a threat source successfully exploiting a vulnerability is known as:
   a. Qualitative risk analysis
   b. Risk mitigation
   c. Quantitative risk analysis
   d. Business impact analysis
4. Selecting this type of alternate processing site would be appropriate when an organization needs a low-cost recovery strategy and does not have immediate system recovery requirements.

   a. Cold site
   b. Warm site
   c. Hot site
   d. Mobile site
5. When initially responding to an incident, it is critical that you:
   a. Share information related to the incident with everyone in the organization
   b. Follow organizational incident response procedures
   c. Notify executive management
   d. Restore affected data from backup
6. The type of data backup that only backs up files that have been changed since the last full backup is called:
   a. Full backup
   b. Incremental backup
   c. Partial backup
   d. Differential backup
7. Which RAID level uses block level striping with parity information distributed across multiple disks?
   a. RAID 0
   b. RAID 1
   c. RAID 4
   d. RAID 5
8. Which of the following are threat sources to information technology systems?
   a. Natural threats
   b. Human threats
   c. Environmental threats
   d. All of the above
9. This concept refers to the point in time to which data could be restored in the event of a business disruption:
   a. Recovery time objective
   b. Business impact analysis
   c. Recovery point objective
   d. Maximum tolerable downtime
10. What is the first type of disaster recovery testing that should be performed when initially testing a disaster recovery plan?
   a. Simulation testing
   b. Structured walkthrough testing
   c. Parallel testing
   d. Full interruption testing
11. This concept refers to the magnitude of harm that could be caused by a threat's exercise of a vulnerability:
   a. Vulnerability
   b. Threat

    c. Impact

    d. Risk

12. This expected monetary loss to an organization from a threat to an asset is referred to as:

    a. Single loss expectancy

    b. Asset value

    c. Annualized rate of occurrence

    d. Exposure factor

13. Which risk mitigation strategy would be appropriate if an organization decided to implement additional controls to decrease organizational risk?

    a. Risk avoidance

    b. Risk reduction and limitation

    c. Risk transference

    d. Risk acceptance

14. When documenting evidence chain of custody, which of the following should be documented?

    a. Who handled the evidence since it was obtained

    b. Where the evidence traveled since it was obtained

    c. Why the evidence was handled after it was obtained

    d. All of the above

15. This data backup strategy allows data backup to an offsite location via a WAN or Internet connection:

    a. RAID

    b. Remote journaling

    c. Electronic vaulting

    d. High-availability clustering

16. During which phase of the risk assessment process is technical settings and configuration documented?

    a. Risk determination

    b. Results documentation

    c. System characterization

    d. Control analysis

17. Which type of control is designed to directly control system actions?

    a. Administrative controls

    b. Detective controls

    c. Activity controls

    d. Technical controls

18. During which phase of incident response are the final results of incident response activities documented and communicated to the appropriate parties?

    a. Post-incident activity

    b. Detection and analysis

    c. Containment, eradication, and recovery

    d. Preparation

19. Which of the following is an example of a detective control?
    a. Password constraints
    b. Audit logging
    c. Segregation of duties
    d. Firewall
20. This document documents the steps that should be performed to restore IT functions after a business disruption event:
    a. Critical business functions
    b. Business continuity plan
    c. Disaster recovery plan
    d. Crisis communications plan

Appendix

Questions and Answers

Access Controls

1. Which is of the following is not one of the three principal components of access control systems?
   a. Access control objects
   b. Biometrics
   c. Access control subjects
   d. Access control systems

   The correct answer is b. Answers a, c, and d are the three principal components of an access control system. While biometrics devices are used in some access control systems to confirm an individual's identity, they are not considered to be one of the three principal components of an access control system.

2. Which of the following are behavioral traits in a biometric device?
   a. Voice pattern
   b. Signature dynamics
   c. Keystroke dynamics
   d. All of the above

   The correct answer is d. Voice pattern, signature dynamics, and keystroke dynamics all are behavioral traits in biometric devices.

3. In the measurement of biometric accuracy, which of the following is commonly referred to as a "type 2 error"?
   a. Rate of false acceptance—False Acceptance Rate (FAR)
   b. Rate of false rejection—False Rejection Rate (FRR)

c. Cross-over error rate (CER)

d. All of the above

The correct answer is a. FRR is a type 1 error, FAR is a type 2 error, and CER is the intersection when FRR equals FAR.

4. Which is of the following is not one of the three functional areas of TACACS known as AAA (triple A)?

a. Authentication

b. Authorization

c. Availability

d. Accounting

The correct answer is c. Authentication, authorization, and accounting are the three functional areas of AAA.

5. Which of the following is an International Telecommunications Union— Telecommunications Standardization Sector (ITU-T) recommendation originally issued in 1998 for indirect authentication services using public keys?

a. Radius

b. X.509

c. Kerberos

d. SESAME

The correct answer is b. X.509 is the International Telecommunications Union—Telecommunications Standardization Sector (ITU-T) recommendation originally issued in 1998 for indirect authentication services using public keys.

6. Which of the following is NOT one of the three primary rules in a Biba formal model?

a. An access control subject cannot access an access control object that has a higher integrity level.

b. An access control subject cannot access an access control object that has a lower integrity level.

c. An access control subject cannot modify an access control object that has a higher integrity level.

d. An access control subject cannot request services from an access control object that has a higher integrity level.

The correct answer is a. An access control subject cannot access an access control object that has a "higher" integrity level is not one of the three primary rules in the Biba formal model.

7. Which of the following is an example of a firewall that does not use Context-Based Access Control?

a. Application proxy

b. Static packet filter

c. Stateful inspection

d. Circuit gateway

The correct answer is b. Context-based access control also considers the "state" of the connection, and in a static packet filter no consideration is given to the connection state. Each and every packet is compared to the rule base regardless of whether it had previously been allowed or denied.

8. In consideration of the three basic types of authentication, which of the following is incorrect:

a. Knowledge based = password   c. Required usage of letters, case, numbers, and symbols in the makeup of the password

d. All of the above

The correct answers are a and c. Minimum password length and the required usage of letters, case, numbers, and symbols in the makeup of the password are typical criteria for password selection. Authorizations, rights, and permissions are associated with account creation, not password selection criteria.

11. Which of the following should be considered in the routine monitoring of an access control system?

a. The regular monitoring of changes to accounts can help to mitigate the risk of misuse or unauthorized access.

b. All changes to accounts within the access control system should be logged and reviewed on a regular basis.

c. Particular attention should focus on any newly created accounts as well as any escalation of the privileges for an existing account to make certain that the new account or the increased privileges are authorized.

d. All of the above.

The correct answer is d. All of the above tasks should be considered in the routine monitoring of an access control system.

12. Which of the following is not true in the consideration of Object Groups?

a. It is a common practice to assign the appropriate permissions to a directory, and each object within the directory inherits the respective parent directory permissions.

b. Although configuring individual objects affords maximum control, this granularity can quickly become an administration burden.

c. By incorporating multiple objects with similar permissions or restrictions within a group or directory, the granularity is thereby coarsened and the administration of the access control system is simplified.

d. Configuring individual objects affords maximum control; this granularity can reduce administration burden.

The correct answer is c. Although configuring individual objects affords maximum control, this granularity can quickly become an administration burden.

13. In the three basic types of authentication, which of the following are related to "something you have"?
    a. Synchronous or asynchronous token
    b. Biometric
    c. Smartcard
    d. All of the above
    The correct answers are a and c. Synchronous or asynchronous token and a Smartcard are something you have while a biometric is something you are.

14. Which of the following is an asynchronous device?
    a. Time-based token
    b. Event-based token
    c. All of the above
    The correct answer is b. Event-based tokens are asynchronous as the password is changed with every use and is not based on time. Time-based tokens change their password based on a time interval and are therefore synchronous.

15. Which of the following are characteristics in biometric behavioral-keystroke dynamics?
    a. The length of time each key is held down
    b. Tendencies to switch between a numeric keypad and keyboard numbers
    c. Acceleration, rhythm, pressure, and flow
    d. All of the above
    The correct answers are a and b. The length of time each key is held down and the tendencies to switch between a numeric keypad and keyboard numbers are characteristics of biometric behavioral-keystroke dynamics. Acceleration, rhythm, pressure, and flow are characteristics of signature analysis.

Cryptography

1. Applied against a given block of data, a hash function creates
    a. A chunk of the original block used to ensure its confidentiality
    b. A chunk of the original block used to ensure its integrity
    c. A block of new data used to ensure the original block's confidentiality
    d. A block of new data used to ensure the original block's integrity

The correct answer is d. Applied against a block of data, hash functions generate a hash of the original data that verifies the data has not been modified from its original form.

2. In symmetric key cryptography, each party should use
   a. A previously exchanged secret key
   b. A secret key exchanged with the message
   c. A publicly available key
   d. A randomly generated value unknown to everyone
   The correct answer is a. In symmetric key cryptography, each party must exchange a private key in advance of establishing encrypted communications.

3. Nonrepudiation of a message ensures that
   a. A message is always sent to the intended recipient.
   b. A message is always received by the intended recipient
   c. A message can be attributed to a particular author.
   d. A message can be attributed to a particular recipient.
   The correct answer is c. The idea of nonrepudiation is to link the actions of an individual to those actions with a great deal of certainty.

4. Digital signatures can afford
   a. Confidentiality
   b. Encryption
   c. Nonrepudiation
   d. Checksums
   The correct answer is c. Digital signatures can afford nonrepudiation by comparing the hash generated off of the message and the hash generated off of the digital signature. If they match, the message is from who it is supposed to be from.

5. In Electronic Code Book (ECB) mode, data are encrypted using
   a. A different cipher for every block of a message
   b. The same cipher for every block of a message
   c. A user-generated variable-length cipher for every block of a message
   d. A cipher-based on the previous block of a message
   The correct answer is b. ECB uses the same cipher for each block resulting in identical cyphertext blocks when encrypting identical plaintext blocks.

6. In Cipher Block Chaining (CBC) mode, the key is constructed by
   a. Reusing the previous key in the chain of message blocks
   b. Generating new key material completely at random

c. Modifying the previous block of ciphertext
d. Cycling through a list of user defined choices
The correct answer is c. CBC Xor is the previous block of ciphertext with the current block of plaintext to produce the key used to encrypt the block.

7. Cipher Feedback (CFB) mode allows for data to be
   a. Transmitted and received in a stream
   b. Encrypted in no particular order
   c. Decrypted in no particular order
   d. Authenticated before decryption
   The correct answer is a. CFB's decryption process allows for CFB to perform as a self-synchronizing stream cipher.

8. Stream ciphers are normally selected because of
   a. The high degree of strength behind the encryption algorithms
   b. The high degree of speed behind the encryption algorithms
   c. Their ability to encrypt large chunks of data at a time
   d. Their ability to use large amounts of padding in encryption functions
   The correct answer is b. Stream ciphers tend to be faster than block ciphers while generally being less robust and operating on single bits of information.

9. Asymmetric cryptography uses
   a. One of five modes of operation
   b. Keys of a random or unpredictable length
   c. One single key for all cryptographic operations
   d. One or more pairs of public and private keys
   The correct answer is d. Asymmetric cryptography uses at least one pair of public keys but does not use a mode of operation like in symmetric cryptography.

10. A key escrow service is intended to allow for the reliable
    a. Recovery of inaccessible private keys
    b. Recovery of compromised public keys
    c. Transfer of inaccessible private keys between users
    d. Transfer of compromised public keys between users
    The correct answer is a. Key escrow services are third-party organizations that can provide a customer organization with archived keys should the recovery of the customer organization's encrypted data be required.

11. Cipher-based method authentication code (CMAC) subkeys 1 or 2 is respectively used when

a. The first subkey is a negative multiple of the block length or the second subkey when the message length is a negative multiple of the block length

b. The first subkey is a positive multiple of the block length or the second subkey when the message length is not a positive multiple of the block length

c. The first subkey is not the positive inverse of the block length or the second subkey when the message length is not the negative inverse of the block length

d. The first subkey is the positive inverse of the block length or the second subkey when the message length is the negative inverse of the block length

The correct answer is b. Subkey 1 or 2 is used in CMAC when the first subkey is a positive multiple of the block length or the second subkey when the message length is not a positive multiple of the block length. Subkey 2 pads the message to make it a positive multiple.

12. In Counter with Cipher Block Chaining Message Authentication Code Mode (CCM), choosing the size of the authentication field is a balance of
   a. Message content and availability
   b. Message content and confidentiality
   c. Message size and integrity
   d. Message size and privacy

   The correct answer is c. When choosing the size of the authentication field, the choice is between a small message and one with a high degree of integrity assurance.

13. The correct choice for encrypting the entire original data packet in a tunneled mode for an IPSec solution is
   a. Authentication Header (AH)
   b. Encapsulating Security Payload (ESP)
   c. Point-to-Point Tunneling Protocol (PPTP)
   d. Generic Routing Encapsulation (GRE)

   The correct answer is b. An IPSec solution that uses ESP will encapsulate the entire original data packet when implemented in a tunnel mode.

14. Security concerns with Rivest Cipher 4 (RC4) stem from
   a. The commonly known nonce hashed with the key
   b. A faulty pseudo random number generator
   c. Slow rates of operation in block mode
   d. A weak key schedule

   The correct answer is d. RC4 suffers from a weak key schedule.

15. A significant advantage to selecting a Feistel Cipher for implementation is that
    a. All encryption functions rely on a complex random shuffling of the key schedule before attempting operation.
    b. All decryption functions rely on a complex random shuffling of the key schedule before attempting operation.
    c. The encryption and decryption functions are often the reverse of each other.
    d. An implementer can choose from multiple native stream ciphers.

    The correct answer is c. The biggest advantage to a Feistel-type cipher is that their encryption and decryption functions are often the reverse of each other, thus allowing the size of the required hardware solution to be cut in half.

16. The AES standard fixes the size for a block at
    a. 96 bits
    b. 128 bits
    c. 256 bits
    d. 512 bits

    The correct answer is b. The block size for an AES standard implementation is fixed at 128 bits.

17. When implementing an MD5 solution, what randomizing cryptographic function should be used to help avoid collisions?
    a. Salt
    b. Message pad
    c. Modular addition
    d. Multistring concatenation

    The correct answer is a. A cryptographic Salt is a series of random bits added to a password or passphrase to help avoid a possible hash collision.

18. Key clustering represents the significant failure of an algorithm because
    a. A single key should not generate the same ciphertext from the same plaintext, using the same cipher algorithm.
    b. Two different keys should not generate the same ciphertext from the same plaintext, using the same cipher algorithm.
    c. Two different keys should not generate different ciphertext from the same plaintext, using the same cipher algorithm.
    d. A single key should not generate different ciphertext from the same plaintext, using the same cipher algorithm.

    The correct answer is b. In key clustering, two different keys end up generating the same ciphertext from the same plaintext while using the same cipher algorithm.

19. A related key attack occurs when a cryptanalyst
    a. Exploits impossible differences at some intermediate state of the cipher algorithm
    b. Attempts to use every combination and permutation possible for a given key
    c. Studies a cryptographic function based on the details of its implementation such as, performance, power consumption, and user load
    d. Observes the operation of a working cipher in an effort to understand the mathematic relationships between the encrypted messages

    The correct answer is d. Related key attack requires some degree of knowledge of how two or more keys are related when studying multiple encrypted messages but the goal is to learn sufficient information to break the keys used by furthering that understanding through observation.

20. Elliptical curve cryptography achieves acceptable levels of security with comparably shorter key lengths in asymmetric cryptography through
    a. The algebraic calculation of an elliptical curve over a large but finite field
    b. The algebraic calculation of an elliptical curve over an infinite field
    c. The natural logarithmic calculation of an elliptical curve using noncyclic subgroups
    d. The natural logarithmic calculation of an elliptical curve using cyclic subgroups

    The correct answer is a. ECC uses curves generated through the algebraic calculation of an elliptical curve over a finite field where the larger the curve ends up being, the greater protection it ends up providing.

Malicious Code

1. A blended threat infects legitimate documents within the My Documents directory and sends them to users in the address book of the victim to spread in the wild. This is primarily an example of a security breach of which CIA element?
   a. Confidentiality
   b. Integrity
   c. Availability
   d. None of the above

   The correct answer is a. It can be argued that all of the above apply, but not "None of the above." Most malicious codes impact some levels of each element of the CIA triangle. However, the best answer is Confidentiality since personal documents are being sent to others by the malcode. Obviously integrity has been compromised via a blended attack, and availability may be a factor if the mass mailing component is resource intensive. With the information provided, the sharing of the documents is the primary element of concern to the CIA triangle.

2. What is the name of the international malcode naming standard used by all antivirus vendors today?
   a. Common Malware Enumeration (CME)
   b. Computer Antivirus Research Organization (CARO)
   c. VGrep
   d. None of the above

   The correct answer is d. There is no international standard for the naming of malcode. Most companies loosely follow CARO standards put forth in the early 1990s. CME was an attempt to cross-correlate names with a unique identifier that lost funding, and is limited in scope and impact today. VGrep is used to cross-correlate malcode names assigned by vendors.

3. "VBS" is used in the beginning of most antivirus vendors to represent what component of the CARO general-structure?
   a. Modifier
   b. Suffix
   c. Platform
   d. Family

   The correct answer is c. VBS is short for Visual Basic Script and is a prefix commonly associated with VBS threats. The general structure of CARO as presented in this chapter is Platform.Type.Family_Name.Variant[:Modifier]@ Suffix.

4. W32.Rispif.AB is what variant of this malcode?
   a. Rispif
   b. A
   c. B
   d. AB

   The correct answer is d. The variant is commonly the last element added to a malcode name, AB in this example.

5. W32.Sober.O@mm spreads through what primary vector, according to Symantec naming conventions?
   a. Mass Mailer
   b. Windows 3.X
   c. Windows 95/98/ME
   d. Windows 32-bit

   The correct answer is a. Symantec uses the @SUFFIX mailing convention to identify how malcode spreads. In this case the suffix is @mm, which stands for mass mailer. The other three answers are specific to the platform, not to how the malcode spreads.

6. A SysAdmin discovers an antivirus message indicating detection and removal of Backdoor.win32.Agent.ich. What should the SysAdmin do to monitor to the threat?
   a. Use rootkit detection software on the host
   b. Update antivirus signature files
   c. Run a full host scan
   d. Monitor egress traffic from the computer

   The correct answer is d. The CARO name indicates that this is a backdoor Trojan. Backdoor Trojans provide attackers with remote access to the computer. Monitoring of network communications is critical in identifying egress communications related to the Trojan. Installation or use of various rootkit or antivirus solutions is not helpful in monitoring the threat. Additionally, antivirus has already detected the threat on the system.

7. Antivirus software detects malcode on a computer. Why would a SysAdmin want to perform additional antivirus scans on the infected host using different antivirus software?
   a. To locate additional threats that may exist, not detected by the host antivirus
   b. To identify a second antivirus vendor name for the code
   c. To identify and remove any threats found on the system
   d. None of the above

   The correct answer is a. No single antivirus program does it all, requiring that more than one be used to identify other threats that may be undetected on the infected host. For this reason, most incident responders use a host of tools, anti-rootkit tools, and antivirus programs to scan hostile files and infected systems. Identifying a second antivirus name for code is not meaningful and can be done more easily with a multiscanner submission of the quarantined code from the first scanner detection. Relying on antivirus software to mitigate a threat is foolish once integrity has been compromised on a computer.

8. Which of the following assists an analyst in cross-correlating malcode samples by name?
   a. VGrep
   b. Public Multiscanners
   c. CME
   d. All of the above

   The correct answer is d. All of the above tools are useful in cross-correlating samples by name. VGrep is a search tool for identifying names assigned to the same binary sample. Public multiscanners report signature names for a binary. CME includes known names for a binary but is largely a discontinued effort by 2008.

9. Malcode that infects existing files on a computer to spread are called what?
   a. Trojans
   b. Viruses
   c. Worms
   d. Rootkit

   The correct answer is b. Viruses require a host file to infect. Trojans do not replicate but masquerade as something legitimate. Worms create copies of themselves as they spread. Rootkits are used for stealth to increase survivability in the wild.

10. A Trojan that executes a destructive payload when certain conditions are met is called what?
   a. Keylogger
   b. Data Diddler
   c. Logic Bomb
   d. None of the above

   The correct answer is c. Keyloggers are not destructive but merely steal keystrokes on a system. Data diddler is defined online by Virus Bulletin as a destructive overwriting Trojan, but it does not have a "time" or conditional component to when the payload is executed like that of a logic bomb.

11. Where does a cavity virus infect a file with malcode?
   a. Prepends Code
   b. Appends Code
   c. Injects Code
   d. None of the above

   The correct answer is c. Cavity viruses inject code into various locations of a file. Prepend is to put code before the body of a file. Append is to put code following the body of a file.

12. What is the family name of the first Macro virus discovered in the wild in 1995?
   a. Concept
   b. AntiCMOS
   c. Melissa
   d. Bablas

   The correct answer is a. Concept is the first Macro virus in the wild. AntiCMOS is not a Macro virus. Melissa and Bablas came long after the emergence of Macro viruses in the wild.

13. Mebroot is unique because it modifies what component of a computer to load on system startup?
   a. Windows registry keys
   b. Startup folder

c. MBR

d. Kernel

The correct answer is c. Mebroot is a kernel-level rootkit that modifies the Master Boot Record to load before the operating system even runs in memory. Modifications to the Windows registry keys and startup folder are not unique, used by many codes to load with the operating system.

14. SYS and VXD hostile codes are commonly associated with what type of threat?

a. Trojans

b. Worms

c. Userland Rootkits

d. Kernel Rootkits

The correct answer is d. Kernel-level rootkits normally have SYS and VXD filenames. Userland rootkits are typically a DLL extension. Trojans and Worms are general classifications for malcode that are not as specific as the answer Kernel rootkits.

15. A PUP refers to software that may include what?

a. EULA

b. Monitoring

c. Capture Sensitive Data

d. All of the above

The correct answer is d. PUP is short for Potentially Unwanted Program. This is technically legal software that includes an End User License Agreement (EULA) but may monitor or capture sensitive data.

16. What is the name of the first highly destructive malcode designed to activate a payload on Friday the 13th?

a. Jerusalem

b. Lehigh

c. Internet Worm

d. Cascade

The correct answer is a. Jerusalem first emerged in the wild in 1987 and infected COM and EXE files with a destructive payload for Friday the 13th. The other examples are also early malcode examples but do not have a Friday the 13th specific payload.

17. Onel de Guzman is known to be one of the authors for ILoveYou who could not be prosecuted for his crimes because he lived in a country without laws prohibiting his behavior. What is the name of his country of residency?

a. Indonesia

b. Philippines

   c. United Kingdom

   d. Germany

The correct answer is b. He lived in the Philippines. Shortly after this fiasco, laws were changed in the country to prohibit such behavior. This situation increased awareness and changed the legal landscape globally for other countries.

18. Social engineering refers to what?
    a. Social networking sites like MySpace and Facebook
    b. Individuals who study the behavior and actions of specific people groups
    c. Training techniques useful in a corporate environment
    d. Techniques and communication strategies for deceiving people

    The correct answer is d. It is a big term for how to trick people, such as make them click on an e-mail attachment.

19. What is an example of rogue security software?
    a. Antivirus Pro
    b. AntiVir
    c. VirusTotal
    d. GREM

    The correct answer is a. Antivirus Pro is one of the examples provided in this text as rogue software. AntiVir and GREM are both legitimate antivirus programs. VirusTotal is a multiscanner.

20. What is one of the most common types of DDoS attacks that take place on the Internet today?
    a. Teardrop
    b. Naptha
    c. TCP SYN
    d. Smurf

    The correct answer is c. TCP SYN attacks are the most common by far and first to be mentioned of DDoS types in this chapter.

21. To evade detection by SysAdmins, malcode typically uses what TCP port in 2008 for remote C&C communications?
    a. 80
    b. 443
    c. 6667
    d. 65000

    The correct answer is a. TCP port 80 is used for legitimate Web traffic and is difficult to monitor for malicious traffic.

22. "0.0.0.0 avp.ch" is a string found within a Trojan binary, indicating that it likely performs what changes to a system upon infection?
    a. Communicates with a remote C&C at avp.ch
    b. Contains a logic bomb that activates immediately
    c. Modifies the HOSTS file to prevent access to avp.ch
    d. Downloads code from avp.ch
    The correct answer is c. The structure of the string is that of a HOSTS file, indicating that it likely modifies the HOSTS file on the computer. Additionally, AVP.CH is a known antivirus Web site used in a HOSTS file modification example in this chapter.

23. Which of the following programs is useful in identifying common modifications made to the Windows registry by malcode?
    a. Autoruns
    b. FPort
    c. Filemon
    d. PeID
    The correct answer is a. Autoruns is the only program in the options above that includes information about the Windows registry. FPort is used to monitor processes and ports. Filemon monitors file activity. PeID is used to identify file information.

24. What does it mean when a SysAdmin does not see explorer.exe in the Windows Task Manager on a host machine?
    a. It is normal for explorer.exe to not appear in Windows Task Manager.
    b. Explorer.exe is likely injected and hidden by a Windows rootkit.
    c. Explorer.exe does not need to be visible if svchost.exe is visible.
    d. Internet Explorer is open and running in memory.
    The correct answer is b. Explorer.exe is Windows and should always be visible within the Windows Task Manager. If it is not visible, a Windows rootkit is likely concealing the process after having injected into it.

25. If a SysAdmin attempts to analyze code within VMware and nothing executes, what might be the next steps to further analyze the code?
    a. Modify advanced settings of VMware to disable hardware acceleration and similar components and execute the code again.
    b. Run the malcode in a native test environment to see if it is anti-VMware.
    c. Submit the code to an online sandbox scanner to compare behavioral results.
    d. All of the above.
    The correct answer is d. All of the above examples are great next steps in dealing with code that may be corrupt or anti-VMware.

Monitoring and Analysis

1. A security audit is best defined as
   a. A covert series of tests designed to test network authentication, hosts, and perimeter security
   b. A technical assessment that measures how well an organization uses strategic security policies and tactical security controls for protecting its information assets
   c. Employing Intrusion Detection Systems (IDs) to monitor anomalous traffic on a network segment and logging attempted break-ins
   d. Hardening systems before deploying them on the corporate network

   The correct answer is b. Answer a is a good example of a type of security audit, but does not answer the question of what a security audit is. Answer c is a good example of a type of security audit, but does not answer the question of what a security audit is. Answer d is a security control check used to harden a host against vulnerabilities.

2. Why is it important for organizations to have a security framework?
   a. To show that the organization has exercised "due care"
   b. So they can adhere to regulations developed by an institutional or governmental body
   c. To avoid possible legal action or financial penalties
   d. All of the above

   The correct answer is d. Having a security framework shows that the organization has exercised "due care" and cares about mitigating security risks. "Organizations will often incorporate the security guidelines and standards published by policy development organizations or regulatory bodies which dictate requirements for the purpose of standardizing their security framework to harmonize with 'accepted' or required practices."

3. Creating incident response policies for an organization would be an example of an
   a. Administrative control
   b. Technical control
   c. Physical control
   d. Logical control

   The correct answer is a. Administrative controls are "managerial" and are a part of corporate security policy. Technical controls (b) implement specific technologies. A policy would not constitute a specific technological process. Physical controls (c) constitute elements such as Closed Caption Television (CCTV), padlocks, or any other physical barrier or device to bar access. Logical control is a fictitious term.

4. Which of the following would be a good example of a host isolation security control?
   a. Encrypting syslog activity on the network
   b. Applying the most recent patches to a system
   c. Installing antivirus on a local machine
   d. Setting up a DMZ between the public and private network (This would provide protection for internal hosts when communicating with untrusted networks.)

   The correct answer is d. Setting up a DMZ between the public and private network would provide protection for internal hosts when communicating with untrusted networks. Answer a is an example of a monitoring control check. Answer b is an example of a patching or system hardening check. Answer c deals with mitigating threats such as worms or viruses.

5. What is the most important reason to analyze event logs from multiple sources?
   a. They will help you obtain a more complete picture of what is happening on your network and how you go about addressing the problem
   b. The log server could have been compromised
   c. Because you cannot trust automated scripts to capture everything
   d. To prosecute the attacker once he can be traced

   The correct answer is a. By analyzing various logs sources, it is possible to piece together a timeline of events and user activity. Answer b is partially correct, but not the most fitting answer. This is only a small picture of what the attacker could have done. c may be true, but again is not the most important reason. This answer is meant to distract. d may apply in some cases, but this is not the primary goal of correlating event logs.

6. Security testing does not include which of the following activities?
   a. Performing a port scan to check for up-and-running services (This is part of security testing. Using a network mapping technique such as nmap will reveal security holes.)
   b. Gathering publicly available information
   c. Counterattacking systems determined to be hostile
   d. Posing as technical support to gain unauthorized information

   The correct answer is c. Counterattacking systems determined to be hostile is never something an organization wants to do, and does not constitute security testing. Answer b can involve "googling" an organization to determine information for future attacks. Answer c is never something an organization wants to do, and does not constitute security testing. Answer d is an example of social engineering and part of an organizations security.

7. Why is system fingerprinting part of the security testing process?
   a. Because it is one of the easiest things to determine when performing a security test
   b. It shows what vulnerabilities the system may be subject to
   c. It shows the auditor whether a system has been hardened
   d. It tells an attacker that a system is automatically insecure

   The correct answer is b. Some versions of an OS or software may be vulnerable, and this information is useful to an attacker. Answer a may or may not be true depending on the system, and is not a reason to determine the OS or other system details. Answer c is true, but it does not answer why system fingerprinting is part of the security testing process. Answer d is not true. Just because a machine is running a particular OS, for example, does not mean it has not been updated and patched to prevent certain vulnerabilities.

8. What is the difference between vulnerability and penetration testing?
   a. Vulnerability testing attempts to exploit a weakness found from penetration testing.
   b. Penetration testing attempts to exploit a weakness found in vulnerability testing.
   c. Vulnerability testing uses scripts to find weaknesses while penetration testing uses a GUI-based program.
   d. Penetration testing is used to uncover vulnerabilities without harming the system.

   The correct answer is d. This is not the situation in all cases. In some cases, testers want to gain the attention of management by showing the possible harm a security breach can cause. Answer a is incorrect. It should be the other way around. Answer c is untrue as both can use either scripts or a graphical tool.

9. The following are benefits to performing vulnerability testing except
   a. They allow an organization to study the security posture of the organization.
   b. They identify and prioritize mitigation activities.
   c. They can compare security postures over a period of time when done consistently.
   d. It has the potential to crash the network or host.

   The correct answer is d. Sometimes innocent tests have the ability to crash a system, and thus this answer would be a disadvantage. Answer a is true as vulnerability testing will give a picture of how secure the network is at a point in time. Answer b is true as systems can be ranked according to how vulnerable they are. Answer d is true because a vulnerability test is a snapshot in time. Many snapshots over a period of time will give a good overall picture of security postures.

10. What is the primary purpose of testing an Intrusion Detection System?
    a. To observe that the IDS is observing and logging an appropriate response to a suspicious activity
    b. To determine if the IDS is capable of discarding suspect packets
    c. To analyze processor utilization to verify whether hardware upgrades are necessary
    d. To test whether the IDS can log every possible event on the network

    The correct answer is a. The primary purpose of an IDS is to detect known attacks or anomalous activity. Answer b would fall more along the line of an Intrusion Prevention System or a firewall. Answer c is not correct because CPU utilization is not the primary concern of an IDS, but rather load balancing or bandwidth limiting. Answer d is an unrealistic and storage-consuming goal unrelated to the primary purpose of an IDS.

11. Which of the following is true regarding computer intrusions?
    a. Covert attacks such as a Distributed Denial of Service (DDOS) attack harm public opinion of an organization.
    b. Overt attacks are easier to defend against because they can be readily identified.
    c. Network Intrusion Detection Systems (NIDS) help mitigate computer intrusions by notifying personnel in real-time.
    d. Covert attacks are less effective because they take more time to accomplish.

    The correct answer is c. NIDS can monitor data in real-time and notify appropriate personnel. Answer a, a DDOS attack, is an example of an overt attack. Answer b is not true, as overt attacks can be just as complex and hard to defend against as covert attacks. Answer d is certainly not true. A waiter can steal a credit card number just as fast as any overt method.

12. The main difference in real-time vs. non–real-time monitoring is
    a. Non–real-time monitoring is not as effective as real-time monitoring.
    b. Real-time monitoring provides a way to immediately identify disallowed behavior, while non–real-time monitoring can be used to trace an attacker's activity.
    c. Non–real-time monitoring is more effective in catching overt activity.
    d. Real-time monitoring is more effective in catching covert activity.

    The correct answer is b. Real-time is concerned more with immediate discovery while non–real-time is more concerned with data preservation. Answer a is false because both are effective in capturing network or system data. Answer c is false because neither is better than the other at catching overt or covert activity. Answer d is false because neither is better than the other at catching overt or covert activity.

13. Why is security monitoring necessary?
    a. Because logging activity can show the steps an attacker used to modify or gain access to a system
    b. Log files can be correlated to form a timeline of events to be used in a forensic investigation
    c. Log files can show deviance from a security policy
    d. All of the above

    The correct answer is d. All of the above are reasons to maintain system logs and monitor activity. Answer a is true because logs can show what files or systems an attacker used in the process of "escalating privilege" or compromising a system. Answer b is true because log times can be pieced together to form a timeline that will help investigators. Answer c is true because if security policy or access rights are changed, a log file can show evidence of this.

14. NIDS and HIDS generally employ the following techniques except
    a. Using a database of known attack signatures and comparing that to current traffic flow
    b. Analyzing traffic flow to determine unusual activity
    c. Monitoring for specific file changes by referencing known good file sets
    d. Counterattacking a system to cut off communication and prevent possible damage

    The correct answer is d. Counterattacking is not the goal of any NIDS or HIDS. Answer a is widely used by NIDS and HIDS, known as misuse detection. Answer b is the technique of anomaly detection used by some NIDS and HIDS. Answer c is the technique of anomaly detection used by some NIDS and HIDS.

15. Why are secure methods of logging system or device data important?
    a. The hosts storing the log files are often easily compromised
    b. Common transport methods of log files are insecure and can be easily sniffed
    c. Unencrypted and unprotected log files are easily altered
    d. Both b and c

    The correct answer is d. Both b and c show how insecure data can be used by an attacker. Answer a is false because system storing the data has nothing to do with security holes. The system may quite likely be hardened. Answer b is false because syslog is a common device logger that sends data over an insecure UDP protocol. Answer c is false because attackers can easily alter data if the log file is unencrypted or file permissions are set improperly.

Networks and Telecommunications

1. Match the topology with the appropriate description and vulnerabilities.
    1. Star
    2. Bus
    3. Ring
    4. Point to point
    a. In its most basic setup, the traffic flows in one direction. A break in the link and all traffic flow is severely limited.
    b. One of the more secure topologies due to the limited opportunities to intercept the traffic.
    c. The type of topology used in older networks or by cable companies. It is easy to listen to all of the traffic being broadcast on the wire.
    d. If the center point fails or is compromised, the traffic can be completely stopped.
       The correct answers are 1–d, 2–c, 3–a, and 4–b.

2. Match the following protocols with their descriptions:
    1. SMTP
    2. ICMP
    3. TFTP
    4. DHCP
    a. This protocol is used as an unauthenticated protocol to transfer data.
    b. This protocol is used between two mail servers to determine how they will communicate.
    c. This protocol is used to transmit the health and status of a network.
    d. This protocol is used in assigning IP addresses, default gateways, and DNS information.
       The correct answers are 1–b, 2–c, 3–a, and 4–d.

3. True or False: It is not important to look at the syslog files because they are being backed up and can be reviewed at any time.
       Answer: False. It is very important to look at all of your log files. These files are the keys for how you understand what is happening to your network.

4. Choose the best description for the following protocols:
    1. SSL
    2. IPSEC AH
    3. IPSEC ESP
    4. NAT
    a. Message confidentiality is provided by encrypting the payload.
    b. Originally designed to compensate for a decreased number of IP addresses; has been used for security purpose of hiding IP addresses.

    c. Message integrity is performed by authenticating the payload and the origin of the information.

    d. Operates at the session layer and is often used with Digital Certificates.
    The correct answers are 1–d, 2–c, 3–a, and 4–b.

5. Which of these protocols is not normally used to help make E-Mail more secure?

    a. PGP

    b. S/MIME

    c. PEM

    d. MSP

    e. SNMP

    The correct answer is e. Simple Network Management Protocol is used for network monitoring and management while the other protocols are often used to help make e-mail more secure.

6. Match the network equipment with its most common PRIMARY function:

    1. Firewall

    2. Router

    3. Switches

    4. VPN Termination Points

    a. Will pass traffic from one network to another network based on IP address

    b. Will pass traffic to the appropriate network segment based on the MAC address

    c. Enforced access control policy at given points of the network

    d. Terminates encrypted communications and forwards them to the internal network

    The correct answers are 1–c, 2–a, 3–b, and 4–d. There can be some reference made that some switches can route traffic based on IP address; some routers and firewalls can terminate VPN connections; and firewalls, routers, and VPNs can often pass traffic to host on the directly connected network via their MAC address. The idea was to understand and define the primary functionality of these devices.

7. Choose the descriptions and benefits/risks that best match the following remote access solutions:

    1. RAS

    2. VPN

    3. Clientless VPN

    a. Allows the user to access the network without necessarily having to have his own device with him. Using a third-party device might increase the network vulnerability by the use of hidden Trojans or keystroke monitoring tools.

   b. Does not require Internet access and can be secured by other means like two-factor authentication; is not easily sniffed. Usually requires a large phone bank to receive calls, can be expensive for long distance bills, and subject to discovery by War dialing.

   c. Allows for the user to have a strong means of authentication and verification. Often requires the IT department to touch and maintain every device, and the device is required to connect to the network.

   The correct answers are 1–b, 2–c, and 3–a.

8. Choose which of the following actions will help secure a wireless access point:
   a. Choosing WPA2 over WEP
   b. Hiding the SSID
   c. Activate MAC address filtering
   d. Having an access control technology with authentication capability built into the device or having this access control product immediately behind the access point
   e. All of the above
   The correct answer is e.

9. Which of the following is true?
   a. Full-mesh topology is less expensive to deploy than other topologies.
   b. Full-mesh topology is just as expensive to deploy as other topologies.
   c. Full-mesh topology is typically used in local area networks.
   d. Full-mesh topology is the less fault tolerant than other topologies.
   e. None of the above is true.
   The correct answer is e.

10. Which of the following is typically deployed as a screening proxy for Web servers?
   a. State inspect firewalls
   b. Packet filters
   c. Reverse proxies
   d. Intrusion prevention devices
   e. Kernel proxy
   The correct answer is c.

11. Which of the following 802.11 specifications support MIMO?
   a. 802.11b
   b. 802.11n
   c. 802.11g
   d. 802.11a
   e. 802.11h
   The correct answer is b.

12. Which of these attacks use an intentionally malformed packet to cause DoS?
    a. LAND
    b. SYN Flood
    c. Session Hijacking
    d. Redirection
    e. Port Scan
    The correct answer is a.

13. Which of these is not true?
    a. MPLS differs from ATM in that it supports IP natively
    b. MPLS supports both cell- and frame-based traffic
    c. MPLS is packet switching technology
    d. MPLS is an OSI Layer 4 technology
    e. MPLS is expected to gain popularity
    The correct answer is d.

14. What is the difference between DRM and IRM?
    a. DRM is completely supported by common law.
    b. DRM's best feature is its interoperability.
    c. IRM is intended to be used on multimedia only.
    d. IRM generally refers to DRM for enterprise content.
    The correct answer is d. IRM is intentionally intended to separate the copyright protection controversy that persists with DRM for corporate content.

15. True or False: IRM technologies strictly deal with the encryption of protected content.
    The correct answer is False. IRM technologies use a variety of technologies, including metadata tagging and watermarking.

16. Which of the following is true?
    a. NAT "hides" private IP addresses behind a single public IP address.
    b. PAT "hides" private IP addresses behind a single public IP address.
    c. NAT and PAT cannot be used simultaneously.
    d. None are true.
    The correct answer is b. Port Address Translation maps requests for a public IP address using IP ports and is the most commonly used address translation scheme due to its use of a smaller number of IP addresses.

17. Select the most correct statement:
    a. Derivative copies of content of documents are best prevented by using metadata tagging.
    b. Derivative copies of content of documents are best prevented by using file-level rights.

   c. Derivative copies of content of documents are best prevented by using encryption and IRM technologies.

   d. None are true.

   The correct answer is c. Derivative copies of documents (cut and paste of content) can only be done using a combination of technologies, including encryption.

18. True or False: Disabling of IM should be part of routine operations in an enterprise.

   The correct answer is False. The suitability of IM should be weighed as part of an overall risk management process balancing the benefits of enhanced collaboration with threats introduce by IM service.

19. What is the primary advantage of a fully meshed network?

   a. It has the lowest operating cost to the end customer.

   b. It has the highest operating cost to the end customer.

   c. It has the lowest fault tolerance.

   d. It has the highest fault tolerance.

   The correct answer is d. A fully meshed network has the highest fault tolerance but also has the burden of the highest operating cost.

20. Which of the following is a common network configuration error?

   a. Using Telnet instead of SSH

   b. Leaving default, factory settings

   c. Copying and using "sample" configurations from technical support Web sites

   d. All of the above

   The correct answer is d. Network and security practitioners should be on the "look out" for poor configuration habits that lead to serious vulnerabilities.

Risk, Response, and Recovery

1. Which of the following terms refers to a function of the likelihood of a given threat source exercising a potential vulnerability, and the resulting impact of that adverse event on the organization?

   a. Threat

   b. Risk

   c. Vulnerability

   d. Asset

   The correct answer is b. A threat (a) is the potential for a threat source to exercise (accidentally trigger or intentionally exploit) a specific vulnerability.

A vulnerability (c) is a flaw or weakness in system security procedures, design, implementation, or internal controls that could be exercised (accidentally triggered or intentionally exploited) and result in a security breach or a violation of the system's security policy. An asset (d) is anything of value that is owned by an organization.

2. The process of an authorized user analyzing system security by attempting to exploit vulnerabilities to gain access to systems and data is referred to as
   a. Vulnerability assessment
   b. Intrusion detection
   c. Risk management
   d. Penetration testing
   The correct answer is d. Vulnerability assessments (a) only attempt to determine if vulnerabilities exist but do not attempt to actively exploit identified vulnerabilities. Intrusion detection (b) is an automated technique for identifying active intrusion attempts. Risk management (c) is the process of assessing and mitigating risk.

3. The process for assigning a dollar value to anticipated losses resulting from a threat source successfully exploiting a vulnerability is known as
   a. Qualitative risk analysis
   b. Risk mitigation
   c. Quantitative risk analysis
   d. Business impact analysis
   The correct answer is c. A qualitative risk analysis (a) assesses impact in relative terms such as high, medium, and low impact without assigning a dollar value. Risk mitigation (b) describes a process of applying risk mitigation strategies to reduce risk exposure to levels that are acceptable to the organization. A business impact analysis (d) assesses financial and nonfinancial impacts to an organization that would result from a business disruption.

4. Selecting this type of alternate processing site would be appropriate when an organization needs a low-cost recovery strategy and does not have immediate system recovery requirements:
   a. Cold site
   b. Warm site
   c. Hot site
   d. Mobile site
   The correct answer is a. A cold site is the lowest cost type of alternative processing site. The warm site, hot site, and mobile site are all higher-cost solutions that support quicker recovery requirements.

5. When initially responding to an incident, it is critical that you
   a. Share information related to the incident with everyone in the organization.
   b. Follow organizational incident response procedures.
   c. Notify executive management.
   d. Restore affected data from backup.

   The correct answer is b. You should always follow the organization's incident response policy when responding to an incident. Information related to the incident should only be shared on a need-to-know basis. Many types of incidents will not require notification to executive management. The incident response policy and procedure should define when notification to executive management is required. Data restoration should not be performed until forensic analyses and evidence gathering is complete.

6. The type of data backup that only backs up files that have been changed since the last full backup is called
   a. Full backup
   b. Incremental backup
   c. Partial backup
   d. Differential backup

   The correct answer is d. In a full backup (a), the entire system is copied to backup media. Incremental backups (b) record changes from the previous day or previous incremental backup. A partial backup (c) is not a widely accepted backup type.

7. Which RAID level uses block-level striping with parity information distributed across multiple disks?
   a. RAID 0
   b. RAID 1
   c. RAID 4
   d. RAID 5

   The correct answer is d. RAID 0 stripes data across multiple disks but no parity information is included. RAID 1 uses mirroring to store identical copies of data on multiple disks. RAID 4 implements striping at the block level and uses a dedicated parity disk. RAID 4 is not used in practice.

8. Which of the following are threat sources to information technology systems?
   a. Natural threats
   b. Human threats
   c. Environmental threats
   d. All of the above

   The correct answer is d. Natural threats, human threats, and environmental threats are all threat sources to information technology systems.

9. This concept refers to the point in time to which data could be restored in the event of a business disruption:
   a. Recovery time objective
   b. Business impact analysis
   c. Recovery point objective
   d. Maximum tolerable downtime

   The correct answer is c. The recovery time objective (a) indicates the period of time within which a business function or information technology system must be restored after a business disruption. A business impact analysis (b) assesses financial and nonfinancial impacts to an organization that would result from a business disruption. Maximum tolerable downtime (d) is the maximum amount of time that a business function can be unavailable before an organization is harmed to the degree that puts the survivability of the organization at risk.

10. What is the first type of disaster recovery testing that should be performed when initially testing a disaster recovery plan?
    a. Simulation testing
    b. Structured walkthrough testing
    c. Parallel testing
    d. Full interruption testing

    The correct answer is b. Simulation testing (a) simulates an actual disaster and is a more in-depth testing approach than structured walkthrough testing. Parallel testing (c) uses testing performed at alternate data processing sites. This test involves significant cost to the organization and should not be performed before structured walkthrough testing. Full interruption testing (d) requires that business operations are actually interrupted at the primary processing facility.

11. This concept refers to the magnitude of harm that could be caused by a threat's exercise of a vulnerability:
    a. Vulnerability
    b. Threat
    c. Impact
    d. Risk

    The correct answer is c. A vulnerability (a) is a flaw or weakness that could be exercised and result in a security breach or a violation of the system's security policy. A threat (b) is the potential for a threat source to exercise a specific vulnerability. A risk (d) is a function of the likelihood of a given threat source exercising a potential vulnerability, and the resulting impact of the adverse event to the organization.

12. This expected monetary loss to an organization from a threat to an asset is referred to as
    a. Single loss expectancy
    b. Asset value
    c. Annualized rate of occurrence
    d. Exposure factor

    The correct answer is a. Asset value (b) is the value of a specific asset to the organization. Annualized rate of occurrence (c) represents the expected number of occurrences of a specific threat to an asset in a given year. Exposure factor (d) represents the portion of an asset that would be lost if a risk to the asset was realized.

13. Which risk-mitigation strategy would be appropriate if an organization decided to implement additional controls to decrease organizational risk?
    a. Risk avoidance
    b. Risk reduction and limitation
    c. Risk transference
    d. Risk acceptance

    The correct answer is b. Risk avoidance (a) is a strategy that is used to reduce risk by avoiding risky behaviors. Risk transference (c) is a strategy to transfer risk from the organization to a third party by methods such as insurance or outsourcing. Risk acceptance (d) is a strategy in which the organization decides to accept the risk associated with the potential occurrence of a specific event.

14. When documenting evidence chain of custody, which of the following should be documented?
    a. Who handled the evidence since it was obtained
    b. Where the evidence traveled since it was obtained
    c. Why the evidence was handled after it was obtained
    d. All of the above

    The correct answer is d. Who handled the evidence, why the evidence was handled, and where the evidence traveled should all be documented when creating and maintaining a chain of custody.

15. This data backup strategy allows data backup to an offsite location via a WAN or Internet connection:
    a. RAID
    b. Remote journaling
    c. Electronic vaulting
    d. High-availability clustering

The correct answer is c. RAID (a) refers to a method for writing data across multiple disks to provide redundancy or improve performance. Remote journaling (b) transfers journals and database transaction logs electronically to an offsite location. High-availability clustering (d) uses multiple systems to reduce the risk associated with a single point of failure.

16. During which phase of the risk assessment process is technical settings and configuration documented?
    a. Risk determination
    b. Results documentation
    c. System characterization
    d. Control analysis

    The correct answer is c. In the risk determination phase (a), overall risk to an IT system is assessed. During the results documentation phase (b), results of the risk assessment are documented. In the control analysis phase (d), controls are assessed to evaluate their effectiveness.

17. Which type of control is designed to directly control system actions?
    a. Administrative controls
    b. Detective controls
    c. Activity controls
    d. Technical controls

    The correct answer is d. Administrative controls (a) are controls such as policies, procedures, and guidelines that dictate how activities should be performed. Detective controls (b) are used to detect actual or attempted violations of system security. Activity controls (c) are not a control type as documented within this section.

18. During which phase of incident response are the final results of incident response activities documented and communicated to the appropriate parties?
    a. Postincident activity
    b. Detection and analysis
    c. Containment, eradication, and recovery
    d. Preparation

    The correct answer is a. During the detection and analysis phase (b), security incidents are initially identified and analyzed to determine if an actual incident has occurred. During the containment, eradication, and recovery phase (c), security incidents are contained, corrected, and systems are restored to normal operations. During the preparation phase (d), incident response policies and procedures are documented and training is provided to enable the incident response team to be prepared to respond to an incident.

19. Which of the following is an example of a detective control?
    a. Password constraints
    b. Audit logging
    c. Segregation of duties
    d. Firewall

    The correct answer is b. Password constraints (a) prevent unauthorized access to systems and applications. Segregation of duties (c) prevents fraud by requiring more than a single person to perform a task. Firewalls (d) prevent unauthorized communications between systems and networks.

20. This document documents the steps that should be performed to restore IT functions after a business disruption event:
    a. Critical business functions
    b. Business continuity plan
    c. Disaster recovery plan
    d. Crisis communications plan

    The correct answer is c. Critical business functions (a) are functions that are integral to the success of an organization, without which the organization is incapable of operating. Business continuity plans (b) focus on the continuity and recovery of critical business functions during and after disaster. A crisis communications plan (d) details how organizations will communicate internally and externally during a disaster situation.

Security Operations and Administration

1. Security awareness training aims to educate users on:
    a. The work performed by the information security organization
    b. How attackers defeat security safeguards
    c. What they can do to maintain the organization's security posture
    d. How to secure their home computer systems

    The correct answer is c. The aim of security awareness is to make the organization more resistant to security vulnerabilities and therefore maintain the organization's security posture.

2. The following are operational aspects of configuration management (CM):
    a. Documentation, control, accounting, and auditing
    b. Identification, control, accounting, and auditing
    c. Identification, documentation, control, and auditing
    d. Control, accounting, auditing, and reporting

The correct answer is b. Configuration management begins with identification of the baseline configuration as one or more configuration items within the configuration management database (CMDB). Once the baseline is established, all changes are controlled throughout the lifecycle of the component. Each change is accounted for by capturing, tracking, and reporting on change requests, configurations, and change history. Finally, auditing insures integrity by verifying that the actual configuration matches the information captured and tracked in the CMDB and that all changes have been appropriately recorded and tracked.

3. An access control model that supports assignment of privileges based on job function is called
   a. Discretionary Access Control
   b. Distributed Access Control
   c. Role-Based Access Control
   d. Mandatory Access Control

   The correct answer is c. Role-based access control associates each role or function within the organization with a set of access privileges. Discretionary access control assigns users and groups certain privileges based on associations made by the administrator or owner of the target object. Mandatory access control determines access privileges based on the intersection of an object's sensitivity level and the subject's clearance level. Distributed access control is not a model per se, but may be used to describe any system in which the access control rules follow instances of an object.

4. The security management cycle described by ISO/IEC 27002 contains the steps
   a. Plan, Check, Document, Act
   b. Document, Plan, Act, Check
   c. Plan, Organize, Check, Act
   d. Plan, Do, Check, Act

   The correct answer is d. The PDCA cycle is iterative, but always begins with planning or establishing scope and selecting controls as part of a risk treatment plan. The plan is then implemented and controls are operated (Do), measured against the plan (Check) for effectiveness, and then analyzed to determine variances and correct deficiencies (Act).

5. The systems certification process can best be described as a
   a. Method of testing a system to assure that vulnerabilities have been addressed
   b. Means of documenting adherence to security standards
   c. Process for obtaining stakeholder signoff on system configuration
   d. Method of validating adherence to security requirements

   The correct answer is d. Certification reviews the system against the requirements specified in the system security plan to ensure that all required control specifications are met. Answer a is incorrect because while the process may include vulnerability testing, this is only one component of the process and residual risks do not preclude certification against requirements. Answer b is incorrect because the controls specified in the security plan are requirements, not standards. The answer is not c, because the certification process results in a recommendation only; accreditation is the process of obtaining signoff to operate the system.

6. A degausser is a device that is used to
   a. Reformat a disk or tape for subsequent reuse.
   b. Eliminate magnetic data remanence on a disk or tape.
   c. Render media that contain sensitive data unusable.
   d. Overwrite sensitive data with zeros so that it is unreadable.

   The correct answer is b. Degaussing eliminates remanence by applying and then removing a strong magnetic field, removing magnetic signals from media. Reformatting does not actually erase data, so a is incorrect. While degaussing may render some media unusable, this is not the aim, so c is also incorrect. Answer d is incorrect because data are not overwritten by degaussing; it is removed.

7. A protection profile is
   a. A set of security requirements for a specific type of system
   b. A documented security configuration for a specific system
   c. A hierarchical classification denoting a system's assurance level
   d. A description of how security requirements must be implemented on a system

   The correct answer is a. In the Common Criteria, the protection profile is a description of the security requirements for a specific system, known as the target of evaluation (TOE). It is not a description of how the system meets these requirements or how controls are implemented, so neither b nor d is correct. Answer c is not correct; this refers to the evaluation assurance level (EAL) for the system; that is, the level of assurance or confidence gained through formalized testing that the requirements specified in the protection profile are met.

8. A Web application software vulnerability that allows an attacker to extract sensitive information from a backend database is known as a
   a. Cross-site scripting vulnerability
   b. Malicious file execution vulnerability
   c. Injection flaw
   d. Input validation failure

   The correct answer is c. An injection flaw occurs when user-supplied data can be sent directly to a command processor or query interpreter; attackers can exploit this flaw by supplying a query string as input to a Web application to extract data from a database. Answer a is incorrect; cross-site scripting vulnerabilities allow an attacker to execute scripts, typically in a user's browser. Malicious file execution (b) is a vulnerability in applications that accept file names or object references as input and then execute the files or objects. Answer d is also incorrect, as failures in input validation can have many adverse consequences (not necessarily disclosure of database content).

9. The security practice that restricts user access based on need to know is called
   a. Mandatory access control
   b. Default deny configuration
   c. Role-based access control
   d. Least privilege
   The correct answer is d. Least privilege grants users and processes only those privileges they require to perform authorized functions, that is, "need to know." Mandatory access control (a) limits access based on the clearance of the subject and the sensitivity of the object, and may provide access to objects of lower sensitivity where there is no business purpose for access; therefore, a is incorrect. Answer b is also incorrect; a "default deny" configuration refers to rule-based access control in which only that which is explicitly authorized is allowed; this is implemented in most firewall rule sets and is the premise behind whitelisting. Role-based access control (c) is not correct because while it provides access based on a role a user is associated with, it does not allow for granting individuals access to specific objects based on a need to know and may provide more access than is required to perform a certain function.

10. A security guideline is a
    a. Statement of senior management expectations for managing the security program
    b. Recommended security practice
    c. Set of criteria that must be met to address security requirements
    d. Tool for measuring the effectiveness of security safeguards
    The correct answer is b. A guideline is a recommended security practice, but is not required (as in a or c) or enforced. As a recommended practice, there is no standard of measurement, so d is also incorrect.

11. A security baseline is a
    a. Measurement of security effectiveness when a control is first implemented
    b. Recommended security practice
    c. Minimum set of security requirements for a system
    d. Measurement used to determine trends in security activity
    The correct answer is c. A baseline is a special type of security standard that specifies the minimum security controls or requirements for a system. Answer a is incorrect because this more accurately describes a configuration

baseline established in a CMDB, but does not indicate whether requirements have been met. Answer b refers to a guideline and is incorrect. Answer d is incorrect; a benchmark, not a baseline, is a value used in metrics against which to measure variations in performance.

12. An antifraud measure that requires two people to complete a transaction is an example of the principle of
    a. Separation of duties
    b. Dual control
    c. Role-based access control
    d. Defense in depth

    The correct answer is b. Dual control requires two people to physically or logically complete a process, such that one initiates and the other approves, or completes, the process. Dual control operates under the theory that controls that require more than one person operating together to circumvent are more secure than those under the control of a single individual. Answer a is incorrect; under separation of duties, two individuals may perform two separate, although perhaps similar, processes; that is, they perform separate functions. Answer c is incorrect; this refers to an access control model. Answer d is incorrect because dual control is actually a single control mechanism, not a series of layered controls.

13. The waterfall model is a
    a. Development method that follows a linear sequence of steps
    b. Iterative process used to develop secure applications
    c. Development method that uses rapid prototyping
    d. Extreme programming model used to develop Web application

    The correct answer is a. The waterfall method is a linear sequence of seven steps used in application development. It is not iterative, does not make use of prototypes, and does not use rapid application development (RAD) or extreme programming techniques; thus b, c, and d are incorrect.

14. A buffer overflow attack
    I.   Can be used to execute code supplied by the attacker
    II. Can be used to escalate privileges on a target server
    III. Can be prevented by appropriate bounds checking
    IV. Can be prevented by appropriate error handling
    a. I, II, and III
    b. I, II, and IV
    c. II, III, and IV
    d. I, III, and IV

    The correct answer is a. Buffer overflows allow an attacker to replace data in a program buffer and thus execute code of the attacker's choosing with effects ranging from system crashes to taking complete control of a system. Most overflow attacks can be prevented using appropriate bounds checking. Errors may not be detected by the system because the instructions that are executing may not produce an error; thus, any answer that includes IV is incorrect.

15. Code signing is a technique used to
    a. Ensure that software is appropriately licensed for use
    b. Prevent source code tampering
    c. Identify source code modules in a release package
    d. Support verification of source code authenticity

    The correct answer is d. Code signing using hash functions and a digital signature is used in the release process to insure that the code that is moved to production is the same as that which was approved for production release. Answer a is not correct because the signature is not the same as a license key. Answer b is not correct because signing itself does not prevent tampering, although it can be used to detect tampering. Answer c is not correct; code signing verifies authenticity of the signed code, but does not identify discrete components or packages.

16. Advantages of using thin client architecture include
    I. Ability to support a wide variety of applications
    II. Ease of maintaining a limited number of configurations
    III. Rapid deployment of security patches
    IV. Simplified policy enforcement
    a. I, II, and III
    b. I, II, and IV
    c. I, III, and IV
    d. II, III, and IV

    The correct answer is d. Thin client architecture, using centrally configured and maintained desktop images, simplifies configuration management, patch management, and policy enforcement. It is not suited for organizations that have a wide variety of desktop applications and configurations to support.

17. Most security breaches that have occurred in the past decade are a result of
    a. Attackers exploiting zero day vulnerabilities
    b. Poor password management
    c. Attackers exploiting known vulnerabilities
    d. Poor configuration management

    The answer is c. Most security breaches have occurred as a result of attackers exploiting known, unpatched vulnerabilities. Attack code and instructions for these vulnerabilities have a long shelf life on the Internet and are successful long after patches are made available. Zero day vulnerabilities, for which patches are not yet available, are an issue but not nearly as widespread. While password management and configuration management are important security measures, the majority of attackers go for easy and well-known exploits.

18. A firecall account is used to
   a. Grant administrator privileges to production programs
   b. Confer authority using the "run as" command
   c. Administer critical systems
   d. Provide temporary access to production systems

   The correct answer is d. Accounts with administrator-level IDs and passwords should not be hardcoded into production programs, nor should production programs run with administrator privileges; thus, a is incorrect. Answer b is not correct because the "run as" command allows any authorized user to switch to an administrator account to run a specific process. Answer c is incorrect; firecall accounts are for temporary access and not for routine administrative tasks.

19. The Common Criteria security-assurance-level EAL4 is awarded to systems that have been
   a. Structurally tested
   b. Semiformally designed and tested
   c. Methodically tested and checked
   d. Methodically tested, designed, and reviewed

   The correct answer is d. Answer a, structurally tested, is EAL2. Answer b, semiformally designed and tested, is EAL5. Answer c, methodically tested and checked, is EAL3.

20. The role of Information Owner in the system security plan includes
   a. Determining privileges that will be assigned to users of the system
   b. Maintaining the system security plan
   c. Authorizing the system for operation
   d. Assessing the effectiveness of security controls

   The correct answer is a. The information owner determines who can access the system and the privileges that will be granted to users. The system owner is responsible for b, maintaining the system security plan. The approver or authorizing official is responsible for c, authorizing the system for operation, at the end of the certification and accreditation process. Assessing the effectiveness of security controls (d) is the responsibility of the system security officer.

Index

3DES (Triple DES), 67

A

AAA (triple A), 34
Abuse notifications, 130
Access control logs, 32–33
Access control matrix, 26–27, 278–279
Access control models, 280–281
Access controls, 3–4
    key areas of knowledge, 3
    objects, 5–6
    physical security, 36
    remote access, 33
    subjects, 4–5
    See also DAC
Access Points, 232–233, 245–246
Account numbers, 14
Accountability, 32, 273–274
Accreditation, 330–331
ACL (Access Control Lists), 25–26
    routers, 174–175
Active network attacks, 249
AD (Active Directory), 27
ADSL (Asymmetrical DSL), 223
Adverse events, 371
Adware, 95
AES (Advanced Encryption Standard), 53,
    67–68, 245
AESA (ATM End Station Address), 224
Agile Development, 322–323
AH (Authentication Header), 220
Airsnort, 181
ALE (Annualized Loss Expectancy), 365
Algorithms, 46
    aging, 64–65

Anna Kournikova worm, 104
ANSI (American National Standards Institute),
    148
Anti-Trojan utilities, 102
Antispyware, 341
Antivirus gateways, 179
Antivirus solutions, endpoint security, 341
Antivirus XP 2008/9, 105, 111
AppDetective, 174
Application layer
    OSI model, 206
    security protocols, 226–227
    security solutions, 118–119
Application proxy firewalls, 238
Applications, security evaluation tools, 174
ARO (Annualized Rate of Occurrence), 365
ARP (Address Resolution Protocol), 216
Assets, 358
Asymmetric cryptography, 46
ATM (Asynchronous Transfer Mode), 224
Attackers, security monitoring, 163–164
Audit
    security frameworks, 150–153
        response to, 158–159
AuthenTec Fingerprint device, 24
Authentication, 15–16, 47
    by characteristic, 18–22
    by knowledge, 16
    by ownership, 16–18
    See also Certificate-based authentication;
        Continuous authentication; Dual
        control; Multifactor authentication;
        Periodic authentication; Reverse
        authentication; time outs
Authentication logs, 32–33
Authorization, 273–274

439